T0365034

God's Truth vs Satan's Doctrine

THE
SECRET
IS OUT

God's Truth vs Satan's Doctrine

THE SECRET IS OUT

INNOCENT NANGOMA

iUniverse

THE SECRET IS OUT: GOD'S TRUTH VS SATAN'S DOCTRINE

Copyright © 2019 Innocent Nangoma.

All rights reserved. No part of this book may be used or reproduced by any means, graphic, electronic, or mechanical, including photocopying, recording, taping or by any information storage retrieval system without the written permission of the author except in the case of brief quotations embodied in critical articles and reviews.

Scripture quotations marked GNT are taken from the Good News Translation — Second Edition. Copyright © 1992 by American Bible Society. Used by permission. All rights reserved.

'Scriptures and additional materials quoted are from the Good News Bible © 1994 published by the Bible Societies/HarperCollins Publishers Ltd UK, Good News Bible© American Bible Society 1966, 1971, 1976, 1992. Used with permission.'

Unless otherwise indicated, all scripture quotations are from The Holy Bible, English Standard Version® (ESV®). Copyright ©2001 by Crossway Bibles, a division of Good News Publishers. Used by permission. All rights reserved.

Scripture quotations from the Holy Bible, King James Version (Authorized Version). First published in 1611. Quoted from the KJV Classic Reference Bible.

Scripture quotations marked NKJV are taken from the New King James Version. Copyright © 1982 by Thomas Nelson, Inc. Used by permission. All rights reserved.

iUniverse books may be ordered through booksellers or by contacting:

iUniverse
1663 Liberty Drive
Bloomington, IN 47403
www.iuniverse.com
1-800-Authors (1-800-288-4677)

Because of the dynamic nature of the Internet, any web addresses or links contained in this book may have changed since publication and may no longer be valid. The views expressed in this work are solely those of the author and do not necessarily reflect the views of the publisher, and the publisher hereby disclaims any responsibility for them.

Any people depicted in stock imagery provided by Getty Images are models, and such images are being used for illustrative purposes only. Certain stock imagery © Getty Images.

ISBN: 978-1-5320-8894-0 (sc)
ISBN: 978-1-5320-9353-1 (e)

Library of Congress Control Number: 2020906262

Print information available on the last page.

iUniverse rev. date: 04/25/2020

PREFACE

What's the secret? Has this title got you curious? Good. This secret is about the author that involves the lives of every reader that picks up this book. According to oxford dictionary, the definition of doctrine is a belief or set of beliefs held and taught by church, political party, or another group. However, this doctrine is not something that a mere human being can be taught or would want to learn. It is broken down into many different concepts. To achieve one goal which is to deceive both the readers and author from a truth, the one truth, God's truth. What is God's truth? Even the author who wrote this book did not know the truth when he began to write it. He began to write this book all in hopes to find the one truth. He had realized that nothing in his life brought him happiness because there was something inside him that kept itching for him to find the answer to life's mysteries. The author of this book turned his back on everything he was ever taught and everything he ever felt for the sole goal to find the one truth. The author of this book had enough of the many religions, ideologies, laws, and opinions that he had to reject his own religion, ideologies, laws, and opinions. He cleared his very disturbed head and wanted to study the very thing that claimed to be the truth. He wanted to do this on his own without prejudice or bias upbringing that his family or the world had said about it. He put the little trust he had left and studied it from the beginning to the end but failed to understand it. Therefore, he searched harder and decided to go to the very source itself and spoke to it. It was at that very moment where the author stumbled upon a resistance; the very enemy that the source had warned about. In this book, one will find what that resistance said to him and how it behaves towards not only the author but to everyone.

Yet, the resistance made one slight mistake, by speaking to the author it revealed its secrets. This resistance is Satan and he has developed false doctrines that has been responsible for mental health issues, addictions, lawlessness, unfaithfulness, loneliness, hardships, suicides, destruction, war and many more things. He torments the author with all these things all in hopes to prevent him from ever connecting with the one truth. The author gives everything that is left inside of him to fight against the resistance but loses. He then remembers why he began to write this book so asks God for help. He confesses all his deepest darkest secrets for even the readers to read just to reveal how broken he is, so God could see how genuine he really is. The author begins a relationship with the one truth, but the resistance refuses to let him go so it wrestles with the author with its voice and temptations. The author finally realizes that he has to make a decision to decide which relationship he wants to keep between the resistance and the one truth.

What started off as a simple mission for the author, turned into a spiritual warfare that will show the readers what it takes just to find the one truth and remain with it. The author searched for the one truth so that he could use it to change and better his life and maybe others too. Little did the author know that the one truth knew he was searching, and it had a secret for him too. The secret is out: God's truth vs Satan's Doctrine. #TheSecretIsOut

*Important message to all the readers: The structure of this book is designed like a narrative to the bible. Each quoted Scripture is used as a trail to get to the core of the message and I did that because as I was writing, I myself was learning. The bible is not an easy book to understand and I myself am no bible expert. Which is why I depended on it in my writing because it will serve as a guide to understanding the meaning behind the secret of God's truth. My narration comes in two forms: One as the author who is attempting to study and talk about the bible to his audience. Secondly as the main character, who the author disguises as a nameless person but is actually himself. He speaks in the form of a prayers to God because he needs help to continue his journey as the author. This starts to happen in the fourth chapter *Battling Egypt* *and Babylon*, right after *the birth of the doctrine* chapter because the author begins to lose control of his narration. Which happens when he hears the first chilling voice that comes from the doctrine of Satan poem which is directed at him.

The reason why I structured the book this way is to give the readers a perspective of what goes on in my mind and how my mind articulated what it read. However, that is not what is noteworthy or even something to get excited about because my perspective means nothing. I allow the readers to see this so they can understand that human perspective has no value when trying to have a genuine relationship with God. Whether it is my perspective or the reader's perspective. The truth is not in us because we all have our own perspectives so what then is truth? Therefore, it is not in my perspective where the secret of God's truth is revealed but it is by the genuine admission of the second narrative. The second narrator is the author speaking in the form of prayers. He allows everyone to hear and understand the Spirit of God's poem which will reveal the truth and expose the doctrine of Satan's lies.

So, don't read this book like its some sort of autobiography about myself, or even think that I am claiming to be righteous. I am not a religious leader, bible expert or even academically qualified to write a book. The idea of writing this book was influenced by my realization that I was spiritually broken. Therefore, I decided to do what I love the most which was to write about the best loving thing I knew about which is Jesus Christ. But what the readers will come to realize is that the source of this book's power comes from faith in God and not faith in myself. My faith allowed me to hear, see and experience God's perspective- the truth.

I did my absolute best to reference Scripture for the sole purpose that everyone understands that everything written in the bible was in fact written by humans. But those humans were inspired/influenced by God's Spirit. However, little did I know that most biblical translations are copywritten. Personally, I prefer the Good News Translation Version because it is easy to read but I was limited in its use. Therefore, you will notice the use of other translations. Altogether they all mean the same thing but are written in a different style of English based on the interpretation of the Hebrew language. But do not be alarmed! If you remember the thing about human perspective. No one can have a genuine relationship with God by relying on their perspective but by faith in God's perspective. In other words, although the bible has many translations (perspectives) of what was originally written in Hebrew- the truth still remains the same. It remains the same because all the writers who wrote from their perspectives wrote it from the standpoint of faith in God. Which is why it is not an ordinary book because they are God's words. The biblical authors had faith in God and heard God's voice which gave it the power to spread all across the world and be titled the best-selling book of all time.

I have no doubt in my mind that it is only by faith that by the end of this book, you will not only have a better understanding of the Word but see the Word as God. It is journey to a forever relationship with God. It is not this story nor my story that will make it so but God's words that allow that journey to be so.

All Scripture is inspired by God and is useful for teaching the truth, rebuking error, correcting faults, and giving instruction for the right living, so that the person who serves God may be fully qualified and equipped to do every kind of good deed. **(2 Timothy 3:16-17) – Good News Translation**

"Take in what you read, highlight what you must and open up your hearts to God's Word.
Enjoy!"

–The Author & Innocent Nangoma

CHAPTER 1

THE VISIONS

"Behold three visions are to be received to a particular individual. I, the Spirit of God, am ready to reveal it to the reader of this book."

Vision #1:

A voice calls out, "Who can I use to be the messenger of the truth? Who is ready for such responsibilities? Who will put me first before themselves just so that they put all the souls of this universe before them for my sake? I have found the person who fits this description, but first I must make him jealous because he has forgotten his one true love. I will remind him of who I am, and I will do so by using someone his heart won't accept so he remembers that I am the God who loves all. I will keep his name a secret until he is ready to acknowledge me."

The man whose name shall be kept a secret is found sitting in a lobby of a five-star hotel when all of a sudden, the elevator doors open. Donald J Trump, the 45th president of the United States, walks out from the elevator door. The lobby is filled with many people and when they see the president, they are caught off guard. Well-known for his outrageous comments and unpopular leadership, the crowd are not pleased to see him. Donald J Trump proceeds to walk past the crowd and invites them to the banquet hall within the hotel. Everyone is unsure of what is about to happen, but they follow out of curiosity. Donald then finds a pulpit in the hall and walks towards it. He then begins to pray over everyone in the group by speaking about the holy texts from the bible. Astonished at his behavior the man whose name shall be kept a secret becomes angry. He cannot

1

accept Donald's prayers because he thinks Donald is making a mockery out of God. The unnamed man starts to speak against the 45ᵗʰ president of the United States of America by cursing him. "Shut up! You're a piece s★★★! How dare you quote God when you have done and said all sorts of horrible things!" Donald J Trump ignored the insult and continued to pray for the crowd. As the crowd continued to listen, they soon start to feel moved by his words. Within the group was a young lady who had been blind since birth. Donald asked a few people in the crowd to bring her forward. She was brought to the president and he laid his hands on her eyes to pray for her to gain sight. As soon as the president touched her, she was able to see at once! When the people witnessed this miracle, they began to believe that God was in fact with the president, so they began praying with him. Everyone in the crowd started to worship God with the president of the United States, all except for one person. The unnamed man refused to participate because he was enraged that God would pick a man like Donald J Trump. However, he loved everyone in the crowd who were listening to the president so he continued to stay and watch, just to see if Donald would slip up. All of sudden, everyone in the group began to speak in God's holy language. This baffled the unnamed man. It was at that time when Donald J Trump said to the unnamed man, "Are you sure you are on the right side of truth? Do not be afraid, because God has changed me. Come join and pray with us so that you may be forgiven by God and we can all worship together." The unnamed man became sad because he noticed he was all alone. All his friends were now being healed and blessed by God's Spirit. He felt left out but still could not find it within his heart to trust a man like Donald J Trump.

A voice then called out, "All that you see before you is not to deceive you. It is to show you that I, the Spirit of God, can use anyone for my works. You're struggling to accept that I have used a man like Donald J Trump, the leader of the United States of America. You have always been a follower of the world and because of this, you follow the world's point of view. Therefore I have put to the test your heart and made it jealous because you felt conflicted about what you think you know about me and what you know of the world. You have heard the world speak negatively against Donald so you followed with them, but when I used Donald to talk about me, you could not accept it. Yet it is the same world that also speaks poorly about me, but you still follow it? You have been a follower all your life and it has only led you to destruction! You saw the world begin to worship me and that saddened your heart. Surely, I tell you, you did not become sad because the world forgave Donald; you were sad because you were ashamed of yourself for always neglecting me. You have always known about me but somewhere along the line, you have forgotten about me. So therefore I ask you, 'Do you wish to come back to me?' I chose Donald to make you jealous because he represents leadership. So, therefore I ask another question, 'Do you wish to lead?' You have always followed, but you saw all your friends go to the first thing that you once loved. So therefore I ask another question, 'Are you ready to follow me?' For your friends did not choose Donald, they accepted me. I can choose to use anyone if you reject me, but I have a name I wish to give you. So, therefore I ask one last question, 'What shall it be?' The unnamed man began to cry and responded back to the voice, 'I do not wish to be a follower of the world anymore, but I will follow you! I want to come back to you not because I felt left out but for the sole reason that I just miss you.'

Then the voice said to the unnamed man,

'Write this upon your heart: Those who wish to be great in the kingdom must first put themselves in a position of servanthood. Although you once loved me and then deliberately abandoned me for the world, I still came back for you because of my love for you. However, because of that, surely I tell you the feeling you felt towards Donald will be the same feeling the world will have towards you but do not be afraid because I will be with you. Be prepared to be my servant and pray to me for a humble heart and I will make you great amongst nations. I can choose to use anyone for my glory and if they obey me they will see my glory which will be called greatness. So remember today I have chosen to use you.'"

Vision #2:

The unnamed man is taken to a wasteland in the middle of nowhere. He then heard the voice call out to him, "You shall design a coliseum for the world, and it will become famous. You will name this coliseum, 'The Secret Is Out.' Many people will talk about this building for years to come." Then the unnamed man said, "Spirit of God, if this coliseum will be famous shouldn't I have a name then? People will wonder who designed this great coliseum, shouldn't they have a name to remember me by?" The voice then replied, "I will give you a name, but you have misunderstood what I have told you. The building will become famous not you. It will become famous because the world will know that I was with you when you designed it. They will forget you but remember the building and what it represents. Therefore the name that I will give you is architect."

The architect was pleased with his name and began to fantasize about how glorious the building would be. A month went by and the architect had finished his design for the coliseum. The architect then called out to the Spirit of God, "I have finished the design for the coliseum but now I need money to hire construction workers and for equipment to provide them the proper tools. What shall I do?" The Spirit of God replied, "Go into the city and you will find a wealthy man. Show the wealthy man your plans and he will be pleased with the design of the coliseum. He will then offer to fund the construction of the coliseum and place you in charge. That is how you will fund the construction of coliseum." The architect obeyed the Spirit of God and went into the city, and everything that the Spirit of God said to him came true. So he then searched for workers to begin construction. However, the architect did not treat his workers kindly and was not honest with the workers because he told them they were going to get paid more if they worked overtime. The architect underpaid them and would make them work overtime just so the coliseum would be built faster but he would never pay for their overtime hours. The Spirit of God saw what the architect was doing and became angry and said, "Because this architect is mistreating his workers and using my plans for his own motives, I will use that very building as the court to bring him to judgment!" Months had passed and the construction workers began to complain because of how the architect was treating them and they questioned why they weren't getting their overtime pay. Whenever they asked the architect, he would blame the wealthy man for delaying the funds. When the wealthy man had received word of what was going on with the coliseum project, he began an investigation against the architect. 6 months had passed and the building was almost complete, when the architect was approached by the state authorities. They arrested him and subpoenaed his financial records. They had found that the architect had spent all the money that was to be used to pay for the construction worker's overtime hours, so he was immediately put under trial. Many people heard about the architect's cruel behaviour and wanted him to be punished immediately! They decided to use the very building that the workers had worked so hard on to bring judgment to the architect. The architect saw the building and his heart became crushed. He felt guilty because he had taken advantage of the construction workers and the wealthy man. He knew God was angry at him for using the money for his own motives when God had blessed him to build the coliseum. He thought to himself, "What have I done? I hurt many people and disobeyed God because I only cared about getting famous. I should have been honorable and obeyed God's plan."

The day finally came for the architect to be prosecuted and a multitude of people came to watch, what was known as the easiest prosecution in history. The judge ordered everyone to wear masks that covered their faces before entering the coliseum. This was done to discourage the architect so he would not see any familiar faces like family or friends. He made this order so that the architect would feel alone. The only thing he was to see was the name of his beloved building, 'The secret is out,' which would come to haunt him to the time he was to be sentenced. "After careful consideration, I have decided that the architect is guilty and will be sentenced to death! But before he is put to death, he must be branded all over his body and suffer then we will end his life," said the judge. The architect began to cry once the judge slammed his gavel and denounced his fate. He was shocked at the sentencing but the whole crowd began to cheer with the judge's decision. The architect looked around his unfinished coliseum and began to remember God's voice. So he closed his eyes and began to pray for forgiveness. When all of a sudden a pen and paper appeared in front of him. So he picked it up and started to write out an apology to God and all the people he had let down. He wrote, 'I deserve this punishment and God will not forgive me for what I did, but I just want him to know I am sorry....'" The judge saw what the architect was doing and became angry. The judge removed his mask and the moment he did, the architect saw a brand written on his forehead. It read, 'The Devourer.' The judge grabbed the branding iron which read, 'Sinner, death to you!' and branded the architect's chest. As the crowd cheered at this, the judge looked directly at the eyes of the architect and yelled, "Stop writing!" He took away his pen and walked away from the architect. It was at that moment when another pen appeared before the architect. Despite being in pain, he grabbed the pen and continued writing. The judge became even more furious and branded the architect's forehead. This made him lose all hope, and the crowd began chanting, "Sinner, death to you! Sinner, death to you!"

Suddenly, a loud noise from the sky was heard which caused the foundations of the coliseum to shake. The judge heard the sound and knew what it meant so he ran out of the coliseum. The people in the coliseum were unaware of what the sound meant and became angry that the judge had stopped branding the architect. They all plotted to ambush the centre of the coliseum where the architect was at so that they could finish the job. As people were preparing to leave their seats, they heard a voice from the sky, "Freeze! For you all wish to brand the architect for his sins but what of all your sins?" All of a sudden the whole coliseum began to groan and cry out in pain because the names of all their sins began to appear as brands all over their bodies. Once they were all branded, they froze as if they were like statues. Then the heavens opened up and a light shown directly down to the coliseum. The architect looked up to the sky and saw a figure too bright to stare at. It was only the architect who saw this happening but he could not look directly at the figure's face because of how bright the light was. The architect became extremely afraid and bowed his face down to the ground because he knew that it was the voice that had given him his name. The figure spoke, "Do not be afraid for I have come to help you finish what you have failed to do. I have seen your sins and gave the world power to bring judgment onto you, but because you have prayed and asked for forgiveness, I am here to do that very thing." The figure then asked the architect, "Do you wish to be forgiven?" The architect replied, "yes."

All of a sudden five cups appeared before the architect and the figure told him to grab the first one and drink it. The first cup had the writings, 'Holy Spirit.' The architect obeyed and grabbed the first cup and drank it. All of sudden the brandings that the judge had branded onto the architect disappeared. It was as if his skin was never harmed from the brandings. The architect was then filled with God's Holy Spirit, and he looked up to the figure and saw the writings on the figure's forehead written, 'Lamb of God.' Overjoyed that his sins were forgiven he asked the Lamb of God to unfreeze everyone in the crowd so that he could help remove the brands that were on the crowds. The Lamb of God accepted his request and he unfroze all of them.

The architect prayed for everyone in the coliseum and as soon as he did the brands that God had given them were gone. Everyone in the coliseum were shocked to see that the architects brandings disappeared and that he was able to rid them of theirs. The architect spoke out loud, "I did not do this with my own strength but by the power of God, who has made his presence known! He has heard my cries of forgiveness and has come to not only forgive me but all of us. I was to design this coliseum for the world so that all of you would come to know that God's love for us is no longer a secret. Look up in the sky!" But everyone in the coliseum could not see the Lamb of God and were confused about what he was saying. Then the Lamb of God said, "They cannot see me, but if you wish for them to see me, you must drink from the second cup."

The second cup had the writings, 'Journey Not Story.' The architect drank from the second cup, and all of a sudden angels from heaven came down to the coliseum and removed the face masks from everyone. Once this happened the architect saw that everyone had the branding, 'Sinner, death to you!' on their foreheads. The angels touched everyone's forehead and the brandings disappeared. Everyone in the crowd was then able to see the Lamb of God. The architect spoke out, "God has removed your masks because you all entered this building hiding your identities from me, but you could not hide it from him. For none of you even knew that before this trial came to be, you were branded the very thing I was to be stamped. God brought me to this trial to expose that my story deserves death, but because of the Lamb of God, he has allowed me to journey with all of you to be one with his loving story! I may have not known your stories because you all masked it from me, but God knew it and didn't care about how sinful they were. He has exposed your stories by removing all your masks which is why you are all shocked of the branding you thought you never had. My story was exposed in this trial, and all of you were just to say death to me, but God has removed the branding from all of us so we may journey to him. The secret is out!" When the whole coliseum heard this speech from the architect, some were moved and got up from their seats to join him, but others were not convinced because they were focused on his story, so they walked out of the coliseum. They did this regardless of what God had done for them.

Then the Spirit of God told the architect to drink from the third cup. The third cup had the writings, 'I Am Nothing Without God.' The architect drank from the third cup and began speaking in God's holy language which translated to, "I was branded justly, but God forgave me and removed my brandings! I Am Nothing Without God! Who then can call themselves righteous? Just because a *person gives to the poor doesn't make that person generous. A person who kisses their children good night, doesn't make them loving. If all this is true for such actions what then of those who sneak off at night and enter the houses of others just to steal? We will brand them as thieves! Or what if a person who kills another person? We will brand them as murderers! It is easy to brand goodness on people, but it enrages the hearts of everyone if the brand of evil is removed from a person! Now let me challenge all your thoughts. Who has the authority to correctly brand a person as righteous and good? It cannot be humans because there are some who treat their families with great love but outside are murders and thieves! There are some who give to the poor and help those in need but get their wealth by using dishonest scales. We can only brand actions as good but how can we know what they do in secret? If what they do in secret is exposed it becomes easy for us to remove the brand of goodness from them. What then of those who have been branded as evil? Anyone who has been branded as evil cannot remove it on their own, nor does any man or woman have the authority to remove it for them. What then is that person to do? How can we trust those branded righteous and good to remove the evil brand, if they have secrets? Only the righteous and perfect God can eliminate such a brand! For human branding is of no value but God can correctly give and take away just brandings! Everyone rejoice because all our sinful brandings have been removed! We Are Nothing Without God!"* However, no one could understand his speech so the Lamb of God told him to translate it to english.*

The Lamb of God then told the architect to share the first, second and third cup to everyone in the coliseum. So the architect obeyed and gave the cup to pass around so that the people would drink, and the drink within each cup never ran out. Then the Lamb of God told the architect to drink the fourth cup and then share it with everyone else. The fourth cup had the writings, 'Purpose.' After they all drank from the cup, they all gathered together and assigned to each other jobs to help complete the unfinished coliseum. Not a single person in the coliseum, even the architect, did not know what their role was. They all worked according to their strengths and talents. The court that was used to bring the architect to trial was torn down, and they built a sanctuary for the Lamb of God so that they would have a place to worship him. Then the Lamb of God told the architect to drink from the last cup and then share it with everyone else. The fifth cup had the writings 'Victory.' They all drank from the fifth cup.

The judge who had fled from the coliseum, the one who had the brandings, 'The Devourer,' had been plotting against everyone in the coliseum. He declared war against everyone in the building. He convinced the state authorities that the architect and everyone in the building had committed treason against his administration. He had lied to the state that he had placed judgment on the architect, but the people in the coliseum disobeyed his decision so they threw him out. He was given permission to declare war against everyone in the building, so he gathered an army to not only kill everyone in the coliseum but also destroy the building. However, the Lamb of God told everyone in the coliseum about the Devourer's plan, so they were prepared.

When the Devourer and his army approached the coliseum with all their weapons, everyone in the coliseum began to sing, "The LORD is my protector; he is my strong fortress. My God is my protection, and with him I am safe. He protects me like a shield and keeps me safe, he is my savior; he protects me and saves me from violence. I call to the LORD, and he saves me from my enemies. Praise the LORD! **(2 Samuel 22:2-4). - Good News Translation"** *As they sang the song of David, the skies opened up, and arrows that were on fire shot down from the sky and struck down everyone in the army. Everyone in the army was killed except the Devourer.*

Then a mighty angel spoke out in a loud voice from the heavens and said to the Devourer, "Leave from this place, I have spared you to show you that these people are protected by the blood of the Lamb. Leave from this place for the Lamb of God is with these people, and you cannot harm them! Leave from this place before I reveal to them your real name. For your time is fast approaching and when it comes, they will see your fate and the secret will be out." The Devourer immediately ran from the place and never attempted to touch the sacred building. When everyone in the building saw what had happened, they rejoiced and praised the Lamb of God. They all worshipped him, and the architect baptized everyone in the coliseum with water and by the name of the Lamb.

The Lamb of God then spoke out from the heavens, "The coliseum has been built, and now the secret is out to the whole world about what I have done to the Devourer and those who accept me." He then instructed everyone in the coliseum to leave the building and go preach to nations about the Lamb of God. The Lamb of God said, "I will never depart from you so do not be afraid of the Devourer or any state authorities. I will be with you as you go out from this coliseum. Now go and tell everyone outside what I have done for all of you. Do not keep it a secret! Tell them everything so that they too may come to know me." All of a sudden brandings appeared over the foreheads of everyone in the coliseum. It read, 'God's Truth.'

"I have revealed to the reader of this book the first two visions, but they will misunderstand and misinterpret them. They will not be able to understand or interpret the two visions because the one I am going to use to write these visions has yet to receive them. The reader will then ask themselves, 'How is it ever possible for us to understand or interpret these visions if the one who wrote it has yet to receive it, but we have received it? If we are reading it, then that must mean he has already received it since he has written it.' I, the Spirit of God, will reply this:

'What has been written last shall be made known and understood for the first. What is written here, the visions, shall be made known last in the conclusion. Skipping to the last will do no one any good because the words I speak are not of the human mind. They are too prophetic for both the reader and author. It is only through the journey from the beginning of this book to the end when all secrets shall be revealed. For the last was given to the author so that he may come to know these visions and understand them so he could write them here. For what is written first are for only the readers, not the author, so that they may come to see and understand the conclusion. Only the author knows what is written in the end because I was with him when he wrote it. But when the author began writing this book he was not with me, so he did not know what I had willed for him to write in the beginning. It was only at the end where I revealed to him the message he did not know existed, which are these visions. Therefore it will be in the conclusion where the readers will understand what he wrote here, the visions; the very message that was hidden from the author. The end was where the author became aware of the visions I had hidden from him because he finally became one with me. How can anyone come to understand something that is written by someone who doesn't understand what he or she has written? How much more is the confusion for any reader if they were to go into the future to read something that the author has yet to write? That is why I have said he will not know what

is written in the beginning. Only the readers are given the advantage because this is the first thing that their eyes will see. However, it is the author's advantage to understand the meaning because his story became a journey to the truth.'"

"Behold, the final vision that has yet to be received by the author. I, the Spirit of God, am ready to reveal it to the reader of this book."

Vision #3:

The one with the writing, 'The Devourer,' had been roaming the earth day and night. He had been going around causing mischief to many nations and deceiving the world by exchanging the truth for a lie. He could shapeshift into anything he pleased so that no one could know his real form. He was feared by many because of his relentlessness and for this he ruled over the earth. However, each passing day that went by, he lived it as if it was his last because he knew that a day was to come where he was to face full judgment for his crimes. Therefore his favorite form to take was that of a judge so that whosoever he devoured would also join judgment.

One day one of his top generals came running into his ancient palace and said, "Bright morning star, we have caught word of two visions sent from the heavenly beings that regard you! Unfortunately, we have been unable to understand or interpret it. I have written them down on these scrolls for you to read." The one with the writing, 'The Devourer,' picked up the scrolls and read what his top general had written down. He studied the words carefully from start to finish but could not understand nor interpret the meaning. He saw how his name was mentioned in the second vision and what was to happen to him. This infuriated the Devourer, so he threw the two scrolls on the ground. He began to wonder who this architect was. So he left his ancient palace and scoured all over the earth to try and determine who the individual known as the architect was. But he could not figure it out because the visions did not give much description of who this secret person was. The Devourer then became restless, so he returned back to his ancient palace to reread the scrolls. But the more he read it, the more he became frustrated because he could not figure it out. Then the Devourer instructed every single person in his ancient palace to stop at nothing to find out who the secret person was. He emphasized the seriousness of his task and gave a strict order to *kill whoever the person was so that neither the first nor second vision would come to pass. After he issued the order, the one who had written down the visions on the two scrolls asked, "Bright morning star, how are we to determine who this individual is? Judging by the first vision, it seems as the individual himself does not even know of his purpose? How then are we going to narrow down who this person is if he himself doesn't even know about the visions?" Then the Devourer changed his form into a dragon and flew off into a dark abyss without replying.*

A few days had passed by, and the Devourer returned back in the same form as he left. Still in the form of a dragon, he let out a ferocious roar calling back all that dwelled in his ancient palace. The dragon spoke this, "Here is a list of all people on earth who still have the brand, 'Sinner, death to you!' on their forehead. We know this secret person is a male. We know this person is a follower of the world. We know he once loved God but has fallen short of his love for him. We know that he must have some sort of creativity to him or else the Spirit of God would not give him the name architect. Spirit's of my kingdom, go and search all over the earth for anyone who still attends church but has his heart in other things. Spirit's of my kingdom, search high and low for this person! Spirit's of my kingdom, I am issuing a warrant for this man's soul! He must be found so that I may devour him. This secret person must not know about these visions! Spirit's of my kingdom, we must stop at nothing so that he never receives it. Spirit's of my kingdom, for if he does, then it means that the coliseum has been built." Then the dragon changed his form back into a judge and went into a secret room. He returned back with a book and stood in front of all that dwelled in his ancient palace and said, "Here is my book which we will use to defeat him. This is the book that I use to govern the souls of everyone on earth. Once we find him we will allow him to read this book so he becomes obsessed by all the secrets within the book. He will be so entertained by what is written within it that he won't search for the truth. Once the writings has his attention, the words on the pages will act as my voice and speak to him. We will use this against him and if followed properly it will lead this individual right into my paws. For the vision spoke about God's truth so we will use this to confuse him from ever knowing the truth." The title of the book read, 'The Doctrine of Satan.' The judge then made extra copies of the book and handed it out to everyone in the palace. He then said, "Now go out and find this man! Once found steal, kill and destroy him!"

After he finished speaking, he dismissed everyone from his presence. The judge then transformed himself into a lion and walked out back of this ancient palace. The ancient palace was built on a mountain so when he walked out back, he faced the cliff of the mountain. The cliff of the mountain stared face down at all the nations of the world. As the lion stared at all the nations he began to growl at all the souls of the earth with hatred. For it had been his mission to destroy all of them since the very beginning of their creation. For it is written:

Be alert, be on watch! Your enemy, the devil, roams around like a roaring lion, looking for someone to devour. (1 Peter 5:8) – Good News Translation"

-The Spirit of God

CHAPTER 2

CORRUPTION IN HEAVEN

So the great dragon was cast out, that serpent of old, called the Devil and Satan, who deceives the whole world; he was cast to the earth, and his angels were cast out with him. **(Revelations 12:9) – New King James Version**

King of Babylon, bright morning star, you have fallen from heaven! In the past you conquered nations, but now you have been thrown to the ground. You were determined to climb up to heaven and to place your throne above the highest stars. You thought you would sit like a king on that mountain in the north where the gods assemble. You said you would climb to the tops of the clouds and be like the Almighty. But instead, you have been brought down to the deepest part of the world of the dead. **(Isaiah 14:12–15) – Good News Bible**

The book of Isaiah is a section within the bible that gives an overview of the prophet Isaiah. Prophets in biblical times were anointed people that God specifically chose to either proclaim messages or prophecies to the people of God. Prophets also performed miracles, which are supernatural acts that God displayed through them. They only performed such powers to get people to believe in God or even punish the wicked. In this specific Scripture, Isaiah is delivering a message to the people of Israel about the fate that awaits the king of Babylon. God doesn't explicitly say or call out Satan by name, but he does call this king of Babylon 'bright morning star.' Satan's original name is Lucifer which also means bright morning star, so this tells us that this king is in fact Satan. The prophet Isaiah mentions that this king of Babylon had fallen from heaven, as indicated in Revelations 12:9.

"Son of man take up a lamentation for the king of Tyre, and say to him, 'Thus says the Lord GOD: "You were the seal of perfection, Full of wisdom and perfect in beauty. You were in Eden, the garden of God; every precious stone was your covering: The sardius, topaz, and diamond, Beryl, onyx, and jasper, sapphire, turquoise, and emerald with gold. The workmanship of your timbrels and pipes was prepared for you on the day you were created. "You were the anointed cherub who covers; I established you; you were on the holy mountain of God; you walked back and forth in the midst of fiery stones. You were perfect in your ways from the day you were created, till iniquity was found in you. "By the abundance of your trading you became filled with violence within, and you sinned; therefore I cast you as a profane thing out of the mountain of God; and I destroyed you, O covering cherub, from the midst of the fiery stones. "Your heart was lifted up because of your beauty; you corrupted your wisdom for the sake of your splendor; I cast you to the ground, I laid you before kings, that they might gaze at you.
(Ezekiel 28:12-17) – New King James Version

Within this passage, we see another prophet named Ezekiel receive a message from God regarding another king. However, this king is of Tyre instead of Babylon. When we read the Scripture regarding this king, it doesn't sound like a king that reigned on earth. Who else could God have been talking about? This king supposedly also lived in the garden of Eden. In the Good News bible translation, it states, "How wise and handsome you were! You lived in Eden, the garden of God." The only characters in the garden of Eden were God, Adam, Eve and the serpent. It's already been established that the serpent is the devil, who has the reputation of being the deceiver of the world. Therefore, Ezekiel was being notified about Satan. When we read both Isaiah 14 and Ezekiel 28, we are being given an exact description of who Satan is.

The Word of the LORD came to me again, saying, "Son of man, say to the prince of Tyre, 'Thus says the Lord GOD: "Because your heart is lifted up, and you say, 'I am a god, I sit in the seat of gods, in the midst of the seas,' yet you are a man, and not a god, though you set your heart as the heart of a god. **(Ezekiel 28:1-2) – New King James Version**

The Scriptures give us a clear understanding of Satan's background and how he got booted from the garden of Eden and heaven. However, this raises another question: Why didn't God just say that he was talking about Satan instead of referring to the devil as the king of Babylon and Tyre? In biblical times, these kingdoms were enemies of Israel, and Israel is originally known as the first nation to acknowledge God. Hence why they are referred to as God's nation, but I will elaborate on that later in this book. The kings at the time that ruled Babylon and Tyre were nations that belonged to someone well known as the devil.

Then the devil, taking him up on a high mountain, showed him all the kingdoms of the world in a moment of time. And the devil said to him, "All this authority I will give you, and their glory; for this has been delivered to me, and I give it to whomever I wish. Therefore, if you will worship before me, all will be yours." **(Luke 4:5-7) – New King James Version**

In this passage, we read how the devil is attempting to get Jesus Christ to worship him. The devil fails to tempt Jesus into sin, but we learn a vital piece of information about Satan. He shows Jesus all the kingdoms of the world, and says, "All this authority I will give you, and their glory; for this has been delivered to me, and I give it to whomever I wish." From all the information that we retrieve from this Scripture, it seems that Satan has some sort of dominion over the world. Which could mean that the devil wasted no time in conquering the kingdoms of the world after he was banished from heaven. But Satan's fate is prophesied when God speaks to Isaiah.

When he does this, they are to mock the king of Babylonia and say: "The cruel king has fallen! He will never oppress anyone again! The LORD has ended the power of the evil rulers who angrily oppressed the peoples and never stopped persecuting the nations they had conquered. Now at last the whole world enjoys rest and peace, and everyone sings for joy. The cypress trees and the cedars of

Lebanon rejoice over the fallen king, because there is no one to cut them down, now that he is gone! **(Isaiah 14:4-8) - Good News Bible**

This prophecy that Isaiah receives from God tells us that a day is coming when he will no longer rule over the nations that he had conquered, and the world will witness the devil's fate.

"Those who see you will gaze at you, and consider you, saying: 'Is this the man who made the earth tremble, who shook kingdoms, who made the world as a wilderness and destroyed its cities, who did not open the house of his prisoners?' **(Isaiah 14:16-17) – New King James Version**

Satan's downfall started when he couldn't appreciate his position in heaven. I was puzzled by this because he was created with such high authority. What was the point in fighting God? God had created him handsome and wise to the point where he was an example of perfection. Nonetheless, that wasn't enough for him and those very qualities influenced his heart to turn against God. His pride and jealousy eventually turned into hate which is why he was cast out of heaven.

You did such evil in buying and selling that your places of worship were corrupted. So I set fire to the city and burned it to the ground. All who look at you now see you reduced to ashes. You are gone, gone, forever, and all the nations that had come to know you are terrified, afraid that they will share your fate. **(Ezekiel 28:18-19) – Good News Translation**

What was God talking about here? Well, Lucifer was once one of the highest-ranked angels in God's kingdom. He was in charge of worship in heaven which is why he was made perfect because he was to perfect worship for God. That is why God tells Ezekiel how Lucifer was an example of perfection. Lucifer was an example of perfect worship for the other angels. The other angels looked up to Lucifer because he led the worship that was for God. Which is why it is written in Isaiah 14:11, "You used to be honoured with the music of harps," because he used music as a tool of worship.

17

You used to be honoured with the music of harps, but now here you are in the world of the dead. You lie on a bed of maggots and are covered with a blanket of worms. **(Isaiah 14:11) – Good News Bible**

It's ideal for us to connect the dots and find the similarities of Isaiah 14, Ezekiel 28 and Revelations 12. The evidence is right in front of us because they are all describing Satan. In Revelations 12, Satan isn't alone. It mentions that Satan and his angels were also banished from heaven. God tells the prophet Ezekiel that Satan began evil in buying and selling in his places of worship. This demands an answer to the question: What was he buying and selling that made it so evil? Well, if we take little pieces of information from the books Isaiah, Ezekiel and Revelations we find the answer. Angels below Satan saw him as an example of perfection, and this made him think he was higher than God. This then got him to not only crave attention, but he also desired for the worship to go to him rather than God. Satan was selling, or in other words, kicking out the angels that refused to worship him and buying those into his alliance that accepted him as king. That is why it is written, "You were busy buying and selling, and this led you to violence and sin." This violence must have occurred whenever angels refused to buy into his lies and did not pledge their allegiance to him. Which could explain why Isaiah described him as a violent tyrant. That is why his places of worship became corrupt because there was no longer peace, but a revolution against God was about to unfold.

And war broke out in heaven: Michael and his angels fought with the dragon; and the dragon and his angels fought, but they did not prevail, nor was a place found for them in heaven in longer. **(Revelation 12:7-8) – New King James Version**

God reveals to his prophets about Satan's character but what surprises me is that he never once speaks about a relationship with him. Which leads me to believe that they never had a relationship in the first place. As a matter of fact, God never once reveals to us about any sort of relationship with his angels. Which also makes me wonder if God even loves angels? Now before I give this answer, I have to reference a few

Scriptures so that we get a glimpse of what it was like to be near God's presence. I am giving everyone this reference because it will tie in with why there is no mention of angels having a relationship with God.

In the year that king Uzziah died, I saw the Lord sitting upon a throne, high and lifted up, and the train of his robe filled the whole temple. Above it stood the seraphim: each one had six wings: with two he covered his face, with two he covered his feet, and with two he flew. And one cried to another and said: "Holy, holy, holy is the LORD of hosts; The whole earth is full of his glory!" And the posts of the door were shaken by the voice of him who cried out, and the house was filled with smoke. **(Isaiah 6:1–4) – New King James Version**

Each one of the four living creatures had six wings, and they were covered with eyes, inside and out. Day and night, they never stop singing: "Holy, holy, holy, is the Lord God Almighty, who was, who is, and who is to come." **(Revelation 4:8) - Good News Translation**

In both Isaiah and the book of Revelations, we hear the mention of strange creatures that each have six wings. Isaiah 6:1-4 is about a vision of when Isaiah saw the Lord sitting on his throne. Wherein the book of Revelation describes what the disciple John saw. In the New King James Version, they refer to these strange creatures as a Seraphim which are highly ranked angels. Isaiah sees these creatures but doesn't identify how many there are, where John says he saw only four. But what I would like us to focus on is Isaiah's vision because the book of Revelations is a vision given to the Apostle John, who had already seen Christ in flesh. In Isaiah's vision the six-winged creatures are using their wings in a unique way: Two of their wings covered their face, the other two covered their bodies, while the other two were used for flying. This just goes to show how marvelous it must be to be in front of God's presence.

I said, "There is no hope for me! I am doomed because every word that passes my lips is sinful, and I live among a people whose every word is sinful. And yet, with my own eyes have seen the King, the LORD Almighty." **(Isaiah 6:5) - Good News Translation**

19

Isaiah is filled with guilt when he sees the Lord sitting on his throne while also witnessing these strange creatures that worship God, day and night. He proclaims that he is doomed because every word that passes from his lips is sinful. God's presence causes Isaiah to feel this way. The Seraphim did not look at the Lord directly in the face and I get this suspicion because it covered its eyes and body with its wings. The Seraphim's actions and Isaiah's guilt give us a glimpse of what it must be like to be in the presence of God. Isaiah is quoted saying, "And yet, with my own eyes I have seen the King, the LORD Almighty," but it is through his previous words which shows us just how overwhelming God's presence truly is. Isaiah says, "There is no hope for me! I am doomed because every word that passes my lips is sinful, and I live among people whose every word is sinful." All of Isaiah's actions in this encounter with God is like a ripple effect. Seeing the Seraphim must have been fascinating enough, but it was seeing God's glory in a vision that really got to him. The sight before him resulted in him feeling guilty because he did not feel worthy enough to join in on the worship.

Then one of the creatures flew down to me, carrying burning coal that he had taken from the altar with a pair of tongs. He touched my lips with the burning coal and said, "This has touched your lips, and now your guilt is gone, and your sins are forgiven." **(Isaiah 6:6-7) - Good News Translation**

The Seraphim in Isaiah's vision were showing reverence for God's glory by covering their whole being. The reason why I'm going in depth about seeing the presence of God is to emphasize God's power and glory. I had mentioned that the bible does not mention any sort of relationship with God and angels simply because there didn't need to be one. All the angels, even Lucifer, have stood and witnessed God's glory. I am using Isaiah's vision as an example to show how the highest-ranking angels cannot look at God directly but still marvel at his glory by singing to him, day and night. How is it that I know why the Seraphim had to cover their eyes and bodies in front of God? Well 1 Timothy 6:16 answers that.

He alone is immortal; he lives in the light that no one can approach. No one has ever seen him; no one can ever see him. To him be honor and eternal power! Amen. **(1 Timothy 6:16) - Good News Translation**

1 Timothy does state that no one can approach God or has ever seen him. But Isaiah is quoted saying he did in fact see the Lord sitting on his throne high and exalted. So which is it? Is the bible contradicting itself here? No, not at all! Actually, this is the coolest part about God, and I will expand the theological concepts of the physical and spiritual.

He is the image of the invisible God, the firstborn over all creation. For by him all things were created that are in heaven and that are on earth, visible and invisible, whether thrones or dominions or principalities or powers. All things were created through him and for him. **(Colossians 1:15-16) – New King James Version**

The Seraphim could not look at God because they were in presence of the invisible God which no one can approach because of the light that shines from him. Whereas, Isaiah saw the Lord's physical presence in a vision which can only mean he saw the glory of Jesus Christ because Christ is the visible likeness of the invisible God. Isaiah was not aware that it was Jesus Christ because his name was yet to be revealed but he knew that it was the Lord because of his glory. No one has seen the invisible God and cannot see him due to his unapproachable light but because God loves us, he allowed us to see himself in Christ. Why were the angels and the Seraphim subject to the unapproachable light of God, where Isaiah was subject to the physical presence of the Lord? Simple. Because we are humans and angels are spirits! I promise I will elaborate all this in the book to help further the knowledge but because of sin, we humans see things only in the physical which is why it is hard for us to believe in God. Isaiah became weary of his worthiness when he witnessed what it was like to be before the Most High.

And suddenly there was with the angel a multitude of the heavenly host praising God, and saying, "Glory to God in the highest, and on earth peace, good will toward men!" **(Luke 2:13-14) – New King James Version**

And I beheld, and I heard the voice of many angels round about the throne and the beasts and the elders: and the number of them was ten thousand times ten thousand, and thousands of thousands; saying with a loud voice, "Worthy is the Lamb that was slain to receive power, and riches, and wisdom, and strength, and honour, and glory, and blessing." **(Revelations 5:11-12) - King James Version**

Angel's worship in this way because of how powerful and overwhelming God's glory is. The angels that are in God's presence see God's love through his glorious power which is why the Scriptures never speak about a relationship with them.

The LORD would speak with Moses face-to-face, just as someone speaks with a friend. Then Moses would return to the camp. But the young man who was his helper, Joshua son of Nun, stayed in the Tent. **(Exodus 33:11) - Good News Translation**

We are not like Moses, who had to put a veil over his face so that the people of Israel would not see the brightness fade and disappear. **(2 Corinthians 3:13) - Good News Translation**

Moses is a special character in the bible because he is the only human to have spoken to God in his spiritual form. But how was it possible for Moses to speak to God's spiritual form? The Scriptures clearly state that no one has seen him. Exodus 33:20-23 explains how.

"But he said, "You cannot see my face; for no man shall see me, and live." And the LORD said, "Here is a place by me, and you shall stand on the rock. So it shall be, while my glory passes by, that I will put you in the cleft of the rock, and will cover you with my hand while I pass by. Then I will take away my hand, and you shall see my back; but my face shall not be seen." **(Exodus 33:20-23) – New King James Version**

When Moses went down from Mount Sinai carrying the Ten Commandments, his face was shining because he had been speaking with the LORD; but he did not know it. Aaron and all the people looked at Moses and saw that his face was shining, and they were afraid to go near him. **(Exodus 34:29-30) - Good News Translation**

It is by this very reason why Moses' face lit up and the people were afraid to approach him. God's presence that is before the angels is so abundant that they do not require a relationship or any sort of assurance of God's love. But God had established a relationship with Moses by allowing him to be the first human being to see his spiritual form. This was something that had never been done before since Moses was a mere human being. Yet, God had allowed him to be in the presence of his Spirit while he was only a mortal being. To the angels they see God in his spiritual form because all they know is the things of the spirit. Whereas for someone like Moses, who only knows the physical, was given the opportunity to be in his spiritual presence as an act of friendship and love.

But since then there has not arisen in Israel a prophet like Moses, whom the LORD knew face to face, in all the signs and wonders which the LORD sent him to do in the land of Egypt, before Pharaoh, before all his servants, and in all his land, and by all the mighty terror which Moses performed in the sight of Israel. **(Deuteronomy 34: 10-12) – New King James Version**

So, it's not that God did not love the angels that decided to leave (this includes Satan himself). The angels are different from us because they were created as spiritual beings that reside in God's presence. It would be false to say that God does not love angels because if he did not love them, he would have not created them. By dwelling in his presence as spiritual beings, all they do is obey and worship. This is what Satan wanted for himself and since he was in the authoritative position of leading worship, he took it upon himself to force the other angels to worship him. That is why it is written in Isaiah 14:14-15, "You said you would climb to the tops of the clouds and be like the Almighty. But instead, you have been brought down to the deepest part of the world of the dead." He saw the worship that God received and grew jealous, so he sought it out for himself. The angels that worshipped did not receive anything from singing or obeying. It was unconditional worship, but it lacked unconditional love because they were always in awe of God's glory. Does that mean that the angels do not love God? Well, the ones that abandoned God clearly didn't but for the ones who remained loyal to him do. The angels who still stand before God, worship God unconditionally because God's presence radiates unexplainable love. It's love that does not require any action and that is why the angel's worship unconditionally. In other words, God does not have to do anything for the angels to prove his love for them because his presence that surrounds them executes that. Love is understood by the angels because they know God made them, but unconditional love is something they cannot comprehend for it requires being one with God. What do I mean by this statement? To understand it, I need to differentiate the love that angels understand versus God's unconditional love that they do not understand. We know that angels were created way before us(humans) so when God was creating the earth, they witnessed creation unfold before their eyes. We know God doesn't make anything without love. This love itself isn't easy to fathom for our own understanding because we will question why God even created Satan. The answer to that just shows us only a glimpse of God's love because he made Satan fully knowing that Satan was going to turn against him. This repetitive 'love' that I keep repeating will only drive our thoughts closer to insanity if we continue questioning God's choices of creation. Even as I write this, I struggle to understand it but because I exist, I can boast that I possess the basic minimum knowledge of love. This is the same for the angels themselves because they know love through their creation as well. What then is God's unconditional love? This is what baffles the minds of angels because they have not and cannot receive God's unconditional love because if they sin, they are not forgiven. Angels are unable to understand unconditional love because they fear judgement. This judgment is basically immediate punishment for angels because they have no excuse to sin. They don't have an excuse to sin because they have always been in the presence of the righteous and perfect God.

There is no fear in love; perfect love drives out all fear. So then, love has not been made perfect in anyone who is afraid, because fear has to do with punishment.
(1 John 4:18) – Good News Translation

On the other hand, because of Jesus' sacrifice when we sin, we are not only able to receive forgiveness, but we can also receive God's Spirit and be apart of him. Now some may have it in their minds that, "If there is no fear in love, why is there a hell? Doesn't that strike fear?" It's a good question but hell wasn't made for human beings but for the devil and his angels because they did not want anything to do with God's love. Therefore, hell is home to those who reject God's love. Except the ironic part is that it is no 'home' but a place of eternal torment and destruction. For us humans, hell becomes a reality if we reject God's unconditional love. Now it is not our actions that essentially get us into hell, but it is dependant on our relationship with God which begins once we receive God's Spirit. Those who reject unconditional love reject a relationship with God which is why hell becomes a reality for human beings because they have put themselves under the same bracket as the devil. They do not reject it out of fear but by hate which is the very fear they associate God with. However, I will speak about all those things later on in this book.

God revealed to these prophets that their work was not for their own benefit, but for yours, as they spoke about those things which you have now heard from the messengers who announced the Good News by the power of the Holy Spirit sent from heaven. These are things which even the angels would like to understand.
(1 Peter 1:12) – New King James Version

1 Peter 1:12 speaks about the Holy Spirit that has been sent down from heaven so that we may receive it. This Holy Spirit is God's way of saying, "I love you all so much that I want you to be one with me." This is God's way of having a relationship with us because no one can have a spiritual relationship with God without his Spirit. By possessing God's Holy Spirit, we begin a connection with God which grants us a higher privilege than the angels themselves. This is a phenomenon that the angels wish to understand because God has granted us an opportunity to be one with him- the definition of unconditional love which they cannot receive.

Do you not know that we shall judge the angels? How much more, then, the things of this life? (**1 Corinthians 6:3**) **- Good News Translation**

It also acts as the thing that prevents us from desiring sin which I will also explain later in this book (don't hate the suspense). The angels in heaven wish to understand this phenomenon because although they may be in God's presence, they are expected by God to live perfectly in their service. The angels may see God's love in his presence, but we are in God's love through his Spirit. So, does that mean anyone who does not have God's Holy Spirit is not in God's love? No, because we became aware of God's unconditional love through Jesus Christ's sacrifice which is called the 'Good News.' Unconditional love was always in God, which is why he sacrificed himself for us, so it is up to us to accept his unconditional love (Which exists in his Spirit). Therefore, anyone who does not have God's Holy Spirit has yet to begin a spiritual relationship with him and those who have received it are in a spiritual relationship with him. But God has always loved us regardless, but it takes his Spirit to be apart of that unconditional love. This is what 1 Peter 1:12 was also referring to regarding the prophet's work that did not benefit them but benefited us. The prophets spoke for years about a hope named Jesus Christ who was to come to deliver the power of God's unconditional love to the world.

By this we know that we abide in him, and he in us, because he has given us of his Spirit. And we have seen and testify that the Father has sent the Son as Savior of the world. Whoever confesses that Jesus is the Son of God, God abides in him, and he in God. And we have known and believed the love that God has for us. God is love, and he who abides in love abides in God, and God in him. (**1 John 4:13-16**) **– New King James Version**

Anyone who believes in Jesus Christ and repents of their sins can receive God's Holy Spirit. How does one know that they have God's Holy Spirit? Well, God's Spirit is a gift by God that we receive when we ask for forgiveness and turn away from our sins. The evidence of God's Holy Spirit in a person is found through the very act of speaking in God's holy language. There are people who have God's Spirit but have never spoken in God's holy language. This is usually because they have not asked God for such gifts and it can be granted through faith. By receiving God's Holy Spirit, we are accepting his unconditional love for us which will then transpire to the very relationship that God so longed for.

So, this leads to another question: Why won't God forgive angels if they sin? Or a better question would be: Why didn't God forgive Satan and the angels that followed him? Well, I will go into more depth to answer those questions later on, but the quick response to that question is that they never asked to be forgiven. God may love the angels, but he loves us unconditionally and that is proven through the sacrifice of Jesus Christ. His unconditional love was shown in that action and because of that action, he offered us his Spirit so that it may dwell in us. By living in us, we can come to understand unconditional worship but also give him that worship.

I keep mentioning worship as if its some sort of cult-based behavior. The concept of worship is something that I will also go into depth about in this book, but I will provide a basic definition of it. The unconditional worship that angels provide God is something that cannot be understood by us because we are cause and effect beings. We place our worship in things like money, technology, social media, music, people, and many more things. Those things become valuable in our hearts because they provide us with entertainment, some sort of emotion or even knowledge (knowledge can be a form of pleasure). We would not worship these things if they didn't give us something in return but the sad truth about our choices of worship are that they are temporary and meaningless. The moment they stop providing us with whatever return that it once gave us, we become spiritually thirsty and search for that return in other things. It is only through God's Holy Spirit that any human being can worship God unconditionally because the spiritual union (The Father & The Son) of himself will be in us. That is the difference between us humans, and the angels.

Angels worship God unconditionally because of how overwhelming and eternal God's presence is. They can and will not seek out the latest new iPhones, for example, because God's presence supersedes all material things and desires. Even as I write this, I begin to wonder about how great God's presence must be but the only way for us to know that is to recieve his Spirit. It is only through God's Spirit where we can experience such things because it will reveal to us the overwhelming glory of God. This complete love story was in God's heart and is proven in 1 John 4:18 because there is no fear in love. The meaning behind that shows us why God made us because although the angels worship God unconditionally; they are incapable of understanding unconditional love. Satan and the angels that followed him are proof of that because they deliberately rejected the love that came from God's presence. Although they know of God's love through their creation, they cannot experience unconditional love because it means being one with God which defines relationship. Proving that relationships are not something that the heavenly beings can attain because the presence of unconditional love dwells in God. That is when he created man and woman for the sole purpose to show his love so that it would be returned right back through a relationship. God sought out for love in our creation so that we would love him back.

Then the LORD God took some soil from the ground and formed a man out of it; he breathed life-giving breath into his nostrils, and the man began to live. **(Genesis 2:7) – Good News Translation**

When Satan saw all this happening, he got angry because he had been exiled from his place of worship in the heavens. Satan never cared for love nor a relationship but just wanted to be above God. So, why was Satan enraged by our creation? The book of Ezekiel 28 states that Satan became, "puffed up with pride, and claimed to be a god." That very pride that he developed was because he was created perfect and felt that he should be above God. When Satan saw God form man and woman in God's own image, his anger grew because we reminded him of God. He saw us as lesser beings compared to who he once was, yet God had created us in his image, and he could not stand it.

So, God created human beings, making them to be like himself. He created them male and female. **(Genesis 1:27) - Good News Translation**

We were made out of love, which to the devil was an insult because it reminded him of that unconditional worship that God receives from his throne. The only difference with what Satan wants and the praise God gets, is that Satan doesn't care how he gets that worship. Although the angels do not understand unconditional love, they continue to worship because of God's glory. Whereas we were shown unconditional love through Christ's sacrifice making our worship worthy to be received by God. The prophet Isaiah is a testimony to that because during his time, Christ had yet to come. But the remarkable thing about Isaiah's vision is he saw Christ before Christ was even born. Even though he may not have known that it was Jesus Christ, he knew it was the Lord. He trembled in fear because he felt unworthy to worship Christ because he knew he was full of sin. Sin prevented the prophet Isaiah from worshipping God but since our sins are now forgiven because of Christ, our worship is worthy to be received by God.

Now faith is the substance of things hoped for, the evidence of things not seen. For by it the elders obtained a good report. Through faith we understand that the worlds were framed by the Word of God, so that things which are seen were not made of things which do appear. **(Hebrews 11:1-3) - King James Version**

Faith is the one and the only element in the entire universe that kickstarts a genuine relationship with God. Faith is the act of believing in God without seeing him. Angels do not require faith to believe in God because they were created to reside in heaven (God's holy throne). This is also why God is strict towards angels because they do not need faith since they believe by seeing his glory (Angels may not need faith but the ones who still live in heaven are called faithful due to their obedience).

Love never gives up; and its faith, hope, and patience never fail. **(1 Corinthians 13:7) - Good News Translation**

Anyone who has faith in God will worship and begin to develop that unconditional love for God due to their faith. We are unable to know unconditional love without his Spirit. Now I hesitated to write that because I have seen people exhibit unconditional love before (well so I thought). Unconditional love is perfect love, and that is something no human can live by because we are not God. Only God can love unconditionally and luckily for us we are who he loves unconditionally. Take for instance forgiveness. If we've ever found it difficult to forgive someone its because we do not possess unconditional love. As a matter of fact, it is humanly impossible to exhibit perfect love because perfect love never dies. It is only God who loves perfectly because he has lived forever. 1 Corinthians 13:7 ties faith, hope, and patience with love because those are just some of the attributes for unconditional love. The angels do not need to have faith, hope or patience because their existence lies solemnly on their absolute worship to God. Satan never cared about love, but when he saw God not only show it but speak it, he grew angrier because it reminded him of God's presence that he rejected. Therefore, he thought to himself, "Since I cannot defeat God, I will destroy the very thing he loves the most because they were made out of his presence." How does he do it though? Do not worry because the secret is out!

CHAPTER 3

BIRTH OF THE DOCTRINE

Jesus answered them, "I saw Satan fall like lighting from heaven." **(Luke 10:18) – New King James Version**

He who sins is of the devil, for the devil has sinned from the beginning. For this purpose, the Son of God was manifested, that he might destroy the works of the devil. **(1 John 3:8) – New King James Version**

What did the devil do? Well, Satan knew Adam and Eve were in God's presence in the garden of Eden. Therefore, he devised a plan to separate them from God's presence by getting them to sin. By doing this, it would disconnect them from God's presence because he knew God did not tolerate sin. Satan thought to himself, "By getting them to sin, God will do to them as he did to me." In other words, Satan himself was unaware of God's unconditional love because he thought that God would dispose of them for good.

Now the serpent was more cunning than any beast of the field which the LORD God had made. And he said to the woman, "Has God indeed said, 'You shall not eat of every tree of the garden'?" And the woman said to the serpent, "We may eat the fruit of the trees of the garden; but of the fruit of the tree which is in the midst of the garden, God has said, 'You shall not eat it, nor shall you touch it, lest you die.'" Then the serpent said to the woman, "You will not surely die. For God knows that in the day you eat of it your eyes will be opened, and you will be like God, knowing good and evil." So when the woman saw that the tree was good for food, that it was pleasant to the eyes, and a tree desirable to make one wise, she took of its fruit and ate. She also gave to her husband with her, and he ate. **(Genesis 3:1-6) – New King James Version**

Eve forgot about God's instructions and started to daydream about how amazing it would have been to be like God. Her mind started thinking in favor of herself rather than listening to God's commandment. Satan knew exactly what angered God and the best way he exercised that tactic was by targeting us.

And the LORD God commanded the man, saying, "Of every tree of the garden you may freely eat; but of the tree of the knowledge of good and evil you shall not eat, for in the day that you eat of it you shall surely die." **(Genesis 2:16-17) – New King James Version**

Once Adam and Eve ate from the tree that gave knowledge of what is good and bad, they didn't physically die. But God wasn't talking about physical death but spiritual death. It was at that moment where we became spiritually disconnected from God and sin entered into us.

For the wages of sin is death, but the gift of God is eternal life in Christ Jesus our Lord **(Romans 6:23) – New King James Version**

Sin broke us off spiritually from God because God and sin cannot be with one another. Romans 6:23 states that, "the wages of sin is death," and Satan knew this since he had committed the same act. Except he was a spiritual being which is why he was kicked out of heaven and could not be forgiven. Pause. I really have to explain this because the pace that I am going at is unfair to the readers. I say its unfair because I myself had to study it deeper. Yes, it is true Satan never asked for forgiveness and he took things to the next level by trying to be above God. However, if everyone is like me, I'd be wondering why forgiveness is not offered to the spiritual beings (angels)? Yes, it is true they should know better because they were in the presence of the invisible God but what was it that really ticked God off? Well, fortunately for us Jesus does give us the answer and it relates to the previous chapter corruption in heaven.

And whoever speaks a word against the Son of Man will be forgiven, but whoever speaks against the Holy Spirit will not be forgiven, either in this age or in the age to come. **(Matthew 112:32) – English Standard Version**

This is what the devil and his angels committed. They spoke against the Holy Spirit (the invisible God). Jesus Christ is the visible likeness of the invisible God and is also referred to as the Son of Man because he came to earth in human form. Even though we shouldn't, the majority of us say horrible things about Jesus but it is not an unforgiveable sin. Now I have to be extremely careful in my explanation here because I do not want to confuse anyone or sin myself when talking about this matter. When the prophet Isaiah saw the Lord in a vision, he saw Christ. Whereas the Seraphim saw the invisible God, or the Holy Spirit of God. Isaiah was incapable of speaking against the Holy Spirit because he had not known of it. But the Seraphim were aware of it which is why they showed the reverence in their actions due to God's power. Satan is aware of the Holy Spirit, but he did not care for it and spoke against it which defied God. But I am talking about the Holy Spirit right now so if someone was to speak against it, are they not forgiven? Here is the answer: For someone to do such a thing they must know and possess the Holy Spirit. For if they were to speak against the Spirit of God, they are no different than the devil himself because they deliberately received God's Spirit as a gift and spoke against it. This is because when someone receives the Holy Spirit, it becomes one with the person and their bodies become a temple of the Lord. That person opened themselves up to God and are then cursing God in his own temple (body) which is the act of rejecting the spiritual presence of God (unforgiveable sin). Which is exactly what the devil did except he was never joined with God but was in front of God's Spirit as a spiritual being which made his actions so despicable.

Or do you not know that your body is the temple of the Holy Spirit who is in you, whom you have from God, and you are not your own? **(1 Corinthians 6:19) – New King James Version**

To get someone who has the Holy Spirit to speak against the Spirit is not an easy task because that person knows better (just like the devil and his angels knew better). But it is something that the devil himself will attempt to do. Those who do not possess it, even if they were to speak against it, are only speaking nonsense since they have never experienced the Holy Spirit. Although it is a sin to speak poorly about Jesus Christ, it is still forgivable. The human body is temporary whereas our spirits are authentic and made to receive eternal life; it is through the spirit that we communicate with the invisible God (Holy Spirit).

And do not fear those who kill the body but cannot kill the soul. But rather fear him who is able to destroy both soul and body in hell. **(Matthew 10:28) – New King James Version**

Now that I have given the knowledge to the public that there is an unforgivable sin, it is still difficult to commit unless the person was to receive God's Spirit. Receiving God's Spirit is not something of a transaction which a person can just go out and get.

Simon saw that the Spirit had been given to believers when the apostles placed their hands on them. So he offered money to Peter and John, and said, "Give this power to me too, so that anyone I place my hands on will receive the Holy Spirit." But Peter answered him, "May you and your money go to hell, for thinking that you can buy God's gift with money! You have no part or share in our work because your heart is not right in God's sight. Repent, then, if this evil plan of yours, and pray to the Lord that he will forgive you for thinking such a thing as this. For I see that you are full of bitter envy and are a prisoner of sin." **(Acts 8:20-24) – Good News Translation**

It requires the steps of believing in Jesus Christ and crying out to him for forgiveness. A person doesn't have to be in church to receive the Holy Spirit either. But it does help to have someone who has the Holy Spirit pray with the person seeking it. But if the person without the Holy Spirit were to pray to God, believe in Jesus Christ and repent of their sins, it can be done by themselves. All in all, for such things to happen, faith and a genuine plea from the heart cannot go unnoticed to God. Therefore, even if a prankster was to attempt to be 'funny' and say they have committed the unforgiveable sin, they are not only walking on thin ice but also fooling themselves. Someone who will make a joke about such things will not obtain God's Spirit but because of God's love he will forgive that person. Even if that person was to go to great lengths to receive God's Spirit, they would need to genuinely plea to God for it and that is a task that cannot be faked. This is because no one can fool God because he knows all. I mean who would go to such great lengths just to commit the unforgivable sin? But sin itself knows no limits and this is found true in humanity because we have done some unthinkable, unspeakable and disturbing things which is why I would not put it past us to do such a thing. But thanks be to God, that God is who he is, and he cannot be fooled (I say that for those who would even think or attempt such things). That is the definition of the unforgiveable sin and Satan and his angels committed it in the presence of God's holy temple (heaven). Now if a person was to go their whole life denying the Spirit, or not believing in it- they have rejected God's unconditional love. This is not the same as the unforgivable sin because the person is not speaking against the Holy Spirit, but they are denying God's truth (due to a lack of faith) which is in the Holy Spirit. But that is not an unforgivable sin because God's unconditional love in the Spirit waits for that person in patience to accept its truth. But that person must accept the Spirit's truth which states: Those who deny him, he too will also deny them back because of their unbelief.

If we continue to endure, we shall also rule with him. If we deny him, he also will deny us. If we are not faithful, he remains faithful, because he cannot be false to himself. **(2 Timothy 2:12-13) – Good News Translation**

Unbelief is a form of rejection to his unconditional love which promises eternal life that he shares with us through the Holy Spirit. Because of his love, his Spirit will accept a person's denial found in their own spirit but that also means that the person will get exactly what they believed in, which in truth isn't eternal life since that is only found in him.

Those who declare publicly that they belong to me, I will do the same for them before my Father in heaven. But those who reject me publicly, I will reject before my Father in heaven. **(Matthew 10:32-33) – Good News Translation**

Now let's get back on topic! Satan knew if he got Adam and Eve to eat from the forbidden fruit, they would become tolerant to sin. That forbidden fruit was our disobedience towards God's presence because it rejected truth for slavery to a sinful nature.

That evening they heard the LORD God walking in the garden, and they hid from him among the trees. **(Genesis 3:8) - Good News Translation**

There was once a time when God's presence walked amongst Adam and Eve. But when they disobeyed God, they were afraid to face his presence because they knew they had done something terrible.

Then the LORD God called to Adam and said to him, "Where are you?" So he said, "I heard your voice in the garden, and I was afraid because I was naked; and I hid myself." And he said, "Who told you that you were naked? Have you eaten from the tree of which I commanded you that you should not eat?" **(Genesis 3:9-11) – New King James Version**

I've heard stories about people who have gotten extreme discomfort, like a sixth sense of some sort, to find out that their child was harmed or even died. I don't know what it's called (or if there is even a term for it). But I think God felt it in Genesis 3:9-11. Thing is it's not like God did not know where Adam was or had not known that he had eaten from the forbidden fruit. God asked where he was because the connection between God and humanity had been disconnected. Yes, eating the tree introduced us to sin but it also did another devastating thing. It killed us off from the presence of God. This was Satan's plan from the very beginning. By getting us away from God's presence, he had thought he won because Adam and Eve were kicked out of the garden. Satan received jurisdiction on our lives because we were no longer connected to God, but we became connected to a sinful nature. Now, this didn't mean Satan made people do things by force. However, God's Spirit was no longer among us which meant Satan had the spiritual authority to enslave us to sin. What that essentially meant was whenever someone had sinned, they had to pay for it. Asking for forgiveness wasn't enough because of the power of the law (will explain the power of the law later in this book).

And he shall do with the bull as he did with the bull as a sin offering; thus he shall do with it. So the priest shall make atonement for them, and it shall be forgiven them. Then he shall carry the bull outside the camp and burn it as he burned the first bull. It is a sin offering for the assembly. **(Leviticus 4:20-21) – New King James Version**

Animal sacrifices were required every time someone sinned because it served as the repayment to the sin committed. Undoubtedly this was a tiresome task to do every time people sinned which inevitably became an issue since they would continue sinning.

Wherefore the Lord said, "Forasmuch as this people draw near me with their mouth, and with their lips do honour me, but have removed their heart far from me, and their fear toward me is taught by the precept of men." **(Isaiah 29:13) – King James Version**

The people continued to sin against God throughout the whole Old Testament which is why we read about God's angry side. In the Scriptures, God even complains through many prophets about how meaningless their offerings and sacrifices were. Although, they were following the procedures to purify themselves, God saw it as pointless because he knew they were going to continue living in sin. This was the problem and the very thing 1 John:3-8 was referring to.

In another vision the LORD showed me the High Priest Joshua standing before the angel of the LORD. And there beside Joshua stood Satan, ready to bring accusation against him. **(Zechariah 3:1) – Good News Translation**

We see another interesting character trait of Satan in Zechariah 3:1. The High Priest Joshua was standing before the angel of the LORD, but Satan was also there to basically 'snitch' on him because he kept a tally of all our sins. This is what the devil did all throughout the whole Old Testament. He would go before God each time a sin was committed and state his case against our souls. Satan's doctrine was to eliminate us from God's presence and by doing so we did not have a spiritual backbone.

Sacrifice and offering you did not desire; my ears you have opened. Burnt offering and sin offering you did not require. Then I said, "Behold, I come; in the scroll of the book it is written of me. I delight to do your will, O my God, and your law is within my heart." **(Psalms 40:6-8) – New King James Version**

For it is not possible that the blood of bulls and goats could take away sins. Therefore, when he came into the world, he said: "Sacrifice and offering you did not desire, but a body you have prepared for me. In burnt offerings and sacrifices for sin you had no pleasure. Then I said, 'Behold, I have come in the volume of the book it is written of me to do your will, O God.'" Previously saying, "Sacrifice and offering, burnt offerings, and offerings for sin you did not desire, nor had pleasure in them" (which are offered according to the law), then he said, "Behold, I have come to do your will, O God." He takes away the first that he may establish the second. By that will we have been sanctified through the offering of the body of Jesus Christ once for all. And every priest stands ministering daily and offering repeatedly the same sacrifices, which can never take away sins. But this man, after he had offered one sacrifice for sins forever, sat down at the right hand of God, from that time waiting till his enemies are made his footstool. For by one offering he has perfected forever those who are being sanctified. But the Holy Spirit also witnesses to us; for after he had said before, "This is the covenant that I will make with them after those days, says the LORD: I will put my laws into their hearts, and in their minds I will write them," then he adds, "Their sins and their lawless deeds I will remember no more." Now where there is remission of these, there is no longer an offering for sin. **(Hebrews 10:4-18) – New King James Version**

Once Adam and Eve were created, Satan influenced them to eat from a fruit that brought us to the enslavement of sin. His first ever doctrine was to remove us from God's presence, but little did Satan know about God's contingency plan. That plan was within Jesus Christ who came to be the one true sacrifice.

Then he took the cup, gave thanks to God, and gave it to them saying, "Drink from it. For this is my blood of the new covenant, which is shed for many for the remission of sins." **(Matthew 26:27-28) - Good News Translation**

These things God has revealed to us through the Spirit. For the Spirit searches everything, even the depths of God. For who knows a person's thoughts except the spirit of that person, which is in him? Do also no one comprehend the thoughts of God except the Spirit of God. Now we have received not the spirit of the world, but the Spirit who is from God, that we might understand the things freely given us by God. **(1 Corinthians 2:10-12) – English Standard Version**

I had difficulty understanding the concept of the Spirit because it did not make sense to me. Whenever I went to church, I saw people worshipping and speaking in God's heavenly language and it looked weird. For the longest time, I found it bogus. But I had every right to think it was fake because I had yet to experience it.

What shall I do with you, O Ephraim? What shall I do with you, O Judah? Your love is like a morning cloud, like the dew that goes early away. Therefore I have hewn them by the prophets; I have slain them by the words of my mouth, and my judgment goes forth as the light. For I desire steadfast love and not sacrifice, the knowledge of God rather than burnt offerings. **(Hosea 6:4-6) – English Standard Version**

Relationship, love, and worship. It has been the sole desire that God wanted from us, but our sin and disobedience drove us away from that path. Yes, it was Satan's plan to get us from ever realizing that. However, it got worse when we ate the very fruit that got us thinking like we are gods. That same corruption Satan caused in heaven, he caused in the garden of Eden. This then led me to ask the question: If God knew we were going to eat from the fruit, why put it in the garden? The answer to that question stems back to the reason for our creation. He wanted a real relationship with us, so he put the tree that gave knowledge of what is good and bad to test our love for him. God knew Satan was going to tempt Eve into eating from the forbidden fruit, and that she would eat it and get Adam to do the same. Although they messed up, he refused to give up on them.

For God so loved the world that he gave his only begotten Son, that whoever believes in him should not perish but have everlasting life. For God did not send his Son into the world to condemn the world, but that the world through him might be saved. "He who believes in him is not condemned; but he who does not believe is condemned already, because he has not believed in the name of the only begotten Son of God." **(John 3:16-18) – New King James Version**

I remember studying all this and thinking how twisted this way of thinking was. But I didn't want to stop because all I wanted was to know God's truth, so I kept pushing myself to learn and found a love that overwhelmed my whole core. Adam and Eve hid from God because they had sinned and were ashamed of their nakedness. I got to thinking about every single time I had done wrong to others and how ashamed I was of my own mistakes. My sins, if stacked up, would go nose to nose with the Eiffel Tower or even exceed the altitude of Mount Everest. Yet, there is this strange but incredible love that is open to forgiving us despite all the mistakes we make.

And yet, I am the God who forgives your sins, and I do this because of who I am. I will not hold your sins against you. **(Isaiah 43:25) – Good News Translation**

Personally, I cannot remember when or where I first read Isaiah 43:25, but I remember becoming so emotional when I read it. I loved it so much that I got it tattooed on my right wrist to always remind me. I did not get it for the sole excuse that I can continue making mistakes with the knowledge that he would always be willing to forgive me. I got it because behind those very words I felt his unconditional love. Even though I still cannot comprehend his unconditional love for us. I have difficulty forgiving myself at times because I introspect the magnitude of my mistakes and always think about how it affects others. Then there is God, whose qualities are beyond my understanding and he just accepts forgiveness and forgets it as if it never happened. My own parents have a hard time forgetting all the stupid things I've done, but then there's God. Whether it is my mistake or a wrong done to me, I always ask myself, "How does someone obtain a heart like that? If it is even possible?"

Now there was a man of the Pharisees named Nicodemus, a ruler of the Jews. This man came to Jesus by night and said to him, "Rabbi, we know that you are a teacher come from God, for no one can do these signs that you do unless God is with him." Jesus answered him, "Truly, truly, I say to you, unless one is born again, he cannot see the kingdom of God." Nicodemus said to him, "How can a man be born when he is old? Can he enter a second time into his mother's womb and be born again?" Jesus answered, "Truly, truly, I say to you, unless one if born of water and the Spirit, he cannot enter the kingdom of God. That which is born of the flesh is flesh, and that which is born of the Spirit is spirit. Do not marvel that I said to you, 'You must be born again.' The wind blows where it wishes, and you hear its sound, but you do not know where it comes from or where it is goes. So it is with everyone who is born of the Spirit." Nicodemus said to him," How can these things be?" Jesus answered him, "Are you the teacher of Israel and yet you do not understand these things? Truly, truly, I say to you, we speak of what we know, and bear witness to what we have seen, but you do not receive our testimony. If I have told you earthly things and you do not believe, how can you believe if I tell you heavenly things? **(John 3:1-12) – English Standard Version**

After Adam and Eve were banished from the garden, they continued to live their lives. It wasn't until the time of Moses and the Israelites when God had made a sacred covenant with his people. I promise, I will explain all this action-packed information later in this book but what needs to be understood is that Israel failed to keep that covenant. God wanted to connect with his people, but they just couldn't commit because they could not come to know or understand who God was. It was all apart of Satan's doctrine for no one to know God. Sin prevented us from knowing God. When I say knowing God, I do not mean the idea or knowledge of his existence but rather that divine connection with God. Only a few people in the Old Testament understood this and are mentioned by God because they pleased him. Now it wasn't because they didn't sin, but it was due to their faith in God which pleased him. However, this wasn't enough for God because he did not create us to just have a relationship with a few people but everyone. That is why the Scriptures say, "He loved the world so much that he gave his only begotten Son." That sacrifice was a worldwide announcement to us about how much he wanted us to 'know him.'

Greater love has no one than this, than to lay down one's life for his friends. You are my friends if you do whatever I command you. No longer do I call you servants, for a servant does not know what his master is doing; but I have called you friends, for all things that I heard from my Father I have made known to you. **(John 15:13-15) – New King James Version**

This is where things get real. Jesus dying on the cross did not just save us from sin, but it opened up a gateway to become one with him. This is why he tells Nicodemus that no one can enter the kingdom of heaven without being baptized by the water and the Spirit. Jesus knew he had to go back into heaven after resurrecting back from the dead, but he could not leave us alone. Sin may have been defeated, but the very thing God wanted from us was accessible to us through the legendary Holy Spirit. Yes, God knew Adam and Eve would screw up in the garden. He knew that because the tree was to test their unconditional love for God and since they failed, he wanted his words to be the testimony to his truth. So, my search led me to dig deeper into God's truth which is defined as his 'Word.' His Word will help us fully understand Jesus' explanation of the Spirit.

In the beginning was the Word, and the Word was with God, and the Word was God. He was in the beginning with God. All things were made through him, and without him nothing was made that was made. In him was life, and the life was the light of men. And the light shines in the darkness, and the darkness did not comprehend it. **(John 1:1-5) – New King James Version**

This passage is puzzling. It suggests many entities yet only describing one entire being: The Spirit of God. The Word was there from the very beginning hence proclaiming the omnipresent abilities of God.

Before God said, "let there be light," it was in him already to declare that action. Inspecting that one line, we know that God is the alpha and omega, but it becomes confusing because John states, "The Word was with God, and the Word was God." Only problem with that statement is it doesn't really make any sense. Or does it? John's statement made complete sense because the Word was with God since he had said the words, and everything came true. This is what blows my mind because when I read it, I thought it sounded contradicting but its because what we define as 'truth' versus 'God's truth' are two different things. Our truth has to be proven, where God's truth just is because of who he is. With just his words he created the whole universe. He didn't snap his fingers or make any crazy hand motions; he just spoke it and it came to be.

He was in the world, and the world was made through him, and the world did not know him. He came to his own, and his own did not receive him. But as many as received him, to them he gave the right to become children of God, to those who believe in his name: who were born, not of blood, nor of the will of the flesh, nor of the will of man, but of God. And the Word became flesh and dwelt among us, and we beheld his glory, the glory as of the only begotten of the Father, full of grace and truth. **(John 1:10-14) – New King James Version**

I think John himself was having a difficult time putting it in his own words. It could be the reason why he phrased it that way because he was speaking about God's truth. That Scripture confirms to us that God is the truth- the one non-negotiable truth. Secondly, John finishes his dumbfounding proclamation by saying, "The Word was God. From the very beginning, the Word was with God." The reason why I'm bringing John is to explain why I had to understand this before learning about the Holy Spirit that Jesus so famously spoke about.

But it was to us that God made known his secret by means of his Spirit. The Spirit searches everything, even the hidden depths of God's purposes. It is only our own spirit within us that knows all about us; in the same way only, God's Spirit knows all about God. We have not received this world's spirit; instead, we have received the Spirit sent by God, so that we may know all that God has given us. **(1 Corinthians 2:10-12) - Good News Translation**

Remember when I asked how does someone obtain a heart as forgiving and loving as God's? I sat in my room and analyzed John 1:1-5, John 3:3-13, 1 Corinthians 2:10-12 and realized that I was missing a massive chunk of the truth. For 24 years of my life, I thought the process of getting into heaven involved reading the bible, going to church and being a good person. I felt this because I knew God would always forgive me anyways and since he is merciful, I was righteous. Well the news hit me hard and the reality was I was so far from the truth. The ironic and funny thing about all of this is if those were the requirements, I had failed on all accounts. Plus, on top of that: Anyone who chooses to continue sinning is living by what I quoted from 1 John 3:8 *(He who sins is of the devil, for the devil has sinned from the beginning -NKJV).* Yeah, I was not walking in the right direction!

John 1:1-5 and John 1:14 taught me that God is truth and his Word is the truth because the Word is who he is since everything he says comes true. This was extremely important for me because I had a terrible habit of picking which Scripture I liked to hear. I would always block out the ones that were undoubtedly an inconvenience for my own life. John 3:3-13 taught me about the Spirit and since God is the truth, then the bogus mindset I had towards people claiming they had the Spirit was not made up. The thing about John 3:3-13 is it has the history of leaving an uncomfortable taste in our mouths because it sounds weird to say that we are 'born-again.' The concept was challenging to absorb for even Nicodemus because he was thinking in the physical sense rather than seeing things in the spiritual. Jesus had to go even further in his explanation by relating it to the way the wind functions. The wind itself is something we cannot see physically, but its presence is made known when we hear the sound it makes or witnesses its power when we look at how it moves things. Nonetheless, Jesus does an exceptional job questioning the knowledge of our own physical senses. We think being born again is strange, yet we do not find natural functions of nature strange. Which is why Jesus asked why it was so difficult for him to not accept the existence of the Spirit. Nicodemus still had a hard time understanding the concept of the Spirit. For me, being baptized under the water wasn't the thing that was confusing because I sort of understood the meaning of being born again. But it was the understanding of the Holy Spirit that confused me. It is until Jesus sends our thoughts over a cliff by basically stating, "How can we come to understand and believe the things of the heavens, when the matters of our physical world dumbfound us?" So, of course, it sounds unusual when we hear Jesus' message regarding the Holy Spirit. It is all apart of Satan's doctrine for us to remain like Nicodemus and always see things in the physical sense. By doing so, Satan blinds us from the truth so that we may never spiritually taste salvation.

Last but not least was 1 Corinthians 2:10-12, which is what got my gears going. If the truth is within the Word, and the being born-again was the only way I could enter the kingdom of heaven, I had to get this Holy Spirit. I studied how the people of the Old Testament struggled with sin but also how they did not know God. I did not want to be like them any longer. The only advantage we have over the people of the Old Testament was the fact that the Jesus Christ had yet to come in that period.

What a record all of these have won by faith! Yet they did not receive what God had promised, because God had deceived on an even better plan for us. His purpose was that only in company with us would they be made perfect. **(Hebrews 11:39-40) - Good News Translation**

Hebrews 11 speaks of the record of all the people who pleased God in the Old Testament, despite never receiving what God had promised. We are lucky enough to receive the blessing of the Holy Spirit, but also, we no longer are required to sacrifice animals like they did in the Old Testament. This gift was prophesied by the prophets, but the time had not come for them to receive it. The sad thing is when the man of the hour finally arrived to deliver the gift, it was the same people who knew the Scriptures that crucified him.

Yet I do proclaim a message of wisdom to those who are spiritually mature. But it is not the wisdom that belongs to this world or to the powers that rule this world- powers that are losing their power. The wisdom I proclaim is God's secret wisdom, which is hidden from human beings, but which he had already chosen for our glory even before the world was made. None of the rulers of this world knew this wisdom. If they had known it, they would not have crucified the Lord of glory. However, as the Scripture says, "What no one ever saw or heard, what no one ever thought could happen, is the very thing God prepared for those who love him." **(1 Corinthians 2:6-9) - Good News Translation**

God may have put the tree in front of the eyes of Adam and Eve to test them, but it was not up to them to understand unconditional love because the world never knew what it was. No one knew it, not even the angels themselves understood it. Even though the angels saw it through the glorious power that was in front of them day and night.

Let us give thanks to the God and Father of our Lord Jesus Christ! Because of his great mercy, he gave us new life by raising Jesus Christ from death. This fills us with a living hope, and so we look forward to possessing the rich blessings that God keeps for his people. He keeps them for you in heaven, where they cannot decay or spoil or fade away. They are for you, who through faith are kept to be revealed at the end of time. Be glad about this, even though it may now be necessary for you to be sad for a while because of the many kinds of trials you suffer. Their purpose is to prove that your faith is genuine. Even gold, which can be destroyed is tested by fire; and so your faith, which is more precious than gold, must also be tested, so that it may endure. Then you will receive praise and glory and honor on the Day when Jesus Christ is revealed. You love him, although you do not see him, and you believe in him, although you do not see him. So rejoice with a great and glorious joy which words cannot express, because you are receiving the salvation of your souls, which is the purpose of your faith in him. It was concerning this salvation that the prophets made careful search and investigation, and they prophesied about this gift which God would give you. They tried to find out when the time would be and how it would come. This was the time which Christ's Spirit in them was pointing in predicting the sufferings that Christ would have to endure, and the glory would follow. God revealed to these prophets that their work was not for their own benefit, but for yours, as they spoke about those things which you have now heard from the messengers who announced the Good News by the power of the Holy Spirit sent from heaven. These things which even the angels would like to understand. **(1 Peter 1:3-12) - Good News Translation**

As my study continued, the more questions I had about the gospel, but I would not understand it without having God's Spirit. I concluded that my life was more than just knowing the truth because according to the Scriptures God isn't pleased with people who only have knowledge of the truth. God is delighted with the person who accepts the knowledge of the truth and wants to be a part of it. Anyone who does this shows God that they have faith in being one with the truth and believe it is superior to any knowledge. Those people please God because they put their trust in God and are no longer spiritually thirsty for anything else. In other words, they are ready to be a part of God's unconditional love and develop the relationship he longed from the beginning. I knew my faults and my sins, and I had things that I consistently struggled with. I wanted to get rid of these things, and I became desperate because I was spiritually exhausted from longing for fullness in other things. I wanted to be made new and the baptism of the water was a step already completed, so I needed the Spirit because it was going to be the guide in my life.

1 Peter 1:3-12 speaks about the beautiful gift of being one with God, and indicates it is something that the angels would like to understand. It is only by his Spirit that we may get to know him. For example, we cannot claim to have a relationship with anyone without first seeing and talking to them. We engage through sight and communication which furthers our relationships with the other person. This is the same with God except the Spirit is required so that we can be one with God. As humans, we are incapable of loving like God because we are not like him. Once we accept his Spirit, we experience that love in ourselves which acts as an antidote towards our sinful nature. When someone says they have been born again, they are spiritually saying that they have been made new with God's Spirit and no longer desire turning back to their sins.

It is true that through the sin of one-man death began to rule because of that one man. But how much greater is the result of what was done by the one man, Jesus Christ! All who receive God's abundant grace and are freely put right with him will rule in life through Christ. **(Romans 5:17) – Good News Translation**

Remember when I thought all that had occurred in Genesis was a twisted way of thinking? If God knew they were going to eat from the tree that gave knowledge of what is good and bad, why would he even put it? That answer is only because of unconditional love. He wanted our love for him to be genuine and the devil thought he outsmarted God by getting Eve to eat from the fruit, but the devil's action triggered God's plan to show love for the world. How can a relationship be genuine without action? No one just loves for the sake of it. Something has to trigger it and God knew we would sin, so he actually allowed it just to show his love for us. Even the actual act of allowing us to sin, shows his love because he wanted us to know that we were not created to be slaves but our freewill gave into disobedience which ironically enslaved us. If a couple has a child and they neglect the child by not taking care of the child, the child will not know what love is. This was and is the same thing with our relationship with God. Adam and Eve's disobedience exposed the flaws of our nature. Satan knew about love through God's omnipotent power. But he did not know about God's unconditional love. Nonetheless he wanted nothing to do with love, instead he wanted worship because to him it was power. Which is why he said, "That's not true; you will not die. God said that because he knows that when you eat it, you will be like God and know what is good and what is bad."

You are the children of your father, the devil, and you want to follow your father's desires. From the very beginning, he was a murderer and has never been on the side of truth because there is no truth in him. When he tells a lie, he is only doing what is natural to him, because he is a liar and the father of all lies. **(John 8:44) – Good News Translation**

This is the thing that I had to learn, it is not like I didn't know Satan was a liar, but that story didn't seem like he lied. But if Jesus called the devil the father of all lies and Jesus is the truth, then it must mean that the devil did, in fact, lie to Eve.

So, Jesus said again, "I am telling you the truth: I am the gate for the sheep. All others who came before me are thieves and robbers, but the sheep did not listen to them. I am the gate. Those who come in by me will be saved; they will come in and go out and find pasture. The thief comes only in order to steal, kill and destroy. I have come in order that you might have life- life in all its fullness. **(John 10:7-10) - Good News Translation**

Jesus answered, "I am the way the truth, and the life; no one goes to the Father except by me. **(John 14:6) - Good News Translation**

What I say is the truth; lies are hateful to me. Everything I say is true; nothing is false or misleading. To those with insight, it is all clear; to the well-informed, it is all plain. Choose my instruction instead of silver; choose knowledge rather than the finest gold. **(Proverbs 8:7-10) - Good News Translation**

It has been established that God is incapable of lying and everything he says is true. Therefore, the dialogue that Eve had with Satan in the garden can only mean that God never lied to Adam and Eve. Satan was the one who lied to Eve. So, why did he lie to Eve? Besides the fact that Satan hates God, how did it benefit him? Satan knew that by convincing Eve to eat of the tree that gave knowledge of what is good and bad, we would not die physically but rather spiritually. The topic of seeing the physical rather than the spiritual began in Genesis. Satan used Eve's mind against her because he knew humans are adept at seeing things only in the physical when it requires a deep spiritual connection with God to see things in the spiritual. It was his goal to have us die a spiritual death, so we became vulnerable to him.

For we do not wrestle against flesh and blood, but against the principalities, against the powers, against the rulers of the darkness of this age, against spiritual hosts of wickedness in the heavenly places. **(Ephesians 6:12) – New King James Version**

49

To conclude, the story of creation is found in the book of Genesis and as simple as the story is, there is much to be understood from it. I have provided the correct Scriptures for everyone to know why God created us. It is also through the Scriptures where we learn more about Satan and his fallen angels (or demons). I had to intensify my research to figure out why there was no mention of God having any sort of relationship with the angels. That was a difficult task because it involved getting to know who God really is and I could not do that on my own. This frustrated me but I had worked too hard to turn back, so I had to understand more about the truth rather than studying the father of lies. As I mentioned in this chapter, the only way to know and understand God is by obtaining his Spirit. Before I took those steps, I had to make sure the validity of all this and I found that within John 1:1-5.

On January 2018, I cannot remember what specific day; I went to a church service that was about to change the whole course of my life. I may not remember what day (besides that it was a Sunday), but I remember that service vividly. The pastor of my church invited anyone who wanted to receive God's Holy Spirit to go to the front of the congregation and pray with the anointed ministers for God's Spirit. I remember my heart began to beat because I had spent so much time studying this Holy Spirit and knew exactly what I had to do and say to get it. I wanted it so badly because I was spiritually broken, and all will see why in this book. I did not want it for research purposes because I had yet to even start writing this book at that time. It may seem like I wanted the Holy Spirit for research purposes because of how I am explaining the process. It sounds like it was a research process because I want everyone to know what triggered me to take the leap of faith. I'm explaining it this way for the good of those who do not know of the Holy Spirit. That way the people who do not have the Spirit will know how to obtain it. I remember being scared because I knew I was full of sin. I felt self conscious because by going forward people would see me, and I felt like I was being judged. Even though that wasn't the case at all but those were my thoughts that caused me to feel afraid and vulnerable. I thank God I still went anyways because my decision was not based on impressing people. I just wanted to get to know God and didn't let anything get in the way of that.

Now the tax collectors and sinners were all gathering around to hear Jesus. But the Pharisees and the teachers of the law muttered, "This man welcomes sinners and eats with them." Then Jesus told them this parable: "Suppose one of you has a hundred sheep and loses one of them. Doesn't he leave the ninety-nine in the open country and go after the lost sheep until he finds it? And when he finds it, he joyfully puts it on his shoulders and goes home. Then he calls his friends and neighbors together and says, 'Rejoice with me; I have found my lost sheep.' I tell you that in the same way there will be more rejoicing in heaven over one sinner who repents than over ninety-nine righteous persons who do not need to repent. "Or suppose a woman has ten silver coins and loses one. Doesn't she light a lamp, sweep the house and search carefully until she finds it? And when she finds it, she calls her friends and neighbors together and says, 'Rejoice with me; I have found my lost coin.' In the same way, I tell you, there is rejoicing in the presence of the angels of God over one sinner who repents." **(Luke 15:1-10) – New King James Version**

I may have not known it then, but God wasn't judging me, but his Spirit was excited to be one with me because of his love for me.

When they finished praying, the place where they were meeting was shaken. They were all filled with the Holy Spirit and began to proclaim God's message with boldness. **(Acts 4:31) – Good News Translation**

Then Peter and John placed their hands on them, and they received the Holy Spirit. **(Acts 8:17) – Good News Translation**

For they heard them speaking in strange tongues and praising God's greatness. **(Acts 10:46) – Good News Translation**

Paul said, "The baptism of John was for those who turned from their sins; and told the people of Israel to believe in the one who was coming after him-that is, in Jesus." When they heard this, they were baptized in the name of Jesus Christ. Paul placed his hands on them, and the Holy Spirit came upon them; they spoke in strange tongues and also proclaimed God's message. **(Acts 19:4-6) - Good News Translation**

I was afraid of doing it because it involved talking to something I could not see, but I felt some overwhelming power drawing me to the front of the church. So, I took a leap of faith and went forward and closed my eyes and prayed. I will never forget that experience. A powerful presence filled my whole body, and I felt extremely warm inside. This presence had me in tears for absolutely no reason, but when I had opened my mouth to speak, I began speaking in a different language. A language that I never had known, and I had no idea what I was saying.

When the day of Pentecost came, all the believers were gathered together in one place. Suddenly there was a noise from the sky which sounded like a strong wind blowing, and it filled the whole house where they were sitting. Then they saw what looked like tongues of fire which spread out and touched each person there. They were all filled with the Holy Spirit and began to talk in other languages, as the Spirit enabled them to speak. **(Acts 2:1-4) - Good News Translation**

Instead, this is what the prophet Joel spoke about: "This Is what I will do in the last days, God says: 'I will pour out my Spirit on everyone. Your sons and daughters will proclaim my message; your young men will see visions, and your old men will have dreams. Yes, even on my servant, both men, and women, I will pour out my Spirit in those days, and they will proclaim my message. I will perform miracles in the sky above and wonders on the earth below. There will be blood, fire, and thick smoke; the sun will be darkened, and the moon will turn red as blood before the great and glorious Day of the Lord comes. And then, whoever calls out to the Lord for help will be saved.'" **(Acts 2:16-21) - Good News Translation**

This is what happened to me on January 2018, and it was at that very moment when I also got the undivided attention of the devil himself. The thing about receiving God's gift, the Holy Spirit, is we mark ourselves as God's children.

And do not make God's Holy Spirit sad; for the Spirit is God's mark of ownership on you, a guarantee that the Day will come when God will set you free. **(Ephesians 4:30) - Good News Translation**

Ephesians 4:30 was my horrible sin because I was so far from knowing the truth. It did not matter that I received God's Spirit because I thought I was set, so I acted like I was free to do as I pleased. That is not how it works because although my prayer to God was genuine, it was at that moment when I should have taken steps to develop a relationship with God's Spirit. This is where Satan's doctrine kicks in once again.

Then I heard a loud voice in heaven saying, "Now God's salvation has come! Now God has shown his power as King! Now his Messiah has shown his authority! For the one who stood before our God and accused believers' day and night has been thrown out of heaven. They have won the victory over him by the blood of the Lamb and by the truth which they proclaimed, and they were willing to give up their lives and die. And so be glad, you heavens, and all you that live there! But how terrible for the earth and sea! For the devil has come down to you, and he is filled with rage because he knows he has only a little time left." **(Revelations 12:10-11) - Good News Translation**

When Jesus ascended into heaven, Satan raged war on the whole earth because his power as the accuser of all sins was no longer valid because Christ had overtaken it.

I cannot talk with much longer, because the ruler of this world is coming. He has no power over me. **(John 14:30) - Good News Translation**

What the devil caused in Genesis was reversed by Jesus, and now Satan can no longer stand before God and accuse us because Jesus had triumphed over sin. He had lost all authority over enslaving us to sin because God's unconditional love poured unto the earth. Although God always loved us unconditionally in heaven, Jesus' resurrection brought forth salvation and grace.

The Scripture says, "Whoever believes in him will not be disappointed." **(Romans 10:11) - Good News Translation**

Jesus reversed the spiritual death caused by Adam and Eve by offering us his Spirit, 'if' we believe in him, we would have a divine connection with him. The Spirit not only acts as our helper but is our mark of ownership to him because he gave himself up for us.

Anyone who strikes you strikes what is most precious to me. **(Zechariah 1:3) – Good News Translation**

But Gods mercy is so abundant, and his love for us is so great, that while we were spiritually dead in our disobedience, he brought us to life with Christ. It is by God's grace that you have been saved. **(Ephesians 2:1-5) – Good News Translation**

This is a true saying: "If we have died with him, we shall also live with him. If we continue to endure him, we shall also rule with him. If we deny him, he also will deny us. If we are not faithful, he remains faithful, because he cannot be false to himself." **(2 Timothy 2:11) – Good News Translation**

We love because God first loved us. If we say we love God but hate others, we are liars. For we cannot love God, whom we have not seen if we do not love others, whom we have seen. **(1 John 4:19-20) – Good News Translation**

After all this victory, the gospel was bestowed onto the disciples to go and preach the Good News to everyone so that they too would know about this incredible love. This infuriated Satan because everything he had done in Genesis and all throughout the Old Testament was ruined. The very 'snitch' himself knew that time was approaching for him to answer to all his wickedness and since he could not reverse or disrupt what Jesus had done, he had to change up his plans.

We've all heard the saying, "If I go down, I'm taking you down with me," and that is exactly what Satan started to do when Christ ascended into heaven. Revelations 12:12 says, "For the devil has come down to you, and he is filled with rage because he knows that he has only a little time left." This little time that the book of Revelations speaks of, does not specify how much time. No one knows precisely when it will

THE SECRET IS OUT

happen but it's not like the Jewish people knew when the Messiah was to come and when he did come, they did not even know it.

The God Abraham, Isaac, and Jacob, the God of our ancestors, has given divine glory to His servant Jesus. But you handed him over to the authorities, and you rejected him in Pilate's presence, even after Pilate had decided to set him free. He was holy and good, but you rejected him, and instead, you asked Pilate to do you the favor of turning loose a murderer. You killed the one, who leads to life, but God raised him from death- and we are witnesses to this. **(Acts 3:13-15) - Good News Translation**

So, this leads to the question: How is it that Satan can bring us down? Well, he had to redevelop his doctrine which does not only apply to believers but non-believers as well. He doesn't care who it is because his rage is beyond understanding. He knows that the only way for anyone to know God is by receiving God's Spirit and the only way to do that is through faith.

To have faith is to be sure of the things we hope for, to be certain of the things we cannot see. It was by their faith that people of the ancient times won God's approval. **(Hebrews:1-2) - Good News Translation**

No one can please God without faith, for whoever comes to God must have faith that God exists and rewards those who seek him. **(Hebrews 11:6) - Good News Translation**

His doctrines key weapon involves manipulating and taking advantage of our physical senses because he knows without God's Spirit we cannot be unified with God. It doesn't just stop there. God's Spirit is available and free to anyone who believes in Jesus Christ, but does that mean they are immune to Satan? That answer is found through my story because I was not immune to his voice, not at all. I had thought everything was going to be all sunshine and rainbows because I had God's Holy Spirit inside me, but I deceived myself. Little did I know I was going to go through hell and back fighting the very dragon the book of Revelations speaks of. Believer or non-believer; what the devil does is to steal, kill and destroy. Even if someone does not believe in God. We all have

55

faith in something and by disrupting that, it breaks the very love within us. That is why 1 Corinthians 13:7 states, "Love never gives up; and its faith, hope, and patience never fail." Faith derives from love and by killing off someone's faith they lose a piece of themselves. To have faith in something, we must have some sort of love towards it and this became my downfall. On March 18th, 2018 my faith was attacked to the point where I couldn't feel nor recognize any sort of love, so I lost my will to live and attempted suicide. It was not attacked by people, but it was because I did not develop a relationship with the Spirit of God. I took steps to find the truth, so the devil held me accountable to my knowledge of the truth. He attacked me through anxiety, addictions, lawlessness, lust, hardships and eventually suicide. Since the devil does not stand before God to accuse us, he accuses us through our thoughts and feelings. Now if he succeeds, we find ourselves in some dark places! It's so sad that I had allowed myself to get to such a low moment, but it was that terrifying moment where I began to understand Ephesians 6:12 which states, "For we are not fighting against human beings but against the wicked spiritual forces in the heavenly world, the rulers, authorities, and cosmic powers of this dark age." The devil's presence has settled itself in this world by deceiving not only me but many others. This book will expose more about his tactics and plans. He does not go easy on anyone, believer of God or not. All he wants to do is to steal, kill and destroy because this war is to anger God. I began to ask myself if that is the case, why doesn't God just destroy Satan for good? The reason why God allows for Satan's existence is to test our love for him. He has already done his part by giving us the gift of the Holy Spirit which is more powerful than anything.

But you belong to God, my children, and have defeated the false prophets because the Spirit who is in you is more powerful than the spirit in those who belong to the world. **(1 John 4:4) – Good News Translation**

Before us, God had the angels in heaven worshipping and obeying him day and night, but there did not exist any relationship. Therefore, he made us out of love, and we prove our love for him through our faith. I mean it makes sense if we think about it. How much greater is our love worth, when we believe in him, whom we have not seen?

Anyone who is not for me is really against me; anyone who does not help me gather is really scattering. **(Matthew 12:30) - Good News Translation**

Even though we are not worthy of his love, God still went to extreme lengths just to show his love for us. We not only became valuable, but we are blessed to be apart of his glory by becoming one with him. Sin is like a financial transaction that is paid with death. The more we sinned, the more Satan accused us, and our value depreciated until we were worth nothing. But Jesus Christ came, and he put himself beneath his glory and worth because he was the only one who could cover the tab that sin was demanding. Jesus gave his life which could not be controlled by death so that we would become valuable and worthy of eternal life.

"The Father loves me because I am willing to give up my life, in order that I may receive it back again. No one takes my life away from me. I give it up of my own free will. I have the right to give it up, and I have the right to take it back. This is what my Father has commanded me to do." **(John 10:17-18) - Good News Translation**

Satan has developed many different ways to get us from being connected with God's Spirit. He either distracts us by keeping us busy or leading our faith into other things. Those who do believe in God are not immune to his temptations and I found that out the hard way. The rest of this book will entail my experience with his voice and the many times I listened or had felt defeated by the guilt of my own sins. It is true that we do not fight against human beings, although we might physically, we are not one another's enemies. I wrote this chapter with just my bare human knowledge but to fight the ancient serpent, named the devil and Satan, I had to give my life to God because he holds the victory. Satan is not invincible because victory exists within God and the only way to know victory is to be one with it. I did not give up and did my best to pick up my broken heart and wavering faith and called for the Holy Spirit's help. When I called out for help, God answered and in ways I could not imagine. Thus, revealing the secret of God's truth and how we can use it to defeat Satan's doctrine.

"You want to write about me? You want to tell the world of all my secrets and expose me into the light? You are pathetic! They won't listen to you because they belong to me. Author, oh author you will fail and fall in my presence, and I will tear through your flesh while you bleed out because you are weak. You're an alcoholic, a slave to depression, and no one loves you. The tears of your loved ones are caused by you and with that said, you tried to kill yourself. How sad are you? You should get up right now and just finish the job or else I will.

I will throw everything at you, and I will take everything from you. I have demons everywhere with names of which you've never even heard. Behold my children: depression, anxiety, addiction, suicide, the disease will all attack you! When they're through with you, you'll have nothing! And that is when your soul will be mine."

-The doctrine of Satan

CHAPTER 4

BATTLING EGYPT AND BABYLON

On September 4th, 2012 Jefferson Bethke posted a spoken word video called, 'Counterfeit Gods,' on his YouTube channel. In the video he asks an underlining question, 'What's on your throne?' This question becomes enlightening once he elaborates on the word throne. Jefferson expands on the metaphor throne by stating that it is what lies within our hearts. A throne is a representation of royalty, power and whoever sits on that throne controls a kingdom, empire or some sovereign power. That then led me to ask myself, "What was on my throne?"

Growing up I have always known who Jesus was but I, like many other teenagers, hated going to church. My favorite time about church was when it was over. I did not know who Jesus truly was and I have a terrible confession to make. I did not want Jesus to be on my throne simply because it sounded boring and non-fulling. I wanted to reap the benefits of what Jesus could do for me (blessing wise) but wasn't interested in putting him first. I was about to find out the hard way of what it was like not to have Christ on my throne.

It wasn't until my first year of university where I would get into drinking alcohol. Alcohol began as something fun to do on a Friday night with friends. The social awkwardness to meet new people disappeared because I become loose and more relaxed. It's not like I'm a shy person and need alcohol, but the more I drank, the more I thought to myself that I needed it. The only problem is it turned into my great escape from reality because I did not want to spend a moment in my mind. I had so much going on in my mind that I did not want to be in my mind anymore. My mind was under attack with the paranoia of never amounting to anything. Whereas my heart was heavy with pride because I didn't want to admit that I needed God. I still wanted to live by my human nature and do the things everyone else was doing. Even if it cost me my happiness, joy and peace. I was mistaking pleasure for joy, and that was messing with my spirit.

Now the works of the flesh are evident, which are: adultery, fornication, uncleanness, lewdness, idolatry, sorcery, hatred, contentions, jealousies, outbursts of wrath, selfish ambitions, dissensions, heresies, envy, murders, drunkenness, revelries, and the like; of which I tell you beforehand, just as I also told you in time past, that those who practice such things will not inherit the kingdom of God. **(Galatians 5:19-21) – New King James Version**

The Spirit (Holy Spirit) sensed this because all the things that surrounded my heart didn't bring any happiness but just dug me deeper into the darkness. Apostle Paul does a great job describing what we are like when we let our bodies, or in other words human nature, take control of our lives (Galatians 5:19-21). Now before I continue, I just want to make sure everyone understands what I mean when I say, "my spirit" vs "The Spirit". "My spirit" relates to the condition of my soul, whereas "The Spirit" relates to God's Spirit residing in me (which also is why I capitalize "spirit" and include "the").

But the fruit of the Spirit is love, joy, peace, longsuffering, kindness, goodness, faithfulness, gentleness, self-control. Against such there is no law. And those who are Christ's have crucified the flesh with its passions and desires. If we live in the Spirit, let us also walk in the Spirit. Let us not become conceited, provoking one another, envying one another. **(Galatians 5:22-26) – New King James Version**

Apostle Paul does a wonderful job comparing the difference between our spirit and The Spirit. Galatians 5:22-26 is what happens when someone obtains the Spirit of God. But for the purpose of this chapter, I'll get back to how I had alcohol on my throne. The thing about getting drunk is we say and do stupid things that we end up regretting the next day. Speaking on behalf of my own experiences, the worst thing it did for me, was it made me lose sense of who I genuinely was or wanted to be.

You are the children of your father, the devil, and you want to follow your father's desires. From the very beginning, he was a murderer and has never been on the side of the truth, because there is no truth in him. When he tells a lie, he is only doing what is natural to him, because he is a liar and the father of all lies. **(John 8:44) - Good News Translation**

As I mentioned in the previous chapter, Satan is a liar. It is Jesus himself who calls Satan, "the father of all lies." There are no buts or ifs or negotiating what Satan's character is.

Then Jesus said to them again, "Most assuredly, I say to you, I am the door of the sheep. All who ever came before Me are thieves and robbers, but the sheep did not hear them. I am the door. If anyone enters by me, he will be saved, and will go in and out and find pasture. The thief does not come except to steal, and to kill, and to destroy. I have come that they may have life, and that they may have it more abundantly. **(John 10:7-10) – New King James Version**

The juxtaposition is evident in these two Scriptures because God in Spirit within Jesus, tells the truth. Where Satan, who also is a spirit, is a liar. The dark humor here is we pick Satan every day without realizing it. I chose not to have Jesus sit on my throne and decided to live for the world.

Do not love the world or anything that belongs to the world. If you love the world, you do not love the Father. Everything that belongs to the world-what the sinful desires, what people see and want, and everything in this world that people are so proud of none of this comes from the Father; it all comes from the world. **(1 John 2:15-16) - Good News Translation**

The world offered alcohol and I gladly accepted it because the world declared that it was okay to have a drink and enjoy ourselves. When I say the world, it must be noted that the world that the bible speaks about is not the things we can see but the things we cannot. As mentioned in the earlier chapters, the devil was thrown down onto the earth and wasted no time setting up his spiritual dominion upon the earth. Therefore, he will use things like alcohol, drugs, pornography, and many more things. The list can go on, but the key is to get any of these things to be on our thrones. The best part, in terms of the devil, is he introduces these things to the world as harmless and innocent. Sin may not have the power to enslave us anymore, but the devil has figured out a way to present such things into our lives as harmless. All in the goal to make us become one with them. If he can get us just to accept the temptations he sets before us, we will find it difficult to accept God in our lives.

What he presented to me was alcohol, and I found that difficult to fight because my flesh eventually began to crave it. It was like I had some sort of relationship with it. The same relationship that God desires with us, Satan attempts to disrupt us from ever being with God by presenting an idol in front of us. Now I will elaborate more on the word 'idol' soon but to simplify things, an idol can be anything that we begin to worship. For other people, it may not be alcohol that will get them, but Satan is no stranger to crossing lines.

All this I will give you, the devil said, "If you kneel down and worship me." Then Jesus answered, "Go away, Satan! The Scripture says, "Worship the Lord your God and serve only him!" **(Matthew 4:9-10) – Good News Translation**

*And God spoke all these words, saying: "I am the LORD your God, who brought you out of the land of Egypt, out of the house of bondage. You shall have no other gods before me." * **(Exodus 20:1-3) – New King James Version**

Satan approached Jesus while he was fasting so naturally his body was weak because he was hungry. Despite being hungry, it is by Jesus' Spirit that gave him the strength to not only fight off the temptation of sin, but he also rebuked Satan. But this is not the only thing that we take away from this Scripture. Satan also asked Jesus to kneel down and worship him, but Jesus responded that no one should be worshipped except God. What Jesus was quoting was one of the Ten Commandments which states, 'You shall have no other gods before me.' Here's where things relate back to us because he does this everyday to us.

You shall not make yourself a carved image- any likeness of anything that is in heaven or above, or that is in the earth and beneath, or that is in the water under the earth; you shall not bow down to them nor serve them. For, I, the LORD your God, am a jealous God, visiting the iniquity of the fathers upon the children to the third and fourth generations of those who hate me. But showing mercy to thousands, to those who love me and keep my commandments. **(Exodus 20:4-6) – New King James Version**

"Did the devil seriously try to tempt Jesus Christ into worshiping him?" that is the one prominent thought that went through my head when I read Matthew 4:9-10. It's like going up to a police officer and offering to sell him drugs and not expecting to get arrested. But here's the thing. I may laugh at that scenario but in my spiritual imagination the devil is looking at me saying, "Oh you want to laugh, when I've gotten you to worship me a million times." Why am I saying this? Because that is what happens when the Holy Spirit (Jesus) is not on our thrones. At that moment of time, Christ was hungry, and we've all heard the term 'hangry'. It is a flesh vs spirit issue but what makes us behave so irrational at times of hunger is much deeper than feeding our bodies food. This chapter will elevate the meaning of temptation even if we think we are in control. We picture the devil as this creature with horns and scary red eyes holding a pitchfork, but the reality is he is a master at deception.

And no wonder! For Satan himself transforms himself into an angel of light. **(2 Corinthians 11:14) – New King James Version**

His sin was to be like the Most High, so he defied God and tried to steal the worship for himself. Guess what he has and is doing in today's day in age! Even as we speak, he has incorporated some sort of worship that is apart of our daily lives which doesn't glorify God.

The first and second of the Ten Commandments intertwine with one another because the devil can use money, possessions, movements, mindsets, feelings, people and many more things just to tempt us to worship it. So, even if someone has never deliberately said, "I worship Satan," he has devised it in his doctrine to get us to worship anything other than God, which is sin. So, what is worship? How does one do it? The concept of worship is held significantly throughout the bible, but why? People don't step outside and want others to kneel and worship them. That is just socially awkward and weird. Or is it?

Then a herald cried aloud: "To you it is commanded, O peoples, nations, and languages, that at the time you hear the sound of the horn, flute, harp, lyre, and psaltery, in symphony with all kinds of music, you shall fall down and worship the gold image that King Nebuchadnezzar has set up; and whoever does not fall down and worship shall be cast immediately into the midst of a burning fiery furnace." So at that time, when all the people heard the sound of the horn, flute, harp, and lyre, in symphony with all kinds of music, all the people, nations, and languages fell down and worshiped the gold image which King Nebuchadnezzar had set up. **(Daniel 3:4-7) – New King James Version**

King Nebuchadnezzar was the king of Babylon at that time and he commanded his people to build him a gold statue. In those days, their worship consisted of gold statues, but in this case the gold statue to Mr. Nebuchadnezzar represented his empire Babylon. King Nebuchadnezzar's intention behind the golden statue was for people of all nations, races, and languages to worship him. Back then it was kneeling and worshiping gold statues, but the concept of worship has not changed because worship is the act of glorying and praising what we hold valuable in our hearts. Just like telephones have been innovated from landlines to the smartphones and iPhones so has worship been innovated from gold statues to glorifying celebrities, love of money, partying, or any human desires. I named this chapter battling Egypt and Babylon for a reason. Babylon represents the temptations of idols, where Egypt represents slavery or in other words addictions. King Nebuchadnezzar was king of Babylon and when he made the decree to worship his gold statue, he was not only speaking to the Babylonians but every single race. Amongst the Babylonians were the Israelites. This is where the story gets interesting because the Israelites were God's people and they knew about God's commandments.

'I am the LORD your God who brought you out of the land of Egypt, out of the house of bondage. 'You shall have no other gods before me. You shall not make yourself a carved image- any likeness of anything that is in heaven above, or that is in the earth beneath, or that is in the water under the earth; you shall not bow down to them nor serve them. For I, the LORD your God, am a jealous God, visiting the inquity of the fathers upon the children to the third and foruth generations of those who hate me. **(Deuteronomy 5:6-9) – New King James Version**

Despite the knowledge of this commandment everyone in the crowd that day bowed to a golden statue that king Nebuchnezzar had set up, all except for three young Hebrew men.

Therefore, at that time certain Chaldeans came forward and accused the Jews. They spoke and said to King Nebuchadnezzar, "O king, live forever! You, O king, have made a decree that everyone who hears the sound of the horn, flute, harp, lyre, and psaltery, in symphony with all kinds of music, shall fall down and worship the gold image; and whoever does not fall down and worship shall be cast into the midst of a burning fiery furnace. There are certain Jews whom you have set over the affairs of the province of Babylon: Shadrach, Meshach, and Abednego; these men, O king, have not paid due regard to you. They do not serve your gods or worship the gold image which you have set up." Then Nebuchadnezzar, in rage and fury, gave the command to bring Shadrach, Meshach, and Abednego. So they brought these men before the king. Nebuchadnezzar spoke, saying to them, "Is it true, Shadrach, Meshach, and Abednego, that you do not serve my gods or worship the gold image which I have set up? Now if you are ready at the time you hear the sound of the horn, flute, harp, lyre, and psaltery, in symphony with all kinds of music, and you fall down and worship the image which I have made, good! But if you do not worship, you shall be cast immediately into the midst of a burning fiery furnace. And who is the god who will deliver you from my hands?" Shadrach, Meshach, and Abednego answered and said to the king, "O Nebuchadnezzar, we have no need to answer you in this matter. If that is the case, our God whom we serve is able to deliver us from the burning fiery furnace, and he will deliver us from your hand, O king. But if not, let it be known to you, O king, that we do not serve your gods, nor will we worship the gold image which you have set up." **(Daniel 3:8-18) – New King James Version**

As we read Daniel 3:8-18, we see the intense pressure that was among all people of Babylon. Well, the Babylonians were not under any pressure because they did not know God so to bow to a gold statue was conforming to their culture and religion. However this was not the case for the Israelites because they were not Babylonians. Babylon at that specific time was a powerful empire that conquered many nations. This is why it was said, "people of all nations, races, and languages!" There were other nations, races and languages that had gathered together in that crowd because Babylon had conquered not just the Israelities but other nations.

Before Babylon, the Israelities were enslaved by the Egyptians but God saved them through Moses which I will discuss later on. Now there were other nations that had also conquered the Israelites but for the purpose of this chapter, I will only be discussing these two nations. After God had saved the Israelities from the enslavement of the Egyptians, he gave them the Ten Commandments. One of those Ten Commandments state not to bow down or worship anything or anyone but God. This commandment put the Israelities to the test in Babylon because if they did not bow down to king Nebuchadnezzar's golden statue they were going to be put in a flaming furance. So that leads me to ask everyone, "What would you do?" I know for a fact that I would be terrified of king Nebuchadnezzar's strict command and probably would have bowed down to the gold statue but that was not the case for Shadrach, Meshach, and Abednego.

Then Nebuchadnezzar was full of fury, and the expression on his face changed toward Shadrach, Meshach, and Abednego. He spoke and commanded that they heat the furnace seven times more than it was usually heated. And he commanded certain mighty men of valor who were in his army to bind Shadrach, Meshach, and Abednego, and cast them into the burning fiery furnace. Then these men were bound in their coats, their trousers, their turbans, and their other garments, and were cast into the midst of the burning fiery furnace. Therefore, because the king's command was urgent, and the furnace exceedingly hot, the flame of the fire killed those men who took up Shadrach, Meshach, and Abednego. And these three men, Shadrach, Meshach, and Abednego, fell down bound into the midst of the burning fiery furnace. Then King Nebuchadnezzar was astonished; and he rose in haste and spoke, saying to his counselors, "Did we not cast three men bound into the midst of the fire?" They answered and said to the king, "True, O king." "Look!" he answered, "I see four men loose, walking in the midst of the fire; and they are not hurt, and the form of the fourth is like the Son of God." Then Nebuchadnezzar went near the mouth of the burning fiery furnace and spoke, saying, "Shadrach, Meshach, and Abednego, servants of the Most High God, come out, and come here." Then Shadrach, Meshach, and Abednego came from the midst of the fire. And the satraps, administrators, governors, and the king's counselors gathered together, and they saw these men on whose bodies the fire had no power; the hair of their head was not singed nor were their garments affected, and the smell of fire was not on them. Nebuchadnezzar spoke, saying, "Blessed be the God of Shadrach, Meshach, and Abednego, who sent his Angel and delivered his servants who trusted in him, and they have frustrated the king's word, and yielded their bodies, that they should not serve nor worship any god except their own God! **(Daniel 3:19-28) – New King James Version**

The three young Hebrew men were pressured into bowing down and worshipping king Nebuchadnezzar's golden statue. All the other Jewish people bowed down out of fear and could not find it within their faith to say no to Nebuchadnezzar. Despite what the crowd was doing the three boys remained faithful to God even when their lives were in danger. Now this might raise the question, "What does this have to do with the present times?" Well, idolatry is something that Satan has found easy to tempt us into because he will use simple things that look harmless so that we worship them. Consequently, this leaves us vulnerable to the spirit of idolatry & addictions because Satan will take what God has handed to the physical world and pervert it spiritually to subdue us. God created everything in the world to be enjoyed so that we may give him praise. What Satan has done is use what God has made and tempts us into worshipping it. It is Satan's way of mocking God because we begin to worship the things God created instead of the maker himself.

The LORD said, "Do not make idols or set up statues, stone pillars to worship. I am the LORD your God. **(Leviticus 26:1) - Good News Translation**

Babylon was known for their idol worshipping but the difference between Babylon and Egypt was that the Egyptians did not make the Israelites worship their idols or false gods. The Egyptians were just cruel to the Israelites and tortured them, where in Babylon they did not treat them like slaves but citizens. Before Shadrach, Meshach, and Abednego defied king Nebuchadnezzar's commandment they were in charge of the province of Babylon. That means they were respected by Nebuchadnezzar because they were put in high political ranks. Now before I continue, I need to emphasize that I am not talking about the actual country Egypt we now know today. Egypt is metaphorical representation of slavery of God's creations which is all of us. So, when I say something like, "It is obvious why we should despise Egypt." The metaphor means no one wants to be a slave and because of Egypt's biblical history with Israel it serves as an example to emphasis spiritual slavery.

Personally, I think Babylon is more dangerous than Egypt because of how it presents itself as modest. If we completely disregard golden statues and the act of bowing down and worshipping them. What are the things that surround us today which tempt us into idolatry? The Babylonians had no problem bowing down to a golden statue because that was their god. However, I did say not to think about golden statues so if we are not bowing down and worshipping golden statues, we must all be in the clear. Right?

"See we all worship something, to an object we're all liable. Ladies, to some your boyfriend is your god, and Cosmo is your bible. Yet, we mock and laugh at the

Israelites Golden calf, but we do the same thing right back; it just looks a little different than that. So, question: "What's on your throne? What do you chase so you don't feel alone? So, what defines you? What do you give ultimate worth? And what if taken will bring ultimate hurt?" Now see, that is your god. And all of us, we've sacrifice deep joy for shallow happiness. To be honest, we look like fools. We're like full grown adults in the kiddie pool, going "oh my goodness, guys! This is like so cool!" Because we're slaves to our possessions; we are always craving something new. Reality check, if you can't give it up, you don't own it, it owns you. And that's why the bible, it says we're all spiritual prostitutes, in fact, it says were much worse because at least prostitutes get paid for their works. All we get paid is a hearse. That's why worship is not just behavior; it goes way into our core. So, ask yourself "What is your God? What do you bow down before?"

For example, some of us, we don't worship God, but we worship what he said. We got theology in our head, but in our hearts, we are poor, pitiful, naked and dead. Or some of us worship in stadiums, while some of us worship in bars. Some of us worship our possessions, while some of us worship our cars. See, some of us worship science, while some of us worship the arts. But I don't care what clothes your idol's wearing for the disease is in the heart."

- Jefferson Bethke, Counterfeit Gods (2012)

In my opinion, Babylon is more dangerous than Egypt because it leads us far past enslavement and straight into the assimilation of Satan's doctrine. What makes Babylon so deadly is that it presents itself as norm or culture that everyone is following and if we do not do what everyone else is doing, we feel left out. The ones who are content with the culture will call themselves Babylonians and see nothing wrong with what they are doing. Babylon attempts to assimilate all nations, races, and languages to conform into a one world order. Where Egypt does not care to bring together any nation, race or language but to torture and enslave people into depression, addictions, and misery. People choose to enter Egypt based off of how Egypt presents itself, which is pleasure, but it is ruthless once the person enters its territory because it refuses to let them go. Where Babylon behaves a bit differently because it pressures people to be like it. Once we become like it, we endanger ourselves of losing out on what God intended us to be because Babylon will award us citizenship to its cultures and way of life in worship.

For our citizenship is in heaven, from which we also eagerly wait for the Saviour, the Lord Jesus Christ. **(Philippians 3:20) – New King James Version**

This is dangerous because Babylon has skilled itself in making evil look good through its structure in government and civilization. Which is why I think Babylon is worse because it has innovated Egypt by creating an order which strives to make everyone like itself and labels that peaceful. When in reality, it is apart of Satan's doctrine to get us away from God. Either way, neither of the two representations are good. Some have been enslaved by their addictions whereas some have been victims to the assimilation of Babylon's ways (worship of idols). Or an even worse situation is if we are conquered by both. This constant talk about being conquered by these two specific nations may cause confusion so what I'll do is elaborate further. I already explained what Egypt and Babylon both represent but what needs to be understood is the representation of nations.

If anyone can recall in the chapter birth of the doctrine, I spoke about the steps I took in determining the legitimacy of being born again. I quoted John 1:1-3 which states, "In the beginning was the Word, and the Word was with God, and the Word was God. He was in the beginning with God." Well what that meant was that the Word is another name for God which also means the Word of God is not something ordinary.

For the Word of God is living and powerful, and sharper than any two-edged sword, piercing even the division of soul and spirit, and of joints and marrow, and is a discerner of the thoughts and intents of the heart. **(Hebrews 4:12) – New King James Version**

What does this have to do with the representation of nations, worshipping of idols, and addictions? Israel is referred to as God's nation because the Israelites of that time acknowledged God as their nation's God before anyone else. Before I go off about the representation of nations, I think it would be vital for everyone to know how Israel even got its name.

And he said, "Your name shall no longer be called Jacob, but Israel; for you have struggled with God and with men and have prevailed." **(Genesis 32:28) – New King James Version**

And God said to him, "Your name is Jacob; your name shall not be called Jacob anymore, but Israel shall be your name." So he called his name Israel. Also God said to him: "I am God Almighty. Be fruitful and multiply; a nation and a company of nations shall proceed from you and kings shall come from your body. The land which I gave Abraham and Isaac I give to you; and your descendants after you I give this land." Then God went up from him in the place where he talked with him. **(Genesis 35:10-13) – New King James Version**

The name Israel was given to Jacob as a continuous blessing /promise which originated from Jacob's grandfather Abraham (Abraham's son was Isaac). God had promised Abraham that he would be the father of many nations. Abraham is called the father of many nations because God had changed his name from Abram (Hebrew for "exalted father") to Abraham (Hebrew for "father of many nations"). It was at that time that Abraham wanted a son but both him and his wife Sarah were old in age (When they had a child; Sarah was 90 years old and Abraham was 100 years old). God gave Abraham and Sarah a son and they named him Isaac. Isaac then had two sons and named them Esau and Jacob. But it was through Jacob where Abraham's promise was fulfilled because Isaac (Abraham's son) gave Jacob the blessing that his father originally gave to him. Therefore, Jacob had twelve children and they became the twelve tribes of Israel. However, it is through Jacob that we recognize Israel as Israel because God had blessed him due to his faith which derived from his father Isaac and Grandfather Abraham. This "faith" gave birth to the nation Israel because God had changed Jacob's name to Israel. The name change was to define the meaning behind Israel because Israel means "to contend or to fight with God" in Hebrew.

Then Jacob was left alone; and a Man wrestled with him until the breaking of day. Now when he saw that he did not prevail against him, he touched the socket of his hip; and the socket of Jacob's hip was out of joint as he wrestled with him. And he said, "Let me go, for the day breaks." But he said, "I will not let you go unless you bless me!" So he said to him, "What is your name?" He said, "Jacob." And he said, "Your name shall no longer be called Jacob, but Israel; for you have struggled with God and with men and have prevailed." **(Genesis 32:25-28) – New King James Version**

This is why God changed Jacob's name because he would not quit wrestling with God until he blessed him. Declaring the representation of Israel as a person that stops at nothing to gain favour with God, which is what Jacob did. As time passed, Jacob passed away and so did his twelve children, but they too also had children which introduced the Jewish identity -Israel. It was then when the nation Egypt enslaved Israel for 400 years. Israel was tortured and tormented by the Egyptians, so they decided to call out to God because they remembered that God was always there for their ancestors (Abraham, Isaac & Jacob). Because the nation Israel knew God through their lineage, they called out to God for help. God then used Moses to save Israel from Egypt and that was when Israel as a nation proclaimed that God was their God. But the thing about this little history lesson was it was not all sunshine and rainbows with Israel and God. Although God had liberated them physically as nation, the Israelites had a habit of disobeying God and that habit was something all nations were enslaved by-sin.

He was in the world, and the world was made through him, and the world did not know him. He came to his own, and his own did not receive him. But many received him, to them he gave the right to become children of God, to those who believe in his name. **(John 1:10-12) – New King James Version**

Fast forward to the New Testament: God being the Word that already existed, went to his own nation (Israel) as Jesus Christ and taught his nation about himself because they did not truly know him. Please refer back to the chapter birth of the doctrine on the actual definition of knowing God (through the Holy Spirit). However, God knew that the

Jews would reject him because sin makes nations care about themselves. In the New Testament, we read about God's nation (Israel) reject Jesus because they read his Word as a hope for the restoration of Israel's land and freedom. They did not expect the Messiah to come in human form because it is blasphemy to call a human God. That is why the Jews of the New Testament rejected him as the Messiah and on top of that, they thought that the Messiah would free them from Rome's reign (or any nation that stood against Israel). But the Word stayed true to itself, since no one knew or understood it. It stayed true to truth and love because it made everything in the beginning out of truth and love. That truth had nothing to do with the physical liberation of nations but the spiritual liberation of all nations which were enslaved by sin. In the Word's complex DNA, it acknowledges that the Jews picked him first. Which is why the Word shows them favour. But it was the Word that chose every race before the Jews even knew the Word, which is why the Word spiritually liberated all nations. Nations are named to help ourselves with identity because we spiritually died in the garden of Eden. But it was God that gave Israel their name because a specific individual believed in him (Abraham). So, when we read about Israel, it technically represents anyone who believes in God because Abraham received his promise by believing in God.

Israel is the representation of having faith in God and the promise that was to be received in the New Testament, which was Jesus Christ. But because of sin, all nations were enslaved by it and as the Old Testament Israel waited for the Messiah, the New Testament Israel misinterpreted what kind of liberation the Messiah was going to provide. God being the Word, then gave the world a greater name than any nation or living being and creature. That name is what the Word calls 'Jesus Christ', which in Hebrew means "to deliver, to rescue." Satan had conquered nations after he was kicked out of heaven, so he was the one in charge of our enslavement to sin. As I mentioned from the earlier chapters, humans died spiritually in the garden and were separated from God. It was at that time when they scattered all over the earth to find an identity which is why nations have names: African, Antarctician, Australian, European, North American or South American. But as we found our physical identities,

God looked at us and saw our spiritual identities as dead because of sin. But Jesus, being the Word and God, reversed the spiritual death that happened in the garden of Eden. To the devil, these are a few of the national identities that he has given us: liar, murderer, theft, cheater, slut, whore, addict, suicidal, worthless, failure, good for nothing, etc. I do not think I could even make a book of all the nasty names the devil has used to bring accusation against us, so I'll end it at that. Our sins became our national identities and since he ruled over sin, we were his spiritual slaves. Which is why the name Jesus is what gives us authority and power to liberate us from any spiritual nation working for Satan's kingdom. That is why I needed to name this chapter Battling Egypt and Babylon because he will either enslave us to our sins (Egypt) or assimilate us into thinking that sin isn't evil (Babylon). Remember in the chapter 'corruption in heaven', when I referenced Scriptures that called Satan, king of Tyre and Babylon? This is where that information comes in handy when understanding the representation of nations. Israel had many enemies with different names, but all of those names had one similar trait, they hated God. In other words, those nations that hated God were influenced by Satan's doctrine because he was the first to sin against God.

This is what the Sovereign LORD *is saying: "You have done all this like a shameless prostitute. On every street you built places to worship idols and practice prostitution. But you are not out for money like a common prostitute. You are like a woman who commits adultery with strangers instead of loving her husband. A prostitute is paid, but you gave presents to all your lovers and bribed them to come from everywhere to sleep with you. You are a special kind of prostitute. No one forced you to become one. You didn't get paid; you paid them! Yes, you are different."* **(Ezekiel 16:30–34) – Good News Translation**

*When the LORD first spoke to Israel through Hosea, he said to Hosea, "Go and get married; your wife will be unfaithful, and your children will be just like her. In the way, my people have left me and become unfaithful." * **(Hosea 1:2) – Good News Translation**

The Lord says, "wine, both old and new, is robbing my people of their senses! They ask for revelations from a piece of wood! A stick tells them what they want to know! They have left me like a woman becomes a prostitute; they have given themselves to other gods. **(Hosea 4:11-12) - Good News Translation**

Jefferson's spoken word about people becoming spiritual prostitutes isn't something that should come to us as a surprise. In the past, God sent many prophets like Hosea and Ezekiel because it was at that very time that Israel began to neglect everything God had done for them. In the bible, God compares idolatry to prostitution because it is the act of giving oneself to something for a price. This comparison to prostitution illustrates God's anger when we neglect his love because his love is like, how a husband loves his wife. Which relates back to one of the second commandments where God states, "For I, the LORD your God, am a jealous God." That is why he says, "You are like a woman who commits adultery with strangers instead of loving your husband." Israel being God's first nation was supposed to love him, but they gave themselves to the other nations who hated God.

When Israel was a child, I loved him, and out of Egypt I called my son. The more they were called, the more they went away; they kept sacrificing to the Baals and burning offerings to idols. Yet it was I who taught Ephraim to walk; I took them up by their arms, but they did not know that I healed them. I led them with cords of kindness, with the bands of love, and I became to them as one who eases the yoke on their jaws, and I bent down to them and fed them. **(Hosea 11: 1-4) - English Standard Version**

Hosea 11:1-4 is so sentimental because God is reminiscing about Israel as a child. The Old Testament Israel rejected God after he had freed them from Egypt, and they began worshipping other gods like Baal. When I read Hosea 11:1-4, I can feel the agony behind God's voice because he feels betrayed by Israel's unfaithfulness. That agony and pain turned into anger which is why we read a lot of God's anger in the Old Testament. The punishments that we read within the Old Testament aligned with the covenant Israel had made with God when they sinned. This covenant dates to the book of Exodus (Which can be found in the Old Testament). It goes back to the story of when God had sent the prophet Moses to free the Israelites from slavery.

Now it happened in the process of time that the king of Egypt died. Then the children of Israel groaned because of the bondage, and they cried out; and their cry came up to God because of the bondage. So God heard their groaning, and God remembered his covenant with Abraham, with Isaac, and with Jacob. And God looked upon the children of Israel, and God acknowledged them. **(Exodus 2:23-25) – New King James Version**

Notice how in this Scripture it says that God heard the Israelites groaning and remembered his covenant with Abraham, Isaac, and Jacob. Since God is God shouldn't he have already known that his people were suffering and acted on that without them asking? Before I answer that, I'll give an example to help better the understanding of this question. In a relationship, there are many things required that make it a healthy one. The most obvious one is the physical attraction between one-another, but physical attraction can only take a couple so far. Having an inner connection is more valuable because that is what glues a couple together despite any one of their flaws. An intimate relationship also helps to tolerate one another even on the person's worst day. Trust, patience, joy, forgiveness, truth, and love are but many more things that are required for a successful relationship. However, there is one condition that will either make or break a relationship and that is communication. A couple that doesn't communicate will inevitably break into pieces, and it doesn't matter how much they love each other. Communication surrounds our whole world and without it nothing could ever move forward because there would be no connection. This not only applies to relationships but also friendships, workplaces, families, politics, technology, etc. The ability to speak is already a remarkable privilege that God has given us, so just imagine how he feels when we don't communicate with him.

What shall I do with you, O Ephraim? What shall I do with you, O Judah? Your love is like a morning cloud, like the dew that goes early away. Therefore I have hewn them by the prophets; I have slain them by the words of my mouth, and my judgment goes forth as the light. For I desire steadfast love and not sacrifice, the knowledge of God rather than burnt offerings. **(Hosea 6:4-6) – English Standard Version**

The prophet Hosea was a peculiar servant of God, he wasn't like Moses who performed incredible miracles. Hosea was used by God as if he was God's personal diary so the people of that time would know how God felt. When Israel was enslaved by the Egyptians, they remembered how God was there for Abraham, Isaac, and Jacob, so they cried out to him. It was at that very moment that started the love story between God and Israel. It started because Israel communicated to God and he heard their cries.

"Ask, and it will be given to you; seek, and you will find; knock, and it will be opened to you. For everyone who asks receives, and he who seeks finds, and to him who knocks it will be opened. Or what man is there among you who, if his son asks for bread, will give him a stone? Or if he asks for a fish, will he give him a serpent? If you then, being evil, know how to give good gifts to your children, how much more will your Father who is in heaven give good things to those who ask him! **(Matthew 7:7-11) – New King James Version**

That is what the Israelites did, and God heard their cries and did something about it. He sent Moses to free them from slavery and through Moses, God showed his extraordinary power and demolished Egypt. Some would think that after such events, the Israelites would be loyal and obey God but that is not how the story goes. Which is why Hosea was bestowed an unfaithful wife and children so that Hosea would know how God felt when Israel broke his heart and disobeyed him. At first, I thought that was a cruel and unusual punishment for Hosea to suffer. Through Hosea we read about God's sadness. The saying, "put your feet in other people's shoes," is what God did to Hosea. God put this burden on Hosea so that the prophet would know how to preach what God was feeling. Hosea's text is influential because we get the inside scoop of God's emotions towards his people. Hosea's own unfaithful wife and children allowed him to see how God felt when his own people were unfaithful to him. By studying all of Israel's errors and disobedience we have to wonder how God still considered Israel as his nation? It is through the prophet Hosea that we get a deeper understanding of God's incomprehensible heart.

So I am going to take her into the desert again; there I will win her back with words of love. I will give back to her the vineyards she had and make Trouble Valley a door of hope. She will respond to me there as she did when she was young, when she came from Egypt. Then once again she will call me her husband—she will no longer call me her Baal. I will never let her speak the name of Baal again. **(Hosea 2:14-17) – Good News Translation**

How can I give you up, Israel? How can I abandon you? Could I ever destroy you as I did Admah, or treat you as I did Zeboiim? My heart will not let me do it! My love for you is too strong. I will not punish you in my anger; I will not destroy Israel again. For I am God and not a human being. I, the Holy One, am with you. I will not come to you in anger. **(Hosea 11:8-9) – Good News Translation**

Remember my earlier explanation about why Israel is God's nation? Hosea was used by God to illustrate to everyone how God felt about Israel. God calls Israel his son because naturally he created all, but it was also God who gave Israel its name. However, the spiritually lost nation that identified themselves as the Jews were the first to call him God. Hosea was given unfaithful children so that he could understand that God's children were unfaithful to him. Unfortunately, it doesn't end there because Hosea was given an unfaithful wife and because Israel had made a covenant with God, he saw them as his wife. Now this does sound a bit twisted because how can Israel be both his children and wife? It all stems back to my earlier explanation of the representation of nations. Israel as a nation acknowledged God as their Father because they believed that he made everything. The Jews acknowledged God's omnipotence, omniscient and omniscience. Due to the spiritual death in humanity, Israel as a nation felt no obligation to their Father and they sinned against him. The story continued because they cried out to their Father when they were in trouble with Egypt, who had enslaved them. After God had saved Israel from Egypt's bondage, he created a covenant with Israel which was a representation of his love for the lost nation Israel. The same love that he asks us to honor when we enter a marriage with our spouses. This covenant was a vow that God and Israel said to one another and it was sealed like a marriage to commemorate what God had done for them. God then gave the lost nation Israel Ten Commandments because he still saw them as his first child, who did not know any better. These Ten Commandments were made as the law that the Jews memorized to help them know what sin is.

"If you love me, you will obey my commandments." **(John 14:15) – New King James Version**

He instructed for the lost nation Israel to know these laws because his first child (Israel- the representation of acknowledging God through faith) did not know any better but because of the covenant he calls them his wife (Israel- the representation of loving God back). The Ten Commandments became Israel's law (representation of knowing sin). Israel ended up breaking God's heart by rejecting and disobeying him. They did not follow the laws that he had given them. Hence, why we hear the term prostitution (representation of selling themselves over to the slavery of many nations) in Hosea's book because they sold themselves back to slavery when they were loved by God. Instead of God divorcing (the representation of giving up on them) Israel for breaking their promise with him, he decided to make a new covenant (the representation of Jesus Christ). This was made possible because the very people who were called, 'God's people' rejected and disobeyed God, so Jesus came to introduce what is well known as salvation to all (The Good News- also known as the gospel of Jesus Christ).

Israel, I will make you my wife; I will be true and faithful; I will show you constant love and mercy and make you mine forever. I will keep my promise and make you mine, and you will acknowledge me as LORD. At that time, I will answer the prayers of my people Israel. I will make rainfall on the earth, and the earth will produce grain and grapes and olives. I will establish my people in the land and make them prosper. I will show love to those who were called "Unloved," and to those who were called "Not-My-People" I will say, "You are my people," and they will answer, "You are our God." **(Hosea 2:19-23) – Good News Translation**

79

But what does it say? "The word is near you, in your mouth and in your heart" (that is, the word of faith which we preach): that if you confess with your mouth the Lord Jesus and believe in your heart that God has raised Him from the dead, you will be saved. For with the heart one believes unto righteousness, and with the mouth confession is made unto salvation. For the Scripture says, "Whoever believes on him will not be put to shame." For there is no distinction between Jew and Greek, for the same Lord over all is rich to all who call upon Him. For "whoever calls on the name of the LORD shall be saved." **(Romans 10: 8-13) – New King James Version**

The love that God showed Israel from the time he saved them from Egypt never died, despite the wrath shown on his people. Israel's unfaithfulness brought out more love for the world through Jesus Christ because his name extended unconditional love to all nations (Jewish & Non-Jewish descendants). This unconditional love provided the liberation from spiritual death (sin) which is what the devil had caused in the garden of Eden. The name Jesus Christ is the name that God gave the world as the new identity (New Covenant) that represented freedom from the empowerment of Satan's spiritual rule. This was the liberation that the Israelites never thought they needed. However, they received it through their own lineage because of their initial faith in acknowledging Jehovah Jireh (Hebrew for "The Lord Will Provide") as their God. In conclusion, God gave Israel the name Israel for their faith and through Israel, he provided the world with the name Jesus to deliver and rescue the "faithful" from spiritual death. It is through his name that we have authority to conquer any nations like Egypt and Babylon.

Concerning the gospel, they are enemies for your sake but concerning the election they are beloved for the sake of the fathers. For the gifts and the calling of God are irrevocable. For as you were once disobedient to God, yet have now obtained mercy through their disobedience, even so these also have now been disobedient, that through the mercy shown you they also may obtain mercy. For God has committed them all to disobedience, that he might have mercy on all. **(Romans 11:28-32) – New King James Version**

CHAPTER 5

CONQUERING EGYPT AND BABYLON

What God did for the Israelites in Egypt, can also be applied to things like addictions, anxiety and even depression because he can free anyone from anything. There are people out in the world that suffer from all sorts of things like addictions to drugs, alcohol, gambling, pornography, etc. These addictions are like our Egypt and the ruler of the state is the well-known tyrant Satan who enjoys watching us suffer. We become enslaved by our addictions because we disobey just like the Israelites disobeyed. There are even times when God delivers us from our enslavements but if we do not truly love him, we will behave just like the Israelites and repeat the mistakes that got us into that ditch. That is what happened to the Israelites because they started to behave like the Egyptians after God had already destroyed Egypt.

When the people saw that Moses had not come down from the mountain but was staying there a long time, they gathered around Aaron and said to him, "We do not know what has happened to this man Moses, who led us out of Egypt; so make us a god to lead us." Aaron said to them, "Take off the gold earrings which your wives, your sons, and your daughters are wearing, and bring them to me." So all the people took off their gold earrings and brought them to Aaron. He took the earrings, melted them, poured the gold into a mold, and made a gold bull-calf. The people said, "Israel, this is our god, who led us out of Egypt!" Then Aaron built an altar in front of the gold bull-calf and announced, "Tomorrow there will be a festival to honor the LORD." Early the next morning they brought some animals to burn as sacrifices and others to eat as fellowship offerings. The people sat down to a feast, which turned into an orgy of drinking and sex. **(Exodus 32:1-6) – Good News Translation**

Jefferson Bethke's reference about how we all have become spiritual prostitutes makes complete sense because we search for happiness in anything but Jesus, when we all belong to him. The Israelites forgot all that God had done and went back to their sinful natures by worshipping other gods. It is no different today because we have forgotten about Jesus Christ and put our worship in other things.

Not unto us, O LORD, not unto us, but to your name give glory, because of your mercy, because of your truth. Why should the Gentiles say, "So where is their God?" But our God is in heaven; he does whatever he pleases. Their idols are silver and gold, the work of men's hands. They have mouths, but they do not speak; eyes they have, but they do not see; they have ears, but they do not hear; noses but they do not handle; feet they have, but they do not walk; nor do they mutter through their throat. Those who make them are like them; So is everyone who trust in them. O Israel, trust in the LORD; he is their help and their shield. **(Psalms 115:1-9) – New King James Version**

The scariest truth about worshipping idols is the fact that they are not gods but are evil spirits imposing as gods which allows Satan easy access into our lives. I can confess in choosing Egypt because Egypt doesn't choose anyone. No one knows the geography of Egypt, unless they choose to enter its land. What do I mean by that? How can anyone ever anticipate that they would become an addict? For example: A person who smokes did not begin smoking to become an addict, but they chose to do so out of curiosity. It is the same for alcohol, drugs, pornography, gambling and many more things. In my case, I picked up alcohol not to become addicted to it but because of curiosity. Does that mean being curious of something is a sin? No, but this was one of the sides affects of the tree that gave knowledge of what is good and bad. I will elaborate more on what that tree represents in another chapter but for the sake of staying on topic let us continue. The law was created by God and passed down to the Israelites because they did not know what sin was. Egypt operates in secret and doesn't bother to spend any money on advertising because it knows the people it wants. It knows that certain people will have that itch of curiosity to see its famous pyramids. In other words, those who fall in trap of addictions are people that are curious of sinful behavior. Their curiosity traps them, even though they know that they shouldn't do certain things. Although millions are enslaved by Egypt, it doesn't bother to ever spend money on ads. It knows it will get more slaves because it has gotten proud of its geography. It knows the shame and the hurt its slaves go through and because of this: Those who are slaves are afraid to escape. How do I know this? Because I was enslaved by it, and when I say it, I'm talking about alcohol.

"Author, oh author why don't you pour another drink? Milliliter? Actually, just make it a liter! One drop turns into 6 cups full of beer and as you urinate it out trying to get rid of what's inside your liver; your mind whispers, 'just one more drink.' Pour a glass of that liquor: Bombay? Brandy? Mm, spiced rum, maybe tequila, vodka, or whiskey? Why don't we watch together, how the flames react to that? Are you an alcoholic? What is your relationship with the bottle that empties you out before you even have a chance to take it out? 'Let's have a relationship?' whispers the drink. 'Let me kiss your lips,' as she continues to whisper. However, there is no relation, just a damn sinking ship! Isn't this beautiful poetry author? Pour me a glass of that red wine, and I want to make this our time. Let me relax you, forget all you know and taste my lips. Don't close your eyes; I know they are drowsy.

The Italians find it romantic or is it the French? Strolling in a mini boat as my head is pressed on your chest. How romantic is this? Private boat tour for two on Lake Como. You and I, dinner for two? As we indulge in some French muenster cheese. That burning session in your throat I know you want some more. Taste me and make me dry to the point that not even water can cure us of this thirsty fantasy. I know you hate me author, but you still cannot resist me. For when it is all said and done, you wake up with a horrid hangover and remember the proverbs. For it is written:

Show me people who drink too much, who have to try out fancy drinks, and I will show you, people, who are miserable and sorry for themselves,

83

always causing trouble and always complaining. Their eyes are bloodshot, and they have bruises that could have been avoided. Don't let wine tempt you, even though it is rich red, and sparkles in the cup and goes down smoothly. The next morning you will feel as if you have been bitten by a poisonous snake. Weird sights will appear before your eyes, and you will not be able to think clearly. You will feel as if you were out on the ocean, seasick, swinging high up in the ringing of a tossing ship. 'I must have been hit,' you will say; 'I must have been beaten up, but I don't remember it. Why can't I wake up? I need another drink. **(Proverbs 23:29-30) – Good News Translation"**

-The doctrine of Satan

I constantly spent years in denial, saying to myself that I was in control when I was never in control. I did not want to advertise it, so I remained in it while it ruled in secret. What do I mean by that? Well when a person is addicted to something, its not hard to see. They may go to great lengths to hide it while what's ruling them hides in secret because it is spiritual. The spirit of addiction is ruthless, and many millions can attest to that by looking at what their addictions has cost them. Emotionally, financially, physically, mentally and if no action is taken against it, it will soon kill them. But as I had said in the Battling Egypt and Babylon chapter, these nations are representations of sinful tactics laid out by the doctrine of Satan. Spiritual warfare is fought by putting faith in the greatest name, Jesus, and by giving our hearts to his Word. His Spirit, which I explained in the earlier chapters is how you spiritually conquer both Egypt and Babylon.

For when you were slaves of sin, you were free in regard to righteousness. What fruit did you have then in the things of which you are now ashamed? For the end of those things is death. **(Romans 6:20-21) – New King James Version**

For the wages of sin is death, but the gift of God is eternal life in Christ Jesus our Lord. **(Romans 6:23)- New King James Version**

Babylon operates differently because it has made its geography known to the public because it uses the media, without the media's knowledge.

They frame it as the good life and do not once advertise what such things are capable of. Babylon is skilled at its craft because it glamorizes anything but God. It focuses to pressure or slowly advises a person to compromise their faith. Now that doesn't really pertain to just Christians, but even the non-believers who do not participate in its lifestyle. Babylon will just hand us a pamphlet through snapchat, Instagram, Facebook or any of Hollywood's entertainment packages. Babylon invests in advertisement because it is obsessed with its nation's appearance. Babylon is proud, the same pride inherited by Satan because it wants to be worshipped. How do I know so much about Babylon? Because Babylon does not keep its ways as a secret. It is bold in its work because it uses entertainment, money, sexual immorality, and more things. Take for instance the story of Shadrach, Meshach, and Abednego. All of Israel was living in Babylon but they had become assimilated and forgotten everything about God, but these three Hebrew boys stood firm to their faith in God and said no to Babylon. Babylon does not look corrupt or evil because it has everyone worshipping in idols that please their natural desires. The spirit of idolatry is wicked because it persuades the person to compromise what God prohibits by pointing at the society that partakes in its culture. The spirit of idolatry has caused us to not want to know God because Babylon hates God so there is always a movement that strives to shun the Word (Jesus). The spirit of idolatry seeks for us to become a citizen of Babylon because it spiritually knows we are denying that God is our Father. This spirit deliberately attempts to mock God and those who give themselves to Babylon are making God jealous. I write this out of love because no spirit that works for Satan's doctrine has any good intentions, but idolatry is a sin that provokes God's anger.

For the LORD your God is a consuming fire, a jealous God. **(Deuteronomy 4:24) – New King James Version**

What then are the idols of today? What is lurking around in our societies that seem harmless and innocent but behind it lies Babylon's investment? To really know the answer to these questions, we have to evaluate our own lives. It is impossible for me to provide a permit/prohibit list. Luckily, I do have an answer to provide how one knows if something is an idol purchased by Babylon. The answer is time. When I said Babylon investments a lot, I was not talking about actual money. There is something more valuable than money itself and it is time. We can tell how wealthy someone is by how much freedom of time they have. Those who can afford freedom of time will use it to travel whenever they want, shop while others are working and many more things. But this isn't a discussion of whose poor, middle class, or rich. Idols do not care about what's in peoples bank accounts because it invests to own our time. Babylon is so devious it will suggest compromises like, "Give this idol 30% of your time and indulge in it only on weekends and give 20% to another idol and indulge in it only on special occasions. Then you can give the rest of your time dedicating it to family, friends and maybe God." It may sound all good in our heads, but we are sadly deceiving ourselves. Once an idol has realized we have given it our time, whether singular or plural, it doesn't matter what percentage we give because it will find a way to make sure it has 100% of our time. For example, my favourite soccer team is Liverpool FC. I think back at how invested I am in watching them play. There is nothing wrong with watching sports. Now, if Liverpool played on a Sunday, there is a dangerously good chance that I will most likely miss church. Now some will say, "Oh, common that's just soccer. How could that be evil?" That's the thing, it isn't evil, but idols want our time because if it has our time it has our hearts. Which makes the spirit of idolatry so sneaky because all the things it has invested in use people. Are our favourite celebrities evil? How about our favourite actors, musicians, athletes, writers, comedians, or politicians? See the thing is they are just people who have become well-known for something they're good at or done. But at the end of the day they all face spiritual warfare like anyone else. They have reached a certain status in life where the doctrine of Satan can use that very status for Babylon's motives.

Yet Michael the archangel, in contending with the devil, when he disputed about the body of Moses, dared not bring against him a reviling accusation, but said, "The Lord rebuke you!" **(Jude 1:9) – New King James Version**

This Scripture pertains to a dispute between the archangel Michael and the devil. The devil wanted the body of Moses for some reason. What's twisted about this Scripture is Jude does not elaborate on what the devil wanted to do with Moses' body. Especially since Moses had already died. My theory, and this is just a theory. I think the devil wanted to use Moses' body as an idol prop. The Israelites already had a history of disobeying God and worshipping golden statues. Since Moses was one of the greatest prophets of God, what better way to get the people of God to sin by worshipping someone they already respected and loved. That's just a theory, but here is the reality. Moses performed great miracles, led the people out of Egypt and spoke to God like a friend. If we began worshipping Moses does that make Moses evil? No, and this is what spirit of idolatry does. If we are not educated by the Word of God, we will not worship God and unknowingly begin to worship people or things. I'll go even deeper and relevant. Take for instance the Roman Catholic Church, they idolize saints for different reasons based on the things those saints have done while they were alive. Does that make the saints evil? Absolutely not! But, the doctrine of Satan has crept into the minds of people who are not spiritually equipped by God's Spirit to know such things. Mary was the earthly mother of Jesus, but what was it that made someone think that God wanted us to pray to or worship Mary? Satan was a powerful angel and regarded the perfectionist of worship for God, but then wanted it for himself. It doesn't take a genius to see the similarities of what he has done. Satan knows we view the earthly mother of Jesus as good so why not use that tactic to piss off God and get us to think that we should pray to her (praying to something or someone is a form of worship). In the chapter 'Corruption in heaven,' I had mentioned how he was buying and selling the angel's worship that belonged to God. In other words, Satan went from the worship provider to the worship thief. He knew how to do it because he was created perfect in the craft of worship. So now that he no longer resides in presence of God, he will use whatever or whomever as a scapegoat to receive worship, just as long as it doesn't go to God. Satan will not use someone like Adolf Hitler because we will reject a person like that due to our knowledge of the evil crimes he committed. Satan's doctrine does not fear crossing such lines and since he used to be the example of perfect worship, just imagine the lengths he will go to just to make sure we do not worship God. This is why the Holy Spirit came down on earth and is received to anyone who believes in Jesus Christ. The Spirit assists us in prayer and worship that supersedes the fraudulent one who was kicked out of heaven because we become one with the Almighty God.

This Book of the Law shall not depart from your mouth, but you shall meditate in it day and night, that you may observe to do according to all that is written in it. For then you will make your way prosperous, and then you will have good success. **(Joshua 1:8) – New King James Version**

Therefore, you shall lay up these words of mine in your heart and in your soul, and bind them as a sign on your hand, and they shall be as frontlets between your eyes. **(Deuteronomy 11:18) – New King James Version**

For if you carefully keep all these commandments which I command you to do- to love the LORD God, to walk in all his ways, and to hold fast to him- then the LORD will drive out all these nations from before you, and you will dispossess greater and mightier nations than yourselves. **(Deuteronomy 11:22-23) – New King James Version**

The spirit of idolatry knows the Word of God as well and as I had mentioned in the chapter birth of the doctrine, Satan had conquered nations and will use them to manipulate and confuse us from the truth. I used something as simple as Liverpool FC, because the love of sports is something that the world enjoys. It brings people together and creates friendships. It keeps us active and healthy. But this is what Babylon does: it takes what God intended to be good and perverts it. I cannot, just for the sake of the length of this book, write everything that the devil has perverted. God himself never bothered to write every single sin down because if we focus on studying evil, our hearts will read evil. Instead he taught us truth and he used broken people to write his Word, all the while changing those broken people for the better. Not one asked for credit in their writings but gave the Word credit because the Word helped them battle nations. But that wasn't the Word's core intention because it wanted us to not only love it back but save us from all the nations of the world. Therefore, the Word became a person and because of his name, Jesus conquered all nations (Satan). That way we don't have to ever battle because the Word gave us authority over all nations by the name Jesus.

And in the days of these kings the God of heaven will set up a kingdom which shall never be destroyed; and the kingdom shall not be left to other people; it shall break in pieces and consume all these kingdoms, and it shall stand forever. **(Daniel 2:44) – New King James Version**

Then the kingdom and dominion, and the greatness of the kingdoms under the whole heaven, shall be given to the people, the saints of the Most High. His kingdom is an everlasting kingdom, and all dominions shall serve and obey him. **(Daniel 7:27) – New King James Version**

Deuteronomy 11:22-23 reveals the perks of listening to his Word. Those who write his Word in their hearts will not be conquered by Egypt, Babylon or any nation. In other words, to write something in our hearts requires us to give our time to it. God instructed the Israelites to read his Word day and night because God knew that the Word would fill their hearts. So, there it is, that is how we know how Babylon has us under its grips!

For where your treasure is, there your heart will be also. **(Matthew 6:21) – King James Version**

My dear friends, do not be surprised at the painful test you are suffering, as though something unusual were happening to you. Rather be glad that you are sharing Christ's sufferings, so that you may be full of joy when his glory is revealed. Happy are you if you are insulted because you are Christ's followers; this means that the glorious Spirit, the Spirit of God, is resting on you. **(1 Peter 4:12-14) – New King James Version**

Whether it's Egypt or Babylon, there will always be a spirit lurking for us to accept it so it can latch onto our very core. So, the question we have to ask ourselves is this: Will we bow to the things of the world? We look to our left and right, our siblings have bowed; our parents have bowed! All our friends are calling us names and telling us to bow. Will we bow down?

As soon as Jesus got out of the boat, he was met by a man who came out of the burial caves there. This man had an evil spirit in him and lived among the tombs. Nobody could keep him tied with chains anymore; many times, his feet and his hands had been tied, but every time he broke the chains and smashed the irons of his feet. He was too strong for anyone to control him. Day and night, he wandered among the tombs and through the hills, screaming and cutting himself with stones. He was some distance away when he saw Jesus, and he screamed in a loud voice, "Jesus, Son of the Highest God! What do you want with me? For God's sake, I beg you, don't punish me!" (He said this because Jesus was saying, "Evil spirit, and come out of this man!") So, Jesus asked him, "What is your name!" The man answered, "My name is 'Mob' – there are many of us!" And he kept begging Jesus not to send the evil spirits out of that region. There was a large herd of pigs nearby, feeding on a hillside. So, the spirits begged Jesus, "Send us to the pigs, and let us go into them." He let them go, and the evil spirits went out of the man and entered the pigs. The whole herd- about two thousand pigs in all- rushed down the side of the cliff into the lake and were drowned. **(Mark 5:2-13)- Good News Translation**

When Jesus saw that the people came running together, he rebuked the unclean spirit, saying to it, "Deaf and dumb spirit, I command you, come out of him and enter him no more!" Then the spirit cried out, convulsed him greatly, and came out of him. And he became as one dead, so that many said, "He is dead." But Jesus took him by the hand and lifted him up, and he arose. And when he had come into the house, His disciples asked Him privately, "Why could we not cast it out?" So he said to them, "This kind can come out by nothing but prayer and fasting." **(Mark 9:25-29) – New King James Version**

I quoted these specific Scriptures for the reason of explaining what happens when we battle nations like Egypt and Babylon. All these Scriptures are events that occurred during the time Jesus Christ was on earth. Mark 5:2-13 tells a story about a man possessed by an evil spirit and once Jesus saw this man; he commanded the spirit to leave him. What I find interesting about this story is there is a dialogue between the evil spirit and Jesus. The spirit begs Jesus not to be sent out of the region but to be sent into a herd of pigs. Pause for a second. The evil spirit begged Jesus not to be sent out of the region! Why did it request that? Well, evil spirits have a characteristic of dwelling in specific regions, or in other words they too have identified themselves geographically. To go even deeper with this, remember how in the chapter corruption in heaven, I explained how Satan was buying and selling in his place of worship? Well, those who bought into his lies were the ones who were also casted out of heaven as well.

And another sign appeared in heaven: behold, a great, fiery red dragon having seven heads and ten horns, and seven diadems on his heads. His tail drew a third of the stars in heaven and threw them to the earth. And the dragon stood before the woman who was ready to give birth, to devour her child as soon as it was born. **(Revelations 12:3-4) New King James Version**

That intense Scripture that I just quoted has a powerful meaning that has to do with what happened right before Satan was banished from heaven. "His tail drew a third of the stars in heaven and threw them to the earth." What does that mean? The stars represented the angels who bought into Satan's sinful ways. What I find interesting is how Satan treated these "fallen" angels (evil spirits) because it mentions that he threw them to the earth. Can we please just take that in for a second? A third of the stars in heaven! Or in other words, Satan convinced a third of the angels in heaven to follow him. The fallen angels must have specific spiritual regions because Satan is known as a tyrant and we see his nature by how he treated the fallen angels because it states, "His tail drew a third of the stars in heaven and threw them to the earth." As I mentioned in the birth of the doctrine, the devil came down to earth and claimed it as his spiritual kingdom since he could not do it in heaven. Now that does not mean the devil is the king of the earth but since he has sent forth his kingdom on earth, he spiritually rules and commands the disgraced fallen angels. That is not what I am saying, nor do I mean that. Satan had this spiritual authority over the fallen angels, but he also had it over us because he ruled over death(sin). That is until Jesus took that authority away from him by dying himself so that the Holy Spirit could come down and conquer Satan's spiritual rule over death(sin). Sorry, but I have to pause again because I have to address another thing. When I say Jesus took that authority away from Satan, it doesn't mean Jesus and Satan fought. It was a spiritual drift in power because a new covenant was formed once Christ died which was sealed by his blood. There was no physical altercation between Jesus and the devil, and Jesus did not go into hell to take any keys from Satan. The reason why I feel the need to explain that is because I've heard this falsely preached by religious leaders, but they do not have any Scripture to back it up. It is a man-made claim which has confused many of what Jesus' death meant. The Holy Spirit was and is the key that allows all this to be true because it is the affirmation of our belief in Christ. Therefore, if someone does not have the Spirit, the Good News is just a truth that they have yet to live within which makes Satan's power their truth. This is another reason why being born again is extremely important. The Holy Spirit is the official mark of God on our lives that represents victory over the devil's spiritual reign on earth. Yes, I just said that and if anyone claims that I am a liar, please refer to the Scriptures which I have provided.

It shall come to pass in the day the LORD gives you rest from your sorrow, and from your fear and the hard bondage in which you were made to serve, that you will take this proverb against the king of Babylon and say: "How the oppressor has ceased, the golden city ceased! The LORD has broken the staff of the wicked, the scepter of the rulers; he who struck the people in wrath with a continual stroke, he ruled the nations in anger, is persecuted and no one hinders. The whole earth is at rest and quiet; they break forth into singing." **(Isaiah 14:3-7) – New King James Version**

The devil read these prophecies and worked so hard to prevent them but could not do it.

She bore a male child who was to rule all nations with a rod of iron. And her child was caught up to God and his throne. **(Revelations 12:5) – New King James Version**

Revelations 12 speaks of a woman who is pregnant and about to give birth to a child so the dragon (the devil) waits for her to go into labour so that he may devour the child once it is conceived. This woman is a representation of Israel and the child is Jesus. We know this because of God's relationship with the Jewish people. Israel had a covenant with God (marriage) and because God is faithful, his child being Jesus, was to be of Jewish descendant.

For unto us a child is born; unto us a son is given; and the government will be upon his shoulder. And his name will be called Wonderful, Counsellor, Mighty God, Everlasting Father, Prince of Peace. Of the increase of his government and peace there will be no end. Upon the throne of David and over his kingdom, to order it and establish it with judgement and justice. From that time forward, even forever. The zeal of the LORD will perform this. **(Isaiah 9:6-7) – New King James Version**

It amazes me how much reference there is to nations and kingdoms, but I dragged this elaboration this far for everyone to understand something about the doctrine of Satan. God has already won it all for us and the biggest lie that the doctrine can come up with for this chapter is that we still have to battle him.

I used to suffer from anxiety, and it drove me insane. My first ever anxiety attack happened right after I cheated on my ex-girlfriend. I remember it so vividly because I was in a car and I felt this overwhelming guilt empowered by fear. Not a fear that I was going to get caught for my actions, but this fear caught my whole-body trembling. Personally, I think I deserved it at that time because of my actions but did not know that the anxiety was going to be battling against me for a year and a half. I was with a friend at the time and when I explained it to her she told me I was experiencing an anxiety attack. The reason why I'm telling this story is not to speak like I'm an expert on mental health because I am not a doctor or therapist. I cannot imagine what some people go through because my first ever anxiety attack came from guilt whereas others suffer from it for no reason at all. I went a full year battling it and it kept getting worse and worse. It happened in my sleep, so I was afraid to go to sleep. It even started happening randomly during the day and one time it happened while I was playing soccer. All these occurrences happened way before I even had the thought of writing this book. I am sharing this battle because it made me feel weak, defeated and vulnerable. I took many trips to the hospital and what drove me even more insane were my results. "Your vitals are where they should be at your age, and you are healthy," the doctor would say. This confused me because I felt how real it was and every time, I had one, I felt like my heart was voluntarily trying to stop- which caused me to call 911. Yes, my doctors educated me about mental health and gave me many options to cope with it. But I was deeply saddened because I did not want to have to cope with it, I wanted it to stop forever.

Jesus answered them, "Those who are well have no need of a physician, but those who are sick. I have not come to call the righteous, but sinners, to repentance." **(Luke 5:31) New King James Version**

When I was 14 years old, I rolled my right ankle playing soccer. I did not think much of it until the next day, when I could not walk on it at all. One would think the swelling would give me a hint, but I thought I was fine. My dad took me to the hospital and after a few hours of waiting, I got news that I fractured my foot. I had to wear a cast for a couple of months and my soccer season was over for that year. When we are sick, we go see a doctor, even Jesus knew this which is why he said it. Doctors are educated and have dedicated their time to their profession, so it is in their hearts to help people. But Jesus came for another sickness that is not visible to any human being. This sickness is spiritual death and it was caused long ago in the garden of Eden by sin. That is why it is written: "I have not come to call the righteous, but sinners, to repentance." A sickness that was transmitted by the devil, and because he is a spiritual being; he had to be defeated spiritually.

For we do not wrestle against flesh and blood, but against the principalities, against the powers, against the rulers of the darkness of this age, against spiritual hosts of wickedness in the heavenly places. **(Ephesians 6:12) – New King James Version**

I gave examples of Scriptures where Jesus encountered people who were possessed by evil spirits. But what I really want everyone to take away about these spirits is they operate under Satan's doctrine. They have been strategically placed in different regions within nations and all have different names. We know of Egypt and Babylon, but just like Matthew 5:2-13, some are named Mob, which means many. Some are called "Deaf and dumb" but the ones we all are familiar with today are: anxiety, depression, suicide, addiction, bipolar, panic. Others live in different regions and are called lust, jealousy, hate, greed, gluttony and laziness. All these spirits lurk in different nations and were assigned there when the devil threw them down to the earth. Please remember that I am not talking about physical countries, but the spiritual realms of the earth. For example, Egypt represents addictions. Chances are if a person is fighting the spirit of addiction, they will also be in danger of encountering anxiety, depression, panic and even suicide.

"I pray for them. I do not pray for the world but for those whom you have given me, for they are yours. And all mine are yours, and yours are mine, and I am glorified in them. Now I am no longer in the world, but these are in the world, and I come to you. Holy Father keep through your name those whom you have given me, that they may be one as we are. While I was with them in the world, I kept them in your name. Those whom you gave me I have kept; and none of them is lost except the son of perdition, that the Scripture might be fulfilled. But now I come to you, and these things I speak in the world, that they may have my joy fulfilled in themselves. I have given them your Word; and the world hated them because they are not of the world. I do not pray that you should take them out of the world, but that you should keep them from the evil one. They are not of the world, just as I am not of the world. **(John 17:9-16) – New King James Version**

There is a lot of reference to the world in Jesus' prayer for his disciples. When I first read this Scripture, I had thought that he was talking about the physical world which does make sense. But we also have to remember that Jesus hardly ever spoke to entertain the physical realm but to open our minds to the spiritual. In this prayer Jesus is referring to the influence of the evil one, Satan, on the world. He prays for his disciples and distinctly mentions that they do not belong in the world, just as he doesn't either, but he doesn't pray for them to be taken from the world. In other words, he is saying that although they don't belong in the world, the disciples had to stay in the world to deliver the Word to the whole world after Jesus spiritually defeated the world (Satan).

"These things I have spoken to you, that in me you may have peace. In the world you will have tribulation; but be of good cheer, I have overcome the world." **(John 16:33) – New King James Version**

The world is not a representation of the physical earth but the spiritual world that Satan had established. This is what I meant by evil spirits in different regions because they all operate differently in the spiritual realm. That is why Jesus is quoted saying, "I have given them your Word; and the world has hated them because they are not of the world, just as I am not of the world." This quote has the potential to mean the physical world but since the spiritual world is not limited to travel, evil spirits exist in every country. Which is why mental illnesses and health don't discriminate any race, they come for everyone! Our mental health is so important, because we all suffer from mental issues. Some are small, others are big, and there are some extremely serious. Serious to the point where they need to seek medical attention, and there is nothing wrong with that at all. Did I make that list to say that we are possessed by evil spirits? No not at all! We are human beings and the thing about being human is we are made up of the mind, body, heart and soul. If we do not take care of all four of these things, we will reap the consequences. They all link together and when one fails, all will soon begin to suffer. What the devil desires is the spiritual because once he has ownership of that he has access to the other three (body, heart and mind). If one takes care of the mind, body and heart but doesn't care for their spirit. What then does the doctrine of Satan have planned for such a person?

"When an unclean spirit goes out of a man, he goes through dry places, seeking rest, and finds none. Then he says, 'I will return to my house from which I came.' And when he comes, he finds it empty, swept, and put in order. Then he goes and takes with him seven other spirits more wicked than himself, and they enter and dwell there; and the last state of that man is worse than the first. So

shall it also be with this wicked generation." **(Matthew 12:43-45) – New King James Version**

So, what is a person to do to protect themselves spiritually?

Therefore, take up the whole armor of God, that you may be able to withstand in the evil day, and having done all, to stand. Stand therefore, having girded your waist with truth, having put on the breastplate of righteousness, and having shod your feet with the preparation of the gospel of peace; above all, taking the shield of faith with which you will be able to quench all the fiery darts of the wicked one. And take the helmet of salvation, and the sword of the Spirit, which is the Word of God; praying always with all prayer and supplication in the Spirit, being watchful to this end with all perseverance and supplication for all the saints— **(Ephesians 6:13-18) New King James Version**

The possibilities are endless but what I am trying to explain is that when dealing with spiritual care, we already have a medication. Just as a doctor would prescribe medication for someone who is suffering from a bipolar disorder, schizophrenia, or depression. Or how we go to the gym as the solution to getting healthier for not just our physical appearance but for our lungs and hearts. Let's not forget a healthy diet to keep our bodies healthy and strong. We all have a solution for our spirits when they are under attack by things we cannot see.

"Come to me, all you who labor and are heavy laden, and I will give you rest. Take my yoke upon you and learn from me, for I am gentle and lowly in heart, and you will find rest for your souls. For my yoke is easy and my burden is light." **(Matthew 11:28-30) – New King James Version**

As this chapter comes to an end, I feel the need to say one last thing because it would not be fair for me not to address this. How do we know whether something is actually mental or spiritual? For the thing about mental issues are that they too are things that we cannot see. I sit back myself and ponder on that question. I spoke about the antidote of spiritual protection but sometimes because we are human and we all struggle. It would be ignorant of me to not mention that sometimes we need assistance from medical professionals. Didn't I not go to the hospital when I twisted my ankle? Although that example is physical and open to the human eye. Mental health is not like fracturing or breaking a bone. We have to accept that we are humans and the best thing we can do for ourselves is to take advantage of the solutions available to us. Help is available for anyone that is suffering from addictions, mental health and illness. It's available through therapy, medication and also just from the support of our loved ones. Mental health awareness is constantly improving but what I write about is bringing forth an awareness of God's love that cannot be forgotten. Yes, I am writing to help people, but it would be a lie to say that I am not also writing to journey with God for myself.

"Spirit of God,

I give you great thanks for allowing me to get to this stage of the book. You did not allow me to finish without addressing such issues. You put pressure on my heart to dive deep in your Word and reminded me that I am human. You reminded me that I do not always have to be in control which is why you provide me assistance.

I tried to keep Egypt and Babylon a secret. I did this because I was ashamed of my interaction with addictions and feared Babylon's influence. I have constantly let you down with my own false worships. I may have never said, 'Oh this is what I worship.' But it was what I invested my time which is how they became my idols. My pupils shifted left to right. Whether on YouTube, Instagram, Facebook and Snapchat. I was so driven by specific lifestyles that brought emptiness, but you are the God that sets his people free!

Spirit of God,

I pray for the readers: Christians, Muslims, Jews, Buddhists, Shinto's, Sikh's, Hinduism, non-believers or any other ones which I am not familiar with. I pray not for what our nation's call religions, but I pray for what you see us as. Your beautiful creations! We have caused war and murdered the innocent. Blood has been shed and hateful messages have been proclaimed. All for the sake to claim supremacy of one's nations beliefs and traditions. I cannot imagine what some have been through just because of the nation they were born into. But my heart prays for the hearts of all races. I am only a mere man and I speak because my nation was once Catholic but then I abandoned that to become an Apostolic Pentecostal. Yet, to you, you look at me as your beautiful creation. For it is written:

Then the Word of the LORD came to me saying: "Before I formed you in the womb I knew you; before you were born I sanctified you; I ordained you a prophet to the nations." (Jeremiah 1:5) – New King James Version

My God, my God you spoke those words to the prophet Jeremiah and with purpose and faith he preached that message. Reminding us all that you knew us before the world claimed ownership of us. But the world has no power over us because of you! So I write to rebuke Egypt and Babylon for all their evil motives. You never named me any of those nations. You came not for the sake of those nations; you came for the sake of your beautiful creations! You were seeking for a relationship with us.

Spirit of God,

You saw how we struggled and saw the one responsible for all our torment. That is why I pray for all because they will read this and think that I claim to have all the answers. Yet, I am a nameless nation who is after your kingdom. Not to rule but to dwell in with you because I belong to you. You made this clear when you came and delivered and rescued us from worldly imprisonment. You came and rescued me! Tears fall on this page but that is this book's secret. For it is written:

Therefore I endure all things for the sake of the elect, that they also may obtain the salvation which is Christ Jesus with eternal glory. This is a faithful saying: For if we died with him, we shall also live in him. If we endure, we shall also reign with him. If we deny him, he will also deny us. If we are faithless, he remains faithful; he cannot deny himself. (2 Timothy 2:10-13) – New King James Version

Spirit of God,

There are people out there who don't know you. My goodness how I wish they sought to know you. Not the knowledge of you but searched for you like David.

A man after God's own heart! Surely that is wonderful religion and because of such a heart you allowed him to be king of Israel and set forth a family tree that reached Jesus. For it is written:

But now your kingdom shall not continue. The LORD has sought for himself a man after his own heart, and the LORD has commanded him to be commander over his people, because you have not kept what the LORD commanded you." (1 Samuel 13:14) – New King James Version

And when he removed him, he raised up for them David as king, to whom also he gave testimony and said, 'I have found David the son of Jesse, a man after my own heart, who will do all my will.' From this man's seed, according to the promise, God raised up for Israel a Savior- Jesus (Acts 13: 22-23) – New King James Version

Spirit of God,

This is one of your beautiful creations speaking. I write on behalf of the unknowing. Because I do not know how they feel, think or go through. Neither do they know how I feel, think or go through. Which is why I have made it known to all of them. At the cost of my story, which is meaningless, so that they may come to somewhat desire to know you. Because your Word is truth and your truth is the story that never ends. Your story includes us since you made us which is why I rely on your Word because it sings forgiveness, love, salvation, grace, mercy and purpose. It gives us victory over the one called Satan.

My name is unknowing and because I am unknowing, I come off as annoying to the readers. How can I understand humanities mental issues? How can I assist them? Can I write a guideline or step by step process to help them? Surely you know all those questions are rhetorical. Because 'I' cannot do anything for them because 'I' am not you, Jesus. So they will look at me and say, 'Author, oh author we are looking at your God, what can he do for us? Can he heal us?' For it is written:

And he was withdrawn from them about a stone' throw, and he knelt down and prayed, saying, "Father, if it is your will, take this cup away

from me; nevertheless, not my will, but yours, be done." Then an angel appeared to him from heaven, strengthening him. And being in agony, he prayed more earnestly. Then his sweat became like great drops of blood falling down to the ground. (Luke 22:41-44) – New King James Version

Seeing then that we have a great High Priest who has passed through the heavens, Jesus the Son of God, let us hold fast our confession. For we do not have a High Priest who cannot sympathize with our weakness, but was in all points tempted as we are, yet without sin. Let us therefore come boldly to the throne of grace, that we may obtain mercy and find grace to help in time of need. (Hebrews 4:14-16) – New King James Version

The Word became a person to save us but also teach us that he too understands humanities mental issues. He faced them too and although he was all powerful, he allowed himself to feel weak and vulnerable. His mind felt agony and his heart trembled in fear, but he set forth an example of true strength. For it is written:

But his answer was: "My grace is all you need, for my power is greatest when you are weak." I am most happy, then, to be proud of my weakness, in order to feel the protection of Christ's power over me. (2 Corinthians 12:9) – Good News Translation

I pray for the unknowing to understand that I may not know them, but I do love them. My prayer to them is to not boast of their weaknesses. For I write knowing the cruelty of things like depression and anxiety. I may not be able to relate to the unknowing's struggles but I announce to the unknowing that I know weakness. So since I can only write from the standpoint of knowing, I must admit that I know nothing of your true strength. Yet I rely on it by faith and you defeat the nations that stand before me. It is the purpose of this book to reveal to the unknowing that I too am unknowing of you. But because of your omnipotence I write as if I am holding hands with all reading this. For the sole goal of chasing after the Lord's own heart.

Spirit of God,

I pray for you to help my mind, body, heart and soul to close this chapter with the help of your voice.

Amen."

To better oneself is to give thanks to God who made us. He made us in such a unique way that he allowed us to love ourselves mentally, spiritually, whole heartedly and physically. Let us do just that and love ourselves mentally, spiritually, whole heartedly and physically. To love ourselves we have to respect ourselves in all four of those streams because God made us all out of love.

You created every part of me; you put me together in my mother's womb. I praise you because you are to be feared; all you do is strange and wonderful. I know it with all my heart. When my bones were being formed, carefully put together in my mother's womb, when I was growing there in secret, you knew I was there. You saw the days allotted to me had all been recorded in your book, before any of them ever began. **(Psalms 139:13-16) – Good News Translation**

So the LORD answers, "Can a woman forget her own baby and not love the child she bore? Even if a mother should forget her child, I will never forget you. **(Isaiah 49:15) – Good News Translation**

I do not have the word to describe his love because I am still wondering how he loves me. However, whatever it is that we suffer from, the greatest message I can deliver is he knew we would, and he has made it clear in his Word that he longs to comfort and protect us. He saw how Egypt tormented us and how Babylon tried to keep us away from him. Consequently, for those nations, he has not only defeated them but the whole world and now he wants his beautiful creations back.

"Come back to me, my beautiful creations.

Oh, how my beautiful creations love to hear the voice of Egypt! Oh, my beautiful creations how they love to dance like the Egyptians! My beautiful creations have lost sight of where they come from. They have left the promised land and scattered over to foreign land. Unaware of what is to come in such vile lands.

The Egyptians suffer from addictions! They allow themselves to be wrapped up in linen. They say to one another, 'This is Egypt's finest!' Unaware that they are being wrapped up for the world of the dead. My beautiful creations will soon begin to beg! Begging to be freed, their hearts will cry out to me, but their mouths will be shut so they cannot speak! From the bottom of their toes to the top of their foreheads they are wrapped tightly with many layers. The ancient land known as Egypt lays in defeat itself but because my beautiful creations have chosen to reside there, they too have been declared beat. Yet, I am the God who loves his people, I will still free them from their addictions! I will unwrap them from their convictions and air out Egypt's mummy traditions. I will not allow my beautiful creations to be spiritual victims. They will call upon the name that is above all names and I will hear them. I will respond to them, 'My beautiful creations, I have given you a name greater than all nations and kingdoms, for his name is Jesus! My name will free you from all your addictions if you choose to follow me.' Yet, my beautiful creations still find it difficult to come back to me. Although I have freed them.

My creations love their addictions. They are addicted to too many things! I wish my creations would just come back to me. The feeling that alcohol gives my creations; it robs them away from me. They love it, and some of them have even said it allows them to escape their pain. It pleasures them and one day I also heard one of them say, 'it sets me free.' So, I asked, 'Does it really set you free? How much did it pay for you?' But there will be no answer because it didn't pay a single cent for him! It was he who actually paid, just to be a slave. I guess the author forgot about the ultimate sacrifice I made for him just so he would be saved.'

Let me speak to you. Yes, you author! The one that said your idol has set you free. If you looked at its ingredients, they all come from me. Yet you do not put your trust in me? How I wish you relied on me. For it is written:

'Wine, both old and new, is robbing my people of their senses!' (Hosea 4:11) Goods News Translation

However, I do not just put the blame on alcohol. My creations choose alcohol and many other things. I have given my creations the earth to cultivate, but instead, they worship it. They have forsaken me and when they are all alone, sad and depressed, some of them look at me like I am the one who is at fault. Is it me or is it them that they should blame? They have chosen to disobey me, so they face wreckage like a sunken ship. Their bones have been broken, and their eyes cannot see. It's the reason why their minds are delusional because they are without sight, so their thoughts are weak. Some of my creations say they believe in me, but when I look at their hearts their hearts belong to only the things of this earth; they just accept what they can see.

Author, oh author please do not let your addictions beat you. What lie have I ever told you? For it is written:

Jesus answered him, 'I am the way and the truth and the life. No one comes to the Father except through me.' (John 14:6)- Goods News Translation

How much longer will you continue to disappoint me? Come to the desert with me and ditch all the things in your heart. Listen to my voice, 'I will not tease you nor will I ever lead you on with words that flirt.' For it is written:

'So I am going to take her into the desert again; there I will win her back with words of love.' (Hosea 2:14) -Goods News Translation

My words are true because the truth is apart of me. Become my people, my child, and marry me. Devote your time to me and have no part with any idols. Then you will truly see me, and my light will shine on you.

My Spirit will defeat any of your addictions and destroy all idols, and you will never want to love them again. If you love them, then you will be one with them. Author, oh author please do not become one with them. For it is written:

'The world of the dead is hungry for them, and it opens its mouth wide. It fills down the nobles of Jerusalem along with the noisy crowd of common people.' (Isaiah 5:14) - Goods News Translation

My beautiful creations do not belong there. My beautiful creations! Why can't you understand that I love you and that my Spirit yearns for all of you? The love of a father, mother, or siblings cannot compare to my love for you. Nor boyfriend, girlfriend, husband, or wife come close to my love for you. Give me an example of unconditional love and my love will triumphant over them.

My beautiful creations do not follow the ways of Babylon! Babylon has given its heart to the worship of idols! Have nothing to do with idols, nor allow them to fool you. They will flirt, but behind their words, they only wish to hurt.

Come back to me, my beautiful creations..."

- Spirit of God

CHAPTER 6
FLESH VS SPIRIT

In the beginning, God had created Adam and Eve who were made in the image of God. Adam and Eve resided in the garden of Eden in the presence of God. The garden of Eden represented peace and happiness between humans and God because sin did not exist, not yet that is. Our souls were without sin until after we had disobeyed God; we were seen by God as unfit to remain in the garden. Sin not only tarnished our soul's but also our human nature, which influences our flesh's desires (to do evil). Before Adam and Eve had eaten from the tree that gave knowledge of what is good and bad, they were not aware of what sin was. That is why they didn't think being naked was something to be ashamed of.

The man and the woman were both naked, but they were not embarrassed. **(Genesis 2:25) Good News Translation**

When we get up in the morning, the first thing that we have to set our minds into doing is selecting what we are going to wear on that day. Depending on the person, their evaluation of fashion is based on what they consider good on themselves. Everyone has their own taste in fashion which in someway reveals their insecurities. For example, I would never get up in the morning and put on my mother's clothing because she wears clothes that are designed for women. It would internally make me uncomfortable if I had to do something like that because I would never wear clothing made for women. What we decide to put on in the morning inevitably puts a label on ourselves whether we like it or not. Before Adam and Eve ate from the forbidden fruit; they did not possess the ability to judge how they looked because they were blessed to be free. The soul had no conflict with the flesh because it was pure and innocent.

The woman saw how beautiful the tree was and how good its fruit would be to eat, and she thought how wonderful it would be to become wise. So, she took some of the fruit and ate it. Then gave some to her husband, and he also ate it. **(Genesis 3:6) Good News Translation**

As soon as they had eaten it, they were given understanding and realized that they were naked; so, they sewed fig leaves together and covered themselves. **(Genesis 3:7) - Good News Translation**

It was only until after they ate from the tree that introduced us to the battle between the flesh and the spirit.

I appeal to you, my friends, as strangers and refugees in this world! Do not give in to bodily passions, which are always at war against the soul. **(1 Peter 2:11) - Good News Translation**

That innocence was not only lost in the spiritual, but the loss showed itself symbolically in the physical. Being naked wasn't something deemed as sinful to God because if it were, he would have clothed Adam and Eve. When Adam and Eve covered themselves, it symbolically exposed our shame when we make mistakes. Their disobedience brought out guilt which caused them to feel ashamed of their nakedness. Their shame became symbolic when they tried to hide their sin with the figs. Before all this, Adam and Eve had no knowledge of what was good and bad. Did this mean that God had made them mindless? That is not the case, Satan knew just how to infiltrate Eve's mind by getting her to forget about God's instruction so that she could think about what it would be like to be like God.

The snake replied, "That's not true; you will not die. God said that because he knows when you eat it, you will be like God and know what is good and what is bad." **(Genesis 3:4–5) - Good News Translation**

Wouldn't it be nice to be like God? It is that very thought process that got Satan kicked out of heaven because he tried dethroning God. That very sin that got Satan kicked out of heaven is the same approach he used on Eve.

Then the LORD *God said, "Now these human beings have become like one of us and have knowledge of what is good and what is bad. They must not be allowed to take fruit from the tree that gives life, eat it, and live forever." So the* LORD *God sent them out of the Garden of Eden and made them cultivate the soil from which they had been formed.* **(Genesis 3:22-23) – New King James Version**

The moment Eve ate from the fruit, she handed it to Adam to eat as well and they became spiritually dead. God immediately made the call that Adam and Eve were not worthy to stay in the garden because they would be among the tree of life.

"If you have ears, then, listen to what the Spirit says to the churches! To those who win the victory, I will give the right to eat the fruit of the tree of life that grows in the Garden of God." **(Revelations 2:7) – New King James Version**

The angel also showed me the river of the water of life, sparkling like crystal, and coming from the throne of God and of the Lamb and flowing down the middle of the city's street. On each side of the river was the tree of life, which bears fruit twelve times a year, once each month; and its leaves are for the healing of the nations. Nothing that is under God's curse will be found in the city. The throne of God and of the Lamb will be in the city, and his servants will worship him. **(Revelations 22:1-3) – New King James Version**

God did not want humans to be immortal at that very moment due to their disobedience, which explains why Adam and Eve were given the boot. We see that God has future plans with the tree of life, hence why we hear about it in the last book of the bible.

When people had spread all over the world, and daughters were being born, some of the heavenly beings saw that these young women were beautiful, so they took the ones they liked. Then the LORD *said, "I will not allow people to live forever;*

they are mortal. From now on they will live no longer than 120 years." In those days, and even later, there were giants on the earth who were descendants of human women and the heavenly beings. They were the great heroes and famous men of long ago. **(Genesis 6:1-4) – New King James Version**

As we read Genesis 6:1-4, we find out that some angels had found some of the women on earth attractive. Now before I continue, I think we should review what we know of the fallen angels. In the previous chapter, I referenced how Satan took a third of the angels in heaven with him. It is quoted that the dragon's tail (the devil) threw them to the ground and they were given specific regions within nations to reside in. But Genesis 6:1-4 is not referring to the fallen angels. Now this is just a theory but it seems as though, there were a few bad apples left in the heavenly realm that did not initially go with the devil.

And the angels who did not keep their proper domain, but left their own abode, He has reserved in everlasting chains under darkness for the judgment of the great day; as Sodom and Gomorrah, and the cities around them in a similar manner to these, having given themselves over to sexual immorality and gone after strange flesh, are set forth as an example, suffering the vengeance of eternal fire. **(Jude 1:6-7) – New King James Version**

That is why Jude writes about these specific angels because they received an unheard punishment that Satan and the other angels didn't receive.

And suddenly they cried out, saying, "What have we to do with you, Jesus, you Son of God? Have you come here to torment us before the time? **(Matthew 8:29) – New King James Version**

I quoted this Scripture in the previous chapter, when Jesus approached the man that was possessed by a demon. I'm referencing this Scripture again because of what the demon said to Christ. It said, "What have we to do with you, Jesus, you Son of God? Have you come here to torment us before the time?" What was the evil spirit referring to? Well in Jude 1:6-7, it speaks of the angels which I am speaking of right now who left their heavenly domain just to have sex with human beings. The evil spirits who were thrown down by Satan's tail must have heard of what happened to those spiritual beings which is why we hear the demons in Matthew 8:29 wonder what Jesus was going to do with them. The rebellious angels that left heaven to go have sex with the women on the earth created Nephilim's, which is Hebrew for Nefilim. What that basically means is that they were the offspring of angels and humans. This enraged God because these angels were disrupting the natural order that God had set out for humanity. Angels are also not like us because they are spiritual beings without the flesh. Which must mean these certain angels who left the heavenly realm must have taken form of human beings. But I want to stay on topic, so we will discuss more about these specific angels in another chapter.

Then the devil, who deceived them, was thrown into the lake of fire and sulfur, where the beast and the false prophet had already been thrown; and they will be tormented forever and ever. **(Revelations 20:10) - Good News Translation**

And I heard a loud voice from heaven saying, "Behold, the tabernacle of God is with men, and he will dwell with them, and they shall be his people. God himself will be with them and be their God. And God will wipe away every tear from their eyes; there shall be no more death, nor sorrow, nor crying. There shall be no more pain, for the former things have passed away." Then he who sat on the throne said, "Behold, I make all things new." And he said to me, "Write, for these words are true and faithful." And he said to me, "It is done! I am the Alpha and the Omega, the Beginning and the End. I will give of the fountain of the water of life freely to him who thirsts. He who overcomes shall inherit all things, and I will be his God and he shall be my son. But the cowardly, unbelieving, abominable, murderers, sexually immoral, sorcerers, idolaters, and all liars shall have their part in the lake which burns with fire and brimstone, which is the second death." **(Revelations 21:3-8) – New King James Version**

Angels are not above humans in the eyes of God even though they worship unconditionally. This may seem like they are better than us because they worship unconditionally, but that is not the case. Angel's may worship unconditionally but do so because they are in God's presence and marvel at his glory. My words cannot collectively come together for even my own mind to explain just how extraordinary God's glory is. I did also mention that it would be a sin for angels to not worship God because that would mean something is of more value than God. We do not understand this way of thinking because of our sinful nature, hence why we live the way we do. What I mean by that is we seek validation in our possessions, careers, or even relationships over God. As mentioned by Jefferson Bethke, 'we all worship something.'

I, John, am the one who heard and saw these things. And when I heard and saw them, I fell down to worship at the feet of the angel who showed them to me, but he said to me, "You must not do that! I am a fellow servant with you and your brothers the prophets, and with those who keep the words of this book. Worship God." **(Revelations 22: 8-9) – English Standard Version**

The Apostle John attempted to worship the angel that accompanied him throughout his whole vision of the end of days. God regarded Apostle John so highly that he showed him what was to happen in the last days. After the vision was revealed to him, John felt honored that he out of all people got to see such sights. He then attempted to bow down to the angel, but the angel had to remind him that the worship belonged to God. The angel told Apostle John, "You must not do that! I am a fellow servant with you and your brothers the prophets, and with those who keep the words of this book. Worship God." I found this interesting because the angel, who hadn't sinned, knew he was at the same level as us. Which got me to wonder: How could that be? Well just because we are not like the angels who have been in front of God's presence. It is through faith that we supersede the unconditional worship that the angels provide God because we worship without seeing! Our worship is seen at an even greater level once we receive the Holy Spirit because we have God in us which exceeds the worship that Satan himself used to perfect.

But the hour is coming, and now is, when the true worshipers will worship the Father in spirit and truth; for the Father is seeking such to worship him. God is Spirit, and those who worship him must worship in spirit and truth." **(John 4:23-24) – New King James Version**

We hope for God to do or change things in our lives but have yet to ever see him. We believe that he exists despite our physical and sinful nature that will always oppose us from following through our faith. The angels worship unconditionally because they see whereas we worship when we don't. To summarize, God still views us as the same, if not higher, because of his love for us. Satan and his angels did not care about God's glory and were seeking to begin their own kingdom, so they got the boot. That specific act should give us a better understanding of how great God's love is for us. For the angels who defied God saw his presence but rejected it for nothing. Where we do not see God's presence but if we exhibit faith through action, he is pleased with us. God has promised to place us above the angels who still worship him unconditionally.

Dare any of you, having a matter against another, go to law before the unrighteous, and not before the saints? Do you not know that the saints will judge the world? And if the world will be judged by you, are you unworthy to judge the smallest matters? Do you not know that we shall judge angels? How much more, things that pertain to this life? If then you have judgments concerning things pertaining to this life, do you appoint those who are least esteemed by the church to judge?
(1 Corinthians 6:1-4) – New King James Version

The battle between flesh and spirit began as soon as we ate from the tree that gave knowledge of what is good and bad. This is because it gave us the understanding to negotiate with sin. The evil one's fundamental doctrine for making humans fall for temptation is found in our very bodies. God did not create us as mindless beings, as a matter of fact, he made us in his own image and granted us the authority over the earth. Having this kind of authority shows us that God did not make us mindless beings.

So God created man in his own image; in the image of God he created him; male and female he created them. Then God blessed them, and God said to them, "Be fruitful and multiply; fill the earth and subdue it; have dominion over the fish of the sea, over the birds of the air, and over every living thing that moves on the earth." And God said, "See, I have given you every herb that yields seed which is on the face of all the earth, and every tree whose fruit yields seed; to you it shall be for food. Also, to every beast of the earth, to every bird of the air, and to everything that creeps on the earth, in which there is life, I have given every green herb for food"; and it was so. **(Genesis 1:27-30) – New King James Version**

Our disobedience made us look stupid because we traded in spiritual life for spiritual death.

For sin pays its wage-death, but God's free gift is eternal life in union with Christ Jesus our Lord. **(Romans 6:23) - Good News Translation**

As a result of our disobedience, sin was born, and it ironically gave birth to death. Foolishness is when we begin to believe that we are like God, which is just how Satan baited Eve into eating from the tree.

To have the knowledge, you must first have reverence for the LORD. Stupid people have no respect for wisdom and refuse to learn. **(Proverbs 1:7) - Good News Translation**

My son, if you receive my words and treasure up my commandments with you, making your ear attentive to wisdom and inclining your heart to understand; yes, if you call out for insight and raise your voice for understanding, if you seek it like silver and search for it as for hidden treasures, then you will understand the fear of the LORD and find the knowledge of God. For the LORD gives wisdom; from his mouth come knowledge and understanding; he stores up sound wisdom for the upright; he is a shield to those who walk in integrity, guarding the paths of justice and watching over the way of his saints. Then you will understand righteousness and justice and equity, every good path; for wisdom will come into your heart, and knowledge will be pleasant to your soul. **(Proverbs 2:1-10) – English Standard Version**

After all this, there is only one thing to say: Have reverence for God, and obey his commands, because this is all that we were created for. God is going to judge everything we do, whether good or bad, even things done in secret. **(Ecclesiastes 12:13-14) - Good News Translation**

The first person to take a ride at arrogance was Satan because he wanted to be above God. Despite all that God had given him through appearance, power, and status. He married sin and became one with it. That marriage that Lucifer engaged himself in, made him change his legal name to Satan. After the honeymoon, sin took the appearance of perfection. The same way Lucifer was created as perfect, sin took the appearance of perfection making it look appealing to the eyes of all humans.

"Mortal man," he said, "grieve for the fate that is waiting for the king of Tyre. Tell him what I, the Sovereign LORD, am saying: "you were once an example of perfection. How wise and handsome you were!" **(Ezekiel 28:12) – Good News Translation**

Well, no wonder! Even Satan can disguise himself to look like an angel of light! **(2 Corinthians 11:14) – Good News Translation**

It shouldn't surprise us that Satan can shapeshift into any being, but he also uses that power to shapeshift into thoughts and nightmares. For example, I had a little sister who passed away. Her name was Neema, who unfortunately was a premature baby. She passed away after 6 months because of pneumonia. This ability to shapeshift has fooled many people simply because Satan can create a sense of comfort to the victim allowing them to trust the voice of whomever he has masked himself. A few years passed after Neema's death. One night I had a dream of Neema walking around wearing a white gown, just slow dancing around my family's living room. I think I was about 13 years old at the time, but I will never forget that dream. I remember a tremendous fear came over me because I didn't understand death. When I asked my mother about this dream, she just briefly told me that it wasn't really Neema but only a spirit trying to pose as her. I was only 13 years old when she told me that and because of my age I didn't really understand her, but I never forgot it. Imagine explaining to a 13-year about spiritual warfare! But the thing is, age does not define ones understanding of any matter. My brother Imani can be a testimony to that since he began preaching at the age of 11. See the thing is God doesn't discriminate on age, color, nationality, sexual orientation or gender. Nor does he overlook status or those with disabilities. Better yet, God does not overlook anyone no matter what they've done or said because these things do not define us in the eyes of God. He overlooks all these things because he is focused on us becoming one with him-which is why my mind is still baffled by his unconditional love for us.

For consider your calling, brothers: not many of you were wise according to worldly standards, not many were powerful, not many were of noble birth. But God chose what is foolish in the world to shame the wise; God chose what is weak in the world to shame the strong; God chose what is low and despised in the world, even things that are not, to bring to nothing things that are, so that no human being might boast in the presence of God. **(1 Corinthians 1:26-29) – English Standard Version**

There was a poster that I once saw that read, "Do you seriously think God can't use you?" Below was a list of famous people in the bible whom God had used and are remembered today as biblical role models. The lesson behind the poster was to reveal to us that God can use anyone no matter what their story is.

The list read:

"Noah was a drunk, Abraham was too old, Isaac was a daydreamer. Leah was ugly, Joseph was abused, Moses had a stuttering problem, Gideon was afraid, Rahab was a prostitute, Jeremiah and Timothy were too young. David had an affair, Elijah was suicidal, Isaiah preached naked, Jonah ran away from God, Naomi was a widow, Job went bankrupt. Peter denied Christ, the disciples fell asleep while praying, Martha worried about everything, the Samaritan woman was divorced, Zacchaeus was too small, Paul persecuted Christians, Timothy was an ulcer, and Lazarus was dead."

The 13-year old me was not ready to understand what my mother said regarding spirits, but I was going to learn very soon.

"Do not go for advice to people who consult the spirits of the dead. If you do, you will be ritually unclean. I am the LORD your God." **(Leviticus 19:31) – Good News Translation**

'And the person who turns to mediums and familiar spirits, to prostitute himself with them, I will set my face against that person and cut him from his people. Consecrate yourselves therefore, and be holy, for I am the LORD your God. And you shall keep my statues and perform them: I am the LORD who sanctifies you. **(Leviticus 20:6-8) – New King James Version**

There shall not be found among you anyone who makes his son or his daughter pass through the fire, or one who practices witchcraft, or a soothsayer, or one who interprets omens, or a sorcerer, or one who conjures spells, or a medium, or a spiritist, or one who calls up the dead. For all who do these things are an abomination to the LORD, *and because of these abominations the* LORD *your God drives them out from before you. You shall be blameless before the* LORD *your God.* **(Deuteronomy 18:10-13) – New King James Version**

And when they say to you, "Seek those who are mediums and wizards, who whisper and mutter," should not a people seek their God? Should they seek the dead on behalf of the living? To the law and to the testimony! If they do not speak according to this word, it is because there is no light in them. **(Isaiah 8:19-20) – New King James Version**

God despises when people not only attempt to communicate with the dead but those who go to people that consult the dead for advice. God doesn't just tell us to not do things for no reason. His reasoning is only because he knows when we do such things, we are consulting Satan's angels (demons). For those who do not have knowledge of the Scriptures, in biblical times the practice of magic was very popular.

Now it happened, as we went to prayer, that a certain slave girl possessed with a spirit of divination met us, who brought her masters much profit by fortune-telling. This girl followed Paul and us, and cried out, saying, "These men are the servants of the Most High God, who proclaim to us the way of salvation." And this she did for many days. But Paul, greatly annoyed, turned and said to the spirit, "I command you in the name of Jesus Christ to come out of her." And he came out that very hour. **(Acts 16:16-18) – New King James Version**

The practice of fortune-telling, consulting the dead, and witchcraft has not died because there are many today who still participate in these acts. It's a disturbing practice that angers God, as mentioned in Deuteronomy and Leviticus. God specifically says that those who do such things will become ritually unclean and be subject to consequences. When I read these Scriptures, I wasn't worried nor concerned about it because I personally have never participated in such acts. Well so I thought.

I am going to share a story which I have never shared with anyone in my whole entire life about witchcraft. Some things happen in our lives that are out of our control and unfortunately this story trends along those lines. After I was born, my umbilical cord was taken by a few family relatives of mine to the graveyard of my grandfather where a ritual was performed. When I gained knowledge of that, I was deeply disturbed. I had this hate in my heart towards them because it made no sense why they would do such a thing. However, when I began this journey to live for God, the Holy Spirit told me not to hate them because they did not know any better. I mean why would relatives wish evil on a newborn of their own blood.

Jesus said, "Forgive them, Father! They don't know what they are doing." They divided his clothes among themselves by throwing dice. **(Luke 23:34) - Good News Translation**

Traditions that are passed on generation after generation are no secret or mystery to some families. They are done for superstitious reasons or are done in an attempt to receive blessings, but the problem about these traditions is it is a direct conversation with the devil. One cannot ask the devil for a blessing because he does not have the power to bless since there is no blessing in him. When these traditions are performed, it violates one of God's sacred commandments. It then brings forth a curse on the person performing the ritual but also to their own offspring.

Do not bow down to any idol or worship it, because I am the LORD your God and I tolerate no rivals. I bring punishment on those who hate me and, on their descendants, down to the third and fourth generation. But I will show my love to thousands of generations of those who love me and obey my laws. **(Exodus 20:5) – Good News Translation**

Whoever believes that Jesus is the Christ is born of God, and everyone who loves him who begot also loves him who is begotten of him. By this we know that we love the children of God, when we love God and keep his commandments. For this is the love of God, that we keep his commandments. And his commandments are not burdensome. For whatever is born of God overcomes the world. And this is the victory that has overcome the world our faith. Who is he who overcomes the world, but he who believes that Jesus is the Son of God? **(1 John 5:1-5) – New King James Version**

God is very firm and strict about this one commandment that he even attaches a curse with it. Some may read this and wonder what he meant of those who hate him. It is better understood in 1 John 5:1-5 because those who love God obey his commandments. On the flip side, those who disobey his commandments hate him. I once wondered how we could really show that we love God, but he provides the answer in that Scripture. By obeying, we are saying we trust in everything he says because we love him. What then happens to those who choose to disobey this strict commandment?

But evil shall come upon you, which you will not know how to charm away; disaster shall fall upon you, for which you will not be able to atone; and ruin shall come upon you suddenly, of which you know nothing. Stand fast in your enchantments and your many sorceries, with which you have laboured from your youth; perhaps you may be able to succeed; perhaps you may inspire terror. You are wearied with your many counsels; let them stand forth and save you, those who divide the heavens, who gaze at the stars, who at the new moons make known what shall come upon you. Behold, they are like stubble; the fires consume them; they cannot deliver themselves from the power of the flame. No coal for warming oneself is this, no fire to sit before! Such to you are those with whom you have laboured, who have done business with you from your youth; they wander about, each in his own direction; there is no one to save you. **(Isaiah 47:11-15) – English Standard Version**

When I read Exodus 20:5 it made me think about what my relatives had done. So, naturally, I began asking myself many questions: How is it fair that the future generations are included on a curse for the sins of past generations? A new-born that is born into a family that has a history of practicing witchcraft and worshipping idols should not be subject to a curse. It isn't the child's fault, nor did the child choose to be apart of those practices. This is when I noticed how doctors have become very adamant on understanding a person's family tree. They tend to ask questions like, "Has anyone in your family ever been affected by so and so infection or disease?" Or on a completely different note: Some people fear unsuccessful marriages, educational failures (not finishing high school, or never going to college or university) or poor finances because these examples have become something that has continued on in their family tree. Some have said, "Drinking runs in the family, so that's why I have a drinking problem. My mother had a smoking addiction, so that's why I have one." Common phrases such as those are inducing curses upon our own lives. These curses come upon our lives because we give authority to such spirits to enter our lives! We have to remember that God gave us authority over the earth. When we speak such things, we invoke spiritual entities on ourselves that were never supposed to be apart of us and Satan knows this which is why we have to watch what we say.

Death and life are in the power of the tongue, and those who love it will eat its fruit. **(Proverbs 18:21) – New King James Version**

Certain behaviors or lifestyles can turn into the very idols God prohibits us from worshipping. Once worshipped the curse is passed down to the child and their child and so forth.

So the LORD became angry with Solomon, because his heart had turned from the LORD God of Israel, who had appeared to him twice, and had commanded him concerning this thing, that he should not go after other gods; but he did not keep what the LORD had commanded. Therefore the LORD said to Solomon, "Because you have done this, and have not kept my covenant and my statutes, which I have commanded you, I will surely tear the kingdom away from you and give it to your servant. Nevertheless, I will not do it in your days, for the sake of your father David; I will tear it out of the hand of your son. However, I will not tear away the whole kingdom; I will give one tribe to your son for the sake of my servant David, and for the sake of Jerusalem which I have chosen." **(1 Kings 11:9-13) – New King James Version**

This also includes sickness and diseases that we so calmly accept because our parents or grandparents had them. Satan wants us to think, "Oh, I will probably get so and so disease because it is in my genes." This arouses spiritual warfare and generational curses because we continue to accept the physical rather than focusing on the spiritual. In that event, what can be done? If all this is linked together, what hope do we have against this?

There is therefore now no condemnation to those who are in Christ Jesus, who do not walk according to the flesh, but according to the Spirit **(Romans 8:1) – New King James Version**

Therefore, if anyone is in Christ, he is a new creation; old things have passed away; behold, all things have become new. **(2 Corinthians 5:17) – New King James Version**

The acceptance of Jesus Christ cuts off any generational curses done by our parents or grandparents because we are made new through Jesus Christ. Any sort of curse is nullified rather than being passed down. However, when I was told about the event of what happened on my birth, it was different. It was different because an actual ritual was performed to target my own life in some sort of way. This ritual that was done was not something that my parents or grandparents had passed on. It was a deliberate attempt to perform a curse on my life, even if they thought it was a blessing. I had many questions like, "Why would they conform to witchcraft? Were they trying to harm me? My family comes from Christian values so why resort to such evil? What did that ritual do to me?" But the most important question I had asked myself was: How does one break a curse?

And Balak the son of Zippor saw all that Israel had done to the Amorites. And Moab was in great dread of the people, because they were many. Moab was overcome with fear of the people of Israel. And Moab said to the elders of Midian, "This horde will now lick up all that is around us, as the ox licks up the grass of the field." So Balak the son of Zippor, who was king of Moab at that time, sent messengers to Balaam the son of Beor at Pethor, which is near the River in the land of the people of Amaw, to call him, saying, "Behold, a people has come out of Egypt. They cover the face of the earth, and they are dwelling opposite me. Come now, curse this people for me, since they are too mighty for me. Perhaps I shall be able to defeat them and drive them from the land, for I know that he whom you bless is blessed, and he whom you curse is cursed." So the elders of Moab and the elders of Midian departed with the fees for divination in their hand. And they came to Balaam and gave him Balak's message. And he said to them, "Lodge here tonight, and I will bring back word to you, as the LORD *speaks to me." So the princes of Moab stayed with Balaam.* **(Number 22:2-8) – English Standard Version**

This story relates back to the Old Testament with Israel. After God had freed them from Egypt. In this story, the king of Moab put two and two together and noticed how Israel was going country to country conquering everything. The Scriptures state that Balak, who was king of Moab, became terrified of Israel so he went to the prophet Balaam for help. The ironic part about this was that the Moabites and Midianites worshipped the false god Chemosh, but never consulted their own god; instead, they went to Israel's God. They did this because they saw how God had been protecting them. I think people didn't understand Israel's covenant with God because one moment they'd be conquering other nations, but other times they'd end up losing wars and getting conquered themselves (hence the punishment that stemmed from their disobedience). This fooled many nations because they recognized God's power through Israel but never wanted to commit to him. They refused because the ways of their gods were appealing to their sinful natures. In spite of that, it did not stop king Balak from trying to curse the Israelites.

He attempted to pay off the prophet Balaam so that Israel would be cursed and that his nation would win the war against them.

Then God came to Balaam and said, "Who are these men with you?" So Balaam said to God, "Balak the son of Zippor, king of Moab, has sent me, saying, 'Look, a people has come out of Egypt, and they cover the face of the earth. Come now, curse them for me; perhaps I shall be able to overpower them and drive them out.'" And God said to Balaam, "You shall not go with them; you shall not curse the people, for they are blessed." **(Numbers 22:9-12) – New King James Version**

The conversation between God and Balaam is alluring because he first asks Balaam: "Who are these men with you?" How is it that God, the creator of the universe, had to ask who the men were? Since he is God, wouldn't he have known who these people were? What Balaam failed to understand was that God was angry with him for associating with Israel's enemy (Balaam is remembered negatively because he kept compromising with Israel's enemies). The Moab's and Midianites worshipped the false god Chemosh, so that's why God asked who they were because they had already identified themselves as Chemosh's people. It wasn't that God didn't know who the Moabites and Midianites were, but he was delivering a far greater message to future generations. If we fast forward to Jesus' resurrection which brought victory over sin and gave us salvation and grace; it applied to anyone who chooses Christ and if they do, they become God's people. Since Israel was the first nation to become God's people, he had blessed them. Anyone who becomes apart of Christ becomes his people and are blessed in spirit.

The next morning Balaam went to Balak's messengers and said, "Go back home; the LORD has refused to let me go with you." **(Numbers 22:13) – Good News Translation**

God replies to Balaam to tell Balak's messenger that the people of Israel cannot be cursed because he blessed them. When I had heard what had happened on the day of my birth it had troubled me for years. I even prayed but they were without genuine faith because I had the knowledge that God could do anything, but my heart was exactly like king Balak of the Moabites. I wanted to use God's power to rid of the curse (whatever the curse meant) and then go on with my ungodly life. This is the fantastic thing about salvation though because God did hear my simple prayers and had a plan set to answer them, but they weren't what I expected. King Moab knew the God of Israel and his magnificent powers but chose to serve the false god Chemosh. He preferred the ways of Chemosh because it allowed him to live the life he desired. I had bottled up tons of hate towards my relatives in Tanzania, so I vowed to never go back there.

We may make our plans, but God has the last Word. **(Proverbs 16:1) – Good News Translation**

"I am the LORD, your savior; I am the one who created you. I am the LORD, the Creator of all things. I alone stretched out the heavens; when I made the earth, no one helped me. I make fools of fortune-tellers and frustrate the predictions of astrologers. The words of the wise I refute and show that their wisdom is foolish." **(Isaiah 44:24–25) – Good News Translation**

I was about to get a first-hand taste of what it was like to have God change my own plans. I received the Holy Spirit on January 2018 and said that I wanted to begin a journey to follow Jesus. People can receive the Spirit but it's up to that person to continue living in the Spirit and that was my problem. I gave 60% to God but allowed my flesh to have 40% jurisdiction of my heart, which only craved the things of the world. In the previous chapter, I spoke about how that doesn't work because whatever percentage we give to an idol, it will find a way to become our number one priority. The problem with giving our flesh any sort of jurisdiction power, is it will do exactly what human nature craves.

Now the works of the flesh are evident, which are: adultery, fornication, uncleanness, lewdness, idolatry, sorcery, hatred, contentions, jealousies, outbursts of wrath, selfish ambitions, dissensions, heresies, envy, murders, drunkenness, revelries, and the like; of which I tell you beforehand, just as I also told you in time past, that those who practice such things will not inherit the kingdom of God. **(Galatians 5:19-21) – New King James Version**

My human nature consisted of always being in control because I believed that I was smart enough to handle everything life threw at me. I believed in taking shortcuts rather than working hard and seeing things through. I believed in pleasing others rather than pleasing God. I believed that by picking up the bible from time to time, I wasn't subject to face any consequences of my actions. I could go on about all the things that I believed in, but what matters is I was only lying to myself and was far from the truth.

But if our unrighteousness serves to show the righteousness of God, what shall we say? That God is unrighteous to inflict wrath on us? (I speak in a human way.) By no means! For then how could God judge the world? But if through my lie God's truth abounds to his glory, why am I still being condemned as a sinner? And why not do evil that good may come? —as some people slanderously charge us with saying. Their condemnation is just. **(Romans 3:5-8) – English Standard Version**

"I know your works, that you are neither cold nor hot. I could wish you were cold or hot. So then, because you are lukewarm, and neither cold nor hot, I will vomit you out of my mouth. **(Revelations 3:15-16) – New King James Version**

I used to think I had and would always have control over my life, so I didn't need God. In a way I put myself on such a high pedestal that I considered myself as my own god. God already hates when people worship other gods, so I could only imagine how upset he was with my egotistic mentality.

Do not worship other gods, any of the gods of the peoples around you. If you do worship other gods, the LORD's anger will come against you like fire and will destroy you completely, because the LORD your God, who is present with you, tolerates no rivals. **(Deuteronomy 6:14-15) - Good News Translation**

But as the Scripture says, "Whoever wants to boast must boast about what the Lord has done." For it is when the Lord thinks well of us that we are really approved, and not when we think well of ourselves. **(2 Corinthians 10:17-18) - Good News Translation**

I referenced 2 Corinthians 10:17-18 because God is trying to explain to us what happens when we live by our human nature. If we look back at Satan's story, he became prideful because he wanted to be above God which caused his fall. That is why God warns us not to boast in our own abilities. He says this to protect us from becoming full of ourselves. It serves as a warning because pride can cause us to behave in such a manner where we think we are gods.

Then, when desire has conceived, it gives birth to sin; and sin, when it is full grown, brings forth death. Do not be deceived, my beloved brethren. **(James 1:15-16) – New King James Version**

This nature that I speak of comes off differently in all people. Some may not be egotistic, but others desire different things. It is one of the deadly side-affects of the forbidden fruit because our nature will crave sin naturally. Remember in the battling Egypt and Babylon chapter when I spoke about Satan tempting Jesus? Well, I used the term 'hangry' but for the context of that chapter I could not elaborate on it. Well, this is the chapter where I can speak of it. Our flesh (or bodies) have inherited a sinful nature from the act that was committed in the garden of Eden. Which is why Apostle Paul writes in Galatians 5:19-21 that human nature craves immorality, filth, indecent actions, worship of idols and witchcraft. Sounds harsh but if we think about it, we all have done these things. Apostle Paul goes even further by stating human nature gets jealous, angry, ambitious. He writes, "separating into parties and groups," which essentially is referring to race, culture and arguments of politics and power. Human nature loves getting drunk and participating in immoral and disturbing sexual acts like orgies. I read all these things that Apostle Paul wrote and sadly I have either done some of them or have thought of doing one of them. But what's dangerous about my attitude was that

I thought I was without sin. So what hope do we have if that is our true nature? I mean for my sake; how did I combat my egotistic self?

But the fruit of the Spirit is love, joy, peace, longsuffering, kindness, goodness, faithfulness, gentleness, self-control. Against such there is no law. And those who are Christ's have crucified the flesh with its passions and desires. If we live in the Spirit, let us also walk in the Spirit. **(Galatians 5:22-25)- New King James Version**

It was this very Scripture that gives us the answer to the flesh vs spirit dilemma. The Spirit that Galatians 5:22-25 speaks about is the Holy Spirit because God knew that it would be impossible for us to beat our sinful nature alone. He knew we would always crave its desires-sin. Jesus made it accesible to all of us after he ascended into heaven because he knew that we would need a helper. In relation to my issues, the Spirit examined my spirit and found a boastful spirit that was attached to my spirit. Which in reality was a form of idolatry because to boast of oneself is like worshipping oneself.

"You cannot be a slave of two masters, you will hate one and love the other; you will be loyal to one and despise the other. You cannot serve both God and money." **(Matthew 6:24) – Good News Translation**

I may have been able to fool people, but I couldn't fool God because he looked at my heart and saw that I wasn't 100% for him. I have revealed a few personality traits about myself so far, but I struggled to control my own flesh and spirit. Months passed by in the year 2018 and God began to isolate me by removing the most valuable things I had placed in my heart. Suddenly every opportunity that I had for employment kept falling apart. Friendships that I valued above my relationship with God disappeared and my relationship with my parents began to deteriorate. Remember my vow about never wanting to go to Tanzania? Well, my Dad randomly gave me an ultimatum that if I didn't go to Tanzania, I had to find my own home which I financially couldn't afford. So, I was left with no choice except take the free trip, but I was not happy at all. I never confided in anyone about my vow or about the incident that happened on the day of my birth. As a matter of fact, my parents did not know about my feelings towards my own birthplace. I was angry at the world and at myself but especially at God because I felt like he was punishing me. Little did I know that God was answering my own prayers. I didn't know God's plan until only an hour before landing to Dares Salem, Tanzania. I was sleeping for the majority of the trip when I was awakened on the plane by the Holy Spirit.

"I brought you back to the very land where you vowed to yourself that you'd never return, all because you hated their evil. But what about your evil? You asked for my Spirit and the dove flew down and gave you peace. Yet you took that dove and tormented it. My forgiveness is not like this world's forgiveness; many will curse at you and say bad things about you for all the wrong that you have committed, but I forgive you and will forget your sins. But I'm taking you back to your birthland; your people, so that it will humble you because you are way too cocky. Did you call Tanzania evil? What about your evil? Evil exists all over the earth, in every location. Everywhere you walk, you walk on contaminated land and you breathe out sin while polluting the atmosphere, sharing and contributing to the air of sinners. I have breathed into you the Spirit, my Spirit! You were supposed to bless the air with my Spirit! My Spirit produces love, joy, peace, patience, kindness, goodness, faithfulness, humility, and self-control. But you consistently made my Spirit sad! I should punish you, but I love you so much so I will show you mercy.

So, now I will show you things like poverty that you have not seen in the land that you've grown so comfortable in. By seeing this, it will remain in your memory forever so that you will always remember those who are suffering. You will never complain about money because you will remember those who are poor and appreciate what you have. You will not seek out money for happiness because you will see a nation filled with people who have more happiness than you can imagine. I will show you faithful people who do not care about what they eat, or how they dress but only care about pleasing me. I see you struggle against your flesh, so I have situated your flesh in an environment unrecognizable to it. You have the upper advantage, now focus on me!

I am bringing you to your country to show you that when I will something, it will come to be. When you enter the land, I want you to open your eyes so that you may see what the Spirit sees. Use your ears to hear what the Spirit hears. Read my Word and study it every day so that you may get to know me. Pray to me and familiarize yourself to my voice. Because you will see miracles that will confuse your sight and hear testimonies that will baffle your mind. You called this country evil because of something your own family did to you. But the very land that you were once cursed, I shall bless you. The very country where you were born will be the very country that our relationship will begin. Your hate will turn to love, and your foolishness will turn to wisdom. Your greed will turn into generosity, and your guilt will be transformed into peace. Your depression will turn to happiness because I know you feel defeated and overwhelmed, but my Spirit will give you strength. My Spirit will provide you with rest, and you will become new in the eyes of my sight. Obey and focus on me and live the rest of your life for me."

-Spirit of God

Hearing God's voice on that flight is something I cannot put in words on paper, or voice by my own lips. I cannot describe the feeling, but it was something that wasn't of this world because of how powerful it was. It gave me hope which filled my whole soul.

I will give him complete authority under the king, the descendant of David. He will have the keys of office; what he opens, no one will shut, and what he shuts, no one will open. **(Isaiah 22:22) – Good News Translation**

In Isaiah 22:22, God was prophesying through Isaiah about Jesus' authority as the Savior of the world. When king Balak wanted to curse Israel, God replied, "No!" because God had already blessed Israel. Whatever God blesses cannot be cursed and whatever God curses cannot be blessed.

How can I curse what God has not cursed, or speak of doom when the LORD has not? **(Numbers 23:8) – Good News Translation**

As a result of this, anyone who has given their lives to Christ will have power in his name to remove any curse placed on themselves.

Thomas said to Him, "Lord, we do not know where you are going, and how can we know the way?" Jesus said to him, "I am the way, the truth, and the life. No one comes to the Father except through me. "If you had known me, you would have known my Father also; and from now on you know him and have seen him." Philip said to him, "Lord, show us the Father, and it is sufficient for us." Jesus said to him, "Have I been with you so long, and yet you have not known me, Philip? He who has seen me has seen the Father; so how can you say, 'Show us the Father'? Do you not believe that I am in the Father, and the Father in me? The words that I speak to you I do not speak on my own authority; but the Father who dwells in me does the works. Believe me that I am in the Father and the Father in me, or else believe me for the sake of the works themselves. "Most assuredly, I say to you, he who believes in me, the works that I do he will do also; and greater works than these he will do, because I go to My Father. And whatever you ask in my name, that I will do, that the Father may be glorified in the Son. **(John 14:5-13) – New King James Version**

So, does this mean we have the power to curse anyone or anything? Of course not! God can see into our hearts and if evil motives in our hearts, he is not really in us. Therefore, to even consider such things would deliberately prevent us from doing anything in Christ' name.

Now it came to pass, when the time had come for him to be received up, that he steadfastly set his face to go to Jerusalem and sent messengers before his face. And as they went, they entered a village of the Samaritans, to prepare for him. But they did not receive him, because his face was set for the journey to Jerusalem. And when his disciples James and John saw this, they said, "Lord, do you want us to command fire to come down from heaven and consume them, just as Elijah did?" But he turned and rebuked them, and said, "You do not know what manner of spirit you are of. For the Son of Man did not come to destroy men's lives but to save them." And they went to another village. **(Luke 9:51-56) – New King James Version**

While I was in Tanzania, I followed all that the Holy Spirit instructed me to do. I enjoyed every minute there. I got to see my family, but I saw how people lived without complaining. Yes, some need help and would be extremely grateful for a better life, but they still manage to enjoy life. I was born in Tanzania but moved to Canada when I was 2 years old. So, I do not really know what its like to live there. Throughout my whole life, I have been fooled by what I saw on TV because of how they depict Africa. They show how poor the countries are but never show how beautiful they are. I am happy that I got to see how beautiful my country is. It is not poor all over, but like any country, there are wealthy neighborhoods and poor neighborhoods. Personally, I found that their culture reflects deeply on family. Neighbors were more than neighbors because they treated each other like family. Children were out and about playing together without a care in the world. As a nation, there is no doubt that it needs improvement but what really struck me was their dedication to God. The people in the churches were so spiritual and I saw people worshipping at a level I've never seen before. I witnessed a Pastor cast out an evil spirit out of someone. That experience not only scared me but also made me realize that demons are very real. I went with my mom, little brother Isaiah, aunt and her children. I sat beside this one lady who was extremely kind and seemed put together. It was not until prayer time when my whole world was about to be turned upside down. That same lady who was sitting beside me started screaming and growling as soon as the church began praying. I remember Isaiah and I ran behind my mom because we were terrified at what was going on. This lady was shaking uncontrollably to the point where it took 4-5 ministers within the church to help restrain her. She wasn't the only person in the church who behaved this way, but my attention was only on her because she sat next to me. The ministers carried her to the front of the church but what really shook me is how she stared at me before they grabbed her. When I looked her in the eyes, I just felt this evil presence. It was as if she was not even human. I didn't see any exorcisms happening like the ones shown from the horror films but saw the Pastor begin to pray for this lady. In Swahili, he said, "Father I call out to the name that is above all names. I command this evil spirit to come out of this lady at once! In the name of Jesus, evil spirit come out!" Just like I read in the book of Acts 16:16-18, I witnessed the very same thing. I remember watching him pray for all these people and instantly thought to myself, "If these evil spirits are coming out of people, I better begin praying too, just so they don't come at me." Honestly, that is how frightened I was when I witnessed all this happening. I was in Tanzania for a full month and went to church consistently from Sunday, Monday, Tuesday, and Wednesday and saw many incredible things. The shocking thing was, I wasn't forced to go! I went because I enjoyed it and brought myself to the services. Observing all this, it allowed me to believe even more how we as humans have an adversary and he does hate us.

Be alert, be on watch! Your enemy, the devil, roams around like a roaring lion, looking for someone to devour. Be firm in your faith and resist him, because you know that other believers in all the world are going through the same kind of suffering. **(1 Peter 5:8-9) - Good News Translation**

God took what I hated and turned it into love by explaining to me that those family members, who unfortunately passed away, performed those rituals because they were spiritually lost. I may have the right to hate them for doing what they did but those who hate others do not really possess God in them. Instead, I learned to hate the sin and pray for others all in hopes that one day people may believe in God as well. God has been so patient and merciful with me, so what gives me the right to hate anyone?

"But I say to you who hear: Love your enemies, do good to those who hate you, bless those who curse you, and pray for those who spitefully use you. To him who strikes you on the one cheek, offer the other also. And from him who takes away your cloak, do not withhold your tunic either. Give to everyone who asks of you. And from him who takes away your goods do not ask them back. And just as you want men to do to you, you also do to them likewise. "But if you love those who love you, what credit is that to you? For even sinners' love those who love them. And if you do good to those who do good to you, what credit is that to you? For even sinners do the same. And if you lend to those from whom you hope to receive back, what credit is that to you? For even sinners lend to sinners

to receive as much back. But love your enemies, do good, and lend, hoping for nothing in return; and your reward will be great, and you will be sons of the Most High. For he is kind to the unthankful and evil. Therefore, be merciful, just as your Father also is merciful. **(Luke 6:27-36) – New King James Version**

But you, beloved, building yourselves up on your most holy faith, praying in the Holy Spirit, keep yourselves in the love of God, looking for the mercy of our Lord Jesus Christ unto eternal life. And on some have compassion, making a distinction; but others save with fear, pulling them out of the fire, hating even the garment defiled by the flesh. **(Jude 1:20-23) – New King James Version**

I lived in a household that abided by God all my life, but it didn't do anything for me until I made a choice to see what all the fuss was about. I have found that the Word of God has this source of power that lifts our spirits when we feel lost or defeated. My younger brother Imani has dedicated himself to God but what touches people is his use of God's Word. It's not by his doctrine that people decide to turn to Christ, and it is not by my doctrine that anyone will turn to Christ. If my doctrine were what I typed onto these pages, I would be doing sin a considerable favor. I would've invested every word on these pages to promote every desire my flesh craved: indecency, lust, drunkenness, drinking parties, and the disgusting worship of idols. There is this quote I once found online, but unfortunately the one who said it is listed as unknown. "Two natures beat within my breast; the one is foul; the one is blessed. The one I love, the one I hate; the one I feed will dominate."

"Spirit of propaganda, arise from the graves, detach yourself from that false prophet Balaam. Although he started off good, you filled his head with worldly desires and eventually, he caved into king Balak's will. For it is written:

But there are a few things I have against you: there are some among you who follow the teachings of Balaam, who taught Balak how to lead the people of Israel into sin by persuading them to eat food that had been offered to idols and to practice sexual immorality. (Revelation 2:14-15) - Good News Translation

Spirit of Propaganda your credentials are real, and I am pleased with your outstanding_works. However, I have a new mission that needs to be fulfilled. There's a person who's taken the responsibility of an author, that I have warned to behave. Except he ignored my threat and partnered himself with the name that must not be named. I have warned him because he chose to write about me and he's going to fill the messages of the heavens, page after page trying to rip through my doctrine. I need you to screw up his information and shapeshift into words that sound like wisdom. Make a dish he cannot resist and mix in a strong drink that he will sip, so he gets drunk off your words. Be straightforward in your approach and use words that sound fair, so he digests them and soothes his soul with a drink that makes his tongue speak blasphemy. I know he will be pleased with the words you speak. For it is written:

The time will come when people will not listen to sound doctrine but will follow their own desires and will collect for themselves more and more teachers who will tell them what they are itching to hear. (2 Timothy 4:3) – Good News Translation

Spirit of Propaganda, you must be thorough in your work. Begin with the wine; thus, he will get drunk off your words. Here's a demonstration: take a thermometer and place it in his soul and you'll see how the temperature soars. Passionately warm, full of religion, seeking God's revelation; the soul itches for the truth. Observe a marriage: How can it last if the husband and wife are always quarreling? Observe a family: How can the house be at peace when siblings are fighting? Better observation: How can a family be at any peace when children and parents are not at peace with one another? The soul's kinfolk is the flesh like a family, they are stuck with one another. The soul and the flesh are sworn enemies refusing mediation because they refuse to find peace. I chose you, spirit of Propaganda so you can speak to the soul's weakness. The author's flesh is weak and vulnerable; this is the perfect time to feast! The author's behavior indicates left when it wants to turn right because he's spiritually bipolar due to the conflict within. Spirit of Propaganda, if you do not get this right, he will figure this out!

Wait! Before you go, I must experiment one last thing. Take this thermometer and place it on his body. Watch how the body's temperature goes from hot to lukewarm. See the difference? Do you see the conflict? His soul itches for the truth while his body craves for sin because it doesn't care about the truth. This is the weakness I spoke about! For it is written:

"I know what you have done; I know that you are neither cold nor hot. How I wish you were either one or the other! But because you are lukewarm, neither hot nor cold, I am going to spit you out of my mouth!" (Revelation 3:15-16) – Good News Translation

His flesh is filled with worldly passions, and full of thoughts that are good and bad. Spirit of Propaganda do you know the advantages of a body that has no principles? The body without principle will always refuse to be ruled. You cannot tell it what it can and can't do; it is reckless and will absorb anything like a sponge. Thus, you must feed it words that are unattractive to the soul. The goal is to make the two argue with one another. Upon his throne, he sits watching flesh and spirit argue with one another. The author is unsure of what is right. One day flesh rules, another day the spirit and despite God's Holy spirit assisting him; he has failed to fully commit to it. That throne is what I'm after! Spirit of Propaganda, you must not fail because if I sit on that throne his life is mine. A person who has not decided who sits on their throne loves no one! They walk when they should run, they crawl when they should jump. They say yes when they mean no. They fight when there is no reason at all. Like a broken marriage and house with no discipline is the relationship the person has with his flesh and spirit. Disguise your words with flattery, and you'll notice this: a troubled individual who is holding onto the words of the name we must not name. Therefore, you must confuse him away from the truth.

Spirit of Propaganda, you are now ready to go and say this,

'If you choose to live for God, you lose all fun in everything. Don't do this! Don't do that! How many rules can one have? Aren't you tired of this back and forth battle? The soul makes you look like a fool because when people look at you, they see a man fighting himself. They will mock you and insult you for your delusional ways. Have you ever noticed that you've failed to love anyone or anything because of this? This is because of the conflict within. You'll never love a thing! Instead, the bold truth is you've always been in love with yourself!'

Spirit of Propaganda the author is unaware of this so he will reply,

'You're lying, I have loved before, I've loved so much that I've been hurt.'

This is how you will respond,

'You can lie to me but how sad are you that you continue to lie to yourself! You've never loved anything or anyone. Look at your commitments, you care for a while then lose interest. You don't love your parents because if you did, you'd spend more time with them. You don't love your siblings or else you'd protect them. You don't love your friends, or you would treat them better. Responsibility for anything is beneath you because you devalue everything. What you do love is yourself; hence why you placed that crown on your head. You're trying to settle your affairs between your flesh and spirit. But they cannot be settled, they are to be enemies forever! So, let me help you. Stop writing this book, it's nonsense. How can you ever please God if you're always going to be lukewarm? Quit this now and just go back to the things your flesh wants because I know you cannot resist. Be free, you only live once! You confuse yourself when you try to settle your affairs in this religion crap. Can you really leave this life?'

Well done Spirit of Propaganda! Now let's watch his thoughts be led astray. If we succeed, I'll bring forth the spirit of War and Rebellion, and they will consume the relationship within. As long as it is always flesh versus spirit; rather than them become one called, 'flesh and spirit.'"

-The doctrine of Satan

There comes a time in everyone's life when they must ask themselves, "What is my purpose in life?" But what's the difference between that question and asking yourself, "what do I want to do for a living?" Do our occupations have any correlation to our purpose in life? My parents told me when I was a child, I had said that I wanted to become a firefighter. This is hilarious now because my interests are far from that. As I grew older, I fell in love with soccer, so my dreams consisted of becoming a professional soccer player. However, that dream quickly diminished when I saw players that were far better than myself. This is not a good excuse to give up on a dream, but I'm just telling it how it is. Once I graduated high school, I was forced to pick a degree in which I was interested in so that it would pave the way to a specific occupation.

At first, I thought I would make a good businessman, but I remembered calculus was one of the prerequisites, so I did away with that. As a result, I looked at the path of law and I adored it. I loved pinpointing previous cases that had to be used as precedence to problem solve current cases just to determine how one would win a case. Becoming a lawyer became my obsession and because I had set that out, I believed it was my purpose. Although, things took a different turn and I was about to figure out something about myself. It started from such a young age, not even my parents could notice it. I was continually searching for a purpose and I couldn't make my mind up because I never truly wanted any of those things. There is a very strong correlation with how I kept changing my mind on what I wanted to do for a living and my relationships with others. I could never fully commit. It's not that I wasn't physically capable of doing so, but instead, I was spiritually unable. I made the realization that my flesh and spirit were always going to be enemies with one another. If I continued to let them control my life, I would never find peace or happiness. I keep bringing up the tangible flesh and the intangible spirit but how do any of them have any significance to how we live? The flesh will always want to be loved by peers, thus societies obsession to applications like Instagram, Facebook, Twitter, and Snapchat. We seek gratification from the world in forms of likes, favorites, retweets, and streaks. The flesh goes even so far by searching for pleasures in our own appearances like what car we drive, the size of our home, and how much money we have. It wants more and more but is never satisfied with anything. Whereas our souls long for meaning and a purpose. To conclude, I was spiritually bipolar and that is what God calls lukewarm.

So then, because you are lukewarm, and neither cold nor hot, I will vomit you out of my mouth. **(Revelations 3:16) – New King James Version**

Conflict arises with the flesh and spirit when they disagree with one another. Therefore, can it be argued that the flesh and spirit need something that they both can agree on? Now some may read this and smile because they've found this one thing, whether in their occupation, relationships, or status. However, if that thing were to be taken away, what is left of that person? Such a scenario is very plausible and once it does, what then? Personally, I couldn't find validation from friends, family, school, or work. The poem "Spirit of propaganda" was not only an indication that I couldn't commit to anything, but I was too spiritually self-absorbed to do so. I looked at all the things the world had to offer and became curious, but my soul kept asking me, "Is that really where your purpose lies?" I searched for God because that felt like the obvious answer to my purpose, but then I would hear my flesh ask, "You may have found your purpose but what about all the fun you had with the world and all its pleasures?" I was tearing myself apart because I couldn't decide what I wanted more: purpose(soul) or pleasure(flesh)? I sat on my own throne and placed a crown on my head, while the palm of my hand pressed against my chin, and just watched the two parties (soul and flesh) argue with one another.

When they had finished breakfast, Jesus said to Simon Peter, "Simon, son of John, do you love me more than these?" He said to him, "Yes, Lord; you know that I love you." He said to him, "Feed my lambs." He said to him a second time, "Simon, son of John, do you love me?" He said to him, "Yes, Lord; you know that I love you." He said to him, "Tend my sheep." He said to him the third time, "Simon, son of John, do you love me?" Peter was grieved because he said to him the third time, "Do you love me?" and he said to him, "Lord, you know everything; you know that I love you." Jesus said to him, "Feed my sheep. Truly, truly, I say to you, when you were young, you used to dress yourself and walk wherever you wanted, but when you are old, you will stretch out your hands, and another will dress you and carry you where you do not want to go."(This he said to show by what kind of death he was to glorify God.) And after saying this he said to him, "Follow me." **(John 21:15-19) – English Standard Version**

This dialogue between Jesus and Peter used to confuse me because I did not understand why Jesus asked Peter three times whether he loved him or not. I did not understand until I received insight from the Holy Spirit regarding its meaning. This conversation was right before Jesus ascended into heaven, so Jesus was giving Peter his final instructions before he left earth. Jesus knew that Peter loved him but also knew that Peter himself struggled with his own flesh and spirit.

And the Lord said, "Simon, Simon! Indeed, Satan has asked for you, that he may sift you as wheat. But I have prayed for you, that your faith should not fail; and when you have returned to me, strengthen your brethren." But he said to him, "Lord, I am ready to go with you, both to prison and to death." Then he said, "I tell you, Peter, the rooster shall not crow this day before you will deny three times that you know me." **(Luke 22:31-34) – New King James Version**

Having arrested him, they led him and brought him into the high priest's house. But Peter followed at a distance. Now when they had kindled a fire in the midst of the courtyard and sat down together, Peter sat among them. And a certain servant girl, seeing him as he sat by the fire, looked intently at him and said, "This man was also with him." But he denied him, saying, "Woman, I do not know him." And after a little while another saw him and said, "You also are of them." But Peter said, "Man, I am not!" Then after about an hour had passed, another confidently affirmed, saying, "Surely this fellow also was with him, for he is a Galilean." But Peter said, "Man, I do not know what you are saying!" Immediately, while he was still speaking, the rooster crowed. And the Lord turned and looked at Peter. Then Peter remembered the word of the Lord, how he had said to him, "Before the rooster crows, you will deny me three times." So Peter went out and wept bitterly. **(Luke 22:54-62) – New King James Version**

After reading about Peter's denial of Christ, I can picture Jesus turning around and looking at Peter to see how devastated he was. He was so sure of himself that he wouldn't deny Jesus but did. Only thing is we forget that the disciples were Jesus' friends. I know I shouldn't say 'we' when bringing up this next statement because I cannot really speak on what others think when they read that passage. But I forget that Jesus must have been heart broken as well because his friend just told a bunch of people that he did not even know him. Peter did not just deny him once, but three times and that must have broken Jesus' heart! This is what God feels whenever we deny him today and that really made me think of my battle between flesh and spirit. My spirit desires my purpose in God, but my flesh is so in love with the pleasures of the world. Peter even made the bold statement that he would go to prison with Jesus and die with him. Nonetheless, Peter was beginning to understand his purpose in life but just like Luke 22:31 states: "Simon, Simon, behold, Satan has asked for you, that he may sift you as wheat: But I have prayed for you, that your faith should not fail; and when you have returned to me, strengthen your brethren." Satan was looking to take souls during that time and that list included Jesus' disciples too. Despite Simon Peter's love for Christ, his faith was tested when his own life was on the line. At that certain time, Jesus was about to go through trial and eventually be sentenced to death. The disciples knew of his fate because he had told them about it. But when Peter was being questioned whether he knew Jesus, he became afraid and denied him. Peter may have said he wouldn't deny Jesus, but the real problem was he didn't fully commit himself into loving Christ. Thus, making it easy for him to listen to his flesh's fear of death.

Do not be afraid of those who kill the body but cannot kill the soul; rather be afraid of God, who can destroy both body and soul in Hell. **(Matthew 10:28) – Good News Translation**

Peter feared the consequences of knowing Jesus because he thought he would've shared the same fate as Jesus. Jesus obviously forgave him but questioned Peter's love for him. This was to get Peter to commit to his purpose over his pleasures. Peter once denied Jesus three times, but after all that, Peter declared his love for Jesus three times. It is sort of poetic in a way! When Jesus was asking Peter whether he loved him, he was speaking to both his flesh and spirit. Peter not only needed to realize his purpose, but he realized his happiness in the very purpose that God had set out for him. Peter knew his purpose but had to acknowledge his love for the Savior so that his flesh could never jeopardize that purpose.

In the bible, there is a character named Paul. Everyone will find that I reference him a lot because he is my favourite writer in the bible. Obviously, everything he wrote was under the influence of the Holy Spirit, so technically God is the real author, but I do enjoy Paul's style of writing. I started this paragraph so casually when speaking of Paul, like he was some irrelevant person, so let me rephrase it. The person who is responsible of writing the majority of the New Testament is well known as Apostle Paul. A little backstory about Paul, who was also called Saul. He used to persecute Christians and that is just a soft way of saying he jailed them in inhumane prisons, stoned them to death and humiliated them in public. He was passionate about his crusade and was firm in his delivery when it came to persecuting Christians. So, what caused his change?

But Saul, still breathing threats and murder against the disciples of the Lord, went to the high priest and asked him for letters to the synagogues at Damascus, so that if he found any belonging to the way, men or women, he might bring them bound to Jerusalem. Now as he went on his way, he approached Damascus, and suddenly a light from heaven shone around him. And falling to the ground, he heard a voice saying to him, "Saul, Saul, why are you persecuting me?" And he said, "Who are you, Lord?" And he said, "I am Jesus, whom you are persecuting. But rise and enter the city, and you will be told what you are to do." The men who were traveling with him stood speechless, hearing the voice but seeing no one. **(Acts 9:1-7) – English Standard Version**

God happened! After that happened, he was baptized and received the Holy Spirit and dedicated his whole life writing Romans, Corinthians, Galatians, Ephesians, Philippians, Colossians, Thessalonians, Timothy, Titus and Philemon. Apostle Paul spoke boldly about the gospel of Jesus Christ and did not fear doing so which got him jailed, beaten, whipped but he did not let his purpose wither.

Five times I was given the 39 lashes by the Jews; three times I was whipped by the Romans; and once I was stoned. I have been in three shipwrecks, and once I spent 24 hours in the water. In my many travels I have been in danger from floods and from robbers, in danger from fellow-Jews and from Gentiles; there have been dangers in the cities, dangers in the wilds, dangers on the high seas, and dangers from false friends. There has been work and toil; often I have gone without sleep; I have been hungry and thirsty; I have often been without food, shelter, or clothing. And not to mention other things, every day I am under pressure of my concern for all the churches. When someone is weak, then I feel weak too; when someone is led into sin, I am filled with distress. **(2 Corinthians 11:24-29) – Good News Bible**

Apostle Paul showed the people of the New Testament what it was like to conquer flesh and spirit, and because of this he is remembered today for not just his writing but his deep connection with the Holy Spirit. His closeness with the Spirit was so deep that he put to death his natural human desires and lived for the Spirit. He did not fear anything and stood firm in his faith even at the hour of his death when he eventually was beheaded, which was an order that came from the Roman Emperor Nero.

Therefore, having been justified by faith, we have peace with God through our Lord Jesus Christ, through whom also we have access by faith into this grace in which we stand, and rejoice in hope of the glory of God. And not only that, but we also glory in tribulations, knowing that tribulation produces perseverance; and perseverance, character; and character, hope. Now hope does not disappoint, because the love of God has been poured out in our hearts by the Holy Spirit who was given to us. **(Romans 5:1-5) – New King James Version**

But one of the most beautiful pieces of literature written by him is the one where he writes about the conflict within us humans (flesh vs spirit). It relates to our true purpose which is perfect for this chapter.

For we know that the law is spiritual, but I am of the flesh, sold under sin. For I do not understand my own actions. For I do not do what I want, but I do the very thing I hate. Now if I do what I do not want, I agree with the law, that it is good. For now, it is no longer I who do it, but sin that dwells within me. For I know that nothing good dwells in me, that is, in my flesh. For I have the desire to do what is right, but not the ability to carry it out. For I do not do the good I want, but the evil I do not want is what I keep on doing. Now if I do what I do not want, it is no longer I who do it, but sin that dwells within me. So I find it to be a law that when I want to do right, evil lies close at my hand. For I delight in the law of God, in my inner being, but I see in my members another law waging war against the law of my mind and making me captive to the law of sin that dwells in my members. Wretched man that I am! Who will deliver me from this body of death? Thanks be to God through Jesus Christ our Lord! So then, I myself serve the law of God with my mind, but with my flesh I serve the law of sin. **(Romans 7:14-25) – English Standard Version**

It is indeed a brain teaser when one first reads it. Maybe its just me but I know my brain hurt when I first read it, so I had to read it twice and once I did, I had only one thought. It was beautifully written. Maybe I'm just being bias since I already admire Paul's writing. But let's get back on topic. Jesus made us a promise about a 'Helper' that has already been sent which serves as a connection to him and the Father. I referenced the exact Scripture in the chapter birth of the doctrine (Acts 2:1-4). I've actually spoken about this Helper over 100 times so far so the name shouldn't come to anyone as a surprise. This Helper is called the Holy Spirit, which will also handle the affairs between our own flesh and spirit. That is if we believe in Christ. The same way that Jesus asked Simon Peter whether he loved him is the same process we must go through to get our flesh and spirit intact for the Holy Spirit.

"If you love me, you will obey my commandments. I will ask the Father, and he will give you another Helper, who will stay with you forever. He is the Spirit, who reveals the truth about God. The world cannot receive him, because it cannot see him or know him. But you know him, because he remains with you and is in you. **(John 14:15-17) – New King James Version**

"I have told you this while I am still with you. The Helper, the Holy Spirit, whom the Father will send in my name, will teach you everything and make you remember all that I have told you. **(John 14:25-26) – New King James Version**

If anyone has ever seen Avenger: Infinity War (2018) I will use it as an analogy to help better understand the use of the Holy Spirit. The Holy Spirit is like the infinity stones; except, instead of five stones, the Holy Spirit brings with it 9 infinity stones (qualities). The Gauntlet in this situation are our bodies which were designed by God so that the Spirit may live in us. If we possess the Holy Spirit, we own all nine infinity stones automatically. In the movie Avengers: Infinity War, an evil tyrant named Thanos was looking to possess all five infinity stones: space, reality, power, mind, time, and the soul stone. Thanos had to wear a particular gauntlet to harness all five stones and once collected, he possessed the ability to change the whole universe. Thankfully, this is not the case in our lives but what the Holy Spirit does is it gives us an infinite connection with God. The gauntlet, being our bodies, were specially designed to seek out God because that is our one true purpose. By possessing the Spirit in our "gauntlets" we no longer fight against what our human nature desires to do which is sin. God's spirit empowers our very own spirits with those nine qualities which put to death our flesh and its sinful nature.

But I say, walk by the Spirit, and you will not gratify the desires of the flesh. For the desires of the flesh are against the Spirit, and the desires of the Spirit are against the flesh, for these are opposed to each other, to keep you from doing the things you want to do. But if you are led by the Spirit, you are not under the law. Now the works of the flesh are evident: sexual immorality, impurity, sensuality, idolatry, sorcery, enmity, strife, jealousy, fits of anger, rivalries, dissensions, divisions, envy, drunkenness, orgies, and things like these. I warn you, as I warned you before, that those who do such things will not inherit the kingdom of God. **(Galatians 5:16–21) – English Standard Version**

I've mentioned that Scripture more than once in this chapter, but its message speaks volumes of our human nature. There may be things on that list that some people do not do, but God instructs us to possess his Spirit because if we let his Spirit direct our lives, we will not be subject to our flesh.

"Watch and pray, that ye enter not into temptation: the spirit indeed is willing, but the flesh is weak." **(Matthew 26:41) – King James Version**

Those words came from Jesus himself when he was trying to get the disciples from falling asleep. He wanted them to pray, but their bodies were weary and tired. The concept of the Spirit can be used to our advantages throughout our lives. Whether it is training for a sport or studying for an exam. These are few examples of when our bodies may refuse to cooperate with us. The perseverance to fight and say no to our bodies when we are required to rise to the occasion on such scenarios is exactly the same effort God expects from us. He understands that sometimes it becomes difficult, which is why I used the Avengers: Infinity War analogy because his Spirit will assist us.

The lazy man does not roast what he took in hunting, but diligence is man's precious possession. **(Proverbs 12:27) - New King James Version**

I can do all things through Christ who strengthens me **(Philippians 4:13) – New King James Version**

The 'Helper' will assist our lives if placed onto our gauntlets (our bodies) and we will possess the nine qualities that are mentioned in Galatians 5:22-26. I also took notice that the spirits that are in our world today are just the complete opposites of what the Holy Spirit produces: hate, sadness, war, impatience, rudeness, evil, unfaithfulness, egoism, and self-indulgence. The Holy Spirit is to combat against these qualities not by fists but by people exhibiting its qualities.

"Author, oh author let me tell you about a story not many know about. A long time ago corruption began in the heavens. My Spirit observed the heavenly beings colluding against my throne. Growing restless of these beings I formed human beings. The heavenly begins could not wonder of their purpose. The heavenly beings that betrayed my throne knew why I made them. Their purpose was written on their foreheads, but they chose to abandon their names.

I remember when I made the heavenly being named Love, but it changed its name to Hate and gave itself a last name called Lust. I remember when I made the heavenly being named Joy, but it adopted the name Misery. I remember when I made the heavenly being named Peace, but instead, it changed its name to War. I remember when I made the heavenly being named Patience, but it couldn't wait to change into Impatience. I remember when I made the heavenly being named Goodness, but it changed its name to Wickedness. I remember when I made the heavenly being named Kindness, but it decided to behave rudely and became Abusive. I remember when I made the heavenly being named Faithfulness, but it changed its name to Unfaithfulness. I remember when I made the heavenly being that was named Humble, but it was manipulated, and its name became Arrogant. I remember when I made the heavenly being whose name was Self-control, but it began to behave impulsively and is now called Wild and Destructive.

I do not tolerate their names anymore for my throne is a house for the righteous. Body and spirit are the difference between heavenly beings and human beings. Therefore, I will not discard you like I did those other heavenly beings. For it is written:

For if God spared not the angels that sinned, but cast them down to Hell, and delivered them into chains of darkness, to be reserved unto judgment; And spared not the old world, but saved Noah the eighth person, a preacher of righteousness, bringing in the flood upon the world of the ungodly; (2 Peter 2:4-5) – King James Version

What excuse did the heavenly beings have to abandon the names I had given them? Their purpose was beautiful and written on their own foreheads, but they chose to follow the maker of mischief named Lucifer, but he decided to change his name to Satan.

Those who realize their one true purpose, I will assist them with my Spirit because my Son's death is proof of purchase. For it is written:

Or do you not know that your body is the temple of the Holy Spirit who is in you, whom you have from God, and you are not your own? For you were bought at a price; therefore, glorify God in your body and in your spirit, which are God's. (1 Corinthians 6:19-20) – New King James Version

Those who question their one true purpose I will say to them as I told the prophet Isaiah. For it is written:

Does a clay pot dare argue with its maker, a pot that is like all the others? Does the clay ask the potter what he is doing? Does the pot complain that its maker has no skill? Do we dare say to our parents, 'Why did you make me like this?' The LORD, the holy God of Israel, the one

who shapes the future, says, 'You have no right to question me about my children or tell me what I ought to do! I am the one who made the earth and created human beings to live there. By my power I stretched out the heavens; I control the sun, the moon, and the stars. **(Isaiah 45:9-12) – Good News Translation**

Human beings from all over ask themselves, 'I wonder why I was created? What is my purpose?' Some of these human beings will search far and wide. Some will look for their purpose in their occupations. Some will look for theirs in sexual orientations or relationships. Some will study in hopes to find their purpose in knowledge. Some may give up their search and just solemnly live. No matter who, what, when or where they search, they will not find their true purpose in any of these things. Their purpose is in me and once they search for me, they will find what their souls long for. They will ask for help and receive it. For it is written:

'Call to me, and I will answer you, and show you great and mighty things, which you do not know.' (Jeremiah 33:3) – New King James Version

I will give them strength so that their bodies do not jeopardize their one true purpose. I created human beings for one purpose: to become one with me but only if they want it. In me, they will find the very names those heavenly beings dismissed. They will hold hands together and sing: 'Love, Joy, Peace, Patience, Kindness, Faithfulness, Humility, and Self- Control!' They will be my people, and I will be there one God. For it is written:

"Hear, O Israel: The LORD our God, the LORD is one! (Deuteronomy 6:4) – New King James Version

They will look at each other and notice different things simply because I loved them so much, I made them all unique. Different talents, different skins; some talk differently and others think differently. I took time in their appearances: different eyes and formed every single detail of their mouths, ears, noses, hands, and feet. I made some stocky while others I made skinny. I designed their hearts to feel things. I placed a throne in each and every one of them, in hopes that they choose me and decide to love and worship me. Those heavenly beings knew their purposes but chose to abandon me. However, I did something different for human beings. I gave up my only begotten Son. All the heavenly beings that stuck with me saw that I am the God of love. What Father gives up their son? The heavens praised my name and sang songs and hymns of grace. For it is written:

And they sang a new song, saying: "You are worthy to take the scroll, and to open its seals; for you were slain and have redeemed us to God by your blood out of every tribe and tongue and people and nation, and have made us kings and priests to our God; and we shall reign on the earth." (Revelations 5:9-10) – New King James Version

They bowed to me because they saw how much I was willing to pay. All this just to save human beings. Some will reject me, and I accept that, but they must accept the true sayings. For it is written:

This is a faithful saying: For if we died with him, we shall also live with him. If we endure, we shall also reign with him. If we deny him, he also will deny us. If we are faithless, he remains faithful; he cannot deny himself. (2 Timothy 2:11-13) – New King James Version

To those who accept the true purpose, they will be awarded. However, I know there will be some who will try and say, 'But Lord we did not know, how could you expect us to find the one true purpose?' I will reject such people. Even their own worldly laws reject this. They call it ignorance of the law! Well, my Word calls it ignorance of purpose! I will respond to them, 'How can you stand there and lie to your own Creator?' I will conclude by saying, 'You knew and heard about the one true purpose, but you chose to ignore it. You closed your hearts and blocked it out of your minds.' For it is written:

For I was hungry and you gave me no food, I was thirsty and you gave me no drink, I was a stranger and you did not welcome me, naked and you did not clothe me, sick and in prison and you did not visit me.' Then they also will answer, saying, 'Lord, when did we see you hungry or thirsty or a stranger or naked or sick or in prison, and did not minister to you?' Then he will answer them, saying, 'Truly, I say to you, as you did not do it to one of the least of these, you did not do it to me.' (Matthew 25:42-45) – English Standard Version

Human beings are all different but are all alive for one purpose. You will gather together and form churches. Some will make buildings, and some will use their own houses. Some will use schools, and others will use their own workspaces. But they are all the church because they are both flesh and spirit so human beings unite together because I am your one true purpose."

-Spirit of God

CHAPTER 7

LOVE VS LUST

The absence of love introduces the rival well known as lust, and it has taken down many and reigns to this very day. Generation after generation have spoken to lust and they accept it as a norm while it defeats each generation. It grows stronger and stronger because lust doesn't just stand on the concept of fornication and sexual immorality. Lust appears in our material possessions, social statuses, and wealth. Lust knows no boundaries!

"Ladies, listen to me and listen carefully. I have seen the way men treat you, and no man is worthy of your love. What is love? How many times have you let them in, and they strangle you with their lies? I'll let you on a little secret about weak men. They have no intelligence once you get the attention of their other head. Control them and let them sink under your spell. Succubus is my friend, and because of this it will torment them. Love is just an outdated source that died long ago. I was there when it died that's why I live. Continue living the way you live. If God was there wouldn't he protect you?

I once knew a lady named Eve; she was so beautiful the whole garden sang to her. God only talked to Adam about the tree but never warned Eve. It appears women are always getting the short end of the stick. I went to her and she listened, but it was Eve's beauty that made Adam listen. Be like Eve. For it is written:

The woman saw how beautiful the tree was and how good its fruit would be to eat, and she thought how wonderful it would be to become wise. So

she took some of the fruit and ate it. Then she gave some to her husband, *and he also it.* **(Genesis 3:6) - Good News Translation**

I once knew a lady named Delilah, she was so beautiful; many men fell for her, *but she knew she was too good for them. Yet, my friend Delilah met a dilemma* *named Samson who was equipped with God's strength. With Delilah's sweet* *lips, Samson revealed to Delilah the source of his strength which was in his hair.* *Snip, snip, powerless and defeated all because of love. Ladies, ladies, Delilah* *got what she wanted and so can you. Be like Delilah. I'm here for you. For it* *is written:*

And when she pressed him hard with her word's day after day, and urged **him, his soul was vexed to death. And he told her all his heart, and** **said to her, "A razor has never come upon my head, for I have been a** **Nazirite to God from my mother's womb. If my head is shaved, then my** **strength will leave me, and I shall become weak and be like any other** **man." When Delilah saw that he had told her all his heart, she sent and** **called the lords of the Philistines, saying, "Come up again, for he has** **told me all his heart." Then the lords of the Philistines came up to her** **and brought the money in their hands. She made him sleep on her knees.** **And she called a man and had him shave off the seven locks of his head.** **Then she began to torment him, and his strength left him. And she said,** **"The Philistines are upon you, Samson!" And he awoke from his sleep** **and said, "I will go out as at other times and shake myself free." But he** **did not know that the LORD had left him. (Judges 16:16-20) – New** **King James Version**

I once knew a lady named Herodias. She and I caused a lot of mischiefs. One *ring on her finger by Philip. But she thought to herself, 'this marriage is boring,'* *so I entered her heart and we climbed up the kingdom. I whispered in her ears,* *'Why have one brother when you can have the other?' That is when we caught* *the eye of Herod, Philip's older brother. Oh, Herod had his eyes on the prize.* *That is why Herod and Herodias were the perfect menaces. He married his own* *brother's wife! Herodias and I were so close, so I told her to tell her husband to* *bring me the head of John the Baptist. How dare he question our relationship!*

Herod was king? It was more like Herodias. Ladies be like Herodias. For it is written:

For Herod himself had sent and laid hold of John and bound him in prison for the sake of Herodias, his brother Philip's wife; for he had married her. Because John had said to Herod, "It is not lawful for you to have your brother's wife." Therefore Herodias held it against him and wanted to kill him, but she could not; for Herod feared John, knowing that he was a just and holy man, and he protected him. And when he heard him, he did many things, and heard him gladly. Then an opportune day came when Herod on his birthday gave a feast for his nobles, the high officers, and the chief men of Galilee. And when Herodias' daughter herself came in and danced, and pleased Herod and those who sat with him, the king said to the girl, "Ask me whatever you want, and I will give it to you." He also swore to her, "Whatever you ask me, I will give you, up to half my kingdom." So she went out and said to her mother, "What shall I ask?" And she said, "The head of John the Baptist!" Immediately she came in with haste to the king and asked, saying, "I want you to give me at once the head of John the Baptist on a platter." And the king was exceedingly sorry; yet, because of the oaths and because of those who sat with him, he did not want to refuse her. Immediately the king sent an executioner and commanded his head to be brought. And he went and beheaded him in prison, brought his head on a platter, and gave it to the girl; and the girl gave it to her mother. When his disciples heard of it, they came and took away his corpse and laid it in a tomb. (Mark 6:17-29) – New King James Version

I've skipped rope through time and seen men fall. God says love, I say lust."

- The doctrine of Satan

A woman of Samaria came to draw water. Jesus said to her, "Give me a drink." For his disciples had gone away into the city to buy food. Then the woman of Samaria said to him, "How is it that you, being a Jew, ask a drink from me, a Samaritan woman?" For Jews have no dealings with Samaritans. Jesus answered and said to her, "If you knew the gift of God, and who it is who says to you,

'Give me a drink,' you would have asked him, and he would have given you living water." The woman said to him, "Sir, you have nothing to draw with, and the well is deep. Where then do you get that living water? Are you greater than our father Jacob, who gave us the well, and drank from it himself, as well as his sons and his livestock?" Jesus answered and said to her, "Whoever drinks of this water will thirst again, but whoever drinks of the water that I shall give him will never thirst. But the water that I shall give him will become in him a fountain of water springing up into everlasting life." The woman said to him, "Sir, give me this water, that I may not thirst, nor come here to draw." Jesus said to her, "Go, call your husband, and come here." The woman answered and said, "I have no husband." Jesus said to her, "You have well said, 'I have no husband,' for you have had five husbands, and the one whom you now have is not your husband; in that you spoke truly." **(John 4:7-18) – New King James Version**

I think the story of the woman at the well depicts the feelings of most women in today's age. The constant struggle to find approval in men is the most disconcerting thing in our society.

"Women at the well, oh women at the well. Dressed in seductive garments, I have never been at the well, well not alone that is of course. Author, oh author what gives you the right to write about the woman at the well?

Well I'm dressed in a seductive sundress and I've dyed the colour of my hair to your favourite- the sun will never see your eye lids. Who gave you the right to write about the woman at the well?

Well since you've followed me here why don't you pick up that bucket and fetch water for me. Enslaved by my beauty I see? Isn't it you men who are thirsty for me? So, who gave you the right to write about the woman at the well?

Well author I can smell the weakness from your pores and how your mind is trying to understand us. Yes, 'us' all the women at the well. Well what makes you think we all go to the well? From where I sit you men are there more than us women! I can hear your thoughts:

'What do you mean sitting where you sit...? You aren't a woman so how could you even know what they feel?'

Well author, have you forgotten? I am lust so I am genderless. I see women's weakness just as much as I see men. I lie naked between both and encourage the walk to the well, as a matter I am the well. Well that must have come to you as a shock.

Well author, who gave you the right to write about the woman at the well? When its mostly men fetching water from the well. Have you ever stopped to think? Use your head, not your other head. What if women used the well as a fix to find me? Why don't you leave us alone and stop writing about things you know nothing about! I've seen you at the well drinking from it as well. You've drank my fluids and began to fantasize about me:

How I look without my sundress; what my lips taste like when I when I put on my lipstick? Thinking about how gentle my fingers are when you hold them? How about when I put on my perfume? Are you wondering what I smell like? Are you picturing me wearing one of your long t-shirts or hoodies? Will the scent of me drive you crazy? When I leave your mattress, will the scent of me make your heartbeat skip? Or are you like me? Once you're finished with me, you will drop me like the bucket used to fetch the well's liquid because you only needed me just for a night. But we both know we will be back together at the well – both male and female.

So, author what gives you the right to write about the woman at the well? When both are at the well together? Indulging in my liquid and forever thirsting for me.

Oh well…"

–The doctrine of Satan

Please note I am not referring to all women, but there are many like the woman at the well, who have been hurt but continue to seek gratification from others. This also does not just involve women but men too, but I will address the men side of things later in this chapter.

Remember the question: What's on your throne? Yes? Good. Jesus was well aware of this woman's whole life but spoke to her with such pleasantness. He never judged her, nor did he call her a sinner for her past because he saw the pain and loneliness in her heart. Jesus used the well as a metaphor so that she may understand the spiritual representation of never thirsting again. The lady was so excited to hear about water that would never get her to thirst again. She pictured all the difficult days she had spent going to that well. She was probably having a hard time imagining it. However, what she thought was not what Jesus was referring to. He did not mean real water, but the water was a representation of his Spirit.

On the last day, that great day of the feast, Jesus stood and cried out, saying, "If anyone thirsts, let him come to me and drink. He who believes in me, as the Scripture has said, 'out of his heart will flow rivers of living water.'" But this he spoke concerning the Spirit, whom those believing in him would receive; for the Holy Spirit was not yet given, because Jesus was not yet glorified. **(John 7:37-39) – New King James Version**

If Jesus was referring to his Spirit the whole time, what did he mean about thirst? If we are supposed to take what Jesus said only in the spiritual form of things rather than the physical. What then is the spiritual meaning of thirst? When Jesus spoke of thirst, he was simply stating the conditions of our souls and what they long for. In this case, the woman at the well had her heart set on finding gratification from men but never found it. She just wanted to be loved! Does this mean that God discourages having relationships? Absolutely not! What he doesn't want us to do is to look for fullness in other things.

What is it that quenches our thirst? Is it pornography? Is it having many hookups? Is it dating? Is it marriage? Whatever it is, God wants us to know that it will not fully quench our thirst. Some may read this and ask, "What about marriage? Doesn't God want us to get married and have children?" Yes, this is true but as I mentioned in the chapter flesh vs. spirit: We can search through anything or anyone to find our purpose, but we will never find our purpose in those things. If it can be taken from us, what then happens to our purpose? Take for instance the stock market. People invest their money on companies because they believe that it will make them more money. There isn't a single person in the world that has invested their own money and hoped to lose it all. If that person makes money, they will be happy but if they were to lose money, they would be upset. The way we live and what we choose to invest our time is like the stock market. Our souls are what we are gambling and everything in this world that we put our trust into can temporarily make us but eventually break us. Consequently, the end results are all the same- it will eventually crush us. The woman at the well had put her time in finding a husband, so her soul made that her purpose, all in hopes that she will get back what she put in-love.

Now concerning the things of which you wrote to me: It is good for a man not to touch a woman. Nevertheless, because of sexual immorality, let each man have his own wife, and let each woman have her own husband. Let the husband render to his wife the affection due her, and likewise also the wife to her husband. The wife does not have authority over her own body, but the husband does. And likewise, the husband does not have authority over his own body, but the wife does. Do not deprive one another except with consent for a time, that you may give yourselves to fasting and prayer; and come together again so that Satan does not tempt you because of your lack of self-control. But I say this as a concession, not as a commandment. For I wish that all men were even as I myself. But each one has his own gift from God, one in this manner and another in that. But I say to the unmarried and to the widows: It is good for them if they remain even as I am; but if they cannot exercise self-control, let them marry. For it is better to marry than to burn with passion. **(1 Corinthians 7:1-9) – New King James Version**

When I read Paul's thoughts regarding marriage it seems like he wasn't too concerned for it himself. He was so devoted to God that he thought marriage was a distraction. He doesn't condemn anyone for being single or for being married, but his main focus was for no one to fall under temptation from lust. I do not consider myself an expert on romance which is why I took a lot of time understanding the difference between lust and love. Looking at my own experiences, I found that I needed to learn about self-control. Self-control is one of the nine qualities that the Holy Spirit does give us, which can assist us against the voice of lust. At that specific time, when Jesus was speaking to the woman at the well, Jesus' Spirit had not poured out to the world. So the woman at the well had no idea what he was talking about. Therefore, her story is revealed by Jesus: She began to search for love but the more times she tried to find it, the more times she failed.

In the mean while his disciples prayed him, saying, "Master, eat." But he said unto them, "I have meat to eat that ye know not of." **(John 4:31-32) - King James Version**

That Scripture is still apart of the story of the lady at the well, but Jesus just went from drinking life-giving water to eating food. This confused the disciples because they had not seen him eat anything. If we read all of John 4, we will notice that Jesus never ate once. So what was he talking about?

And when he had fasted forty days and forty nights, he was afterward an hungered. And when the tempter came to him, he said, "If thou be the Son of God, command that these stones be made bread." But he answered and said, "It is written, man shall not live by bread alone, but by every Word that proceeded out of the mouth of God." **(Matthew 4:2-4) - King James Version**

Jesus was referring to the Word as his food which strengthens his Spirit.

"But the hour is coming, and now is, when the true worshipers will worship the Father in spirit and truth; for the Father is seeking such to worship him. God is Spirit, and those who worship him must worship in spirit and truth." The woman said to him, "I know that Messiah is coming" (who is called Christ). "When he comes, he will tell us all things." Jesus said to her, "I who speak to you am he." **(John 4:23-26) – New King James Version**

Jesus was able to look into her heart and saw her emptiness, and the thing that she longed for was to be loved. Each day she kept going to that well for water. The well became symbolic to her lifestyle because it represented her constant urgency to find satisfaction in men. In the physical realm, we see a woman going to drink water which would temporality satisfy her, but she would return again because it wasn't enough. Jesus saw that her spirit was thirsty for love and it had become restless to the constant trips to the well. The well represented the search for love in this world. She searched for this love in husband number one, but that failed. She searched for it in husband number two, but that failed. She searched for it in husband number three, but that failed too. She even brought up the courage in finding it in husband number four, but it broke her heart into pieces when it failed again. When I think of her life, I see a woman that continuously returned to this well but had lost all hope in love. I see a woman that looked down at the well desperately, as warm tears filled her eyes. The woman at the well must have gathered up all her strength and asked herself, "maybe husband number five will love me?" But unfortunately, that failed too. This is when I begin to wonder: "How many of us (both male and female) today feel like the woman at the well? How many times in a year do we consistently walk to that well with our buckets and level it down to have our thirst quenched for a short time?" Thus, we conform to lust just like the woman at the well because she grew tired of searching for love, which is why she gave up on marriage. Jesus was able to summarize her whole life when he said, "You have been married to five men, and the man you live with now is not really your husband. You have told me the truth." She grew tired of searching and let the mask of lust run its course. Jesus saw how this woman searched for love but was hurt by the disappointment, so she became content with lust. Therefore, he spoke about the Spirit because his Spirit cannot be taken away. Once obtained lust would no longer appeal to her. Her soul rejoiced not just for the fact of love but also her desire to worship God as well. In those times, worship had to be done in temples. Where the Holy Spirit was to come and squash that practice because the Spirit would give a person the power to give true worship. We read about her excitement when she hears about this water that doesn't allow anyone to ever thirst. She rejoiced in the news of the Holy Spirit because it was to fulfill both her flesh (desire to be loved) and spirit (her desire to worship God). The very things she looked for gratification kept robbing her but what lust took from her, Jesus' Spirit would end up renewing.

Jesus was not just speaking to the lady at the well but to both men and women today. There is nothing wrong with finding a partner, but the emphasis is on who, what, and where our spiritual thirst is directed. The woman's desperation kept leading her to look in all the wrong places. Where the Spirit, which provides patience and self-control, will guide us to the one we need to be with. Now I have to also state that there was both a physical and spiritual meaning in the dialogue between Jesus and the woman at the well. Yes, she desired to find love, but she also found excitement in the reality of true worship. As I mentioned not to long ago, it was believed that true worship had to be done in the temples, but Jesus assured her that with the Spirit, worship could be done anywhere.

Yes, there is no greater feeling than when we are loved by others but what needs to be understood is that we can love only to a certain extent. Where God's love captures the whole; something that human beings cannot. In the chapter flesh vs spirit, I specifically mentioned that I still find it difficult to understand God's love. I will even rewind further in the earlier chapters where I was trying to understand God's unconditional love. Therefore, what gives me the right to dedicate a chapter to love, all in hopes to shame lust? Have I defeated lust? Or am I exactly like the woman at the well? I knew this chapter was going to be challenging to write about. As a result, I decided to pray for assistance.

"Spirit of God, I'm having a tough time writing about love. How do I sit here and speak about something that I too am still learning about? Even with all my creativity, I cannot write about things that I barely know about. The doctrine of Satan has deemed me as a person who's never loved. I look at my own life and I begin to agree with it. I've lusted more than I've loved. I've even done a poor job loving myself. I cannot sit here and pretend to know about love. Yes, I know my family loves me; Yes, I know my friends love me; However, even if all their love were combined together, it just isn't enough. It cannot save me. It cannot heal me. Do I sound selfish? Maybe, that's why the doctrine of Satan called my bluff. I'm a liar, liar and my hearts on fire because of it! I'm screaming on the rooftops because I don't know a single thing about love. Spirit of God, please consult me! Teach me about love.

I got this far because I wrote about what I know. How do I even speak to an audience who may or may not know about God? I know I cannot force people to believe everything I write. That's why I made the decision to write about you because I know you cannot lie. Spirit of God, I need insight. I know a lot about lust, but I barely know anything about love. How do you do it? How do you love a whole world filled with people? There is not one soul in the world whose soul is perfect. Yet you still bat your eyes at us. Spirit of God, please consult me. Teach me about true love.

Amen.*"*

What bothers me about lust is that it's easy to get along with. Whether it is a woman or a man seeking love. The first thing that our minds think of are relationships with one another. My problem is that although the physical relationship of having someone is delightful, it doesn't complete us. If we really think about it, without our control, people and things can get taken away from us. I pray and hope one day I can fall in love as well because I know people who have fallen in love. I see it in the marriage of my parents, and I've seen in other families. On the other hand, I've also seen people who looked inseparable but have left one another. I've seen people who have everything but are alone and just want someone to share it with. I've seen people who've been so badly hurt they choose to never trust anyone but that in itself brings them unhappiness. I've seen people who have been happily married their whole entire life, but their partner passes, so all their joy disappears. There just doesn't seem to be a silver lining and that's my problem. I want to know what that silver lining is, so I don't have to reform to lust.

"Author, oh author you say you're searching for my love, but that's not true. Liar, liar at least you admit that your hearts on fire. You desperately want to understand the fruits of my love. I see you've grown restless of your body's lust. I'm surprised you didn't go to the Scripture that speaks about love. For it is written:

If I speak in the tongues of men and of angels, but have not love, I am a noisy gong or a clanging cymbal. And if I have prophetic powers, and

understand all mysteries and all knowledge, and if I have all faith, so as to remove mountains, but have not love, I am nothing. If I give away all I have, and if I deliver up my body to be burned, but have not love, I gain nothing. Love is patient and kind; love does not envy or boast; it is not arrogant or rude. It does not insist on its own way; it is not irritable or resentful; it does not rejoice at wrongdoing but rejoices with the truth. Love bears all things, believes all things, hopes all things, endures all things. Love never ends. As for prophecies, they will pass away; as for tongues, they will cease; as for knowledge, it will pass away. For we know in part and we prophesy in part, but when the perfect comes, the partial will pass away. When I was a child, I spoke like a child, I thought like a child, I reasoned like a child. When I became a man, I gave up childish ways. For now we see in a mirror dimly, but then face to face. Now I know in part; then I shall know fully, even as I have been fully known. So now faith, hope, and love abide, these three; but the greatest of these is love. **(1 Corinthians 13:1-13) – English Standard Version**

Can you understand love now? No? Don't even try to lie to me, I can see your heart and I know you're not satisfied with this knowledge. Author, oh author love isn't something tangible that you can pick up. But its power is evident when you feel it, but you're focused on understanding it. Author, oh author love cannot be studied like the way you study books, but I see your heart and it burns for more knowledge. You're behaving like Jacob, trying to wrestle with one of my angels. For it is written:

Then Jacob was left alone; and a man wrestled with him until the breaking of day. Now when he saw that he did not prevail against him, he touched the socket of his hip; and the socket of Jacob's hip was out of joint as he wrestled with him. And he said, "Let me go, for the day breaks." But he said, "I will not let you go unless you bless me!" So he said to him, "What is your name?" He said, "Jacob." And he said, "Your name shall no longer be called Jacob, but Israel; for you have struggled with God and with men and have prevailed." (Genesis 32:24-28) – New King James Version

You are struggling with the Spirit to give you an answer. You fear the thirst like the woman from the well. You fear you too will become a slave to that well. That is why you are calling me for insight. I see you pleading, you've made your case. You've grown tired of lust, but you fear love? I will give you the answer you search for but before I do you must know: the knowledge of love is not what you need. The love that you know steals, but the love that I provide feeds and it begins from deep within. This is the answer you seek:

'Author, oh author you know your parents because they made themselves known to you. Your mother used every inch of her strength just to get you out. Despite all of her tears and pain, when she saw you, she fell in love. Your father held you and began to fantasize about who you'd become. At that very moment, even though you were young, they became your parents and you became their son. But what then of their story? It may have been years ago, but they knew their parents because their parents made it known to them. That is your story, and that is theirs. What then of those who were, or are born but their parents don't make it known? Some are luckier than others, but regardless someone pushed the child out. If the father leaves, who does the child call father? Or what if the mother chooses to give up her child? Who does that child call mother? That's right that child becomes an orphan because their parents decided to abandon them. Is that love? Of course not!

I created all, but none has ever seen me. Does that mean that I've abandoned all? Not at all! I have made myself known. I am the heavenly Father of all. The Father that created that orphan and the Father that created the woman at the well. For it is written:

God, who lives in his sacred Temple, cares for orphans and protects widows. (Psalms 68:5) – Good News Translation

Therefore I made myself known to all when I sent my own Spirit in the same form of all. The child whose parents did not make themselves known is referred to as an orphan. So, if you think I have not made myself known to you that would make you a spiritual orphan. But none of you are really orphans. Instead, you choose to be orphans. The child whose parents abandoned them has every right to be upset with their own earthly parents. That child never asked for that to happen to them. But no one has the right to be upset with me. I made myself known to all of you. Author you are trying to find the silver lining, but I am here to tell you that 'I AM' the line that you cannot cross. For it is written:

We love because God first loved us. (1 John 4:19) - Good News Translation

To fear love is foolish because I made all to love. For it is written:

There is no fear in love; but perfect love casts out fear, because fear involves torment. But he who fears has not been made perfect in love. (1 John 4:18) – New King James Version

Those who love are closer to me; those who obey show their love for me; those who try to go past me to find love will never be pleased. Whether married; the woman at the well; broken hearts; widow or single. No one will be complete because they choose to be spiritual orphans. Your real desire in your question is to seek out perfection. Your excuse to lust is because you've yet seen perfect love? Is it fair that a child is born and becomes an orphan? Author, when you were born to know both parents. Some will say, 'Oh God, if you truly loved why would you let such things come to be?' Shame on those who ask such things. How are the sins of people directed at me? Shame on those people! They abandoned their child due to their own evil. But I am the God of love and people love because I first loved.

Author, I chose birth as an example so that you may come to know and understand that birth represents firsts. Because you were born, you are subject to love. This ranges from those who have both parents, or one and none. Birth represents firsts because I first loved that's why all shall love; and whether orphan or not, you all exist because I willed it due to my love. I am the alpha and omega; the first and the last so my love will reign forever. What's unfair in the world is made fair through me. What's hurt you in the world will be healed through me. What disappointed you in the world will be fulfilled through me. What ignored and neglected you in the world will be cherished and noticed through me. All this is made true if the child recognizes me. They will no longer be called orphan because they have realized that I have made myself known to them from the very beginning. All this is possible because I am love.

Author, oh author I have answered all your thoughts. Do not be afraid of love because whatever is taken away from you, whether family or friends; I will always remain in you because I am true love."

-Spirit of God

Then the scribes and Pharisees brought to him a woman caught in adultery. And when they had set her in the midst, they said to him, "Teacher, this woman was caught in adultery, in the very act. Now Moses, in the law, commanded us that such should be stoned. But what do you say?" This they said, testing him, that they might have something of which to accuse him. But Jesus stooped down and wrote on the ground with his finger, as though he did not hear. So when they continued asking him, he raised himself up and said to them, "He who is without sin among you, let him throw a stone at her first." And again, he stooped down and wrote on the ground. Then those who heard it, being convicted by their conscience, went out one by one, beginning with the oldest even to the last. And Jesus was left alone, and the woman standing in the midst. When Jesus had raised himself up and saw no one but the woman, he said to her, "Woman, where are those accusers of yours? Has no one condemned you?" She said, "No one, Lord." And Jesus said to her, "Neither do I condemn you; go and sin no more." **(John 8:3-11) – New King James Version**

A very well-known story but the meaning behind it has qualities like wisdom, forgiveness, but most importantly love. Yes, lust was involved too because the woman was caught in the act of adultery. Jesus looked at the woman and saw her pain while everyone else was looking at her sin. Jesus was filled with so much compassion and love, he wasn't seeking to judge her but to forgive her which exhibited the new covenant.

And the Word became flesh and dwelt among us, and we beheld his glory, the glory as of the only begotten of the Father, full of grace and truth. **(John 1:14) – New King James Version**

The world came after the woman and was ready to stone her, but Jesus saw a woman that was bound by sin, so he freed her by forgiving her. Just by forgiving her, she was set free! Sin was speaking through the Pharisees demanding for its dividend of the transaction: "Death, Death,

Death!" yelled sin because the law demanded that death. Little did sin know that its shady transactions were about to be revoked.

"Men,

Made from the ground, hard working and strong why settle for one when you can lust? You know women need you, you know women seek you. There once was a man named Elkanah who was married to Hannah. Hannah was unable to have children and because of this she grieved. For it is written:

Her husband Elkanah would ask her, 'Hannah, why are you crying? Why won't you eat? Why are you always so sad? Don't I mean more to you than ten sons?' (1 Samuel 1:8) – Good News Translation

Poor old Elkanah infused with love. All Hannah cared for was getting a child. Women don't care and even if they do, why take the chance with one when you can have two? Incubus is my friend, he'll torment them. I'm more fun, and I won't restrain you. I lay my hands around my back as I snap my fingers it's on to the next. I assure you that love ends with death.

Want to chuckle? David defeated Goliath with God's help and reigned as king. Does anybody know that David got into bed with me? He stole one of his soldier's wife and got her pregnant. David and I had fun just ask him. The woman's name was Bathsheba. David found her so beautiful and as I whispered into his ear, he listened to every one of my instructions when I advised him to kill her husband. For it was written:

'Put Uriah in the front line, where the fighting is heaviest, then retreat and let him be killed.' (2 Samuel:15) – Good News Translation

My name is lust, and I promise you, I will not disappoint you."

–The doctrine of Satan

As we shift to the doctrine of Satan's letter to men, it boasts about how many men have fallen under its spell. Even the very David, who killed

Goliath, lusted after one of his men's wife. The very David that spoke with so much faith and reverence for the Lord.

David answered, "You are coming against me with a sword, spear, and javelin, but I come against you in the name of the LORD Almighty, the God of the Israelite armies, which you have defied." **(1 Samuel 17:45) – Good News Translation**

Lust doesn't care about our faith for God. It is a spirit that fears nothing which makes it one of the most dangerous spirits to combat against. It is a devious spirit because it is a spirit that tells us we are not harming anyone when we are actually harming ourselves. Thing is, that may be true when it comes to things like watching pornography but those are just the baby steps that it takes to capture our hearts. Eventually what we do in secret will seep into our daily public lives.

Flee sexual immorality. Every sin that a man does is outside the body but, he who commits sexual immorality sins against his own body. **(1 Corinthians 6:18) – New King James Version**

Remember the Scripture that spoke about who our real enemies are?

Finally, my brethren, be strong in the Lord, and in the power of his might. Put on the whole armour of God, that ye may be able to stand against the wiles of the devil. For we wrestle not against flesh and blood, but against principalities, against powers, against the rulers of the darkness of this world, against spiritual wickedness in high places. **(Ephesians 6:10-12) – King James Version**

There is a story that I'd like to share that I've also kept to myself because of how disturbing it is. During my trip to Tanzania, I got the opportunity to go visit the very village my father grew up. It is approximately a two-hour drive from Dar-es-Saleem, which is where I was born. I only stayed in the village for three days, but I got to see where my dad used to sleep, eat and play when he was a child. It was a remarkable experience except for the last day. On my last day in the village, my mother, little brother Isaiah and aunt had just finished dinner and went inside to begin packing for our departure back to

Dar-es-Saleem. Before we went inside, a little girl sat with us while we were having dinner, but she was so quiet and refused to eat anything. I didn't think much of it since I did not know who she was, and it is tradition to eat with your neighbors in Tanzania. After I had finished eating, I went inside with my mom and little brother to pack for the next day. My whole trip was about to be turned upside down when my other two aunts came running inside the house outraged. That little girl who was about 12 years old, refused to speak or eat because she was in a state of shock. She had been sexually assaulted that night by an older man. The only way my two aunts found out was because the sperm of that man was dripping down from her skirt. The little girl decided to confide in both my aunts and told them that a man in his 60's had forced himself on her. He then paid her 10,000 Tanzanian shillings (that is about 5 Canadian dollars) to keep her quiet. I remember feeling so sick to my stomach that I had to leave the room to throw up. My aunts took her to the police station to file a case against this disgusting man.

I began to think to myself how God could let such a thing happen? That little girl is going to be damaged for the rest of her life because of that. I was so angry because I couldn't do anything and that broke my heart. What does God say about things like rape? How does he mend the hearts of those who have been a victim to such things? How does God forgive a man who does not respect women and violates them? They are so sick that they even target little girls. I remember asking my one of aunts about this matter. I asked her specifically because she had devoted her whole life to God. To be honest her answer pissed me off even more. She basically said, "the only thing we can do is pray for that little girl so that God can heal her from that attack. We also have to pray for that man because he is very sick; all in hopes that he may turn away from his sins." I couldn't accept that answer because I didn't even want that man to turn away from his sins. In all honesty, I wanted him to die. My aunt understood my anger because she was angry too, but she reminded me of something.

Whoever breaks one commandment is guilty of breaking them all. For the same one who said, "Do not commit adultery," also said, "Do not commit murder."

Even if you do not commit adultery, you have become a lawbreaker if you commit murder. Speak and act as people who will be judged by the law that sets us free. For God will not show mercy when he judges the person who has not been merciful; but mercy triumphs over judgment." **(James 2:10–13) – Good News Translation**

As they stood there asking him questions, he straightened up and said to them, "Whichever one of you has committed no sin may throw the first stone at her." **(John 8:7) – Good News Translation**

Despite all these Scriptures, I was still angry and couldn't bring myself to change my thoughts and emotions towards that man. Nonetheless, God had his way of communicating with me.

"Author, oh author why do you continue to disappoint me? I see your frustration. I see your anger. So, author let me ask you something: 'When were you born? How old are you? At exactly what time were you conceived?' I can hear your heart out loud asking, 'What do these questions have anything to do with this?' Well, you asked rhetorical questions, so I returned the favor!

24 years later and it took only one sin to make you feel sick? If you're going to throw up from one, you might as well throw up on all. You think I do not hear the cries of the innocent? They are constant victims of sinners. Those who do not know me ask, 'What kind of God allows this?' While they themselves proceed to sin. Those who do not know me ask, 'Why won't God punish this?' Author, do you remember Genesis? For it is written:

Then the LORD saw that the wickedness of man was great in the earth, and that every intent of the thoughts of his heart was only evil continually. And the LORD was sorry that he had made man on the earth, and he was grieved in his heart. So the LORD said, "I will destroy man whom I have created from the face of the earth, both man and beast, creeping thing and birds of the air, for I am sorry that I have made them." But Noah found grace in the eyes of the LORD. (Genesis 6:5–8) – New King James Version

I've flooded the earth; I've commanded fiery sulfur hit the cities of Sodom and Gomorrah for all its wickedness. I've even turned some to a pillar of salt. For it is written:

But his wife looked back from behind him, and she became a pillar of salt. (Genesis 19:26) – King James Version

However, the wicked continue to grow! They grow like unwanted weeds in the garden. Humans may tolerate this in their gardens, but I don't. That's why I kicked Adam and Eve out. Destruction and more destruction; all at the expense of the innocent. It is no use because those who are wicked enjoy their wicked ways! For it is written:

Who can understand the human heart? There is nothing else so deceitful; it is too sick to be healed. I, the LORD, search the mind and test the hearts of the people. I treat each of them according to the way they live; according to what they do. (Jeremiah 17:9) – Good News Translation

When my anger is shown and I proclaim punishments from my throne; the people that do not know me complain by saying, 'What a cruel God!' When things go wrong it is those same people that say, 'Oh my God!' I sit and question them, 'What god are they referring to?' They hate me when there's justice and they hate me when there's an injustice. So, author, oh author what is your excuse? You know me so why do you ask me questions like the heathens? Do you even know the name of that little girl? When she was sexually assaulted, where were you? I saw the evil act in front of me. Do you not forget that I see everything? I have seen all kinds of wickedness. You should see what people do in secret. Some are so sinful they have tattooed their sins. What I call shameful they brag and stick their chests up high because their hearts have become shameless. Some people sin in broad daylight and some who sin at night. There are even people who sin and say, 'It's strictly business.' Author, oh author what would you do? Is your next piece of writing going to be called, The death book? See if I possessed your heart, there would be no mercy or love. Do not let the sins of others contaminate you. There is nothing more contagious than sin. For it is written:

Do not fret because of evildoers, nor be envious of the workers of iniquity. For they shall soon be cut down like the grass, and wither as the green

herb. Trust in the LORD, and do good, dwell in the land, and feed on his faithfulness. Delight yourself also in the LORD, and he shall give you the desires of your heart. Commit your way to the LORD, trust also in him, and he shall bring it to pass. He shall bring forth your righteousness as the light, and your justice as the noonday. Rest in the LORD and wait patiently for him; do not fret because of him who prospers in his way, because of the man who brings wicked schemes to pass. Cease from anger and forsake wrath; do not fret- it only causes harm. For evildoers shall be cut off; but those who wait on the LORD, they shall inherit the earth. For yet a little while and the wicked shall be no more; Indeed, you will look carefully for his place, but it shall be no more. But the meek shall inherit the earth and shall delight themselves in the abundance of peace. **(Psalms 37:1-11) – New King James Version**

As for those who are victims of the violent sinners; I hear their cries. I know their hearts and I know their stories. I even know how many hairs are on their heads. For it is written:

As for you, even the hairs of your head have all been counted. (Matthew 10:30) – Good News Translation

I know their trauma and I know how much they hate their thoughts. They hate them because their brain continues replaying that day over and over. They will say, 'You're an unfair God, how could you just watch? Why didn't you send one of your angels to make it stop?' Some will even say, 'God they violated my body! God, they violated my soul! How can I ever recover from all these violations?' I will say this to all the broken:

'I know they violated the body and I know they violated the soul. I know you're mad and it has turned your heart cold. Come to me and let me take it all away. You've tried it your way but all its done is bring you more loneliness. You will say, 'But Spirit of God no one understands it, I keep seeing it replay over and over in my head.'

This is how I will reply, 'My Spirit watches over all the earth. I see the wicked spirits infiltrating those who are spiritually gone. For it is written:

The LORD remembers what their enemies have done; he waits for the right time to punish them. The LORD will take revenge and punish them; the time will come when they will fall; the day of their doom is near. (Deuteronomy 32:34-35) – Good News Translation

I saw what happened to you, my beautiful daughter, but do not allow the anger to take over you; Let vengeance be mine and allow me to heal your cuts and bruises. I understand your pain, but the enemy Satan was trying to destroy you! That pain that you feel is trying to lay its eggs. If you continue like this, it will grow and grow and soon hatch inside of you. That pain is trying to give birth to sin, you must not let it hatch! Or else it will infiltrate you too! You must overcome it! The memory is replaying to taunt and make fun of you. It's no different from the wicked spirit named Anxiety. It plots to steal, kill and destroy.' For it is written:

The thief comes only in order to steal, kill and destroy. I have come in order that you might have life-life in all its fullness. (John 10:10) – Good News Translation

Call upon my name, and I will not let your pain hatch! You are not its slave! You are free! For it is written:

But you do see; you take notice of trouble and suffering and are always ready to help. The helpless commit themselves to you; you have always helped the needy. Break the power of the wicked and evil people; punish them for the wrong they have done until they do it no more. (Psalms 10:14-15) – Good News Translation

Whoever goes to the LORD for safety, whoever remains under the protection of the Almighty, can say to him, "You are my defender and protector. You are my God; in you I trust." He will keep you safe from all hidden dangers and from all deadly diseases. He will cover you with his wings; you will be safe in his care; his faithfulness will protect and defend you. (Psalms 91:1-4) – Good News Translation

God says, "I will save those who love me and will protect those who acknowledge me as LORD. When they call to me, I will answer them; when they are in trouble, I will be with them. I will rescue them and

honor them. I will reward them with long life; I will save them." **(Psalms 91:14-16) – Good News Translation**

It will continue to use your very thoughts, but you must remember this. For it is written:

The LORD is my shepherd; I shall not want. He makes me lie down in green pastures; he leads me beside the still waters. He restores my soul; he leads me in the paths of righteousness for his name's sake. Yea, though I will walk through the valley of the shadow of death, I will fear no evil; for you are with me; your rod and your staff, they comfort me. You prepare a table before me in the presence of my enemies; you anoint my head with oil; my cup runs over. Surely goodness and mercy shall follow me all the days of my life; and I will dwell in the house of the LORD forever. (Psalms 23) – New King James Version

What shattered into broken pieces, I will pick up and put back together. The body that you now think is disgusting, I shall wash and make whiter than snow! I will let you hear the sounds of joy and gladness. These sounds will remind you that you are beautiful. They will outplay and out sing your thoughts; the memories that tried to steal, kill and destroy you will seize at once! Your story will become a strength to many. What the wicked committed brought you to my glory! Then you will be courageous and strong becoming a voice of hope. You will ask for my Spirit and receive it. Then you shall share your story and teach others how I restored you.' For it is written:

Then will I teach transgressors your ways, and sinners shall be converted to you. Deliver me from the guilt of bloodshed, O God, the God of my salvation, and my tongue shall sing aloud of your righteousness. O Lord open my lips, and my mouth shall show forth your praise. (Psalms 51:13-15) – New King James Version

Author, oh author I have returned my attention to you. I have prepared a date; a date where the righteous will no longer be victims to those who are evil. I have arranged a time; a time where the wicked will face their fate. For it is written:

Now I saw a new heaven and a new earth, for the first heaven and the first earth had passed away. Also, there was no more sea. Then I, John, saw the holy city, new Jerusalem, coming down out of heaven from God, prepared as a bride adorned for her husband. And I heard a loud voice from heaven saying, "Behold, the tabernacle of God is with men, and he will dwell with them, and they shall be his people. God himself will be with them and be their God. And God will wipe away every tear from their eyes; there shall be no more death, nor sorrow, nor crying. There shall be no more pain, for the former things have passed away." Then he who sat on the throne said, "Behold, I make all things new." And he said to me, "Write, for these words are true and faithful." And he said to me, "It is done! I am the Alpha and the Omega, the Beginning and the End. I will give of the fountain of the water of life freely to him who thirsts. He who overcomes shall inherit all things, and I will be his God and he shall be my son. But the cowardly, unbelieving, abominable, murderers, sexually immoral, sorcerers, idolaters, and all liars shall have their part in the lake which burns with fire and brimstone, which is the second death." **(Revelation 21:1-8) – New King James Version**

This day approaches because I want to be together with my righteous people. Those that choose me will be apart of my everlasting garden. There will be no annoying wicked evil weeds to mess up my garden! For it is written:

I am now giving you the choice between life and death, between God's blessing and God's curse, and I call heaven and earth to witness the choice you make. Choose life. (Deuteronomy 30:19) - Good News Translation

I patiently wait for this day, the day that I have set. A day that neither heaven nor earth, or the world of the below knows. I have placed my covenant and proclaimed it upon the land, skies, and sea. I patiently hold back my anger towards the wicked because I am the God of love. I patiently wait for people to become righteous because I am merciful but tolerate no evil. I fear no human, no angels and no demons.

Author, oh author I have one last thing to say to you. Never wish death upon anyone! Or else you will be judged! If I were to act now, where would your name be? For it is written:

Those who did not have their name written in the book of the living were thrown into the lake of fire. (Revelation 20:15) – Good News Translation

Author, oh author show mercy and forgive; hate the sin but do not catch its flu! For it is written:

Show mercy toward those who have doubts, save others by snatching them out of the fire, but hate their clothes, sustained by their sinful lusts. (Jude 1:22-23) – Good News Translation

Sin is highly contagious and exists in every season. My Spirit is the antidote, and it must live in you. So, remain in me and I will remain in you. For it is written:

Remain united to me, and I will remain united to you. A branch cannot bear fruit by itself; it can do so only if it remains in the vine. In the same way, you cannot bear fruit unless you remain in me. I am the vine, and you are the branches. Those who remain in me, and I them, will bear much fruit; for you can do nothing without me. Those who do not remain in me are thrown out like a branch and dry up; such branches are gathered up and thrown into the fire, where they are burned. If you remain in me and my words in you, then you will ask for anything you wish, and you shall have it. My Father's glory is shown by your bearing much fruit, and in this way, you become my disciples. I love you just as the Father loves me; remain in my love. If you obey my commands, you will remain in my love, just as I have obeyed my Father's commands and remain in his love. I have told you this so that my joy may be in you and that your joy may be complete. My commandment is this: love one another, just as I love you. The greatest love you can have for your friends is to give your life for them. And you are my friends if you do what I command you. I do not call you servants any longer, because servants do not know what their master is doing. Instead, I call you friends, because I have told you everything I heard from my Father. You did not choose me; I chose

you and appointed you to go and bear much fruit, the kind of fruit that endures. And so, the Father will give you whatever you ask of him in my name. This, then is what I command you: love one another. (John 15:1-17) – Good News Translation"

– Spirit of God

All these Scriptures have one thing in common: forgiveness, mercy, trust and love. Even the ones that spoke of punishments, did not include us executing revenge because God is our protector. Not one of them promoted hate or violence, and that was what I was exhibiting. To others, it may seem like I was saying that man deserved death because of the magnitude of the sin he committed. However, God exposed the real motive behind my rage which mainly consisted of me thinking that I am a better person than that old man because I've never committed such a disgusting act. It's a fair statement to make, but that doesn't fly with God. That is why James 2:11 makes the bold statement that there is no distinction with sin because they are all the same in the eyes of God. The reason why I was angry at that man was due to the nature of his sin, but if we dig spiritually into his soul- he has indulged the spirit of lust to such a point where he no longer feels remorse or care for righteousness. Lust is the driving force behind such a disgusting act. My aunt referred to him as a "sick" man because he is spiritually infected by the spirit lust. If our bodies can be infected by sicknesses. What then stops our spirits from being infected? Lust influences many but expresses itself in different ways depending on the person. Can we really say that a person who commits infidelity is better than a man that rapes? A man who commits adultery is also hurting others as well. He is hurting his significant other and if that man has a family, he is hurting his children. The roles can be switched, but at the end of the day, sin is still sin. I may have never committed such a sin but for me to sit here and wish death upon that man would mean that I am without God.

If we say that we have no sin, we deceive ourselves, and the truth is not in us. If we confess our sins, he is faithful and just to forgive us our sins, and to cleanse us from all unrighteousness. If we say that we have not sinned, we make him a liar, and his Word is not in us. **(1 John 1:8-10) – New King James Version**

Some may read this and ask, "So whenever I sin can I just blame it on so and so spirit because it made me do it?" Of course not! That is not what I mean when I bring up this spiritual warfare. A spirit cannot force one to do anything because God has given us the free will to choose our own actions. In the garden, Adam and Eve had the choice to eat from the tree that gave knowledge of what is good and bad. Satan influenced Eve to eat it and then she got Adam to do the very same thing. No one forced anyone to do anything. Any evil spirit that works for Satan's kingdom will shapeshift into scenarios and will attempt to influence our will. The spirit of lust can impact anyone and depending on the person, it will either affect the person severely or begin with baby steps.

Put on the whole armour of God, that ye may be able to stand against the wiles of the devil. For we wrestle not against flesh and blood, but against principalities, against powers, against the rulers of the darkness of this world, against spiritual wickedness in high places. Wherefore take unto you the whole armour of God, that ye may be able to withstand in the evil day, and having done all, to stand. **(Ephesians 6:11-13) - King James Version**

If that one sinful act made me so sick to my stomach, so should all sins. We cannot pick and choose which ones we are content with because even those ones have a way to dig us deeper into Satan's doctrine. The person who lies could have never imagined that their lies would get them to steal. They started off with little white lies that did not harm anyone, but the spirit of untruthfulness has other ideas with the person. The person who has a short temper could have never imagined that their anger would result in them to commit murder, but the spirit of rage tricks the person. This is the same with people who lust because they begin to lust simply because they find another person attractive. There is no harm in that right? Consequently, the spirit of lust has its tricks too. As a result, to those who listen to lust, they find themselves with unwanted pregnancies, abortions, suicide, infidelity, lies, sickness, sexual assault, and even murder. I called lust a sly spirit because it's friends with many other spirits.

"When an unclean spirit goes out of a man, he goes through dry places, seeking rest, and finds none. Then he says, 'I will return to my house from which I came.' And when he comes, he finds it empty, swept, and put in order. Then he goes and takes with him seven other spirits more wicked than himself, and they enter and dwell there; and the last state of that man is worse than the first. So shall it also be with this wicked generation." **(Matthew 12:43-45) – New King James Version**

When it calls its other friends the person who's committed to lust find themselves in situations they never even dreamed of. Lust disguises itself in almost anything. It infiltrates the mind slowly and without realizing it, we find ourselves hooked.

You have heard that it was said, "Do not commit adultery" But I tell you that anyone who looks at a woman to lust after he has already committed adultery with her in his heart. **(Matthew 5: 27-28) - Good News Translation**

There's this thing called selective hearing which means we listen to the things we want to hear and block out the things we do not want to hear. I can fully admit that reading that passage had me selectively reading. Which in my definition means: I chose to ignore what I read. The Scripture above are words by Jesus, and he was teaching about how lust leads to adultery. How does lust lead to infidelity? Trust me, I did not want to know the answer to the question because I was guilty of it. But what needs to be understood is nothing that comes from Satan is good. Remember the serpent that deceived Eve with just one lie, and it cost the human race spiritual death? When God says, "do not do this," he's saying it because there is a spiritual reason as to why we shouldn't. In the doctrine of Satan poem forwarded to the ladies, it says, "Succubus is my friend, she'll torment them." Succubus, which derives from late Latin for succubae (sub- "under" and cub are "to lie in bed") is a name of a demon that preys on victims of lustful men while they are sleeping. It's something that I could not wrap my head around until I thought about wet dreams. This disgusting phenomenon is not something new, and as a matter of fact, this process of spiritual beings having sexual intercourse with humans is noted in the bible. If I want to be all scientific or professional, the proper term for a wet dream is nocturnal emission (Yes, I googled that). Which basically happens to us males when we are sleeping. We may experience an orgasm without anyone touching us, and at times it could result to ejaculation.

Some of the heavenly beings saw that these young women were beautiful, so they took the ones they liked. **(Genesis 6:2) - Good News Translation**

That is the only account in the bible regarding this disgusting and vile act. The male counterpart spirit for women is called Incubus, which is derived from late Latin as incubo (a nightmare induced by such a demon from incubare "to lie upon"). So, what does the spirit of incubus do to women? Well, the reality of these spirits are they influence the body to behave lustfully. It is why terms like 'sex addict' or 'nympho' are brought into the discussion. This does not only pertain to women but men as well! The person who behaves this way is acting on these spirit's influences, but the sad and scary part is they can never be sexually satisfied. But what do the spirits gain from doing such things?

Therefore, a man shall leave his father and mother and be joined to his wife, and they shall become one flesh. **(Genesis 2:24) – New King James Version**

The reason why lust is such a dangerous spirit is because once a person is influenced by the spirit of lust, whatever other spirits that are latched onto them will latch onto the person they sleep with or vice-versa. This is because sexual intercourse involves becoming one flesh. But the thing about us humans is that we are more than just flesh but also spirit as well. Therefore, whomever we sleep with, we now share whatever spirit that lies with them. For example, if that person has a generational spirit that involves divorce in their family tree, that person has now just welcomed the generational curse of unsuccessful marriages to their life. That spirit is now being passed down to another family tree! It could legit be anything; a spirit that is generational or a spirit that is specific to that certain person. I didn't go into this much depth for the chapter flesh vs spirit, but this is what lust does because it knows flesh and spirit go hand in hand. The demons that left heaven to go have sexual intercourse with women introduced the act of infiltrating human beings sexually. But we know due to the Scriptures that they are now caged in eternal darkness (Jude 1:6). But that did not stop the angels who left with Satan to adopt these methods which is why Incubus and Succubus are spiritual realities. Now since that is the only evidence within the bible that we have regarding these spiritual beings, how can we affirm that all this is true? Simply by connecting the dots. Jesus said, "by looking at a woman lustfully you have already committed adultery." We know that committing adultery is a sin because it is one of the Ten Commandments but what if we're not married and are single? Isn't adultery being unfaithful to our significant other?

"All things are lawful for me," but not all things are helpful. "All things are lawful for me," but I will not be dominated by anything. "Food is meant for the stomach and the stomach for food"—and God will destroy both one and the other. The body is not meant for sexual immorality, but for the Lord, and the Lord for the body. And God raised the Lord and will also raise us up by his power. Do you not know that your bodies are members of Christ? Shall I then take the members of Christ and make them members of a prostitute? Never! Or do you not know that he who is joined to a prostitute becomes one body with her? For, as it is written, "The two will become one flesh." But he who is joined to the Lord becomes one spirit with him. Flee from sexual immorality. Every other sin a person commits is outside the body, but the sexually immoral person sins against his own body. Or do you not know that your body is a temple of the Holy Spirit within you, whom you have from God? You are not your own, for you were bought with a price. So glorify God in your body. **(1 Corinthians 6:12-20) – Good Standard Version**

The Scripture that once didn't make any sense has now made complete sense due to the help of the Holy Spirit. I tried to find a loophole in the Scripture: "Anyone who looks at a woman lustfully has committed adultery" But there is no loophole! Sexual immorality is a sin because it disgraces our bodies. If we trace back to the chapter flesh vs. spirit;

our bodies are like a gauntlet which were designed for the Holy Spirit so that we can become one with Christ. Lust looks so satisfying, but it's pickpocketing love from our hearts. Thus, if a man looks at a woman lustfully, they have already committed adultery because behind the mask of lust are the spiritual beings that are trying to become one with the man's body. We have to ask ourselves this: Would we rather a demonic spirit latched onto us or Jesus Christ? 1 Corinthians 6:12-20 states: "Our bodies belong to Christ because he paid the price for all so that we may not be slaves to sin." Before Christ, our bodies belonged to sin, so in other words Satan. In 1 Corinthians 6-10, it states: "we are free to do whatever we want, but not all things are good." With that information revealed in God's Word, the onus is on us to hold onto God's Word. The doctrine of Satan will lecture our minds by saying, "You are free to express your free-will so just do what you want!" He yells, "encore, encore" to all our actions that do not bring glory to God.

"I still have many things to say to you, but you cannot bear them now. However, when he, the Spirit of truth, has come, he will guide you into all truth; for he will speak on his own authority, but whatever he hears he will speak; and he will tell you things to come. He will glorify me, for he will take what is mine and declare it to you. All things that the Father has are mine. Therefore I said that he will take of mine and declare it to you." **(John 16:12-15) – New King James Version**

It is only through the Spirit that I understand and fear the disgusting consequences of listening to lust. For without the Spirit, I looked at Scripture and didn't understand or want to understand it. The ugly truth about lust has been exposed but what more did we expect? We know that the Spirit of God produces love, joy, peace, patience, kindness, goodness, faithfulness, humility and self-control (Galatians 5:22). All that the Spirit produces cannot be shared with what lust produces. Before the Spirit, I walked with lust day and night. I did not see it as harmful because it knocked on my door with a mask but underneath it plotted to steal, kill and destroy (John10:10). Lust also has a way of taking away our own vision by applying its own set of eyes. It does this, so we become blind from seeing what we're doing which is actually hurting people. Lust can destroy friendships, relationships, and even marriages. The Holy Spirit produces many things and one of those things is self-control, which combats against lust. However, if we choose to receive the Holy Spirit, we cannot revert back to lust. The Holy Spirit can only do so much, but if the person decides not to listen to it, the Spirit becomes sad. It allows us to do this because of God's unconditional love but we must remember that we cannot serve two masters.

You cannot drink from the Lord's cup and also from the cup of demons; you cannot eat at the Lord's table and also at the table of demons. Or do you want to make the Lord jealous? Do we think we are stronger than he? **(1 Corinthians 10:21-22) – Good News Translation**

And do not make the God's Holy Spirit sad; for the Spirit is God's mark of ownership on you, a guarantee that the Day will come when God will set you free. **(Ephesians 4:30) – Good News Translation**

That mask named lust wants to rule us by attaching itself on our souls so that it can conquer us. Resting and giving up isn't apart of lust's nature because spirits aren't accustomed to time, but they love taking our time. On the other hand, there will come a time when Satan's wicked doctrines and demons will face their punishment.

I refuse to be a part of that punishment and I pray that anyone who reads this may feel the same way. The devil uses lust and many more spirits so that we are blinded from the truth. He will do anything to make flesh and spirit battle while he hides in the darkness. Satan loves making enemies out of us while his demonic spirits feed on our souls.

Once I was looking out the window of my house, and I saw many inexperienced young men, but noticed one foolish fellow in particular. He was walking along the street near the corner where a certain woman lived. He was passing near her house in the evening after it was dark. And then she met him; she was dressed like a prostitute and was making plans. She was a bold and shameless woman who always walked the streets or stood waiting at a corner, sometimes in the streets, sometimes in the marketplace. She threw her arms around the young man, kissed him, looked him straight in the eye, and said, "I made my offerings today and have the meat from the sacrifices. So I came out looking for you. I wanted to find you, and here you are! I've covered my bed with sheets of colored linen from Egypt. I've perfumed it with myrrh, aloes, and cinnamon. Come on! Let's make love all night long. We'll be happy in each other's arms. My husband isn't at home. He's on a long trip. He took plenty of money with him and won't be back for two weeks." So she tempted him with her charms, and he gave in to her smooth talk. Suddenly he was going with her like an ox on the way to be slaughtered, like a deer prancing into a trap where an arrow would pierce its heart. He was like a bird going into a net—he did not know that his life was in danger. Now then, sons, listen to me. Pay attention to what I say. Do not let such a woman win your heart; don't go wandering after her. She has been the ruin of many men and caused the death of too many to count. If you go to her house, you are on the way to the world of the dead. It is a shortcut to death. **(Proverbs 7:6–27) – Good News Translation**

"Stay away from a woman like that," warns king Solomon. The same Solomon who asked God for wisdom rather than gold or silver. Unfortunately, the story of Solomon doesn't end with a happily ever after. The irony of king Solomon's demise is that he couldn't practice what he preached. There was one truth that lust spoke about that is sadly true; it has taken down many men and one of them was king Solomon.

Now king Solomon loved many foreign women, along with the daughter of Pharaoh: Moabite, Ammonite, Edomite, Sidonian, and Hittite women, from the nations concerning which the LORD had said to the people of Israel, "You shall not enter into marriage with them, neither shall they with you, for surely they will turn away your heart after their gods." Solomon clung to these in love. He had 700 wives, who were princesses, and 300 concubines. And his wives turned away his heart. For when Solomon was old his wives turned away his heart after other gods, and his heart was not wholly true to the LORD his God, as was the heart of David his father. For Solomon went after Ashtoreth the goddess of the Sidonians, and after Milcom the abomination of the Ammonites. So Solomon did what was evil in the sight of the LORD and did not wholly follow the LORD, as David his father had done. Then Solomon built a high place for Chemosh the abomination of Moab, and for Molech the abomination of the Ammonites, on the mountain east of Jerusalem. And so he did for all his foreign wives, who made offerings and sacrificed to their gods. And the LORD was angry with Solomon, because his heart had turned away from the LORD, the God of Israel, who had appeared to him twice and had commanded him concerning this thing, that he should not go after other gods. But he did not keep what the LORD commanded. Therefore the LORD said to Solomon, "Since this has been your practice and you have not kept my covenant and my statutes that I have commanded you, I will surely tear the kingdom from you and will give it to your servant. Yet for the sake of David your father I will not do it in your days, but I will tear it out of the hand of your son. However, I will not tear away all the kingdom, but I will give one tribe to your son, for the sake of David my servant and for the sake of Jerusalem that I have chosen." **(1 King 11:1-13) – English Standard Version**

Solomon really messed that one up, and it cost him his whole kingdom. The saddest part of the story was the person that was to pay the price of his sins. It was his son! God didn't let Solomon off the hook that easily though because the protection that God provided Israel left and many different nations began to turn on Solomon's Israel. But, how did this all start? That's right. Lust entered king Solomon's heart and even with all his wisdom, it infiltrated all his defenses and he caved into the voice of lust. Solomon was the son of David, the same David that killed Goliath. Now before we begin saying, "like father like son." David did repent of his sin that he committed when he slept with one of his soldiers' wife'. But lust entered Solomon's heart like a tsunami, and he lost all connection with God. The Scriptures state that Solomon married 700 princesses and had 300 mistresses! I know my lustful mind at first wanted to give Solomon props for scoring such numbers but after realizing what lust really is, I too am disgusted. Lust brought the downfall of a well-respected king, and it slipped past all of Solomon's wisdom. Imagine that! The son of king David abandoned his faith in God and began worshipping other gods (Ashtoreth, Milcom, Chemosh and Molech – strongly advise to google those gods). But how did lust achieve that? It's because he slept with over 1000 different women that worshipped other gods and whatever spirits that were latched onto them, soon latched onto him!

The world promotes this lifestyle, and many have or continue to live by the standards held by the world. I do not need to recap what happens when lust has its grip around someone because that very thing it promises, it also takes away. Lust flirts with pleasure and excitement but behind our backs, it is poisoning our hearts and then we find ourselves in a bottomless pit. God patiently waits for us to turn away from it because all he can do is love us but be sure that he hates our sins.

But do not forget one thing, my dear friends! There is no difference in the LORD's sight between one day or a thousand years; to him, the two are the same. The Lord is not slow to do what he has promised, as some think. Instead, he is patient with you, because he does not want anyone to be destroyed, but wants all to turn away from their sins. **(2 Peter 3:8-9) - Good News Translation**

Lust came into Solomon's life so rapid and it got him to commit one sin, but once it removed its mask, Solomon began to commit many sins. He disobeyed God and abandoned his faith. The very proverb he wrote about regarding the immoral woman, he ditched and got with over 1000 women. Solomon's lust did not just end in the sexual manner, but it motivated him to please every one of those foreign women. Therefore, he proceeded to worship their gods while forgetting the one true God.

But you, LORD, are the true God, you are the living God and the eternal king. When you are angry, the world trembles; the nations cannot endure your anger. (You people must tell them that the gods who did not make the earth, and the sky will be destroyed. They will no longer exist anywhere on earth.) **(Jeremiah 10:10-11) - Good News Translation**

In conclusion, it is fair to say that it is only in faith in the Spirit of God and Jesus that we are saved from sin.

Now Joseph had been brought down to Egypt, and Potiphar, an officer of Pharaoh, the captain of the guard, an Egyptian, had bought him from the Ishmaelites who had brought him down there. The LORD was with Joseph, and he became a successful man, and he was in the house of his Egyptian master.

*His master saw that the L*ORD *was with him and that the L*ORD *caused all that he did to succeed in his hands. So Joseph found favor in his sight and attended him, and he made him overseer of his house and put him in charge of all that he had. From the time that he made him overseer in his house and over all that he had, the L*ORD *blessed the Egyptian's house for Joseph's sake; the blessing of the L*ORD *was on all that he had, in house and field. So he left all that he had in Joseph's charge, and because of him he had no concern about anything but the food he ate. Now Joseph was handsome in form and appearance. And after a time, his master's wife cast her eyes on Joseph and said, "Lie with me." But he refused and said to his master's wife, "Behold, because of me my master has no concern about anything in the house, and he has put everything that he has in my charge. He is not greater in this house than I am, nor has he kept back anything from me except you, because you are his wife. How then can I do this great wickedness and sin against God?" And as she spoke to Joseph day after day, he would not listen to her, to lie beside her or to be with her. But one day, when he went into the house to do his work and none of the men of the house was there in the house, she caught him by his garment, saying, "Lie with me." But he left his garment in her hand and fled and got out of the house. And as soon as she saw that he had left his garment in her hand and had fled out of the house, she called to the men of her household and said to them, "See, he has brought among us a Hebrew to laugh at us. He came to me to lie with me, and I cried out with a loud voice. And as soon as he heard that I lifted up my voice and cried out, he left his garment beside me and fled and got out of the house." Then she laid up his garment by her until his master came home, and she told him the same story, saying, "The Hebrew servant, whom you have brought among us, came to me to laugh at me. But as soon as I lifted up my voice and cried, he left his garment beside me and fled out of the house." As soon as his master heard the words that his wife spoke to him, "This is the way your servant treated me," his anger was kindled.* **(Genesis 39: 1-19) – English Standard Version**

On the other hand, we see a different character in the bible who goes toe to toe with lust but rejects it. Joseph may have not been blessed with wisdom like king Solomon, but it was his faithfulness in God which saved him. Joseph held unto his faith in God, so no evil spirit or temptation of sin was capable of infiltrating him.

I found something more bitter than death- the woman who is like a trap. The love she offers you will catch you like a net and her arms around you will hold you like a chain. A man who pleases God can get away, but she will catch the sinner. **(Ecclesiastes 7:26) – Good News Translation**

For if you want to save your own life, you will lose it; but if you lose your life for my sake, you will find it. Will you gain anything if you win the whole world but lose your life? Of course not! There is nothing you can give to regain your life. **(Matthew 16:25-26) – Good News Translation**

Solomon was blessed with wisdom and treasures that were beyond his imagination through his faith in God. God was once so pleased with him and made him a wealthy king. However, he lost his way and no amounts of wisdom was capable of combating against the temptations. He became so content in his wisdom that he forgot the very thing that prompted him to ask God for that wisdom. The faith that his father David taught him, which was to worship and obey God. He lost his way because he tried to be his own savior which resulted in him to lose his life to another spirit rather than giving his life to the Spirit of God.

Who can find a virtuous woman? For her worth is far above rubies. The heart of her husband safely trusts her; so he will have no lack of gain. She does him good and not evil all the days of her life. She seeks wool and flax, and willingly works with her hands. She is like the merchant ships; she brings her food from afar. She also rises while it is yet afar. She also rises while it is yet night, and provides food for her household, and a portion for her maidservants. She considers a field and buys it; from her profits she plants a vineyard. She girds herself with strength and strengthens her arms. She perceives that her merchandise is good, and her lamp does not go out by night. She stretches out her hands to the distaff, and her hand holds the spindle. She extends her hand to the poor. Yes, she reaches out her hands to the needy. She is not afraid of snow for her household, for all her household is clothed with scarlet. She makes tapestry for herself; her clothing is fine linen and purpose. Her husband is known in the gates, when he sits among the elders of the land. She makes linen garments and sells them and supplies sashes for the merchants. Strength and honor are her clothing; she shall rejoice in time to come. She opens her mouth with wisdom, and on her tongue is the law of kindness. She watches over the ways of her household and does not eat the bread of idleness. Her children rise up and call her blessed; her husband also, and he praises her: "Many daughters have done well, but you excel them all." Charm is deceitful and beauty is passing, but a woman who fears the LORD, she shall be praised. Give her of the fruit of her hands, and let her own works praise her in the gates. **(Proverbs 31:10-31) –New King James Version**

That is the last proverb written in the book of proverbs that Solomon wrote. Which is highly ironic. It is as if his own wisdom was mocking his legacy. There is a saying, "behind every successful man is a sensible woman," and Solomon threw that away for the claws of lust.

"It's funny how in this chapter called lust, the author of these pages uses fancy words to bring me down. He recites the Scriptures of God vindicating both male and female. The strategy he plays is clever because he wants the public to think he's never gotten in bed with me as well! Well author, if you incriminate me so shall I bring accusation towards you!

The author of these pages has met girls alike from the very garden of Eden. The author of these pages has picked up a guitar and played melodies that sounded like this, 'Hey there, Delilah!' Yes, the same Delilah that did and said anything to take down God's servant Samson. The author of these pages has beheaded a friend for a Herodias. The author of these pages' mocks Solomon for the 700 princesses and 300 mistresses that made him turn away from God. Who wants to make a bet that if I seduced him with all those women, he too would fall?

Author, oh author you know so much about God, right? Yet you have failed to testify that you and I have become so close. You've used my power and sorcery; magic you know very well God wouldn't permit. Oh no folks, do not worry. I do not speak about wands, for he is no magician. But the author of this book forgot to mention after they hurt him, he made it his life's mission to hurt them.

Author, oh author did you forget to mention that sweet lady you once dated? She loved and trusted you, but I came knocking on your door and just like all my victims you eventually listened. You've used lies and manipulation to make her stay and even when she had enough you kept using my powers. I unveiled my mask and you saw my true colors. The only difference is I am not ashamed of what is under my mask why don't you take off yours? Oh, that's right because the thing that's under your mask is a weak man who has no idea what to do with love. Like many of this generation, you find strength and validation in how many girls you get with. The mask that all you wear is to hide your loneliness and sinful ways. I sit at the table when all you men gossip and give props to one another for your current and next conquests. Don't worry author, you're not my only victim, maybe Jesus should have gone to a man at the well rather than the woman. It's okay though, I will always be here for you.

Author, oh author you saw me for who I was and accepted everything. Yes, I am lust, and I grant temporary and meaningless wishes. I lie and tell my victims that I'm all they want and I'm all they need. I tell them to not worry and when they swallow my pill, they become addicted. I do not sleep; I arise in the morning, jump in the afternoon and attack with full force at night. I do it because it is my mission.

The author of these pages became my friend but what a horrible friend he is! Author, oh author don't you remember all our laughs? I have taught you all you know! I taught you what to say at certain situations even if it was at the cost of my other victims!

Author, oh author why don't we talk about all those times you've spent on those perverted websites? See what the world fails to understand is how vulnerable sight is. Maybe that is why it is written:

So, if your right eye causes you to sin, take it out and throw it away! It is much better for you to lose a part of your body than to have your whole body thrown in Hell. (Matthew 5:29) – Good News Translation

Yes, that's right author, I too know the Word but are you willing to take out your right eye? I laugh because the sin of lust is too pleasurable, no one would be willing to do such an act. You know the saying, 'You are what you eat?' The more you indulge in such things, the stronger I become. Those warped into that industry live under lust so in hindsight I am everywhere. I have spell bounded them under my control and the more you indulge, the more you fall under my control! Don't you fret! Continue living the way you want to live, soon you and

I will be with all my friends together. I'm so excited for you to meet all my friends but mainly my master. You'll enjoy him!"

-The doctrine of Satan

To say that I have overcome lust's dirty tricks would be a lie. I think that is evident in the doctrine of Satan poem regarding my own behavior. It really is difficult to get rid of the old habits that we've become so accustomed doing. I'm no saint and praying to God for the definition of love was the best decision because I have not truly expressed love. I try to express love, but I feel vulnerable whenever I do. I'm not going to lie but I think the real problem is lust. I think I have consumed so much of the lustful spirit that whenever I try to express love, I can hear lust call me out saying, "You're not doing it right!" Now, this might sound strange especially because love does not always mean romantically, it could be towards friends and family. I'm not saying I am feeling lustful towards them. That is not what I am saying (ew)! However, I have noticed a shift in my spirit because lust does more than just immorally rob us of love, but it also brings on selfishness. It's as if the only thing I care about is myself and I strive to please only myself which is selfish. When God said, "love", he did not just mean for us to focus on the people in our lives but also to strangers and people that we despise. I've spent a good chunk of my life like that and before I even started writing this chapter, the Holy Spirit brought that to my attention. In 1 Corinthians 13, it defines the characteristics of love accurately. I then got to thinking if Satan wants us lusting rather than loving, it just means he's perverted what love is. If love is patient and kind; not jealous or conceited or proud; or ill-mannered, selfish, and irritable; doesn't keep a record of wrongs. What is lust really? Besides it being shown through sexual immorality, lust must have characteristics as well! I sat down one day and studied my whole being and noticed that I exhibit many of lust's personalities. I am not patient nor am I kind; I get jealous, and I am conceited, proud; ill-mannered, selfish, and irritable. Lastly, and definitely, I do keep records of everyone who's wronged me. All the while that I was searching for the definition of love, I forgot to ask God to get rid of the one thing that prevents me from receiving the one true

THE SECRET IS OUT

love. It is why in the poem by the Spirit of God, it distinctively said, *"Author, oh author love cannot be studied like the way you study books."* No, for me to get rid of the spirit of lust from myself, I need to stop studying it. It is a sly spirit for a reason and the more we converse with it, the more we empower it. It is by that very reason why Joseph ran away from his master's wife because she was not looking for a reason to not sleep with him. She had already committed herself to the lustful spirit. If the lustful spirit is ill-mannered, what good comes from speaking to it? What do I mean by all this? Well, it could mean anything. Spirits tend to infiltrate our thoughts and if we do not condemn our thoughts or feelings when we begin to feel or think in a lustful way, then we have already lost the battle. A spirit's goal is to enter our hearts because once it does, it has control over our emotions which influence our actions.

"Who can understand the human heart? There is nothing else so deceitful; it is too sick to be healed." **(Jeremiah 17:9) – Good News Translation**

It is by our free will that can reason with our thoughts, but when it comes to emotions, it becomes more difficult to control. If anyone wants to know what kind of person they are, they can just analyze their own feelings because it will tell us what our hearts are like. God tells the prophet Jeremiah that our hearts are deceitful because our feelings do not listen to reason. This becomes dangerous because even if our thoughts have come up with the conclusion to not commit an immoral sin, it is our emotions that can turn the tables on us. "It just feels right," as lust whispers to our hearts. That is a phrase that has doomed both men and women, and it will continue to condemn us if we don't get rid of all traces of lust from ourselves. Does this mean that dating is sinful? Are we not supposed to act on our emotions? No, dating is not a sin (just do not let it become a lifestyle) nor is having feelings because God made us as beings that express emotion. The thing I find tricky about this sly spirit is it can manipulate us into thinking it isn't even in us so what hope do we have?

In the same way, the Spirit also comes to help us, weak as we are. For we do not know how we ought to pray; the Spirit himself pleads with God for us in groans that words cannot express. And God, who sees into our hearts, knows what the thought of the Spirit is, because the Spirit pleads with God on behalf of his people and in accordance with his will. **(Romans 8:27) – Good News Translation**

One of the most dangerous things we can do to ourselves is medically diagnose ourselves. I've done it countless times and when I do that, I tend to go on google and search my symptoms which makes my worry go through the roof. One minute I think I just have the common cold but google then tells me I have the Ebola virus or cancer. This is no different spiritually speaking because when I received the Spirit on January 2018, I had thought that I was no longer a lustful person. Boy was I wrong! As sly and cunning as the serpent was, so is the lustful spirit and it doesn't just go away overnight. Yes, it is by God's Holy Spirit that examines our whole being but how can we ever know what it found if we never pray? This was my problem.

"Spirit of God,

I give you great thanks and praise for the wisdom you have instilled in me while I write. I have prayed to ask what love was and you have answered me, but there still remains one more thing. You warned me that understanding was not what I needed because it would not do away from what is inside of me. I have read about the many people who have fallen for lust in the Scriptures. Even king David, who slew Goliath, fell for lust's unfaithful ways. He then had a child with Bathsheba, and they decided to name him Solomon. It was you who went to Solomon and asked him what he would like from you because he was the heir to the throne. For it is written:

At Gibeon the LORD appeared to Solomon in a dream by night; and God said, "Ask! What shall I give you?" And Solomon said: "You have shown great mercy to your servant David my father, because he walked before you in truth, in righteousness, and in uprightness of heart with you; you have continued this great kindness for him, and you have given him a son to sit on his throne, as it is this day. Now, O LORD my God, you have made your servant king instead of my father David, but I am

a little child; I do not know how to go out or come in. And your servant is in the midst of your people whom you have chosen, a great people, too numerous to be numbered or counted. Therefore give to your servant an understanding heart to judge your people, that I may discern between good and evil. For who is able to judge this great people of yours?" The speech pleased the Lord, that Solomon had asked this thing. Then God said to him: "Because you have asked this thing, and have not asked long life for yourself, nor have asked riches for yourself, nor have asked the life of your enemies, but have asked for yourself understanding to discern justice, behold, I have done according to your words; see, I have given you a wise and understanding heart, so that there has not been anyone like you before you, nor shall any like you arise after you. And I have also given you what you have not asked: both riches and honor, so that there shall not be anyone like you among the kings all your days. So if you walk in my ways, to keep my statutes and my commandments, as your father David walked, then I will lengthen your days." (1 Kings 3: 5-14) – New King James Version

Solomon did not ask for riches or power but humbly asked for wisdom for the sake of being a good king to your own people. For it is written:

For wisdom is better than rubies, and all the things one may desire cannot be compared to her. "I, wisdom, dwell with prudence and find out knowledge and discretion. (Proverbs 8:11-12) – New King James Version

"The LORD possessed me in the beginning of his way, before his works of old. I was set up from everlasting, from the beginning, or ever the earth was. (Proverbs 8:22-23) – New King James Version

You were so pleased with his request that you gave him everything a king could ever desire. Unfortunately, king Solomon turned his back on you! Despite all his wisdom, it wasn't enough to save him from the sly wicked spirit lust. For it is written:

From the nations of whom the LORD had said to the children of Israel, "You shall not intermarry with them, nor they with you. Surely they

will turn away your hearts after their gods." Solomon clung to these in love. And he had seven hundred wives, princesses, and three hundred concubines; and his wives turned away his heart. For it was so, when Solomon was old, that his wives turned his heart after other gods; and his heart was not loyal to the LORD his God, as was the heart of his father David. **(1 Kings 11:2-4) – New King James Version**

Spirit of God, it was king Solomon himself who warned about certain women. For it is written:

And I find more bitter than death the woman, whose heart is snares and nets, and her hands as fetters: He who pleases God shall escape from her, but the sinner shall be trapped by her. (Ecclesiastes 7:26) – New King James Version

Spirit of God, I do not want to end up like king Solomon and turn away from you because of lust. I know you created women and you love them the same as you love us men. There is no point hiding the next few things that I have to say because you can see my heart and every single one of my thoughts. What darkness is too dark for you not to shine your glorious light and expose what lurks in the dark? For it is written:

And the light shines in the darkness, and the darkness did not comprehend it (John 1:5) – New King James Version

I have noticed that the doctrine of Satan has developed a plan to accuse me even though he no longer stands before you. I am ashamed to say this, but Spirit of God I struggle to get rid of the spirit lust. I have consumed so much lustful thoughts and emotions that I cannot get rid of it alone. I struggle with pornography and sexual immorality. I can hear lust itself speak through me saying, 'Stop talking! You do know family and friends will read this!' But I will stop at nothing to be one with you, so please help me. My God, my God who has shown me love that I still cannot comprehend, it is only by your power which will get rid of this sly spirit. How am I to grow with you when lust acts as an anchor to my connection with you? How can I ever expect to be in a healthy relationship with someone when lust has consumed my every thought? How can I expect to find a wife and love her the same way she loves me when my eyes are always committing adultery? How can I ever call myself faithful if my eyes, heart, and mind are not? How can I ever be a good father and an example to my children if I am always fighting against this disgusting spirit called lust? How can I ever live for you when I exhibit lust's destructive attributes?

Spirit of God,

I've lived such a lustful life that it feels impossible to turn back from, but I know only you can save me! For it is written:

But if the Spirit of him who raised Jesus from the dead dwells in you, he who raised Christ from the dead will also give life to your mortal bodies through His Spirit who dwells in you. (Romans 8:11) – New King James Version

Spirit of God,

I know you did not create women to be avoided. Nor did you create them to tempt us men. I've heard about unthinkable and vile things that men commit onto women; crimes against women that are done in secret. When I hear of such things, my own heart groans in agony about these disgusting acts. It even tells me that I am not capable of such things.

Spirit of God,

This prayer cannot be said with fibs and you know I am telling the truth! I believe with all my heart that I am incapable of doing such things, but it is by your words that question our hearts motives! For it is written:

Who can understand the human heart? There is nothing else so deceitful; it is too sick to be healed. (Jeremiah 17:9) - Good News Translation

Spirit of God,

If this is so, what can I trust? If my own heart can lie to me, then does that mean that I am capable of such vile sins? Who knows what us humans are capable of! Those people who have done such vile things to women in secret probably thought *they weren't capable of doing such things either. Please oh God, just get rid of this sly spirit from me! For it is written:*

There is no one who is righteous. *(Romans 3:10)* **- Good News Translation**

Spirit of God,

I need your help! Tell me what I must do. It is no secret that I have not respected women! My thoughts are always perverted and thinking lustfully towards every one of them. I behave like my very environment. Whenever I try to rebuke the spirit, it replies, 'Everyone else is doing it! There is no harm in finding someone attractive!' It's as if it is just a game to this sly spirit. The whole city and nation are under lascivious behavior! Oh, Spirit of God, please free me from this enslavement. I have heard your Spirit convicting me in the past, but I have shamelessly ignored it.

Spirit of God,

I will no longer ignore your Spirit, please answer me! Help me destroy these thoughts, or they will lead me to the world of the dead. Spirit of God, I cannot change my past, but I know if I am with you, I can reroute my future. Spirit of God you have taught me about love, but now all I ask for is to help me get rid of lust!

Amen.*"*

"Author, oh author put down your pen and listen to the sound of my voice. Close your eyes and picture this: Walking through nature's forest as the birds are chirping. You look up in the sky but beware not to look at the sun directly, for I have made its rays too bright for the human eye to face. As your eyes are closed picture breathing in and out. Describe to me what your body feels like? That's right! Author, oh author your body is at peace with its surroundings. Look down on the ground, can't you see the beautiful plants that I have made? What about the trees and those squirrels that race each other on it? Now author, watch how all that vanishes from your sight. Do not worry for I am now changing the scenery for you. Picture this: You are now walking through a battlefield! On the left-hand

side, you will see how they fought long ago before technology was a destructive force. Where on the right-hand side you will see how human beings fight today. Author, oh author look to the left-hand side and watch how the soldiers fight. A group of men have surrounded one of their enemies! They have beaten him up sensibly and are preparing to end that man's life. That one man wearing all red, who is the leader, has drawn his sword. Author, oh author do not look away, watch what happens to that man's fate! The man wearing all red decapitates the head of that man, and all his men cheer at the gruesome act. Author, oh author now turn your attention to the right-hand side. Watch as a young soldier, who has stepped on a mine, cries in agony because both his legs have been blown off. His heart is beating rapidly because he is thinking about his family! Author, oh author on Sunday evenings his family sits together and eat dinner. Laughing and sharing their week's experience. He knows he will never see his mother and father again. His heart is in his throat because he is the only child, the only child to his loving mother and father. He thinks to himself, 'Even if I survive through this, I will never be the same. All this death, all this hate, all this evil; how can I ever be the same?' His enemy finds him weeping alone, so he decides to put that young soldier out of his misery. The enemy shoots him in the forehead! Author, oh author do not look away! Watch how the insides of his head scatter over the ground and just like that he is dead. Author, oh author now look up in the sky! What do you see? The future has learned from the past and has taken their war up to the skies! What once was just regular fighting planes are now drones and jets flying in the clouds! They have polluted the air with all this destruction from their weaponry! Author, oh author tell me what do you smell now? How does your body feel now? I can hear your heart saying, 'fear and death!' Author, oh author let me tell you the smell of one dead body is already discomforting, just imagine many!

Author, oh author you may now open your eyes for you have called upon my holy name for help. Pay attention to the message I have for you. How was it that you were able to see and imagine such things yourself when you have never even picked up a gun? You have never held a sword and cut through someone's neck to have their head come off. Nor have you been in the air to control a drone, plane or jet. You have not worn your country's uniform and gone to war! All that you have seen are imposter thoughts. It was easier for you to picture the beautiful trees and birds chirping because such sights are available to everyone. They are apart of my creation, so your body felt peace and happiness to it. It's as easy as walking outside and taking a deep breath in and out just to experience it. Let me tell you and all your readers why all of you are struggling with the disgusting spirit lust. For none of you are born with it even if you were conceived because of it! The author of these pages was able to picture death and fear because he has allowed himself to see such things. It has changed the whole course of his body because of how much death and fear he has consumed. For it is written:

The lamp of the body is the eye. If therefore your eye is good, your whole body will be full of light. But if your eye is bad, your whole body will be full of darkness. If therefore the light that is in you is darkness, how great is that darkness! (Matthew 6:22) – New King James Version

**Therefore take heed that the light which is in you is not darkness. If then your whole body is full of light, having no part dark, the whole body will be full of light, as when the bright shining of a lamp gives you light."
(Luke 11:35-36) – New King James Version**

Author, oh author can't you see what you have done to your own sight? You have consumed so much lust in the things you watch! Just as you have consumed so much fear and death, so have you consumed lust. That is why you struggle with this disgusting spirit lust! For picturing nature was easy because I had made it good, but I did not create destruction and war; that was done by all of you! By your sins, you all created fear and death! Author, oh author you looked to the left and then to the right. You saw the past and the present but because fear and death are what is stored in all your hearts; war has advanced into more fear and death! It is for this reason why I told you to look up to the sky. Sin gave birth to fear and death, and the more you all indulged in it, the worse it got! It has claimed territory to even the clouds! Author, oh author fear and death has advanced and elevated themselves to the height of the skies! Author, oh author I see how you struggle day and night with lust. When you're alone in your room, it speaks to you by saying, 'no one is watching so let us go on that phone or laptop and celebrate! Do not be ashamed; everyone else does it.' It speaks to you during the day whenever you look at a woman lustfully. Anyone who listens to its voice is only giving it more power! Surely, I tell you, that spirit is as deceitful as its father, Satan! He has instructed that spirit to enter the houses of many people. Author, oh author I am not talking about your real homes. I'm talking about all the people's hearts. Those are the houses that I speak of. Lust cannot storm into anyone's home without the homeowner's permission. It knocks politely at the front door, and it is up to the homeowner to not let it in! Author, oh author I can hear your heart asking, 'How does it knock? Are our eyes the door?' Surely I tell you author, Satan has orchestrated a meeting place daily with all his unclean spirits. They sit at a round table discussing many things. They have developed a plan to not only enter the eyes but the ears too! For it is written:

Gossip is so tasty! How we love to swallow it! (Proverbs 26:22) – Good News Translation

It is in what you hear that also acts as the knock on the door! For if you listen to more lust, then you have already tasted it and allowed it in! It gossips with your heart and the heart is forced to listen. The heart has no intelligence to know that it has absorbed darkness. It opens its mouth like an infant opens its mouth to be fed by his or her parents. The heart puts its trust in the homeowner to feed it love, but if the homeowner has not known love then they are both doomed! The heart will complain to the homeowner by saying, 'You have deceived me why have you allowed me to see such things, now I am craving for more.' While the homeowner will reply, 'No, you deceived me how could you allow me to desire such things.' They will argue with one another while lust drags both of them down to the world of the dead. Author, oh author I have taught you that love comes from me and to know love is only through me because I am true love! Guard your heart for it does not know any better! If you choose to consume more lust, it will consume you! But if you choose to deny it, it will begin to hate you and flee. For it is written:

Keep your heart with all vigilance, for from it flow the springs of life. (Proverbs 4:23) – English Standard Version

Keep me from paying attention to what is worthless; be good to me, as you have promised. (Psalms 119:37) – Good News Translation

You asked what you should trust if not your heart? Author, oh author have you forgotten what the Spirit produces? For it provides self-control needed to combat this sly spirit. Those who put their trust in me will be made new! For it is written:

Trust in the Lord with all your heart and lean not on your own understanding; In all your ways acknowledge him, and he shall direct your paths. **(Proverbs 3:5-6) – New King James Version**

Author, I am telling you the truth! It is by the power of my Word in which you will seize all sly comments made by that spirit or any other. For it is written:

For the Word of God is living and powerful, and sharper than any two-edged sword, piercing even to the division of soul and spirit, and of joints and marrow, and is a discerner of the thoughts and intents of the heart. And there is no creature hidden from his sight, but all things are naked and open to the eyes of him to whom we must give account. (Hebrews 4:12-13) – New King James Version

Author, oh author I can hear your heart asking, 'What then can I not watch or listen to? How do I know what darkness is and what is light?' Author, oh author have you not wondered how you were able to picture such violence? All that death and fear that your thoughts conjured up when I asked you to picture it! It was not new images that your mind presented so vividly but rather old memories that your mind has stored up. Author, oh author you were able to feel fear and death because your heart has also stored such things in itself because of what you have allowed it to see. For how would you have the knowledge of fear and death without not exposing yourself to fear and death? Surely, I tell you the enemy has knowledge of this too! He has devised a way to take the lewd behavior of the past and present it in today's day and age! He has advanced his reach on all of you and elevated his weaponry up to the skies for all to see! It is by this reason why lust is not only found in shameful things like pornography but also in television shows and news reports! It has expanded its reach in movies that all you are so gladly entertained by. Author, oh author the sly spirit that follows Satan's doctrine has influenced celebrities and musicians which is why they sing and gossip about lustful things! Beware and guard yourselves! It is only by the Spirit in which will convict and warn you to lock your doors! You must not allow it into your homes!

Who has seen the face of lust? Surely, I tell you if I showed you its true form you would be in pure disgust! Its feet do not point forward, but backward yet it walks forward! Author, oh author use wisdom for the way it walks signifies disturbing perversion! Its posture has no shape because it has no spine to stabilize it. It spends day and night blasting disgusting and foul things from its mouth because of its shameless ways. It does not eat for the sole purpose of ever becoming full but devours anything because its stomach disintegrates everything due to all the acid inside of it. That is why the spirit of lust is without appetite so whenever you indulge in it, it leaves the person feeling empty and unsatisfied. Its eyes are directionless, so they just wander in all directions. The left eye does not follow what the right eye is doing and vice versa! Author, oh author this spirit is a ghoul and its pervasion knows no limits. It comes in all sorts of shapes and sizes, and those who have chosen to submit to it are doomed to walk where it is destined to go! For it is written:

Their bodies waste away to nothing; you can see all their bones; they are about to go to the world of the dead. (Job 33:21-22) – Good News Translation

Bury them all in the ground; bind them in the world of the dead. (Job 40:13) – Good News Translation

Author, oh author I have seen those who have committed to this spirit! For the steps needed to turn back are difficult for both man and woman but plausible through me! But who is it that has the authority to bring people back from the world of the dead? It is only I who has such power! For it is written:

Perhaps an angel may come to their aid– one of God's thousands of angels, who remind us of our duty. In mercy, the angel will say, 'Release them! They are not to go down to the world of the dead. Here is the ransom to set them free.' Their bodies will grow young and strong again; when they pray, God will answer; they will worship God with joy; God will set things right for them again. Each one will say in public, 'I have sinned. I have not done right, but God spared me. He kept me from going to the world of the dead, and I am still alive.' God does all this again and again; each one saves a person's life and gives him the joy of living. (Job 33:23-30) – Good News Translation

Author, oh author I have heard your prayer, but you must not let the enemy fool you! This spirit has manipulated the world into thinking that the cause of lust comes from women! I see how the world treats women and the unjust acts that are done to them! Author, oh author have you not wondered why the serpent went after Eve instead of Adam? He knew the glorious presence Eve was blessed with. He targeted her to give birth to the lustful spirit into the world! For a child is not born without the womb of a woman! For it is written:

I will make you and the woman hate each other; her offspring and yours will always be enemies. Her offspring will crush your head, and you will bite her offspring's heel. (Genesis 3:15) - Good News Translation

It is by this very reason why women are blamed for things like lust, but there is a greater force at work! It was part of Satan's plan to target women because once they are targeted so are their offspring! No man or woman whether righteous or wicked are born without the womb of a woman. Even my own Son came into the earth this way, but he was conceived by my Spirit rather than a man's sperm. For it is written:

This was how the birth of Jesus Christ took place. His mother Mary was engaged to Joseph, but before they were married, she found out that she was going to have a baby by the Holy Spirit. (Matthew 1:18) - Good News Translation

The serpent went after the most beautiful thing in the garden because I made man first from my love and through that very same love, I took a piece out of him and made even more love! For it is written:

Then the LORD God made the man fall into a deep sleep, and while he was sleeping, he took out one of the man's ribs and closed up the flesh. He formed a woman out of the rib and brought her to him. Then the man said, "At last, here is one of my own kind- Bone taken from my bone, and flesh from my flesh. Woman is her name because she was taken out of man. (Genesis 2:21-23) - Good News Translation

It was at that very time where the serpent went to the most beautiful thing in the garden and tempted her so that he could give birth to something darker! Does this mean that it is the fault of women that lust exists? Anyone who thinks such things has already shamed their own mothers! The spirit of lust has perverted love and seeks to plant its seed within all of you! Surely you remember when I spoke it upon you that birth represents firsts! Satan is aware of the Scriptures which says, 'the woman's offspring will crush the head of the serpent.' So the snake attempts to plant its seed in them to stomp the heads of both man and woman! Author, oh author for you have not heard nor seen the cries of women! Just like you will never be able to feel what that little girl in Tanzania feels! You should see how the spirit lust torments them! Have you seen them when they are alone at night? Some of them soak their pillows with their tears and ask themselves, 'Am I even beautiful? Will I ever be loved?' Author, oh author some of them cry all night long from the pressures of this world. They know men look at them lustfully so their spirits are saddened because they feel like they must conform to the world's sickness. They long to protect themselves but also want to be loved and respected. Unlike men, they do not put themselves on their own thrones! Their spirits seek for their fleshes attention, but their flesh rejects their own spirit because it is being deceived by lustful spirits. Author, oh author for women do not battle flesh and spirit-like men do! Their spirit has to go chasing after their own flesh because the flesh has yet to recognize their spirits beauty! For as beautiful as they are on the outside; what makes them more beautiful is what is on the inside! That is why a child is nursed inside the womb for 9 months and the mother shares everything with her child! Men will not and will never be able to know such a connection because their flesh and spirit are both egoistic! Their flesh and spirit refuse to chase after one another! The lustful spirit tells the woman they must dress a certain way; walk a certain way; look a certain way and talk a certain way! If the woman listens to this sly spirit, it will begin to plant its seed within the woman! If the enemy corrupts the beauty within the woman, he knows he can continue the cycle with the offspring! Surely, I tell you there are some who attempt to fight this lustful spirit because they have had enough of its torment! For it is written:

Happy are those who remain faithful under trials because when they succeed in passing such a test, they will receive as their reward the life which God has promised to those who love him. If we are tempted by such trials, we must not say, "This temptation comes from God." For God cannot be tempted by evil, and he himself tempts no one. But we are tempted when we are drawn away and trapped by our own evil desires. Then our evil desires conceive and give birth to sin; and sin, when it

is full grown, gives birth to death. (James 1:12-15) - Good News Translation

However, this spirit has not corrupted just women but also men! Surely, I tell you some men have given themselves over to lust and prey on women that are trying to fight off such spirits. For it is written:

They will be treacherous, reckless, and swollen with pride; they will love pleasure rather than God; they will hold to the outward form of our religion but reject its real power. Keep away from such people. Some of them go into people's house and gain control over weak women who are burdened by the guilt of their sins and driven by all kinds of desires, women who are always trying to learn but who can never come to know the truth. (2 Timothy 3:4-7) - Good News Translation

Shame on these kinds of men! I have seen them manipulate and shamefully disgrace women. They do this because they have lost all sense to the shameless spirit lust. For it is written:

And even though I am far away from you in body, still I am there with you in spirit; and as though I were there with you. I have in the name of our Lord Jesus already passed judgment on the man who has done this terrible thing. As you meet together, and I meet with you in my spirit, by the power of our Lord Jesus present with us, you are to hand this man over to Satan for his body to be destroyed, so that his spirit may be saved in the Day of the Lord. (1 Corinthians 5:3-5) - Good News Translation

Author, oh author tell all women this:

'The Spirit of God has not condemned any of you. All condemnation is done by this very world because they judge how you look, how you dress, how you talk and how you behave. Surely, I tell you those who search for me have found the antidote to the sly and disgusting spirit lust! Be free from its torment and conviction! You are to present yourselves as women that love God! Satan planned to have a target on all of you because as the world behaves lustfully, he has tiptoed past you to pervert what is within you. However, I must warn all of you! Your flesh will only covet what you place before it. Your hearts will have no choice to

deceive you through emotions because of what you feed it. If you desire the world, it is the things of the world that you will receive! For it is written:

If you plant in the field of your natural desires, from it you will gather the harvest of death; if you plant in the field of the Spirit, from the Spirit, you will gather the harvest of eternal life. (Galatians 6:8) - Good News Translation

Satan's doctrine has targeted your worth and will always use the disgusting spirit lust to get all of you questioning your beauty and worth. This filthy spirit will knock on your doors and say, 'I have come to provide the beauty you seek! Let me in and I will redesign not only the inside of your home but renovate the outside too! I promise I do not charge anything!' But women, do not listen to it! Behind its back pocket is a bill you cannot afford to pay! It won't show you its blueprints but opens its mouth and speaks uncontrollably making false promises! Those who listen to its voice and open their doors willingly have already put themselves on the route to the world of the dead. Those who listen to its voice will only desire men that their flesh seeks but inside their spirits will cry out warnings. It is by this very reason that all your hearts will be broken! Women! Look at the woman at the well! She kept going day after day seeking to be loved, seeking for a second chance! The more she went, the thirstier she got! That upset spirit that keeps chasing after your own flesh will be muzzled by the spirit lust! That wicked spirit will violently duct tape your spirit's mouth! It will tie it down and throw it at the bottom of the basement! That sly spirit will bolt the basement door shut so that you cannot hear it! It will then claim ownership of your home and consume everything within! You will feel lost and empty. You will ask yourself, 'Why does it feel like something is missing?' But that sadden spirit is unable to respond because you neglected it and it now is trapped in the darkness of your basement! This is what will happen to women who give themselves to that disgusting spirit lust!

Women you must not converse with this spirit! It is a liar and will always lie! It only fears one thing! For it is only by my Spirit that can get rid of its hold on you! There is not one unclean and vile spirit that is too much for me! For it is written:

Do you believe that there is only one God? Good! The demons also believe- and tremble with fear. (James 2:19) - Good News Translation

For the house that has been defiled will be made new through me! Always be at guard, women! For the spirit will influence and use weak men that have given themselves to it to either tempt or pressure you! For you now know the attributes of those who have given themselves to this sly and disgusting spirit! It is perverted and shameless! Stay away from such men! I have created you all with emotion so sweet, honey weeps with jealousy. I have created you with a womb so that you may be blessed with children. I have created you so that you may be an honorable wife to your husband and your husband be a loving and loyal man to you. With that union, you two will serve and love me so that your children may know the truth. Your child will call you, 'mother,' because you are full of loving kindness. You will raise them to serve and know me so that they too may stomp on the head of the serpent. Women do not follow the ways of the world. Your worth is envied by lust, it seeks after you so that you lose sight. Women, if you want to continue drinking the water from the well, you will continue to thirst. I offer you a new deal. Those who drink the water I give will never thirst again.'

Author, oh author write this upon your heart and never forget it:

As vile and deceitful as my heart is, I give and dedicate my heart, body, mind, and soul to the Lord! For as perverted and sinful as I have been, through the Lord I am made new! For I once disrespected women even though the Spirit of God convicted me of such behavior; The Spirit of God has shown me the face of lust and the love he has for women! To disrespect them now is to disrespect that love that God made through them! For it is written:

What I say is this: let the Spirit direct your lives, and you will not satisfy the desires of human nature. For what our human nature wants is opposed to what the Spirit wants, and what the Spirit wants is opposed to what our human nature wants. These two are enemies, and this means that you cannot do what you want to do. If the Spirit leads you, then you are not subject to the Law. (Galatians 5:16–18) - Good News Translation

Author, oh author I have answered all that you have prayed about! For those who put their trust in me shall reap the gifts of the Spirit! Those who reject and refuse to converse with that lustful spirit shall no longer struggle with its temptations. Follow the guidelines I have given you and guard your house with caution! For it is written:

In the Lord's name, I warn you: do no continue to live like the heathen, whose thoughts are worthless and whose minds are in the dark. They have no part in the life that God gives, for they are completely ignorant and stubborn. They have lost all feeling of shame; they give themselves over to vice and do all sorts of indecent things without restraint. That was not what you learned about Christ! You certainly heard about him, and as his followers, you were taught the truth that is in Jesus. So, get rid of your old self, which made you live as you used to- the old self that was being destroyed by its deceitful desires. Your hearts and minds must be made completely new, and you must put on the new self, which is created in God's likeness and reveals itself in the true life that is upright and holy. **(Ephesians 4:17-24) - Good News Translation**

For this reason, I fall on my knees before the Father from whom every family in heaven and on earth receives its true name. I ask God from the wealth of his glory to give you power through his Spirit to be strong in your inner selves, and I pray that Christ will make his home in your hearts through faith. I pray that you may have your roots and foundation in love, so that you, together with all God's people, may have the power to understand how broad and long, how high and deep is Christ's love. Yes, may you come to know his love- although it can never be fully known- and so be completely filled with the very nature of God. **(Ephesians 3:14-19) - Good News Translation**

Author, oh author you may now go in peace for your house has been inspected. Be on guard of the sly and deceitful spirit! For they will seek to revisit you but if you remain in me, they will flee!"

- Spirit of God

"Spirit of God,

I want to thank you for everything. My mind is satisfied with what you have revealed to not only me but the readers as well. For you held my hand in the journey of this chapter.

Spirit of God, you already know where I've come from and what's scary but also amazing is that there is still more for me to receive. Live inside my house and my heart will honor you. For when you send over your holy mailman I will forever and always receive it with diligence. For it is written:

How can young people keep their lives pure? By obeying your commands. With all my heart I try to serve you; keep me from disobeying your commandments. I keep your law in my heart, so that I will not sin against you. I praise you, O LORD; teach me your ways. I will repeat aloud all the laws you have given. (Psalms 119:9-13) – Good News Translation

Spirit of God, when I started writing about this chapter my focus was on relationships, but you wanted to teach me something deeper than companionship. For when you spoke about true love, you exposed the world's definition of love. For love is far more than just human companionship. Love comes from you and we struggle to understand it because we have been lied to by a lying tyrant. Our definition of love; the world's definition of it has been manipulated and perverted. But you showed mercy towards my knowledge and feelings, and, in that mercy, you revealed love. For it is written:

But I tell you who hear me: Love your enemies, do good to those who hate you, bless those who curse you, and pray for those who mistreat you. If anyone hits you on one cheek, let him hit the other one too; if someone takes your coat, let him have your shirt as well. (Luke 6:27-29) – Good News Translation

Spirit of God,

What kind of words are these? There is not one moment where I have exhibited such things. What kind of love is this? For it is written:

Then they spat in his face and beat him; and others struck him with the palms of their hands, saying, "Prophesy to us, Christ! Who is the one who struck uou?" (Matthew 26:67-68) – New King James Version

And they stripped him and put a scarlet robe on him. When they had twisted a crown of thorns, they put it on his head, and a reed in his right hand. And they bowed the knee before him and mocked him, saying, "Hail, King of the Jews!" Then they spat on him and took the reed and struck him on the head. **(Matthew 27:28-30) – New King James Version**

So then Pilate took Jesus and scourged him. **(John 19:1) – New King James Version**

Spirit of God,

I read all this, and my heart became disturbed, but you did all that for us. Not once did you cuss or plot out revenge. For it is written:

Then Jesus said, "Father, forgive them, for they do not know what they do." And they divided his garments and cast lots. (Luke 23:34) – New King James Version

And because of this love, you died fully accepting all the pain, insults and humiliation for our sake. You possessed no pride, being who you are, you allowed yourself to be hit and tortured by sinners. You allowed them to think that they had beaten you because we know death is the end, but you are the first and the last. You are the one who has lived forever and because of this, death could not hold you. For it is written:

But the truth is that Christ has been raised from death, as a guarantee that those who sleep in death will also be raised. For just as death came by means of a man, in the same way the rising from death comes by means of a man. For just as all people die because of their union with Adam, in the same way all will be raised to life because of their union with Christ. (1 Corinthians 15:20-22)- Good News Translation

Spirit of God, due to your actions, we received the Good News which inspired the movement of the faithful. For the faithful went out to the world and preached the original perfect love without fearing death. For it is written:

So he sent and had John beheaded in prison. **(Matthew 14:10) – New King James Version**

They kept stoning Stephen as he called out to the Lord, "Lord Jesus, receive my spirit!" He knelt down and cried out in a loud voice, "Lord! Do not remember this sin against them!" He said this and died. And Saul approved of his murder. **(Acts 7:59-60) – Good News Translation**

Now about that time Herod the king stretched out his hand to harass some from the church. Then he killed James the brother of John with the sword. **(Acts 12:1-2) – New King James Version**

Still others had trial of mocking and scourging, yes, and of chains and imprisonment. They were stoned, they were sawn in two, were tempted, were slain with the sword. They wandered about in sheepskins and goatskins, being destitute, afflicted, tormented— of whom the world was not worthy. They wandered in deserts and mountains, in dens and caves of the earth. **(Hebrews 11:36-38) – New King James Version**

What a story the persecuted had to go through but in reality, they did not live it for the story but rather a journey to see the One whose love is true and perfect.

Spirit of God,

Thank you for revealing to me the truth about love because it did not exist in me. As a matter of fact, it could not exist in me without you! For when you spoke of true love, my heart trembled at the poem you helped me write because I am selfish, hateful, vindictive, impulsive, impatient and evil. I have always had trouble showing love to my brothers, parents and friends. So, what hope did I ever have in showing it to a companion? When my teacher was that disgusting sly spirit named lust!

I was so young when it happened. I saw my friends holding hands and kissing their companions. They gossiped with one another; they gossiped with me, but I had nothing to share with them because I was raised in a home that honored your name. But my God, my God I forgot your teachings; the teachings my mother spent so long instilling in me. She taught me your hymns and told me to cover my eyes from evil, but I grew curious. It was taught to me at such a young age, but I was so rebellious, so I went to that dance. Spirit of God, everyone was at that dance and when I arrived, I saw her smile and her beautiful eyes. She came to me and grabbed my hands and said, 'dance with me.' So, I danced with her and my whole body was filled with passion and delight. She whispered in my ear, 'Put your hands around my waist.' And my heart began to beat faster, not aware that I was falling under her spell. I looked her deep in her eyes and she did the same to mine. Fingers locked, nose to nose as our lips locked.

Spirit of God,

We kissed and my flesh called it perfect. She made me promise to stay by her side and if I did that, it was true love. I obeyed but something inside me cried out, 'My child, my child run away!' But I was so infatuated by her voice. She taught me how to dance; she taught me how to touch; she taught me how to kiss. I will never forget that first dance, touch and kiss. But I heard something inside me cry out, 'Come back to me my beautiful creation!' However, my flesh said to itself, 'Finally I have a story to share for I am now apart of the dancing, touching and kissing.'

Spirit of God, our dance was to a slow song, but little did I know that was going to be our last slow dance. My God, my God after that it was all fast songs. I don't remember any of the songs nor the lyrics because they were so fast. I adjusted to her pace because everyone was dancing at her pace. My God, my God I did all this to impress her because she called it true love. Then one night she proposed an idea. She grabbed a hold of me and said, 'I'm going to be your first.' I was so scared but excited because I would have another story to share with all my friends who had done this. But I heard something inside me, 'My child, my child run away for she is trying to steal something precious from you.' But I ignored the voice. She proceeded to lick my ear-lob and with her saliva her tongue reached my neck. I couldn't resist and I allowed her to be my first. Spirit of God, I did not know what I was getting myself into. I gave her my word and after it was finished, she looked at me and told me that I was hers forever. I agreed and ran back to my home. I gathered all my expensive valuables. I was preparing an offering for her by exchanging my belongings for a ring. But I heard a voice inside me say, 'My child, my child run away from her. She is leading you like an ox on the way to be slaughtered, like a deer prancing into a trap. Where an arrow would pierce your heart. You are like a bird going in a net. You do not know that your life is in danger. My child, my child, do not allow her into your house! She will destroy it and leave it in ruins and that is where you will be buried.'

Spirit of God, I truly believed it was real love, so I sold all my belongings. I sold it for a ring and proposed to her. I was filled with joy when she said yes. But I should have known something was wrong when said we had to marry in secret. We then went to the courtyard and I signed the marriage certificate, but once I had signed it and turned around, she was gone. Spirit of God, I searched day and night for her but could never find her. I thought she was the one, so I asked around for her, but no one knew of her. I asked myself, 'Where could she have gone?' My heart was broken and confused. 'Not even a letter to provide me closure?' I thought to myself. My heart was so broken and hurt, I decided to numb it by finding someone else. So, I met many other women, but I was shocked to find out that they too had the same story. They married the one who taught them how to dance, touch and kiss. But as soon as they signed the marriage certificate and turned around the man disappeared from them.

Spirit of God, so I wept with these women and with some I committed adultery with them, but it did not mend our broken hearts. I then remembered the voice that used to warn me but I could not feel its gentle voice inside me. This is what devastated me because although I ignored it, I found comfort in its warmth. I called out to it saying, 'What is your name? I am all alone and in need of comfort. I know I neglected you but if you are still near can you please come back?' It was at that moment when you spoke back to me. For it is written:

"So I will restore to you the years that the swarming locust has eaten, the crawling locust, the consuming locust, and the chewing locust, my great army which I sent among you. You shall eat in plenty and be satisfied, and praise the name of the LORD you God, who dealt wondrously with you; and my people shall never be put to shame. (Joel 2:25-26) – New King James Version

'My name is deliverer and rescuer, Holy God who made heaven and earth. I will lift you from the world of the dead! Worry not of your belongings down there because they are of no use anymore. For it is written:

Now when he said these things, he cried with a loud voice, "Lazarus, come forth!" Now he who had died came out bound hand and foot with graveclothes, and his face was wrapped with a cloth. Jesus said to them, "Loose him, and let him go." (John 11:43-44) -New King James Version

Take off the graveclothes for they represent your brokenness, sadness, regret, guilt and sins. For I see in your heart you are looking at the past and grieve at how lust influenced you. It robbed you of how to feel and you have forgotten how to express love but worry not! I will clothe you in holy white linen for they represent renewal. I will teach you true love through me because I have always loved you. For that woman you married was not a human, but the spirit well known as lust! And I will reveal to you its true face, and no longer will you desire it. I have nullified your marriage certificate with that disgusting spirit lust! It has fooled many of your generation. I will teach onto you patience, self control, kindness and you will find peace and joy. You will know and experience such things because of your faithfulness but most importantly you will know love. You will love not just yourself but the people in your life, even those who hate you and you will love those whom you declared hate to!' For it is written:

Therefore if there is any consolation in Christ, if any comfort of love, if any fellowship of the Spirit, if any affection and mercy, fulfill my joy by being like-minded, having the same love, being of one accord, of one mind. (Philippians 2:1-2) – New King James Version'

Spirit of God, I have told my story, not like you didn't know it, but I wrote it for those reading this. For I can say more but I have addressed what needed to be said and revealed to all what you have done for me. You defined in me true love, rebuked hate, defined lust, rebuked lust so I close this prayer by saying thank you Jesus. Although I thought all was lost, you renewed something new in me. Love is truly the greatest thing we all have and since I am still learning more about love, I vow to seek out your heart. For I name this prayer, the prayer of a man after God's own heart.

Amen."

CHAPTER 8

LAW VS FAITH

We have finally arrived at the third conflicting chapter and I selected this to be the last one for a good reason. I needed everyone to understand the conflict within (flesh vs spirit) as the first because faith in God starts within. Love vs lust was the second conflict discussed because it is through the Holy Spirit where we tame both flesh and spirit. By taming both flesh and spirit we are no longer distracted by their feud and become one with God. It was then when the Holy Spirit spoke through me in the Spirit of God poems to help the readers and myself know what true love is. The knowledge of love may be comforting but it is when we become one with it that makes it perfect due to the relationship with the Holy Spirit. As we can see, without the Holy Spirit the flesh and spirit does what it wants because it cannot know, nor execute true love which sets us back to the conflict of the flesh and spirit. Carrying on the journey, we are now sitting in front of the law vs faith conflict which doesn't sound conflicting, but they are pivotal in our journey with God. I say it is pivotal because the Holy Spirit has taught me friendship between flesh and spirit which will tame the conflict between law and faith. Just like flesh and spirit were once sworn enemies, we will find that the law and our faith were once sworn enemies but now because of God's love, they work in union to live for Christ. Pause. "What in the world did he just say?" is what most people will think when they read what I just wrote. If that is the reaction, then I have everyone exactly where I want them because it is the reason why this chapter is titled law vs faith.

It would be a lie to say that when I first wrote this chapter, I knew what I was talking about. As a matter of fact, the very sentences that everyone is reading right now are being written after editorial and revision. Yes, I sort cheated, but I will not lie to anyone because I made a vow when I wrote this book to speak earnestly and honestly.

And the tongue is a fire, a world of iniquity. The tongue is so set among our members that it defiles the whole body and sets on fire the course of nature; and it is set on fire by hell. For every kind of beast and bird, of reptile and creature of the sea, is tamed and has been tamed by mankind. But no man can tame the tongue. It is an unruly evil, full of deadly poison. With it we bless our God and Father, and with it we curse men, who have been in the similitude of God. Out of the same mouth proceed blessing and cursing. My brethren, these things ought not to be so. **(James 3:6-10) – New King James Version**

My tongue has done works in favour of God and wicked works in favour of the doctrine of Satan. What do I mean by that? In my life, I have lied and used deceitful tactics that involved manipulation to get what I want, but I refuse to continue living like that. This book is my conversation with Jesus Christ so if I lie to all, I lie to him. I could not in good conscious of the Holy Spirit lie to any of the readers which is why I have no problem bashing and humiliating myself through the embarrassing sinful acts I have done. That courage is provided to me by the Holy Spirit so that all can know I do not write this from the angle of looking good but for glory of Jesus Christ. This book has been received onto whomever by faith so that all can know the oneness of God, the Holy Spirit and Jesus Christ who are all one being. They are all the same just as I, the author and Innocent Nangoma, are the same. Two narrators speaking in different tongues; one of prayer in plea to God, and the other wearing the cap of the author narrating the flow of this book. But I am the same beating heart reaching out to Christ through the Holy Spirit speaking to the Father, who has one beating heart. This is the law of God and the law of our natures. Now that comparison wasn't written as a proclamation that I am like God, but I used that as an example to help our human minds understand the oneness of God the Father, Jesus Christ the Son and the Holy Spirit.

My interpretation and understanding of the law of God was so miscued that when I came back to read this chapter my head began to hurt. I could not leave anyone hanging on the notion that the definition of God's law is the same definition of what humanity describes it to be. There are two core pieces of the law that are forever true. It's creation and its existence. The law is created for a reason and that reason defines its purpose. As a matter of fact, to make things much more interesting, the law is no different than flesh and spirit! For it serves both a purpose and desires pleasure just as we do. In the terms of humanity, we create the law for the purpose of order whereas it pleasures in finding justice and justice is executed by punishment. That is the law of the law. But I will discuss the difference between God's law and humanities law later on in this chapter, which I did not screw up because it was handled by the Spirit of God. This strange and out of character introduction had to be done so that I can explain what I did not understand in the past. It is to talk about the law of God and what it means to believers and non-believers.

Before the creation of this book and far past January 2018 (when I received the Holy Spirit). I saw Jesus Christ, God, the Word as the open discussion of hell. Because it was taught onto me that the laws of God have judged me and deemed me unworthy.

"And this is the inscription that was written: MENE, MENE, TEKEL, UPHARSIN. This is the interpretation of each word. MENE: God has numbered your kingdom and finished it. TEKEL: You have been weighed in the balances and found wanting. **(Daniel 5:25-27) – New King James Version**

I'm doing it again (over exaggerating or bending the truth)! Because my life was not subject to condemnation, but it was I who felt condemnation which made me feel judged. But this was the problem and might be the problem of many believers or non-believers. They do not feel love and the reason why they do not feel it is because they do not know it. I only knew temporary things and what I saw the law to be was an eternal condemnation of my whole being. A perfect way of understanding what

I just said is by analyzing how our laws (earthly laws; or man-made laws) make us feel. When someone applies for a job, the first thing they must do is fill out a job application form. One thing an employer, who is looking to hire, will look for is the past of the applicant. Questions like who, what, when, where and why are pressed onto the applicant of their professional history. These questions help the employer determine whether or not they feel the person is qualified for the job or even worthy of the position. But there is also another section within the job application form that will either make or break the employer's decision. That section is where it questions if someone has a criminal record or not. A criminal record pertains to the law and it is the law that defines whether someone is good or bad. As unfortunate as that sounds, an employer will not feel inclined to hire someone who has a criminal record. Even if it was a petty crime, the stigma exists and subconsciously they will rather hire someone who is without a record. What does this have to do with God's law? Because if anyone has done the due diligence of reading the Old Testament that is what they will feel like. Those feelings will formulate into thoughts which will target how we think of God. I gave the employer and applicant scenario as an example to remind everyone what kind of power the law holds. Someone who has not broken the law are called law abiding citizens whereas someone who has broken the law are called criminals. It is as simple as that and there are no buts or ifs, and to the law that is called justice. Unless there is a retrial of some sort, but the very principle still stands and to the law (if it remains to be the law), it has received its pleasure through its purpose.

For as many as are of the works of the law are under the curse; for it is written, "Cursed is everyone who does not continue in all things which are written in all things which in the book of the law, to do them." But that no one is justified by the law in the sight of God is evident, for "the just shall live by faith." Yet the law is not of faith, but "the man who does them shall live by them." Christ redeemed us from the curse of the law, having become a curse for us (for it is written "Cursed is everyone who hangs on a tree"), that the blessing of Abraham might come upon the Gentiles in Christ Jesus, that we might receive the promise of the Spirit through faith. **(Galatians 3:10-14) – New King James Version**

Just as our man-made laws have two concepts to them so does God's. But because of John 1:1-5, we know that God was the first to establish these two concepts.

Jesus Christ is the same yesterday, today, and forever. **(Hebrews 13:8) – New King James Version**

I quoted this specific Scripture because nothing in the world remains constant. We are always changing, adapting and conforming to different cultures, lifestyles, politics, laws and even religions. We do this to accommodate our nature, which by now everyone should know is sinful. But Jesus Christ has not and will not change because he is without sin. Perfection cannot change. But I can feel my sinful nature playing devil's advocate with that phrase because Satan was made perfect but changed. See the thing is, Satan was made perfect in his talent of worship but was not perfect as a whole spiritual being which is why he is what he is today. Whereas God is omnipotent, omnipresent, and omniscience which details his perfection. The devil was none of these things! Since this is so, then the law of God was not made by mistake. As I mentioned in the chapter Battling Egypt and Babylon, the law was made so that we may come to know what sin is. But just as I said in this chapter, the law itself has a law that it cannot deny. It has a nature that it cannot refute, and that nature exists because of sin. The law of sin demands death. ("For the wages of sin is death")-Romans 6:23 defines the entire law of sin which is why we read things like: If a woman was caught in adultery they were stoned or if a person cursed their own mother they would be put to death. I'm only giving a few examples from the top of my head of some of these barbaric punishments written in the Word. So, what's changed? Did God change? The answer to that question is the covenant changed but God never did.

And the LORD God commanded the man, saying, "Of every tree of the garden you may freely eat; but of the tree of the knowledge of good and evil you shall not eat, for in the day that you eat of it you shall surely die" **(Genesis 2:15-17) – New King James Version**

Does anyone remember this dialogue between Adam and God? Well-the law, sin and all that is of our nature traces back to this one event. The moment we ate from that tree, we disobeyed and sinned which caused spiritual death. As the story went on in Genesis, God eventually created a covenant between Israel and himself after he rescued them from Egypt. The law was included in the covenant which was to act as the physical entity to save them from themselves. But remember God does not change but people do and although the Israelites agreed to the covenant, they broke the covenant (the law). Now since the law demands death, they had to do this thing called animal sacrifices. They did this for the sake of their sins so that they would be forgiven because the law of sin wanted death (It's a nature that cannot deny itself which is why it is the law). That is why God made his law for the people so that we would follow it and avoid death (to combat against the nature of sin). But as the story goes, they kept sinning and would sacrifice animals left, right and center and this became pointless. Now I keep saying 'we', but if someone is not of Jewish descendants (like myself) then the Torah (Jewish law) should not mean anything to a non-Jewish descendant. But does everyone remember the explanation in the chapter battling Egypt and Babylon? The representation of nations! Although the Scriptures refer Israel, it was God who passed down the law to Israel because they were the first to acknowledge God. Since we all are God's creations, the law passed down was in fact intended for the Jews, but the principle of the law applied to all nations.

"And when he has made an end of atoning for the Holy Place, the tabernacle of meeting, and the altar, he shall bring the live goat. Aaron shall lay both his hands on the head of the live goat, confess over it all the iniquities of the children of Israel, and all their transgressions, concerning all their sins, putting them on the head of the goat, and shall send it away into the wilderness by the hand of a suitable man. The goat shall bear on itself all their iniquities to an uninhabited land; and he shall release the goat in the wilderness. "Then Aaron shall come into the tabernacle of meeting, shall take off the linen garments which he put on when he went into the Holy Place, and shall leave them there. And he shall wash his body with water in a holy place, put on his garments, come out and offer his burnt offering and the burnt offering of the people, and make atonement

for himself and for the people. The fat of the sin offering he shall burn on the altar. And he who released the goat as the scapegoat shall wash his clothes and bathe his body in water, and afterward he may come into the camp. The bull for the sin offering and the goat for the sin offering, whose blood was brought in to make atonement in the Holy Place, shall be carried outside the camp. And they shall burn in the fire their skins, their flesh, and their offal. Then he who burns them shall wash his clothes and bathe his body in water, and afterward he may come into the camp. **(Leviticus 16:20-28) – New King James Version**

You do not want sacrifices, or I would offer them; you are not pleased with burnt offerings. My sacrifice is a humble spirit, O God; you will not reject a humble and repentant heart. **(Psalms 51:16-17) - Good News Translation**

God was fed up with Israel and their fake offerings. He looked in their hearts and saw they were only doing it because it had just become something of a routine. The initial creation of the law (Old Testament) was made out of love so that we would be saved but we did not acknowledge that love. We look at God's Old Testament laws and judge it as barbaric, cruel and evil but what eludes us is that what we think of that law is what our nature exhibits. If we want to test out our sinful nature, its quite easy. Watch movies like 'Law Abiding Citizen,' or 'John Wick,' and see how satisfied we become when the main characters enforce their own justice. Those are movies that I love myself so don't worry I'm not trying to throw shade at them. I gave those two movies as a way for us to test what our natures are really like because our nature will praise the violence and justify it as justice. The conclusion in movies like 'Law Abiding Citizen' and 'John Wick' is that the law could not and cannot protect anyone from human nature, yet we praise it when we give into it. To finalize the test, take heed upon the story of Cain and Abel.

So the LORD said to Cain, "Why are you angry? And why has your countenance fallen? If you do well, will you not be accepted? And if you do not do well, sin lies at the door. And its desire is for you, but you should rule over it." Now Cain talked with Abel his brother; and it came to pass, when they were in the field, that Cain rose up against Abel his brother and killed him. **(Genesis 4:6-8) – New King James Version**

There existed no laws at that time and when Cain became jealous of his brother, he killed him. We do not praise nor commemorate Cain's actions because he committed murder. Yet we praise the main characters of Law-Abiding Citizen and John Wick but they themselves committed murder. The only difference between these two examples which I have given are that the law existed in those movies whereas the law didn't in the story of Cain and Abel. We call Cain a murderer but call the main characters in those two movies heroes. But all it really reveals is our true nature because we praise murder when we do not see the law as just. Yet we shun the murderer who had no laws to abide by. When in reality, Cain was acting on his human nature because murder is in our nature and to our nature, murder is just. This exposes that we are all in fact murderers, even if we have not committed it, because the very thing we praise in the movies reveal the dark secret about us. That murder is just and the only thing that separates us from Cain is the law which prohibits us from committing murder. If one was to deny this, that would mean they have never praised the main characters in movies like Law Abiding Citizen or John Wick. "Oh author, are you trying to defend Cain's actions?" No absolutely not! What I am revealing to all is that we are all sinners and our nature has always been evil. I'll go even deeper and state that the main characters in the two movies were acting out of revenge. But what is revenge? Revenge stems from anger and hate. In the two avenging movies (John Wick & Law-Abiding Citizen) they act on both anger and hate. But what did Cain act on? For he did not kill his own brother out of vengeance but rather jealously. There are no laws against having feelings even if they are anger, hate, or jealously because they are emotions that are embedded in our human nature. But there are laws made to combat acts that stem from our very natures (anger, hate and jealously etc.). Revenge is what we cheered for in the avenging movies because we called it 'just' but what executed their actions? Human nature! Our nature executes the act of revenge and we call it 'just' by labeling ourselves avengers because the law failed to avenge us. But if we remove the law what than defends us from sin?

Nothing does but our nature still remains intact! Therefore, in reality, our nature has not changed and will always remain sinful. So, the only thing that really separates us from Cain is the law of God. For God is the same God of both the Old Testament and the New Testament. Nothing changed in him but his love for us grew because he gave the Old Testament Israelites the law as the body which acted as the scapegoat of forgiveness to combat against our human nature. But our human nature rejected the body of forgiveness (the law) because our nature desired the very thing that needed forgiveness- sin. The law was a form of protection from our nature but behind the law was a spirit named death, and just guess who executed this spirit of death? Yes, that's right it was Satan. He would go up to God and state his case against us because he knew that sins are paid out by death. This is why God instructed the people of the Old Testament to offer animal sacrifices because the devil wanted our souls as payment. Hence why Christ came in flesh and took the place of the law through pain and death as the ultimate forgiveness because behind his flesh was unconditional love. His Spirit knew our nature from the very beginning and by dying on the cross, he outsmarted death and Satan by offering us his Spirit which will triumphant over the law of our nature.

As it is written: "There is none righteous, no, not one; there is none who understands; there is no one who seeks after God. They have all turned aside; they have together become unprofitable; there is none who does good, no, not one." "Their throat is an open tomb; with their tongues they have practiced deceit"; "The poison of asps is under their lips"; "Whose mouth is full of cursing and bitterness." "Their feet are swift to shed blood; destruction and misery are in their ways; and the way of peace they have not known." "There is no fear of God before they eyes." Now we know that whatever the law says, it says to those who are under the law, that every mouth may be stopped, and all the world may become guilty before God. Therefore by the deeds of the law no flesh will be justified in his sight for by the law is the knowledge of sin. **(Romans 3:9-20)- New King James Version**

After I read Romans 3:9-20, it felt like a volcano erupted in both my flesh and spirit. Galatians 3:10-14, Paul writes how the law is cursed because of sin and what that really means is that we cursed ourselves in the garden of Eden. We may say, "it was Adam and Eve's fault," but if they weren't going to do it someone else was bound to do it. Remember that Adam and Eve were made without sin and were considered good, but the devil found a way to manipulate Eve, who then convinced Adam to do the same act. We may read about the Israelites of the Old Testament and say, "they pissed off God not us," but even if they followed through and obeyed the law, someone was bound to break it. How do I know this?

For all have sinned and fall short of the glory of God. **(Romans 3:23) – New King James Version**

That is why it is written, "the law is cursed," because it defines our nature as sinful beings and God gave us the law as a provision to ourselves so that we may not behave according to our nature. So in retrospect, the law did not fail us, we failed the law. God then came to us through Jesus Christ, not as the law but as the one to fulfill the purpose (defeat sin) of the law since he was without sin. The Old Testament speaks of animal sacrifices as the repayment of sins (death). It served worthy enough to satisfy the pleasures of the law temporarily but could not sustain our nature because our nature desired pleasure from sin. Animals were selected because within an animal is blood and blood is sacred because it symbolizes life.

But you, shall not eat flesh with its life, that is, its blood. **(Genesis 9:4) – New King James Version**

"Whatever man of the children of Israel, or of the strangers who dwell among you, who hunts and catches any animal or bird that may be eaten, he shall pour out its blood and cover it with dust; for it is the life of all flesh. Its blood sustains its life. Therefore I said to the children of Israel, 'You shall not eat the blood of any flesh, for the life of all flesh is its blood. Whoever eats it shall be cut off.' **(Leviticus 17:14) – New King James Version**

The flesh and spirit of the law could not save us because our flesh and spirit argued within itself for sin. What is the flesh and spirit of the law?

The flesh being the tangible law of God, which was given to Moses, that tells us not to sin. The spirit of the law is punishment which is death because that is what sin desires. God came to earth in flesh and spirit (Jesus Christ) and gave us something the law could never offer. Love, salvation, grace, forgiveness, mercy, peace, humility, kindness, faithfulness, patience, joy, self-control and sacrifice which is why he is called the Lamb of God. Because his blood was worthy enough to sustain all sins. In my heavenly imagination, Jesus' blood spoke to sin and said, "They no longer belong to you because I have paid their long overdue tab. They will no longer be offering anymore animal sacrifices to you because I am eternal life that overcame you, yes you Death!" It may sound strange that I have that kind of imagination, but my imagination does not come out of thin air because blood does speak (in a way).

Then the LORD said to Cain, "Where is Abel your brother?" He said, "I do not know. Am I my brother's keeper?" And he said, "What have you done? The voice of your brother's blood cries out to me from the ground. **(Genesis 4:9-10) – New King James Version**

After Cain had killed his brother Abel, the Scriptures explain that Abel's blood was crying out to God from the ground. This spooky revelation reveals to us how significant our own blood is. A person's blood has a way of speaking itself because there is life inside of it. Notice whenever we go for checkups, a doctor's standard practice is to do blood work. They do this because a person's blood does an outstanding job voicing out a person's health. The blood work cannot lie because the blood itself does not hide anything. Take for instance blood alcohol concentration. If a police officer wanted to know how much a person drank, they could find out by using a breathalyzer. The machine measures how much alcohol is in the bloodstream which gives the police officer a good idea of how much that person drank. The person may lie about it, but their blood will be quick to sell them out.

For it is not possible that the blood of bulls and goats could take away sins. Therefore, when he came into the world, he said: "Sacrifice and offering you did not desire, but a body you have prepared for me. In burnt offerings and sacrifices for sin you had no pleasure. Then he said, 'Behold, I have come-in the volume of the book it is written of me- to do your will, O God.'" Previously saying, "Sacrifice and offering, burnt offerings, and offerings for sin you did not desire, nor had pleasure in them." (which are offered according to the law), then he said, "Behold, I have come to do your will, O God." He takes away the first that he may establish the second. By that will we have been sanctified through the offering of the body of Jesus Christ once for all. **(Hebrews 10:4-10) – New King James Version**

For if that first covenant had been faultless, then no place would have been sought for a second. Because finding fault with them, he says: "Behold, the days are coming, says the LORD, when I will make a new covenant with the house of Israel and with the house of Judah— not according to the covenant that I made with their fathers in the day when I took them by the hand to lead them out of the land of Egypt; because they did not continue in my covenant, and I disregarded them, says the LORD. For this is the covenant that I will make with the house of Israel after those days, says the LORD: I will put my laws in their mind and write them on their hearts; and I will be their God, and they shall be my people. None of them shall teach his neighbor, and none his brother, saying, 'Know the LORD,' for all shall know me, from the least of them to the greatest of them. For I will be merciful to their unrighteousness, and their sins and their lawless deeds I will remember no more." In that he says, "A new covenant," he has made the first obsolete. Now what is becoming obsolete and growing old is ready to vanish away. **(Hebrews 8:7-13) – New King James Version**

And for this reason he is the mediator of the new covenant, by means of death, for the redemption of the transgressions under the first covenant, that those who are called may receive the promise of the eternal inheritance. For where there is a testament, there must also of necessity be the death of the testator. For a testament is in force after men are dead, since it has no power at all while the testator lives. Therefore not even the first covenant was dedicated without blood. For when Moses had spoken every precept to all the people according to the law, he took the blood of calves and goats, with water, scarlet wool, and hyssop, and sprinkled both the book itself and all the people, saying, "This is the blood of the covenant which God has commanded you." Then likewise he sprinkled with *blood both the tabernacle and all the vessels of the ministry. And according to the law almost all things are purified with blood, and without shedding of blood there is no remission.* **(Hebrews 9:15-22) – New King James Version**

He gave up his flesh so that his Spirit would raise it after three days. He then released his own Spirit onto the whole world so it would serve as the key to break the curse that agitated the flesh and spirit within us. Death had to happen so that his blood would be poured out to cover the curse that came with the law. Which in reality is a curse that sin had on us. This is why the law of God is different to our laws because his law did not intend to torture us with barbaric punishments. Although it spoke barbaric punishments its creation was made to protect us from the law of sin. Whereas our laws, in flesh, serve to protect and maintain order to the very desires of our nature and because of this, in spirit, it judges a person permanently and instantly labels them criminals. When in fact, by nature we are all criminals in the eyes of God due to our nature because we have all sinned. This very curse is why the example between employer and applicant is a known reality because our man-made laws have the power to tarnish, devalue, humiliate and destroy one's character when God's law was made to do the opposite.

Jesus answered them, "I told you, and you do not believe. The works that I do in my Father's name, they bear witness of me. But you did not believe because you are not of my sheep, as I said. My sheep hear my voice, and I know them, and they follow me. And I give them eternal life, and they shall never perish; neither shall anyone snatch them out of my hand. My Father, who has given them to me, is greater than all; and no one is able to snatch them out of my Father's hand. I and my Father are one." **(John 10:25-30) – New King James Version**

Our laws change because we change but the dangerous thing about humanity is our nature still stays the same- sinful. Does that mean all our man-made laws are evil and pointless? No, that is not what I'm saying! We have to remember that God made us good from the beginning, and that goodness is recognized in the very intent of having the law. For the law's initial creation reveals our intent of preventing chaos and maintaining order for the sake of peace, even if that law passed is just or unjust. However, our laws have the capabilities of trespassing over to sin because of our nature. We change as a society and if society as a whole comes together to accommodate their nature, they will pass down laws that infringe the laws of God. As I mentioned before, Jesus Christ is the same yesterday, today and forever. I needed everyone to understand this because his nature is righteous and ours is sinful. Our man-made laws once respected the principle of God's law hence incorporating its values in our laws but if we look at our world today, all nations have different laws. They have drifted away and innovated their own laws according to their nation's cultures, politics and beliefs. Now I am not calling out any nation specifically, but I am revealing the reality that sin can and has already seeped into the legislations of the sovereign powers. It has disguised itself underneath man-made laws because our nature desires to sin. This is dangerous because sin holds a power that traces back to the very laws God made for us, which was to prevent what the devil desired (spiritual death). This is a doctrine that Satan holds dearly within his spiritual realm and why I had to make sure everyone knows there is a difference between God's laws and man-made laws. If we despise the Old Testament laws, we are really despising ourselves because they reveal who we really are. Man-made laws are open to change because it is in our nature to give into the compromise of sin. Sin lusts for more sin and Satan knows this which is why he hopes for us to live by our nature so he can manipulate us, just like he manipulated Eve. It is the reason why Jesus Christ said, "My sheep hear my voice and I know them, and they follow me." He refers himself as the shepherd because as the Lamb (flesh) who sacrificed himself, he has now risen to heaven as the shepherd (Spirit). Those who listen to him and follow him will receive eternal life because they received his Holy Spirit, by faith in the Word. The shepherd leads his flock and the flock know his voice because of the Holy Spirit. This is why the Word makes sense and how I am able to deliver this message to all.

In conclusion to the message above, which I had to run back after editorial and revision: Does that mean we disregard God's laws? No and thanks be to God that the Spirit of God assists me in writing what the law should mean to us now. For Christ came to fulfill the law which we had failed to live by. He did this by exchanging his flesh for the law's flesh and the spirit of the law retaliated by taking his flesh to the grave. But the spirit of the law could not contain his Spirit so it broke free while his blood became the eternal scapegoat of forgiveness. All this gave a stronger purpose to the law which is now his body (Jesus Christ) and Spirit (Holy Spirit). This purpose which I speak of is called the Good News or eternal life. That is if we believed in Jesus Christ because those who do not are then subject to the curse of the law which is a permanent death (physically and spiritually). Death or any of the barbaric punishments spoken in the Old Testament are no longer valid in Jesus Christ. They are no longer valid because he allowed our sinful nature to treat him barbarically so that we no longer are tortured by the law's curse.

We use his law as a precedence to know sin, but it is within the Spirit of God (Holy Spirit) which serves as our guide to live righteously because his sheep know his voice and follow him. Now does this mean, if someone has the Holy Spirit, they are perfect? Absolutely not! Even as people read this book, they will notice my nature in how I write. I had mentioned that Apostle Paul was my favourite writer which is why my nature favours referencing him a lot. In a way, my nature has put Apostle Paul on such a high pedestal and that in itself has transpired into sin. "Wait, what? How is that possible?" some will ask. Well, if Paul was physically alive today, he would rebuke my nature and remind me that he did not write what he wrote for praise or glory. He wrote for the glory of Jesus Christ so to favour him over other writers, who wrote before him, is like telling God he made a mistake in choosing the very people that pleased him. How can I say that Paul is my favourite writer? When all he did was behave like the sheep that Christ speaks of and wrote what the shepherd told him to write. It is because of Moses' relationship with God, that we know how God formed the earth since he wrote Genesis (Moses also wrote Exodus, Leviticus Numbers, and most of Deuteronomy). Do I favour Paul over Moses? Even that question itself exposes my human nature because I have now turned the Word of God into some sort of competition. God did not need to use anyone to reveal the Scriptures to us, but he did so for the sake of a relationship with the people that wrote for him and the future generations. All the writers in the Scriptures had their own style of writing and own experiences with God but they needed God constantly. They knew without him; they would be nothing and even the New Testament characters who received the Holy Spirit knew this. The Holy Spirit is Jesus and the Father, but if we do not speak to him then we leave room for our nature to speak. Apostle Paul is not the Word, nor is Moses or any of prophets and none of them ever weighed themselves greater or less than one another.

When one of you says, "I follow Paul," and another, "I follow Apollos"—aren't you acting like worldly people? After all, who is Apollos? And who is Paul? We are simply God's servants, by whom you were led to believe. Each one of us does the work which the Lord gave him to do: I planted the seed, Apollos watered the plant, but it was God who made the plant grow. The one who plants and the one who waters really do not matter. It is God who matters, because he makes the plant grow. **(1 Corinthians 3:4-7) – Good News Translation**

Once we start thinking that we are greater or less than one another, we have allowed the works of our nature to speak. For there is no greater Scripture than the other because they all come from the one who is the greatest, that being Jesus Christ. This is what all the writers knew which is why they are remembered as greats, but they will never call themselves that because they know who made them great.

Therefore God also has highly exalted him and given him the name which is above every name, that at the name of Jesus every knee should bow, of those in heaven, and those on earth, and those under the earth, and that every tongue should confess that Jesus Christ is Lord, to the glory of God the Father. **(Philippians 2:9-11)– New King James Version**

If someone thought that I had meant once they receive the Holy Spirit, they will be perfect; I apologize for making it seem like that. Because if it were like that, then there would be no relationship with God. All the famous characters that pleased God in the Scriptures were once irrelevant, but it was God that made them relevant. None of them were without sin so they all made mistakes, but they are not remembered by their mistakes but by their faith which created a beautiful relationship with God. If it were up to the law, they would have all been doomed. The same principle applies to us because God knows we will never be perfect, but we please God in the pursuit to defeat our imperfections with the Holy Spirit. This is a truth that Satan doesn't want us to know because the Holy Spirit is perfect. By it living in us, it serves as the shepherd to perfection. Now since we can never be perfect, it resembles the perfect relationship that will last forever. This is how we please God and as his sheep, we forever rely on his Spirit to overcome our nature which will show in how we live our lives. It must also be noted that I am not saying that us humans are nothing but evil because the Scriptures do not say we only have evil in us. But this conversation and deep elaboration is to reveal to all that our natures desire to do evil but there still exists a truth in us that seeks to be good because in the beginning God made us as good beings. But because of sin, God has provided the Holy Spirit as the solution to our natures desire to do evil, which is the nature that excels in righteousness.

Abram put his trust in the LORD, and because of this the LORD was pleased with him and accepted him. **(Genesis 15:6) – Good News Translation**

What is it that puts us right with God? Is it through the obedience of the law or the measure of our faith? Can it not be argued that they are the same thing? Don't we obey the law because of faith? See the thing is, that did not answer the question. We start to see the true value of faith versus the law when we look at the conflict between Jesus and the Pharisees. The Pharisees were teachers of the law and were highly respected in society. The law that they were devoted to was passed down generation down to generation but originated from God, who gave it to Moses. As a result, it created tension when Jesus was "not following" the law.

Not afterward Jesus was walking through some wheat fields on a Sabbath. His disciples were hungry, so they began to pick heads of wheat and eat the grain. When the Pharisees saw this, they said to Jesus, "Look, it is against our Law for your disciples to do this on the Sabbath!" Jesus answered, "Have you never read what David did that time when he and his men were hungry? He went into the house of God, and he and his men ate the bread offered to God, even though it was against the Law for them to eat it- only the priests were allowed to eat that bread. Or have you not read in the Law of Moses that every Sabbath the priests in the Temple actually break the Sabbath law, yet they are not guilty? I tell you that there is something here greater than the Temple. The Scripture says, 'It is kindness that I want, not animal sacrifices.' If you really knew what this means, you would not condemn people who are not guilty; for the Son of Man is Lord of the Sabbath." **(Matthew 12:1-8) - Good News Translation**

And when he returned to Capernaum after some days, it was reported that he was at home. And many were gathered together, so that there was no more room, not even at the door. And he was preaching the Word to them. And they came, bringing to him a paralytic carried by four men. And when they could not get near him because of the crowd, they removed the roof above him, and when they had made an opening, they let down the bed on which the paralytic lay. And when Jesus saw their faith, he said to the paralytic, "Son, your sins are forgiven." Now some of the scribes were sitting there, questioning in their hearts **(Mark 2:1-6) – English Standard Version**

'Observe the Sabbath day, to keep it holy, as the LORD *your God commanded you. Six days you shall labor and do all your work, but the seventh day is the Sabbath of the* LORD *your God. In it you shall do no work: you, nor your son, nor your daughter, nor your male servant, nor your female servant, nor your ox, nor your donkey, nor any of your cattle, nor your stranger who is within your gates, that your male servant and your female servant may rest as well as you. And remember that you were a slave in the land of Egypt, and the* LORD *your God brought you out from there by a mighty hand and by an outstretched arm; therefore the* LORD *your God commanded you to keep the Sabbath day.* **(Deuteronomy 5:12-15) – New King James Version**

The third commandment that God had given Moses was about observing the Sabbath day and keeping it holy. God had commanded this to the Israelites so that they would always remember how God had delivered them from the Egyptians reign. It was also to be a sacred day for them to devote their time to God and rest.

By the seventh day, God finished what he had been doing and stopped working. He blessed the seventh day and set it apart as a special day because by that day he had completed his creation and stopped working. **(Genesis 2:1-3) - Good News Translation**

In the books Matthew and Mark, the Pharisees accuse Jesus of 'breaking' the third commandment when they see him eating grain and healing a leper on the Sabbath day. The Pharisees immediately come down on Jesus for these so-called violations. On each occasion where Jesus is found 'breaking' the law, he rebuttals by questioning the Pharisees' understanding of the actual law. The Pharisees were so obsessed with the law that the law itself became their god. This was the problem. They were using the law as a weapon to judge who was righteous. Which relates back to my very question. What is it that God values more: The person who follows the law or the one that has devoted their time getting to know God? The person who devotes their time in knowing God is the one who exhibits faith because they are believing in what they cannot see (seeking out a relationship). Whereas the law is a tangible thing which is seen, but the Pharisees used its power to judge whether a person was righteous.

Saying: "The scribes and the Pharisees sit in Moses' seat. Therefore, whatever they tell you to observe, that observe and do, but do not do according to their works; for they say, and do not do. For they bind heavy burdens, hard to bear, and lay them on men's shoulders; but they themselves will not move them with one of their fingers. But all their works they do to be seen by men. They make their phylacteries broad and enlarge the borders of their garments. They love the best places at feasts, the best seats in the synagogues, greetings in the marketplaces, and to be called by men, 'Rabbi, Rabbi.' **(Matthew 23:2-7) – New King James Version**

How terrible for you, teachers of the Law and Pharisees! You hypocrites! You clean the outside of your cup and plate, while the inside is full of what you have gotten by violence and selfishness. Blind Pharisee! Clean what is inside the cup first, and then the outside will be clean too! **(Matthew 23:25-26) - Good News Translation**

Jesus despised the Pharisees way of life because they were using God's law as a weapon to judge others. This is why he said, "Blind Pharisee! Clean what is inside the cup first, and then the outside will be clean too!" They worshipped the law to such an extent that it became their idol which they used to make themselves feel greater than everyone else. This really ticked off Jesus because it drove people away from God. As I study this today, I can see the very same scenario in todays' society. The purpose of God's law has become miscued and people feel judgement from it because they view it the same way they view man-made laws. When the law of God was made for our benefit to help us recognize our sinful nature. But how can anyone articulate such things when they hear, "You're going to hell because you did this and that." When in truth Jesus, God, The Word says, "Your human nature is spiritually killing you, so I sacrificed myself so you can have my nature which will teach you how to overcome your nature. I did that because I love you so much and cannot let you go." The first voice is what the Pharisees expressed to people and sadly their movement did not die. As a matter of fact, it is a movement that the doctrine of Satan developed because he is the original accuser. It was Satan who would appear before God and state his case against us, according to the law. He was the prosecutor of the law since he was the first to sin. Satan knows that God does not tolerate sin and because of this God cannot go against his own nature, so Satan used the law as a weapon to bring accusation to us. But that plan failed with Jesus Christ. Satan no longer has the authority to bring accusation to God concerning us because sin no longer has jurisdiction over our lives. That is if we believe in Jesus Christ. Satan then developed a sinister plan and it was to make the law look unappealing to us so that we would not go to Jesus Christ. By making the law look like it is constantly judging us, it turns us off from going to God because it involves fear which has nothing to do with love but hate.

There is no fear in love; but perfect love casts fear, because fear involves torment. But he who fears has not been made perfect in love. **(1 John 4:18) – New King James Version**

This is what the Pharisees did which was a doctrine developed by Satan himself because he hates God and since God loves us, he hates us too. What does this have to do with law vs faith? Simple. Because all the devil did was use the law, which would have never existed if he did not trick Eve into eating from the forbidden fruit. He uses the law because the law is apart of God's Word and if we hate the law, we will also hate God. In other words, he has manipulated our thoughts by redefining what the purpose of the law is. We associate God with punishment and hate but fail to realize that the law was given to us to protect us from punishment and hate (the devil, the one who was the first to sin). When Jesus Christ came, he made sure that his disciples, believers and non-believers understood this. Apostle Paul went toe to toe against Satan's doctrine and made sure that we understood that it is not in the means of the law that we are made right with God but by faith.

For the promise that he would be the heir of the world was not to Abraham or to his seed through the law, but through the righteousness of faith. For if those who are of the law are heirs, faith is made void and the promise made of no effect, because the law brings about wrath; for where there is no law there is no transgression. **(Romans 4:13-15) – New King James Version**

The doctrine of Satan's goal was to make the law equivalent to man-made laws for the sole purpose of seeing the law as a way of judging who is righteous. That is the flesh and spirit of man-made laws and he has incorporated that belief in our minds which is why we think, "So and so person is going to hell because they did or said that." By keeping us in that mindset and bubble it doesn't surprise me why people are turned off by God. But nothing the devil has done has ever achieved victory and this is made true through Jesus Christ. As I said before, we did fail the law but that is because our nature was always against righteousness. Our nature desired sin and could not program itself to desire anything else so the law was always against us. Jesus Christ then came to uphold and fulfill the law by taking away its true power; the very power Satan was using to enslave us which was spiritual death.

What then can the devil do now? Since the law essentially does not put us right with God. What can? That answer is faith and since Satan knows that it is by faith that we are put right with God, it is that very thing that he targets.

So Christ was offered once to bear the sins of many. To those who eagerly wait for him he will appear a second time, apart from sin, for salvation. **(Hebrews 9:28) – New King James Version**

Therefore rejoice, O heavens, and you who dwell in them! Woe to the inhabitants of the earth and the sea! For the devil has come down to you, having great wrath, because he knows that he has a short time! **(Revelations 12:12) – New King James Version**

Time is not on the devil's side and because of this he has come down with fury and anger. For he knows that Christ will come a second time but not for the remission of sins but for those who believed in him. Belief is the key word, but we all know its meaning-faith. That is what Satan is after now! Now he hasn't abandoned his principles or core doctrines because if they work then he will gladly use them if it keeps us in the corner of disbelief. It really doesn't matter to him, but he knows if he can get us to doubt just one Scripture, he has access to our faith. Hence the title of this chapter because he will use either the law (man-made or God's) to weaken our faith or he will challenge our faith by using the law (man-made or God's).

Everyone must obey state authorities because no authority exists without God's permission, and the existing authorities have been put there by God. **(Romans 13:1-2) - Good News Translation**

If Romans 13:1-2 is the case, what happens if a particular law is put into place that infringes against God's laws? This is clearly a hypothetical question because Canadians are protected by section 2a of the Canadian Charter of rights which states, "everyone has the following fundamental freedoms: a) freedom of conscience and religion." However, other countries are not as privileged to have such a justice system. Some countries are subject to laws that not only infringe on basic human rights but also prohibit the practice of their faith. Certain nations go so far by implementing imprisonment or even death if the people practice their faith. If the Scriptures have said, "everyone must obey state authorities because no authority exists without God's permission." What then of those countries that prohibit practicing the gospel of Jesus Christ?

"Attention! Attention all readers! Those who are reading this chapter, there is something you must know. The author of these pages did his best to avoid this topic. I've seen him scribble on white pages trying to shut out the thoughts. The author proceeds to go back to his electronic device staring blankly at his Microsoft pages. Type, type, type then backspace and erase. Author, you cannot avoid this fight. Law vs. faith? Law vs. faith? Law vs. faith? You should see the grin on my face. You cannot even defend your own faith. For it is written:

Whoever opposes the existing authority opposes what God has ordered, and anyone who does so will bring judgment on himself. (Romans 13:2) - Good News Translation

Law vs. faith? Law vs. faith? Law vs. faith? You should see the grin on my face. You cannot even defend your own faith. Author, you vowed to speak the truth. So tell the readers this, 'Your Heavenly Father tells you to obey the authorities and if you don't, you will face judgment. The authorities tell you to not worship your Heavenly Father, will you dare disobey them?' Law vs. faith? Law vs. faith? Law vs. faith? You should see the grin on my face. You cannot even defend your own faith. What kind of God puts his people through such humiliation? What kind of God puts such a strain on his people? Law vs. faith? Law vs. faith? Law vs. faith? You should see the grin on my face. You cannot even defend your own faith. Author stop backspacing! The readers are reading; they want to read the truth. If there really is a truth? Or just a damn confusing old book full of contradictions. Author this is it! You wanted to write so answer my questions because now even your readers are confused. If God willed for state authorities and commands his people to obey their leaders. What then of the countries that list your faith as a false religion? Who do they obey? For it is written:

For this reason, you must obey the authorities -not just because of God's punishment, but also as a matter of conscience. (Romans 13:5) - Good News Translation

Author, oh author attest to this: Your spirit versus flesh causes you to break laws and lose faith. Therefore, you will receive no grace. Law and faith? You are lawless and filled with no faith. Backspace that! No, as a matter of fact, backspace this whole book! The real secret is out! You should see the grin on my face. You cannot even defend your own faith."

-The doctrine of Satan

"Spirit of God,

I have come a long way in my life. I have vowed to tell the truth, but I have stumbled upon a problem. I'm afraid to answer incorrectly, and I am scared to lie to not only myself but to all the readers. For it is written:

And we impart this in words not taught by human wisdom but taught by the Spirit, interpreting spiritual truths to those who are spiritual. The natural person does not accept the things of the Spirit of God, for they are folly to him, and he is not able to understand them because they are spiritually discerned. The spiritual person judges all things but is himself to be judged by no one. "For who has understood the mind of the Lord so as to instruct him?" But we have the mind of Christ. (1 Corinthians 2:13-16) – English Standard Version

Every time I have prayed to you in writing, your angels have lifted up each and every word from these pages and delivered them to you. I ask for not only my sake but for the sake of those who are also searching for the answers to Law vs. faith.

Spirit of God, I love your Psalms, specifically number 51. For it is written:

235

Create a pure heart in me, O God, and put a new and loyal spirit in me. Do not banish me from your presence; do not take your holy spirit away from me. (Psalms 51:10-11) - Good News Translation

I have favored that line because I did not find value in myself, but your Spirit has revealed how much you value me. The Spirit that restored my peace, love, and joy. Please do not take away your Spirit from me. I fear that because I fear of the fate you mentioned in your last book Revelations regarding those who abandon the faith. For it is written:

Think how far you have fallen! Turn from your sins and do what you did at first. If you don't turn away from your sins, I will come to you and take away your lampstand from its place. (Revelations 2:5) - Good News Translation

It is written those who abandon faith cannot be brought back to repent. Therefore, I urge you Spirit of God do not take away your Spirit from me. I may pray through paper and pen; the very gifts you instilled in me but please before I continue my prayer do with me what you did to the prophet Isaiah. For it is written:

Then said I, "Woe is me! for I am undone; because I am a man of unclean lips, and I dwell in the midst of a people of unclean lips: for mine eyes have seen the King, the Lord of hosts." Then flew one of the Seraphim's unto me, having a live coal in his hand, which he had taken with the tongs from off the altar: And he laid it upon my mouth, and said, "Lo, this hath touched thy lips; and thine iniquity is taken away, and thy sin purged." (Isaiah 6:5-7) - King James Version

I know you are a merciful God and your love is beyond any love I've ever seen or known. That is why you are so quick to change your mind on our punishments because you forgive and forget our sins. I sinned, not because I live amongst sinners but because I chose to sin. I've lied like the one you banished from your kingdom, not because Satan made me but because I chose to. Despite all these things you continue to love me which is why you have brought me this far in life. For it is written:

But, beloved, we are confident of better things concerning you, yes, things that accompany salvation, though we speak in this manner. For God is not unjust to forget your work and labor of love which you have shown toward his name, in that you have ministered to the saints, and do minister. And we desire that each one of you show the same diligence to the full assurance of hope until the end, that you do not become sluggish, but imitate those who through faith and patience inherit the promises. (Hebrews 6:9-12) – New King James Version

I give you great thanks and praise for everything you've done. From the very beginning, the Word existed; the Word was with God, and the Word was God. Those who remain in you, you will remain in them. Those who believe in your Word will possess the Word. Those who read the Word, the Word will be preached to them. For it is written:

Then Moses said to the LORD, "O my Lord, I am not eloquent, neither before nor since you have spoken to Your servant; but I am slow of speech and slow of tongue." So the LORD said to him, "Who has made man's mouth? Or who makes the mute, the deaf, the seeing, or the blind? Have not I, the LORD? Now therefore, go, and I will be with your mouth and teach you what you shall say." (Exodus 4:10-12) – New King James Version

From the very beginning, you have been 'I AM' and you will remain 'I AM.' Help me write in such a way where those who read it will know it is you, 'I AM,' who writes through me. For it is written:

Then Moses said to God, "Indeed, when I come to the children of Israel and say to them, 'The God of your fathers has sent me to you,' and they say to me, 'What is his name?' what shall I say to them?" And God said to Moses, "I AM WHO I AM." And he said, "Thus you shall say to the children of Israel, 'I AM has sent me to you.' Moreover, God said to Moses, "Thus you shall say to the children of Israel: 'The LORD God of your fathers, the God of Abraham, the God of Isaac, and the God of Jacob, has sent me to you. This is my name forever, and this is my memorial to all generations' (Exodus 3:13-15) – **New King James Version**

I seal this prayer and lock every word written on this page with the name that is above all names. In the name of your Holy Son, Jesus Christ.

Amen."

"Author, oh author walk to your room and shut the door. I have heard your prayer but now listen to my voice. Kneel down and close your eyes. I am putting you through a deep sleep. Now dream! For it is written:

Like the appearance of a rainbow in a cloud on a rainy day, so was the appearance of the brightness all around it. This was the appearance of the likeness of the glory of the LORD. So when I saw it, I fell on my face and heard a voice of One speaking. (Ezekiel 1:28) – New King James Version

And he said to me, "Son of man, stand on your feet, and I will speak to you." Then the Spirit entered me when he spoke to me and set me on my feet; and I heard him who spoke to me. (Ezekiel 2:1-2) – New King James Version

But you, son of man, hear what I say to you. Do not be rebellious like that rebellious house; open your mouth and eat what I give you." Now when I looked, there was a hand stretched out to me; and behold, a scroll of a book was in it. Then he spread it before me; and there was writing on the inside and on the outside and written on it were lamentations and mourning and woe. (Ezekiel 2:8-10) – New King James Version

Moreover, he said to me, "Son of man, eat what you find; eat this scroll, and go, speak to the house of Israel." So I opened my mouth, and he caused me to eat that scroll. And he said to me, "Son of man, feed your belly, and fill your stomach with this scroll that I give you." So I ate, and it was in my mouth like honey in sweetness. (Ezekiel 3:1-3) – New King James Version

Awaken! Wake up, author! Stand up straight for it was written the prophet Ezekiel fell face down to the ground when he heard my voice but obeyed when I told him to stand up. My servant Ezekiel, the prophet that warned Israel. For it is written:

And he said to me: "Son of man, I am sending you to the children of Israel, to a rebellious nation that has rebelled against me; they and their fathers have transgressed against me to this very day. For they are impudent and stubborn children. I am sending you to them, and you shall say to them, 'Thus says the Lord GOD.' As for them, whether they hear or whether they refuse—for they are a rebellious house—yet they will know that a prophet has been among them. "And you, son of man, do not be afraid of them nor be afraid of their words, though briers and thorns are with you and you dwell among scorpions; do not be afraid of their words or dismayed by their looks, though they are a rebellious house. You shall speak my words to them, whether they hear or whether they refuse, for they are rebellious. (Ezekiel 2:3-7) – New King James Version

I named Ezekiel the prophet and when he spoke, the people knew it was my voice. This book has become your treasure and you called it your story, but that is no longer what it will be! It will now be your journey. When you started writing you were still afraid. Unsure of what you would write and hesitant about what truth was. This book has now become a path and the readers will read and call it a story however it will be their journey to the truth as well. Ezekiel's story has been written and I prepared him as Israel's prophet. The name I have given you is the name that I've been calling you. Author, oh author as you write you learn too. However, at this very moment, I'm going to change your name from author to watcher.

Watcher, oh watcher observe as I take away the voice from your mouth. Remain silent for I will finish this chapter. For it is written:

But you have not believed my message, which will come true at the right time. Because you have not believed, you will remain silent until the day my promise to you comes true. (Luke 1:20) - Good News Translation

Watcher, oh watcher how could you allow Satan play with your thoughts? Don't you know that the Spirit inside you provides insight? Then again, how could you hear the Spirits insight when you lack to spend time with me? Watcher, I watch you take my Spirit for granted. I watch you plead to me when you only want answers for this book. What will happen once finished? Will you forget me? For it is written:

"Remember these, O Jacob, and Israel, for you are my servant; I have formed you, you are my servant; O Israel, you will not be forgotten by me! (Isaiah 44:21) – New King James Version

There is no backspacing this because I know your heart. Watcher, oh watcher it is time to test your heart. Law vs. faith? I am the God of truth; there is no contradiction and my Spirit is proof. Write this in your heart. For it is written:

Jesus said to him, "Friend, do what you came to do." Then they came up and laid hands on Jesus and seized him. And behold, one of those who were with Jesus stretched out his hand and drew his sword and struck the servant of the high priest and cut off his ear. Then Jesus said to him, "Put your sword back into its place. For all `who take the sword will perish by the sword. (Matthew 26:50-52) – English Standard Version

Watcher, oh watcher I have a law vs. faith riddle for you to answer:

There once was a rich man who had finished shopping for his family. He was innocently walking out of a store when he was approached by a poor man. The poor man then proceeded to take the items bought by the rich man. The rich man tried to defend himself but was outmuscled by the poor man. The rich man fell to the ground because the poor man had pushed him down during the fight. The poor man could have run with the rich man's belongings but because of his rage from the fight, he took out his knife and brutally stabbed the rich man. The poor man then fled before the state authorities came to the scene of the crime. The rich man was fatally wounded, and his wounds became a concern while he was being rushed to the hospital. The rich man was immediately sent to the emergency room as the doctors operated on him. The rich man was barely conscious, but his thoughts were filled with the images of his family.

The rich man was at the wrong place at the wrong time! The rich man's blood was crying out for his life outside the store where he was stabbed. Rain began to fall that same night, washing away the rich man's blood at the scene of the crime. As time passed and the rain was just about done. The blood was washed away with the rain. It was at that moment when the doctors had realized a punctured organ in the rich man. The life threating organ caused the rich man to enter cardiac arrest. The rain continued to pour onto the earth as the doctors desperately attempted to save the rich man. The rich man's heart began to beat faster, faster then began to slow down, slower and slower. As the rich man took his last breath; his soul knew it was time to go. Unfortunately for the rich man, his family had just arrived at the hospital, but it was too late. 'Tell my family I love them,' as he spoke his last words to the operating doctors. Beep, beep, goodbye.

Watcher, oh watcher which of these two fates would you prefer? The rich man who died by a stab wound or the poor man who robbed the rich man, that committed murder? Watcher, oh watcher I took away your voice for a reason and this very question is proof. I made you silent because I knew you'd remain silent when asked this question. If you were to type I would see you type, then backspace. Type, type, type then backspace and erase. You do not wish to choose because the two fates both don't appeal to you. You want to know more about the man who died. You ask yourself, 'Well, what kind of man was he? Was he a man of God? And if so, will he go to heaven?' However, the real reason why you do not want to choose the fate of that man is because he was stabbed and died. You really do not care about what kind of man he was, but you're just afraid of death. That is why your thoughts are leaning to the poor man who got away with murder. This is why I changed your name from author to watcher. You are not fit to understand the law or faith. Your hesitation to speak is screaming out of your heart yelling, 'I'd rather live a sinner than die innocent.' Watcher, oh watcher if you were to speak at this very moment, you'd try to defend your case by saying, 'O God no I would choose the rich man's fate. I couldn't speak because you took away my voice!' Watcher, oh watcher why do you insist on lying? From your very heart, you know you couldn't choose either fate. It is the reason why when you prayed to me and I answered back with this riddle, but you hesitated to put it on this very page! I caught you on your own lie! I took away your voice so you wouldn't sin against me with your hearts reply because I knew you were willing to lie to me. Watcher, oh watcher you know the Scriptures. For it is written:

Above all, my friends, do not use an oath when you make a promise. Do not swear by heaven or by earth or by anything else. Say only "Yes" when you mean yes, and "No" when you mean no, and then you will not come under God's judgment. (James 5:12) - Good News Translation

But I say to you, do not swear at all: neither by heaven, for it is God's throne; nor by the earth, for it is his footstool; nor by Jerusalem, for it is the city of the great King. Nor shall you swear by your head, because you cannot make one hair white or black. But let your 'Yes' be 'Yes', and your 'No,' 'No.' For whatever is more than these is from the evil one. (Matthew 5:34-37) - New King James Version

These six things the LORD hates, Yes seven are an abomination to him: A proud look, a lying tongue, hands that shed innocent blood, a heart that devises wicked plans, feet that are swift in running to evil, a false witness who speaks lies and one who sows discord among brethren. (Proverbs 6:16-19) – New King James Version

You hesitated to put this riddle in your book because you did not understand it. The reason why you cannot understand it is that you are still a child. For it is written:

For though by this time you ought to be teachers, you need someone to teach you again the basic principles of the oracles of God. You need milk, not solid food, for everyone who lives on milk is unskilled in the Word of righteousness, since he is a child. But solid food is for the mature, for those who have their powers of discernment trained by constant practice to distinguish good from evil (Hebrews 5:12-14) – English Standard Version

But I, brothers, could not address you as spiritual people, but as people of the flesh, as infants in Christ. I fed you with milk, not solid food, for you were not ready for it. And even now you are not yet ready, for you are still of the flesh. For while there is jealousy and strife among you, are you not of the flesh and behaving only in a human way? For when one says, "I follow Paul," and another, "I follow Apollos," are you not being merely human? (1 Corinthians 3:1-3) – English Standard Version

I withheld information to test your heart. The poor man that killed the rich man knew everything about him. He knew the rich man had always carried a lot of cash on him, so he studied his schedule. The rich man was married and had 2 children. He devoted his whole life to the me and the church. Watcher, oh watcher the rich man knew the Scriptures just like you, but the difference is he remained consistent in his worship. The poor man lived all his life by the sword which is why he did not uphold the law. As a matter of fact, he placed the law of the world above my own laws. Watcher, oh watcher I can hear your heart asking, 'Spirit of God, what do you mean by that?' The poor man ran from the scene of the crime because he was escaping the judgment of the law. The sin inside him had already contaminated his heart, so it influenced the poor man to run. However, sin doesn't run away from the law because sin hates the law; sin is actually running away from me because I made the law. For even though sin influenced the poor man to run; the poor man ran from the world's law not thinking of my laws. The poor man placed the world's law above my own because he feared the judgment of the world rather than fearing my judgment. Watcher, oh watcher are you following? By fearing the world's judgment rather than mine, he has completely doomed himself. The poor man was robbing from the rich man for his money, but because he has always lived a violent life, a life that involves a knife! The poor man committed another sin-murder. Watcher, oh watcher if you were to unlock the door behind the law, what do you think you'd find? Behind that door is death. For the accuser stands with sin before the law waiting for people to choose it so he may accuse them according to the law. Those who do not believe in me are subject to be dragged by the curses of the law to death! He does this because he no longer stands before me accusing sinners, for he has lost that power. Watcher, oh watcher it is by this reason why I have said, 'Whosoever believes shall be saved!' Those who do not believe cannot uplift themselves from the law's curse, so they are under the accuser's power, who drags them to death! It is by the blood which saves all from death when belief in the gospel is in their hearts and they plead for forgiveness. Sin and Satan attempt to be like Christ each and every day. My law hates sin and sin hates my law; that is why sin tried to raise itself above the law, but it has been sent to the ground. Beneath the earth and buried in the world of the dead as it awaits. For it is written:

We know that Christ, being raised from the dead, will never die again; death no longer has dominion over him. For the death he died he died to

sin, once for all, but the life he lives he lives to God. So you also must consider yourselves dead to sin and alive to God in Christ Jesus. Let not sin therefore reign in your mortal body, to make you obey its passions. Do not present your members to sin as instruments for unrighteousness but present yourselves to God as those who have been brought from death to life, and your members to God as instruments for righteousness. (Romans 6:9-13) – English Standard Version

Watcher, oh watcher do you see now? The poor man allowed sin to be his master and by doing so, he has surrendered his grace for death. The rich man who had lived his whole life not living by the sword was sadly murdered by the sword. Watcher, oh watcher I can hear your heart asking, 'Spirit of God if he did not live by the sword why did he die by the sword?' My answer to you will provide you true insight and reveal the evil lies of Satan. For it is written:

What then? Are we to sin because we are not under law but under grace? By no means! Do you not know that if you present yourselves to anyone as obedient slaves, you are slaves of the one whom you obey, either of sin, which leads to death, or of obedience, which leads to righteousness? But thanks be to God, that you who were once slaves of sin have become obedient from the heart to the standard of teaching to which you were committed, and, having been set free from sin, have become slaves of righteousness. I am speaking in human terms, because of your natural limitations. For just as you once presented your members as slaves to impurity and to lawlessness leading to more lawlessness, so now present your members as slaves to righteousness leading to sanctification. (Romans 6:15-19) – English Standard Version

The fate of the rich man was the correct answer not because of his fate but because of his faith. For it is written:

Two others, who were criminals, were led away to be put to death with him. And when they came to the place that is called The Skull, there they crucified him, and the criminals, one on his right and one on his left. And Jesus said, "Father, forgive them, for they know not what they do." And they cast lots to divide his garments. And the people stood by, watching,

but the rulers scoffed at him, saying, "He saved others; let him save himself, if he is the Christ of God, his Chosen One!" The soldiers also mocked him, coming up and offering him sour wine and saying, "If you are the King of the Jews, save yourself!" There was also an inscription over him, "This is the King of the Jews." One of the criminals who were hanged railed at him, saying, "Are you not the Christ? Save yourself and us!" But the other rebuked him, saying, "Do you not fear God, since you are under the same sentence of condemnation? And we indeed justly, for we are receiving the due reward of our deeds; but this man has done nothing wrong." And he said, "Jesus, remember me when you come into your kingdom." And he said to him, "Truly, I say to you, today you will be with me in paradise." **(Luke 23:32-43) – English Standard Version**

Watcher, oh watcher do you not see the similarities of these two stories? Out of the two criminals, which of them would you want to be? I can hear your heart say, 'Spirit of God, please forgive me! I can see what you have done. You've removed my own voice to show me mercy. From the first riddle, I was prepared to lie to you. As a matter of fact, you knew I was going to lie to you which is why you took away my voice. My lying tongue would have picked the fate of the poor man, and now I'm ashamed to even answer this question. That being said, I see what you've done; I am in awe of you because your wisdom is beyond me. In my shame- I have seen your glory so thank you, I have seen the similarities.'

Watcher, oh watcher those who live by their natural human desires will pick the poor man's fate. The sword that Christ spoke of is natural human desires. Those who live by their natural human desires will die spiritually! For it is written:

Put to death therefore what is earthly in you: sexual immorality, impurity, passion, evil desire, and covetousness, which is idolatry. On account of these the wrath of God is coming. In these you too once walked, when you were living in them. But now you must put them all away: anger, wrath, malice, slander, and obscene talk from your mouth. Do not lie to one another, seeing that you have put off the old self with its practices and have put on the new self, which is being renewed in knowledge after the image of its creator. (Colossians 3:5-10) English Standard Version

Watcher this is why it was difficult for you to pick the rich man's fate. Those who live by their natural human desires will place themselves over me. They will misinterpret the law because they do not have faith. Those who live by their natural human desires will be too blind for the details of the story. Those who live by their natural human desires will focus on the rich man's wealth. But it isn't the rich man's wealth that makes him the right answer. Neither is it the correct answer because he went to church. The rich man's fate is the correct answer not because he never picked up a sword, but because he put down the sword! The rich man put to death his natural human desires and lived a life that is now the story of grace because he put his faith in me. The law was no concern to the rich man because his faith raised him above the law. This is also true in the story of the two criminals on the cross. Both criminals were lawbreakers. Therefore, it was the law that had decided their fates. The first criminal had accepted his fate but what doomed him was that his sin had contaminated his heart. For it is written:

Take care, brothers, lest there be in any of you an evil, unbelieving heart, leading you to fall away from the living God. But exhort one another every day, as long as it is called "today," that none of you may be hardened by the deceitfulness of sin. For we have come to share in Christ, if indeed we hold our original confidence firm to the end. As it is said, "Today, if you hear his voice, do not harden your hearts as in the rebellion." (Hebrews 3:12-15) – English Standard Version

The first criminal insulted the Lamb of God because he rejected faith; hence no grace was shown to him. The second criminal, on the other hand, had accepted his fate but he rose above the punishment of the law because of his faith in the Lamb of God. That is why Jesus said, 'I promise you that today you will be in Paradise with me.' Watcher, oh watcher do you see now? The poor man and the first criminal are similar to one another because their hearts were consumed with the 'sword.' The poor man ran away from the scene of the crime to escape the punishment of the law not understanding that it is not up to the law to judge but by me. For it is written:

They show that the work of the law is written on their hearts, while their conscience also bears witness, and their conflicting thoughts accuse or even excuse them on that day when, according to my gospel, God judges the

secrets of men by Christ Jesus. (Romans 2:15-16) **– English Standard Version**

Those who do not know me, do not have faith in me. They rely on the law for justice but the law itself fails them and provides no justice. Therefore, they will seek out their own justice by betraying their own faith which was towards the law! The law that lives in them is sinful, so they become the very sin the law rebukes! It is only by faith that people know me and if they know me, they will know the truth in justice and judgment. The first criminal was caught by the law's punishment but did not realize that if he put his faith in me, I would have shown him mercy from real punishment. One ran away and the other was caught, but both will be subject to the punishment of the law rather than being put above the law's punishment to experience forgiveness and grace. For it is written:

For what does the Scripture say? "Abraham believed God, and it was counted to him as righteousness." Now to the one who works, his wages are not counted as a gift but as his due. And to the one who does not work but believes in him who justifies the ungodly, his faith is counted as righteousness, just as David also speaks of the blessing of the one to whom God counts righteousness apart from works: "Blessed are those whose lawless deeds are forgiven, and whose sins are covered; blessed is the man against whom the Lord will not count his sin." (Romans 4:3-8) – Good News Translation

Watcher, oh watcher do you now understand? Those who do not understand will think that by following the law, they are righteous people. I will call those people misguided and foolish for not understanding the purpose of the law. For it is written:

Does this mean that by this faith we do away with the Law? No, not at all; instead, we uphold the Law. (Romans 3:31) – Good News Translation

As serious as it is to follow the law, it isn't the law that declares people righteous. It is the creator of the law, "I AM," that judges the hearts of those who are righteous. Watcher, oh watcher let me ask you this: 'For in the world there exists lawmakers who gather together and come up with unbiased laws to provide to the people so that they may follow it. They do this to provide order for the people, so then which is righteous? The law that they have made or they themselves, who are the lawmakers?' The bill that they decide to pass down is the thing that will be favored over the lawmakers because they are only humans who have broken laws too. However, people must follow their rules to be seen as righteous. Surely, I tell you those who have faith in me have come to the truth because I, the lawmaker am righteous, holy and 'I AM,' without sin. For it is written:

For it is not by hearing the Law that people are put right with God, but by doing what the Law commands. (Romans 2:13) - Good News Translation

Those who know me do what the law commands because of their faith in the righteous and perfect God! For who follows the laws of the unrighteous? Only the unrighteous! Watcher, oh watcher the Scriptures state, 'there is no one who is righteous, no one who is wise or who worships God.' All are born by the sword, but it is up to their faith that decides to put down the sword and live under my grace. Watcher, oh watcher I can hear your heart asking, 'What then of newborn babies, how is it that they are born of sin? They have done no wrong because they have just been conceived.' Watcher, oh watcher do you not forget what you wrote when your name was author? Your very own experience of sin and curses are written in the chapter flesh vs. spirit. Watcher, oh watcher when a child is born, they are an offspring of two. A father and a mother, however, their sins are now passed down to their own offspring. Watcher, oh watcher I can hear your heart asking, 'Spirit of God, how is that fair? I thought you make all things new?' Watcher, oh watcher when a queen gives birth to a child from the king; that child is then destined to take on his or her parents' legacy. This is the natural order of things, and the same goes with sin. It is on that child to seek repentance through the baptism of the water. This creates a new being spiritually that separates the child from the sins of his or her parents. For it is written:

For Christ also suffered once for sins, the righteous for the unrighteous, that he might bring us to God, being put to death in the flesh but made alive in the spirit, in which he went and proclaimed to the spirits in prison, because they formerly did not obey, when God's patience waited in the days of Noah, while the ark was being prepared, in which a few,

that is eight persons were brought safely through water. Baptism, which corresponds to this, now saves you, not as a removal of dirt from the body but as an appeal to God for a good conscience, through the resurrection of Jesus Christ, who has gone into heaven and is at the right hand of God, with angels, authorities, and powers having been subjected to him. **(1 Peter 3:18-22) – English Standard Version**

Watcher, oh watcher those are the laws of things but what puts the child above the sins of his or her parents are based on the child's faith in me. For it is written:

He abolished the Jewish Law with its commandments and rules, in order to create out of the two races one new people in union with himself, in this way making peace. By his death on the cross Christ destroyed their enmity; by means of the cross he united both races into one body and brought them back to God. (Ephesians 2:15-16) - Good News Translation

Watcher, oh watcher the law was made to create order, but it is the faith of people that lift them above the law and make them righteous people. The law cannot prevent the natural human desires from its works just like the natural human desires cannot change the natural order of the law. They both are enslaved to one another but those who put to death their natural human desires can rise above what the law condemns, which is sin, to the grace of God and the forgiveness of sins. For it is written:

But now the righteousness of God has been manifested apart from the law, although the Law and the Prophets bear witness to it— the righteousness of God through faith in Jesus Christ for all who believe. For there is no distinction: for all have sinned and fall short of the glory of God, and are justified by his grace as a gift, through the redemption that is in Christ Jesus, whom God put forward as a propitiation by his blood, to be received by faith. This was to show God's righteousness, because in his divine forbearance he had passed over former sins. It was to show his righteousness at the present time, so that he might be just and the justifier of the one who has faith in Jesus. (Romans 3:21-26) – English Standard Version

Watcher, oh watcher I see great joy in your heart because you now have an understanding. However, you must continue to observe because it is only partially told. This is the difference between humans and me: the human hearts focus on the stories, but I do not focus on their narratives but focus on the characters within the story. Watcher, oh watcher the world is filled with different stories and fates. The world is full of different stories, but it is up to me to judge the person not according to their story but what they store in their hearts. For it is written:

For we conclude that a person is put right with God only through faith, and not by doing what the Law commands. Or is God the God of the Jews only? Is he not the God of the Gentiles also? Of course, he is. God is one, and he will put the Jews right with himself on the basis of their faith and will put the Gentiles right through their faith. (Romans 3:28-30) - Good News Translation

What is in their hearts will determine how they live. The first riddle spoke of the rich man's death, but his situation would have meant nothing without his faith in me. I knew of his faith by how he lived which is what you have read! But what you read was revealed to you as a simple story about a rich man. That is how you interpreted his life — a simple story. But I have interpreted his heart and found faith in my Spirit. Which is why the complete story speaks of him going to church and dedicating his life to me because his nature denied the sword; the sword that is of human nature. The poor man's murder became his fate and that sin caused his heart to reject my grace due to his lack of faith. Watcher, oh watcher I can hear your heart asking, 'Spirit of God, what would you have done if the poor man asked for repentance but didn't mean it?' Watcher don't you know, no one makes a fool out of me. For it is written:

Do not deceive yourselves; no one makes a fool of God. You will reap exactly what you plant. (Galatians 6:7) - Good News Translation

What you don't see in the opaque is transparent in my eyes. I look at the hearts of all, so if a lie comes out of the mouth of a person; I see the truth in their hearts. If the law were the real judge, all would be sentenced to death. That is why I tell all to come to me because those who remain in me will be saved from the powers of death; the law will have no control over you because the law will not be your judge. Watcher, oh watcher why are these words so difficult to let in? Do you really uphold the law above me? There is no love in the law; there is no forgiveness in the law; there is no mercy in the law; there is no grace in the law; there is no salvation in the law. There is only judgement in the law and what it demands is death because the law recognizes sin. For it is written:

For sin pays its wage-death, but God's free gift is eternal life in union with Christ Jesus our Lord. (Romans 6:23) - Good News Translation

Death gets its power to hurt from sin, and sin gets its power from the Law. (1 Corinthians 15:56) - Good News Translation

Those who put their faith in me will see forgiveness in me because I am a merciful God. If the poor man pleas for forgiveness I will search his heart for his faith in the truth. No one makes a fool of me so I will know what they mean and what they don't. Watcher pay no attention to the account of others. It does you no good when you concern yourself of who I consider good and who I consider evil. For it is written:

When Peter saw him, he asked Jesus, 'Lord, what about this man?' Jesus answered him, 'If I want him to live until I come, what is that to you?' Follow me!' (John 21:21-22) - Good News Translation

Watcher, oh watcher you do not seem satisfied with my answer because I can search your heart right now and it is asking, 'Spirit of God, but what if the person sins and his heart is sorrowful, so you forgive them, but they continue to sin?' Watcher write this on your heart and never forget it! For it is written:

But the LORD said to him 'Pay no attention to how tall and handsome he is. I have rejected him because I do not judge as people judge. They look at the outward appearance, but I look at the heart.' (1 Samuel 16:7) - Good News Translation

Watcher, oh watcher have you ever been lied to? Yes, you have been. When this happened to you, you became cautious because it is impossible for you to read the motives of a person. Watcher, oh watcher have you ever lied? Yes, you have lied, and you've gotten away with it too but when you did you also were lying to yourself. Whenever people lie, they devalue their own hearts, that is why they become accustomed to telling lies. There is not one human who has not told a lie. That is why the Scriptures speak about your natures as liars. It is by this very reason why all find it difficult to tell the difference between the truth and the lie. Watcher, oh watcher I am the truth so there doesn't exist a single lie within me. My eyes are clear! That is why I can see through a lie, whether if it comes from the mouth, heart or mind. Humans can only see the outward of others whereas I see the inside. The poor man's sin does not stain grace, but it is his lack of faith in me that will jeopardize grace. Watcher, oh watcher this is also why I have brought your eyes to attend to Luke 23:33-42: The story of the two criminals. The first criminal was unable to ask for forgiveness because his heart was too contaminated by sin. That is why the Lamb of God said, 'those who live by the sword will die by the sword.' Watcher, oh watcher those who live by the sword are proclaiming spiritual suicide. For it is written:

Then the LORD said to Cain, "Why are you angry? Why that scowl on your face? If you had done the right thing, you would be smiling; but because you have done evil, sin is crouching at your door. It wants to rule you, but you must overcome it." (Genesis 4:6-7) – Good News Translation

Those who live by their natural human desires will deceit themselves by saying, 'If faith transcends above the law then my faith will allow me to escape God's punishment so I can do as I please.' Watcher, oh watcher surely I tell you those who think like that possess the heart of the first criminal. The first criminal spoke these words to the Messiah, 'Aren't you the Messiah? Save yourself and us!' Watcher, oh watcher those are not words of faith but rather arrogance. To speak faithfully, one must behave according to the words that come out of their mouth. For it is written:

What good is it, my brothers, if someone says he has faith but does not have works? Can that faith save him? If a brother or sister is poorly clothed and lacking in daily food, and one of you says to them, "Go in peace, be warmed and filled," without giving them the things needed for the body, what good is that? So also faith by itself, if it does not have works, is dead. But someone will say, "You have faith and I have

works." Show me your faith apart from your works, and I will show you my faith by my works. **(James 2:14-18) – English Standard Version**

Watcher, oh watcher this is the difference between the first criminal to the second criminal: The second criminal was just as guilty as the first, but his heart possessed faith in Christ rather than faith in the law. For it is written:

For all who rely on works of the law are under a curse; for it is written, "Cursed be everyone who does not abide by all things written in the Book of the Law and do them." Now it is evident that no one is justified before God by the law, for "The righteous shall live by faith." But the law is not of faith, rather "The one who does them shall live by them." (Galatians 3:10-12) – English Standard Version

Watcher, the heart of the second criminal spoke words of faith when he said, 'Remember me when you become king.' Watcher, oh watcher don't you see that the second criminal could have asked the Lamb of God to free him from the punishment of the law, but instead he asked Christ to remember him. By doing so, the second criminal's faith broke the curse of the law. This is how the second criminal pleased the Lamb of God because his faith was seeking out spiritual rescue rather than physical rescue. It is at this very moment where the riddle of the rich man and the poor man tests the heart of all readers. Those who choose the rich man's fate possess the heart of the second criminal. Those who choose the poor man's fate possess the heart of the first criminal. The rich man's fate is the person who wants to be remembered by Christ. They acknowledge their sins and by their faith, they break the law's curse. Watcher, oh watcher this is made true because we remember the fate of the rich man, not for its tragedy, but of his good conduct that is produced by his faith. Those who choose the poor man's fate are the people who live by their natural human desires, so they want to continue living in sin. They will do and say anything to please the very sword that is slowly killing them. They do not wish, nor care to be remembered because they behave like wild animals. For it is written:

Or do you despise the riches of his goodness, forbearance, and longsuffering, not knowing that the goodness of God leads you to repentance? But in accordance with your hardness and your impenitent heart you are

treasuring up for yourself wrath in the day of wrath and revelation of **the righteous judgment of God, who "will render to each one according to his deeds": eternal life to those who by patient continuance in doing good seek for glory, honor, and immortality; (Romans 2:4-7) – New King James Version**

Watcher, the first criminal spoke empty words and his sin attempted to escape the punishment of the law when he said, 'Save yourself and us.' The first criminal had no intention of changing his life because he lived by the sword. The first criminal is no different from the poor man who murdered the rich man. Although the first criminal was caught, he was in a situation where he could have asked the Lamb of God to remember him in Paradise; instead, the criminal was seeking to flee from the punishment of the law. He did not fear the true judge, but his sin had urged him to flee from his deserved punishment. Watcher, I have shown you two different stories to define both what the law is and what faith is. Watcher, oh watcher you have seen the power of the law and the power of faith. Watcher, oh watcher I have put your heart to the test and taken away the ability to move your lips, so you may understand the difference between law and faith. The riddle exposes the law's unfairness where the story of the criminals shows the law's fairness. Despite what the law deems fair and unfair, my love transcends above the law's curse and brings forth grace to all who accept it. Author, oh author that is the power of faith! For if they believe in me, they will obey me which shows that they accept my love and love me back. For it is written:

For through the law I died to the law, so that I might live to God. I have been crucified with Christ. It is no longer I who live, but Christ who lives in me. And the life I now live in the flesh I live by faith in the Son of God, who loved me and gave himself for me. I do not nullify the grace of God, for if righteousness were through the law, then Christ died for no purpose. (Galatians 2:19-22) – English Standard Version

Watcher, oh watcher I am pleased with how joyous your heart beats. This is no secret; it has been written in the Scriptures and blessed upon the apostles who persevered the faith. You wish to be named back author, but I will not give you back that name nor will I return your voice just yet. Behold, the final answer

*you have longed for. It is through this answer that you will stomp on Satan's
doctrine. For it is written:*

**Be subject for the Lord's sake to every human institution, whether it
be to the emperor as supreme, or to governors as sent by him to punish
those who do evil and to praise those who do good. For this is the will
of God, that by doing good you should put to silence the ignorance of
foolish people. Live as people who are free, not using your freedom as a
cover-up for evil, but living as servants of God. Honor everyone. Love
the brotherhood. Fear God. Honor the emperor. (1 Peter 2:13-17) –
English Standard Version**

*Watcher, oh watcher I can hear your heart asking, 'Spirit of God, what then of
the cruel states and evil authorities?' Watcher, oh watcher just as you watch my
words become one with the page; so, do I view the nations and rulers who abuse
their powers and make slaves out of the righteous. For it is written:*

**"Woe to the shepherds who destroy and scatter the sheep of my pasture!"
declares the LORD. Therefore, thus says the LORD, the God of Israel,
concerning the shepherds who care for my people: "You have scattered
my flock and have driven them away, and you have not attended to them.
Behold, I will attend to you for your evil deeds, declares the LORD. Then
I will gather the remnant of my flock out of all the countries where I have
driven them, and I will bring them back to their fold, and they shall be
fruitful and multiply. I will set shepherds over them who will care for
them, and they shall fear no more, nor be dismayed, neither shall any be
missing, declares the LORD. (Jeremiah 23:1-4) – English Standard
Version**

*Watcher, oh watcher I am now taking away your vision because they will not be
able to withstand the upcoming sight. Therefore, I am now changing your name
from watcher to listener. As my angels touch your ears with the coals from my
altar, I give your ears authority to understand what I have to say. When your
name was Author, I spoke to you regarding the fallen angels. In heaven they
rejected their own blessed names to become Satan's slaves. It is no different now
because Satan has infiltrated the hearts of kings, presidents, prime ministers,*

governors; and many other rulers who have turned corrupt and abuse their political positions. Listener, listen! Their acts have not gone unseen and their punishment will be severe. Listener, I took away your sight because if you saw with your eyes how my people are treated, you would be in great sorrow. Listener, listen! Those who suffer for my sake are indeed my people. For it is written:

"If the world hates you, know that it has hated me before it hated you. If you were of the world, the world would love you as its own; but because you are not of the world, but I chose you out of the world, therefore the world hates you. Remember the Word that I said to you: 'A servant is not greater than his master.' If they persecuted me, they will also persecute you. If they kept my Word, they will also keep yours. But all these things they will do to you on account of my name, because they do not know him who sent me. If I had not come and spoken to them, they would not have been guilty of sin, but now they have no excuse for their sin. Whoever hates me hates my Father also. If I had not done among them the works that no one else did, they would not be guilty of sin, but now they have seen and hated both me and my Father. But the Word that is written in their Law must be fulfilled: 'They hated me without a cause.'" (John 15:18-25) – English Standard Version

Listener, I can hear your heart asking, 'Spirit of God, why would you let your people suffer on earth? Aren't you the God of peace?' Listener, listen! I touched your ears to listen and understand. Have you not heard my words? How do you still not understand? Listen again! For it is written:

Jesus said, 'My kingdom does not belong to this world; if my kingdom belonged to this world, my followers would fight to keep me from being handed over to the Jewish authorities. No, my kingdom does not belong here!' So, Pilate asked him, 'Are you a king, then?' Jesus answered, 'You say that I am a king. I was born and came into the world for this one purpose, to speak about the truth. Whoever belongs to the truth listens to me.' (John 18:36-37) - Good News Translation

Listener, listen! From the very beginning, I existed because my voice spoke it. That is why I talk to you because 'I AM' the truth. You prayed to me through your faith; that is why I respond with the truth. I can take away your voice from your mouth; I can take away the sight from your eyes; I can even make your ears go deaf! All these things are of no use when one wants to get to know me. Listener, oh listener I can hear your heart asking, 'Spirit of God, I am not following? What do you mean by all this?' Listener, listen! It is by means of your faith that you have obtained my Spirit. Human beings may persecute you today, or tomorrow. It might be so that the world may slit your tongue right out from your mouth! It might be so that the world may slash off both your ears! It might be so that the world may even remove your eyes from their lids! However, none of those things are required to know me! As long as you have my Spirit, I will always be with you. For it is written:

Neither the world above nor the world below- there is nothing in all creation that will ever be able to separate us from the love of God which is ours through Christ Jesus our Lord. (Romans 8:39) - Good News Translation

Listener, oh listener that is why it is written, 'they will hate you because they hated me.' Since you've accepted my Spirit, you are bound to be persecuted. You are persecuted because you do not belong here. All those who accept me live because all wait for thy kingdom to come. For it is written:

But even if you should suffer for righteousness' sake, you will be blessed. Have no fear of them, nor be troubled, but in your hearts honor Christ the Lord as holy, always being prepared to make a defense to anyone who asks you for a reason for the hope that is in you; yet do it with gentleness and respect, having a good conscience, so that, when you are slandered, those who revile your good behavior in Christ may be put to shame. For it is better to suffer for doing good, if that should be God's will, than for doing evil. For Christ also suffered once for sins, the righteous for the unrighteous, that he might bring us to God, being put to death in the flesh but made alive in the spirit, in which he went and proclaimed to the spirits in prison (1 Peter 3:14-19) – English Standard Version

Beloved, do not be surprised at the fiery trial when it comes upon you to test you, as though something strange were happening to you. But rejoice

insofar as you share Christ's sufferings, that you may also rejoice and be glad when his glory is revealed. If you are insulted for the name of Christ, you are blessed, because the Spirit of glory and of God rests upon you. But let none of you suffer as a murderer or a thief or an evildoer or as a meddler. Yet if anyone suffers as a Christian, let him not be ashamed, but let him glorify God in that name. (1 Peter 4:12-16) – English Standard Version

Listener, oh listener do not be afraid of the journey ahead. There will be days where your faith will be put to the test, but you must remain strong! There are some who will hear the word suffering and say, 'No thanks!' Listener, oh listener is there one person who does not suffer? Surely, I tell you, it is better to suffer for my sake than to suffer for no purpose. For it is written:

For I consider that the sufferings of this present time are not worth comparing with the glory that is to be revealed to us. For the creation waits with eager longing for the revealing of the sons of God. For the creation was subjected to futility, not willingly, but because of him who subjected it, in hope that the creation itself will be set free from its bondage to corruption and obtain the freedom of the glory of the children of God. For we know that the whole creation has been groaning together in the pains of childbirth until now. And not only the creation, but we ourselves, who have the first fruits of the Spirit, groan inwardly as we wait eagerly for adoption as sons, the redemption of our bodies. (Romans 8:18-23) – English Standard Version

Who shall separate us from the love of Christ? Shall tribulation, or distress, or persecution, or famine, or nakedness, or peril, or sword? As it is written: "For your sake we are killed all day long; we are accounted as sheep for the slaughter." Yet in all these things we are more than conquerors through him who loved us. For I am persuaded that neither death nor life, nor angels nor principalities nor powers, nor things present nor things to come, nor height nor depth, nor any other created thing, shall be able to separate us from the love of God which is Christ Jesus our Lord. (Romans 8:35-39) – New King James Version

Listener, Oh listener! Let me take you back in time. A time where the Israelites refused to listen to me. Listen! For it is written:

Then all the elders of Israel gathered together and came to Samuel at Ramah and said to him, "Behold, you are old, and your sons do not walk in your ways. Now appoint for us a king to judge us like all the nations." But the thing displeased Samuel when they said, "Give us a king to judge us." And Samuel prayed to the LORD. And the LORD said to Samuel, "Obey the voice of the people in all that they say to you, for they have not rejected you, but they have rejected me from being king over them. According to all the deeds that they have done, from the day I brought them up out of Egypt even to this day, forsaking me and serving other gods, so they are also doing to you. Now then, obey their voice; only you shall solemnly warn them and show them the ways of the king who shall reign over them." So Samuel told all the words of the LORD to the people who were asking for a king from him. He said, "These will be the ways of the king who will reign over you: he will take your sons and appoint them to his chariots and to be his horsemen and to run before his chariots. And he will appoint for himself commanders of thousands and commanders of fifties, and some to plow his ground and to reap his harvest, and to make his implements of war and the equipment of his chariots. He will take your daughters to be perfumers and cooks and bakers. He will take the best of your fields and vineyards and olive orchards and give them to his servants. He will take the tenth of your grain and of your vineyards and give it to his officers and to his servants. He will take your male servants and female servants and the best of your young men and your donkeys and put them to his work. He will take the tenth of your flocks, and you shall be his slaves. And in that day, you will cry out because of your king, whom you have chosen for yourselves, but the LORD will not answer you in that day." But the people refused to obey the voice of Samuel. And they said, "No! But there shall be a king over us, that we also may be like all the nations, and that our king may judge us and go out before us and fight our battles." And when Samuel had heard all the words of the people, he repeated them in the ears of the LORD. And the LORD said to Samuel, "Obey their voice and make them

a king." Samuel then said to the men of Israel, "Go every man to his city." (1 Samuel 8:4-22) – English Standard Version

Listener, did you hear how I warned Israel? The Israelites asked for a king, even though I informed them what the king would do. Listener, oh listener from long ago my people came to me and acknowledged my presence by asking for help. When they were slaves to the Egyptians, they cried out to me and I heard their cries. Listener, oh listener when I listened to their cries, I sent Moses for my people. No longer were they supposed to be slaved by other nations. However, they rejected me! They did not want me as king!

Listener, oh listener from the very beginning of time people have sought out for human kings. They all seek out to praise a government that they can see so they neglect me. The nations of long ago did not acknowledge my throne. But Israel! Oh, my Israel! They knew about my kingdom; they knew of my throne! Yet, they desired to be like the rest of the nations. I warned them of the consequences of putting their trust in other human beings, but they refused to listen. Now all countries are subject to their leaders. All countries have rejected my reign because all lacked the faith to acknowledge me. That is why all must obey state authorities because it is how all of you have established yourselves. These authorities exist because I have willed them to exist! I will use these authorities to show my people the real power of my kingdom! For it is written:

Then Pilate said to Him, "Are you not speaking to me? Do you not know that I have power to crucify you, and power to release you?" Jesus answered, "You could have no power at all against me unless it had been given you from above. Therefore, the one who delivered me to you has the greater sin." From then on Pilate sought to release him, but the Jews cried out, saying, "If you let this man go, you are not Caesar's friend. Whoever makes himself a king speaks against Caesar." (John 19:10-12) – New King James Version

I have given authority to nations with military forces; these nations force their children's children to go into war; these nations force their people to pay taxes for the political forces; these nations discriminate against all sorts of races; these nations treat their own people with unjust deals; these nations struggle to find peace! All the world wars and innocent blood spilled! Listener! Oh, listener, I can hear your heart ask, 'Spirit of God, was it not Israel who asked for a king? Why then are we all subject to suffer from wicked rulers?' Listener, oh listener it was not just Israel but all nations. All nations wanted to serve a master; all of them wanted a government. Listener! Oh listener, do not fret because the power of all these kingdoms will soon cease to exist. For it is written:

And in the days of these kings the God of heaven will set up a kingdom which shall never be destroyed; and the kingdom shall not be left to other people; it shall break in pieces and consume all these kingdoms, and it shall stand forever. (Daniel 2:44) – New King James Version

Listener! Oh, listener, those who possess my Spirit and acknowledge me will be welcome into this new and everlasting kingdom. For it is written:

In this manner, therefore, pray: Our Father in heaven, hallowed be your name. Your kingdom come; your will be done on earth as it is in heaven. (Matthew 6:9-10) – New King James Version

Listener! Oh, listener, you have listened and heard what I have said. You have heard of my kingdom that approaches. Listener! Oh, listener, those who put their faith in my Son will rise and have eternal life. For it is written:

Let this mind be in you which was also in Christ Jesus, who, being in the form of God, did not consider it robbery to be equal with God, but made himself of no reputation, taking the form of a bondservant, and coming in the likeness of men. And being found in appearance as a man, he humbled himself and became obedient to the point of death, even the death of the cross. Therefore God also has highly exalted him and given him the name which is above every name, that at the name of Jesus every knee should bow, of those in heaven, and of those on earth, and of those under the earth, and that every tongue should confess that Jesus Christ is Lord, to the glory of God the Father. (Philippians 2:6-11) – New King James Version

Listener, oh listener! I repeat! Do not concern yourself with the fate of the emperors, kings, presidents, prime ministers, or any other sort of ruler. Listener!

Oh, listener, you have come to know my voice; this voice is above all state authorities. For it is written:

No weapon formed against you shall prosper, and every tongue which rises against you in judgment you shall condemn. This is the heritage of the servants of the LORD, and their righteousness is from me," says the LORD. (Isaiah 54:17) – New King James Version

If the state authorities act in such a way that attempt to scatter my people, their punishment will be severe; If the state authorities pass down laws that are influenced by evil, they will be condemned accordingly. For it is written:

Oh, give thanks to the LORD; for he is good! For his mercy endures forever. O give thanks to the God of gods! For his mercy endures forever. Oh, give thanks to the Lord of lords! For his mercy endures forever: To him who alone does great wonders! For his mercy endures forever; To him who by wisdom made the heavens! For his mercy endures forever; To him who laid out the earth above the waters, for his mercy endures forever; to him who made great lights, for his mercy endures forever- The sun to rule by day, for his mercy endures forever; The moon and stars to rule by night, for his mercy endures forever. To him who struck Egypt in their firstborn, for his mercy endures forever; And brought out Israel from among them, for his mercy endures forever; With a strong hand, and with an outstretched arm, for his mercy endures forever; To him which divided the Red sea in two, for his mercy endures forever; And made Israel to pass through the midst of it: for his mercy endures forever; But overthrew Pharaoh and his army in the Red Sea, for his mercy endures forever; To him who led his people through the wilderness, for his mercy endures forever; To him who struck down great kings, for his mercy endures forever; and slew famous kings, for his mercy endures forever- Sihon king of the Amorites, for his mercy endures forever; And Og the king of Bashan, for his mercy endures forever- And gave their land as a heritage, for his mercy endures forever; A heritage to Israel his servant, for his mercy endures forever. Who remembered us in our lowly state, for his mercy endures forever; and rescued us from our enemies, for his mercy endures forever, who gives food to all flesh, for his mercy endures forever.

Oh, give thanks to the God of heaven! For his mercy endures forever. **(Psalms 136) – New King James Version**

Listener! Oh, listener give thanks to the name that is above all names; for my love is truly forever. I have taken away your voice; I have taken away your sight. Your name has been changed twice! However, the time has come to restore your sight. Listener, oh listener your name will now go back to the watcher. Watcher, oh watcher your name will not remain watcher because I am changing it back to the author. By doing so, I have restored your voice. Author, oh author you once could not speak because I took your voice. Author, oh author you once could not see because I took away your sight. Author, you have been restored to one piece. Author, oh author I did these things so that you may understand faith through different themes. For it is written:

The God who said, 'Out of darkness the light shall shine!' is the same God who made his light shine in our hearts, to bring us the knowledge of God's glory shining in the face of Christ. (2 Corinthians 4:6) – Good News Translation

Author, oh author it is through your faith in me that your heart did not need your mouth, eyes or ears to understand who I am. I proved to you that even with your voice, sight, and hearing, it is not enough to know me. Author, oh author it is what you store in your heart that measures your faith. For it is written:

"Do not lay up for yourselves treasures on earth, where moth and rust destroy and where thieves break in and steal; but lay up for yourselves treasures in heaven, where neither moth nor rust destroys and where thieves do not break in and steal. For where your treasure is, there your heart will be also. (Matthew 6:19-21) – New King James Version

Author, oh author those who store up faith in me within their hearts will be put right with me. What will they have to worry about? Yes, that's right nothing! Do you not remember Zechariah, the father of John the Baptist? The angel Gabriel came to him and told him that he would have a son, but he did not believe. The angel Gabriel took away Zechariah's voice until he saw what was promised to him. For it is written:

Immediately his mouth was opened, and his tongue loosed, and he spoke, praising God. (Luke 1:64) – **New King James Version**

Author, oh author it is not by his voice that his heart began to store up faith in what God had promised him. It was in his silence where his heart became patient in the faith and when John was born his voice returned. I too changed his name from Zechariah, a man with a voice to a watcher, a man without a voice. Author, oh author does this mean to develop faith, one must see to believe? Of course not! For it is written:

Now Thomas, one of the twelve, called the twin, was not with them when Jesus came. So the other disciples told him, "We have seen the Lord." But he said to them, "Unless I see in his hands the mark of the nails and place my finger into the mark of the nails, and place my hand into his side, I will never believe." Eight days later, his disciples were inside again, and Thomas was with them. Although the doors were locked, Jesus came and stood among them and said, "Peace be with you." Then he said to Thomas, "Put your finger here, and see my hands; and put out your hand and place it in my side. Do not disbelieve but believe." Thomas answered him, "My Lord and my God!" Jesus said to him, "Have you believed because you have seen me? Blessed are those who have not seen and yet have believed." (John 20:24-29) – English Standard Version

Author, oh author those who store the real treasure, well known as faith, in their hearts will not even need their mouths, eyes or ears to believe. Those who store doubt within their hearts are doomed to ever understanding because it robs faith. Author, oh author I have mentioned that it is only by faith that you are put right with God. Author, oh author you asked what people are to do if a law is passed by the state that infringes against my laws? What I say to you is this: Have you forgotten about my servant Daniel? Author, it is through his story where people will see how the power of faith transcends above the law. A law was passed that forbid anyone in the kingdom to worship any god. Daniel could not obey this law, even though it was passed down by the state authority. Daniel's faith in the LORD was more important than the law. Daniel did not fear the punishment of the law because he valued his relationship with me. For it is written:

Then these men came by agreement and found Daniel making petition and plea before his God. Then they came near and said before the king, concerning the injunction, "O king! Did you not sign an injunction, that anyone who makes petition to any god or man within thirty days except to you, O king, shall be cast into the den of lions?" The king answered and said, "The thing stands fast, according to the law of the Medes and Persians, which cannot be revoked." Then they answered and said before the king, "Daniel, who is one of the exiles from Judah, pays no attention to you, O king, or the injunction you have signed, but makes his petition three times a day." Then the king, when he heard these words, was much distressed and set his mind to deliver Daniel. And he labored till the sun went down to rescue him. Then these men came by agreement to the king and said to the king, "Know, O king, that it is a law of the Medes and Persians that no injunction or ordinance that the king establishes can be changed." Then the king commanded, and Daniel was brought and cast into the den of lions. The king declared to Daniel, "May your God, whom you serve continually, deliver you!" And a stone was brought and laid on the mouth of the den, and the king sealed it with his own signet and with the signet of his lords, that nothing might be changed concerning Daniel. Then the king went to his palace and spent the night fasting; no diversions were brought to him, and sleep fled from him. Then, at break of day, the king arose and went in haste to the den of lions. As he came near to the den where Daniel was, he cried out in a tone of anguish. The king declared to Daniel, "O Daniel, servant of the living God, has your God, whom you serve continually, been able to deliver you from the lions?" Then Daniel said to the king, "O king, live forever! My God sent his angel and shut the lions' mouths, and they have not harmed me, because I was found blameless before him; and also before you, O king, I have done no harm." (Daniel 6:11-22) – English Standard Version

Author, oh author my servant Daniel knew to respect the king because he knew that it was by my will that he was king. However, my servant Daniel also knew and kept the most important commandment. For it is written:

Jesus said to him, "'You shall love the LORD *your God with all your heart, with all your soul, and with all your mind.' This is the first*

265

and great commandment (**Matthew 22:37-38**) **– New King James Version**

Author, oh author don't you understand now? My Word remains true because I am the truth! Rebuke the doctrine and all its thoughts. The enemy will always go for your mind because his principle goes like this: 'He plants his evil doctrine in the minds of humans, all in hopes that the seed will grow and the person harvests what is found in their fields.' Author, oh author you have been warned! Be careful! People will reap what they sow! If my servant Daniel did not plant in the field of the Spirit, he would have not known me, and the lions would have mauled his bones. My servant Daniel did not rest on his relationship with me. He spent time getting to know me; by praying and fasting; by studying my Word. For it is written:

This Book of the Law shall not depart from your mouth, but you shall meditate in it day and night, that you may observe to do according to all that is written in it. For then you will make your way prosperous, and then you will have good success. (Joshua 1:8) – New King James Version

Author, oh author I can hear your heart ask, 'Spirit of God, then the law does have value? I thought it is faith that protected Daniel, not the law?' Author, oh author I can also hear your heart also asking, 'Spirit of God, please forgive me if it seems as though I do not understand. I just want to know everything so that I may not fall.' Author, oh author do not be afraid to speak to me. During this whole speech, you have learned many things. What kind of God would I be if I did not want my people to speak to me? Long ago I delivered the Israelites from Egypt's slavery. I performed many miracles to show not only my people, but also their enemies that I am who I say I am. For it is written:

Then Moses called for all the elders of Israel and said to them, "Pick out and take lambs for yourselves according to your families and kill the Passover lamb. And you shall take a bunch of hyssops, dip it in the blood that is in the basin, and strike the lintel and the two doorposts with the blood that is in the basin. And none of you shall go out of the door of his house until morning. For the Lord will pass through to strike

the Egyptians; and when he sees the blood on the lintel and on the two doorposts, the Lord will pass over the door and not allow the destroyer to come into your houses to strike you. And you shall observe this thing as an ordinance for you and your sons forever. It will come to pass when you come to the land which the Lord will give you, just as he promised, that you shall keep this service. And it shall be, when your children say to you, 'What do you mean by this service?' that you shall say, 'It is the Passover sacrifice of the Lord, who passed over the houses of the children of Israel in Egypt when He struck the Egyptians and delivered our households.''' So the people bowed their heads and worshiped. (Exodus 12:21-27) – **New King James Version**

My servant Daniel knew all of this and obeyed. Author, oh author that was then and this is now. For the people of the old times did not have what you have now. Author, oh author many other authors wrote about the great things I have done. It is by me that they wrote for me in order to show my glory for the future people. Today, you write in this way because of your faith. Author, oh author it was not by Daniel's knowledge of the law that I had my angels go and save him; it was by his faith in me that I had him saved. My servant Daniel studied and understood the law because of his faith in the Author named 'I AM.' The author named, 'King of kings and Lord of Lords.' The author named, 'Mighty God, Prince of peace, Eternal Father, and Wonderful Counselor.' I am the Author of the Word, and it is by your faith that you have received my Word. My servant Daniel recognized that my Word was higher than any law because it is the same Word that made the law. That is why my servant John wrote, 'In the beginning, the Word already existed; the Word was with God, and the Word was God. From the very beginning, the Word was with God.' Author, you came and prayed to me so that I may guide you through my Word. Author, you asked your parents and your brother Imani for help to understand the importance of Law and Faith. Author, you even went so far by asking someone from church, but none could provide you with the answer. Then I sang this to your heart this. For it is written:

I will lift up my eyes to the hills- from whence comes my help? My help comes from the LORD, who made heaven and earth. (Psalms 121:1-2) – **New King James Version**

Your heart sang back,

'Spirit of God, you're the true Author. Every Word written on the biblical pages. It is your Word that gives me strength; it is your Word that made heaven and earth. Spirit of God, you're the true Author. You wrote about the beginning and you wrote about the end. Spirit of God, you're the true Author. You give insight to those who ask for it. Spirit of God, you're the true Author because you help me write about the things that I do not know of.'

I have revealed to you the difference between the law and faith. Author, oh author you titled this chapter law vs. faith but what you fail to realize is that there is no contradiction within my Word. Author, oh author my servant Daniel was safe from the lions because he obeyed the most important commandment: love your Lord God with all your heart, mind and soul. My servant Daniel only followed that commandment because of his faith in my Word. Author, oh author my speech to you in this chapter would mean nothing to you without faith. Passover is remembered because of what I did for Israel. Then those people passed away, so what did the people who did not see my works go off? It is by faith that they believed in my actions and obeyed my Word also. For it is written:

Heaven and earth will pass away, but my words will never pass away. (Matthew 24:35) - Good News Translation

Author, oh author the law is not your enemy, but it opens people's eyes to the real enemy. It is faith that defeats the enemy because it allows people to believe and obey the law. My servant Daniel knew that before the law my Word already existed, so he put his faith in the Word because 'I AM.' The law would have never existed without the Word. Author, oh author you have read from other authors in my book who wrote on my behalf, all the works that I have performed. Author, oh author those who believe in my Word; believe in my Son and me. To please me is not by the law but by faith and by faith they will obey my Word. Author, oh author faith establishes relationship while the law is followed to show your love for righteousness because I AM the Author of righteousness! Those who have faith in me, will obey me because of their love for me and they will have eternal life!"

-Spirit of God

CHAPTER 9
ADVERSITIES AND HARDSHIPS

The year 2018 could have gone anyway when I start to think back on how things turned out. The saying, "you learn from your mistakes," had yet to stick in my head. I often picture God up in heaven just staring down shaking his head at me for all the avoidable situations I got myself into. Maybe it's just me who thinks like that but when I do make mistakes I always think, "I wonder what God thinks of me?" I have opened up a lot in this book, but this is when things get really deep.

A friend of mine once suggested that I should go see a therapist, not because they thought I was crazy (well who knows) but they noticed that I had a serious issue confiding in people. Even as I think about their suggestion, what I did next was horrible. I lied and said I went when I never intended to go. Why did I do that? Well, I didn't like the idea of speaking to a complete stranger. I thought it was a waste of time because I knew what my problem was. It was pride. In the chapter love vs lust, I had mentioned how sin has the powerful ability to deceive us into thinking that we have sin under control when it's the other way around. The dangerous thing about self-diagnosing ourselves is although we may know what our sicknesses are, we become reluctant from doing anything about it. In my case, I had various issues as some might have noticed in previous chapters. In this chapter that speaks about adversities, the common denominator that is similar to my problems is pride. One thing I have to address before I continue, is I am not bashing therapy. Therapy is about having a healthy conversation with a qualified individual who attempts to resolve a person's issues or comforts someone in need without prejudice. I have never stepped foot in a counselor's office because my pride always said, "they don't and won't understand me because no one knows and understands me." What did I mean by that? Well, when I was younger, I'm talking like about 10 years old, I went to a public school. I had a tough time fitting in because I was bullied because of my skin color. I never shared this with my parents and if they were to read this now, it would come as a complete shock. From a very young age, I was too prideful to even say what I felt because I wanted to be seen as put together. The only reason how I even remember how old I was is simply because the grade I was in was always the last digit of the year. When I was in grade 2, the year was 2002. Now I didn't stay at the Bayshore public school for long, but the bullying went on from preschool to grade 3 until my family moved to a different area in Ottawa. Relieved that I did not have to see those bullies anymore, I moved to a Catholic elementary school called, St. Elizabeth Ann Seton. The reason why I am time traveling back to these events is to explain what happens when sin, even at a young age, can grow to something destructive.

I do not think it really matters what kind of school parents enroll their children in because bullying exists everywhere. For me, going to a Catholic school was a better experience. Another great experience that I had growing up was being apart of a team and I think that's why I fell in love with soccer. So, when did it all go wrong? Everyone deals with bullying in different ways; some talk about it with their parents; some ignore it, and others bottle it up inside. I chose to bottle it up inside and let my pride deal with it. Things took a different turn in high school because although the bullying stopped when I moved from a public school to a Catholic school, the memories never went away. That pride that I had inside me from such a young age decided to advise me, "If you cannot beat them, you have to join them." It was then when I unknowably planted the seed of a prideful nature and as we have learned from God's Word: We will reap exactly what we plant.

I got extremely talented at making friends with almost everyone because I became what the Pokémon world calls a ditto (Yes, I'm THAT nerdy). I use that analogy because Pokémon are cartoons, which I used to watch when I was younger. I think subconsciously I inherited the features of the Pokémon named ditto. To quickly sum up what Pokémon are (for those who do not know), they are living creatures in this cartoon universe that all had certain powers. The Pokémon ditto had the power to replicate the image and powers of any other Pokémon it saw. In other words, it was an imposter and copied the abilities of others. I remember the feeling of being made fun of because of my skin color. I remember how much it hurt and how I used to sit alone at recess. I just waited for that final bell to ring so I could go home. Those are things people just cannot forget because that's how real the pain is. Despite all that pain, what I really wanted was to just be liked for who I was, but the bullying made me question God, "Why did you make me black?"

So, God created human beings, making them to be like himself. He created them male and female, blessed them, and said, "Have many children, so your descendants will live all over the earth and bring it under their control. I am putting you in charge of the fish, the birds, and all the wild animals. **(Genesis 1:27) – Good News Translation**

The only issue about living life like the Pokémon ditto was I began to hate myself. My pride prevented me from confiding in anyone because it would expose to people that what they said or did to me hurt. I couldn't allow that, so I decided to spend my whole high school years being someone I was not. Picture this: If someone said they liked green, but my favorite color was actually blue, I would lie and say green just to fit in with that person. It wasn't until my last year in high school when I not only hated who I had become but realized I was spiritually lost.

To some extent, I hated being bullied so much that I became the bully and surrounded myself with the group of people who I thought looked superior. The cold truth that I have realized is it doesn't matter how old we get or what we look like, bullying will always exist. However, what I went through had to happen or else I don't even think I would even be writing this book.

LORD, you have examined me, and you know me. You know everything I do; from far away you understand all my thoughts. You see me, whether I am working or resting; you know all my actions. Even before I speak, you already know what I will say. You are all around me on every side; you protect me with your power. Your knowledge of me is too deep; it is beyond my understanding. Where could I go escape from you? Where could I get away from your presence? If I went up to heaven, you would be there; if I lay down in the world of the dead, you would be there. If I flew away beyond the east or lived in the farthest place in the west, you would be there to lead me, you would be there to help me. I could ask the darkness or the light around me to turn into night, but even darkness is not dark for you, and the night is as bright as day. Darkness and light are the same to you. You created every part of me; you put me together in my mother's womb. I praise you because you are to be feared; all you do is strange and wonderful. I know it with all my heart. When my bones were being formed, carefully put together in my mother's womb, when I was growing there in secret, you knew that I was there- you saw me before I was born. The days allotted to me had been recorded in your book before any of them ever began. O God, how difficult I find your thoughts; how many of them are there! If I counted them, they would be more than the grains of sand. When I awake, I am still with you.
(Psalms 139:1-18) - Good News Translation

From a young age I had pride, and some may think that it is normal for a child to not say anything if they're being bullied. However, that silence was influenced by my own pride. I was more interested in what people thought of me than the actual bullying itself. What do I mean by that? Although it hurt to be bullied, I was more insecure and worried about whether people saw that it affected me. I never developed a tough skin to ignore any insult but instead would deflect an insult right back. This was the start of my change in character because my parents did not raise me to behave that way. That is why I use the ditto analogy because I knew I couldn't change my outward appearance but could become tougher on the inside by combating against those who were evil on the inside. I figured this was poetic justice because the people who were being racist were only doing it because it made them feel stronger on the inside.

"Spirit of Pride! Spirit of Pride! I order you to rise! There's a young boy that has caught the attention of my eyes. I order you to enter his mind and watch over all his thoughts. When the time is right, you will rule over his thoughts. Spirit of Pride! Listen to what I am telling you because this will become your goal. This young boy must always be prideful because those who are, will always want to be in control. Those who are prideful will never be able to save their souls. This is because they will believe they are in control! For it is written:

And so they wear pride like a necklace and violence like a robe; their hearts pour out evil, and their minds are busy with wicked schemes. They laugh at other people and speak evil things; they are proud and make plans to oppress others. (Psalms 73:6-8) - Good News Translation

Pride leads to destruction, and arrogance to downfall. (Proverbs 16:18) - Good News Translation

At such a young he refused to admit that he was hurt. Spirit of Pride take pride in your work! You must mold this child to be prideful! Spirit of Pride, haven't you noticed? Those who turn to God must admit they are full of sin, so what then if they are prideful? They cannot turn to God! This is your goal! Spirit of Pride you have slain many kings that is why I have placed you on my right wing. This child must never see you so I will disguise you as his friend. He will call you, and you must answer him! Spirit of Pride he must see you as his friend! As he grows up, he will always call you his friend! You must gain his trust, so he thinks you will protect him. Once you have earned his trust, we will move to his heart. Spirit of Pride, this is your next mission. Once you have reached his heart this what you will say to him:

'Young child from the beginning you never liked to admit your weaknesses. You cannot stand it! That is why I am here to help; to help you fight! You have named me ditto. No one will ever hurt you; no one will ever make you feel alone. I will put them in their place for you. You must always remember this: What hurts more? The pain you feel on the outside or the pain that hurts the insides? What scares people the most? Things they can see or the things they cannot? My child

273

it is the things they can't see because real pain is felt within! Study the thoughts and desires of those who hurt you so you will be able to double the pain they caused you! The words you speak aren't tangible; that is what I meant about things people cannot see!'

This child, once grown, will be the bully because you will have taught him to never be bullied. For it is written:

Teach children how they should live, and they will remember it all their life. (Proverbs 22:6) – Good News Translation

He will always think he is right and because he has heard all your lies, he will never see that he has sinned. When this child grows up, he will think he is a king. Spirit of Pride, this is your mission! When this child grows, he will be cursed because you sang this to his mind,

'Be prideful my child so that you will never lose control.'

Spirit of Pride this child will grow up to hate the answer 'no' because you will teach him to want anything and everything! Spirit of Pride there will come a time when I will call unto you to abandon him so he will not know what to put his trust in! I will plant onto him other spirits that will torment him in other ways! Spirit of Pride, I am pleased with your works so continue with pride because this child's soul will soon be mine!"

–The doctrine of Satan

As a child, I had prideful thoughts, but those same thoughts soon became an attitude and then changed into my personality. Writing this chapter was an adversity itself because it involved a lot of humility to admit my pride and what stupid situations it got me into. Everyone's high school experience is different, but one thing I have noticed about mine was that we were a bunch of young teenagers that all wanted to be loved. The chronicles of my story are my own story because I am my own person, so do not think that all students behaved as I did. It's not like I spent each day making sure everyone liked me, but I had this ego that I was better than everyone else. I did a good job disguising that ego, but it wasn't until a person got really close to me and that is when they would notice it. On paper, some will read this and wonder how anyone could have liked me, but it was that ditto ability of mine that could blend in with any group of people. I became so good at it that I became a natural at making friends. Before I continue, it must be noted that the ditto analogy became to be because of my prideful nature of always wanting to be liked. I knew I couldn't change my outward appearance, but if I changed who I really was on the inside just well enough. No one could be hateful towards how God made me look. Imagine that! All that ideology came from one hurtful experience in elementary school. In the poem about pride, it mentions a moment where the spirit of pride will abandon me. What did it mean by that? Well, it wasn't until high school graduation when I began to hate who I had become because I was starting to forget who I actually wanted to be. The whole time throughout high school, I spent mimicking different personalities just so I could fit in. It was after high school when the real problems began because it was time to grow up. I became afraid of how I would cope in the real world because I didn't know who I wanted to be in life. That ditto side of myself graduated high school with me and that's when I noticed its destructive behavior.

"Spirit of Pride! Well done, you have succeeded in your mission! The seed has been successfully planted, and his heart has allowed it to sprout. It is now become apart of him and beats within his bloodstream. The time is now right to abandon the child that has grown up clueless of who he really is. Spirit of Pride well done! You should take pride in your work! Now go away I have something to say to the child that has grown up."

"My child, my child who has grown up to be an author! I sent a powerful spirit out to get you a long time ago when you were so young. His name is called Prideful. Author, oh author how I've watched you grow. You want to know where your pride came from? It's something that's been passed down from your own family generations. This should not come to you as a shock! You have grown to be an author, an author for the Lord. Tell me how is that going? The seed prideful was born with you, but I commanded it to stick with you. I empowered your thoughts to be prideful and even though you were such a young baby; you

accepted it and the seed grew inside you. You must be wondering, 'Was this nature in me or nurtured?' The attitude was your nature, but because I am the ruler of all these spirits, I nurtured it to you. All throughout high school, you had pride in your nature, but the truth is what you really are is that scared little boy from elementary school. Therefore, when the time was right, the power of pride left you because you became scared of your own nature. You've been struggling to fit in from such a young boy, and I used this against you. You think I don't know the Scriptures? For it is written:

Everything that happens in this world happens at the time God chooses. He sets the time for birth and the time for death, the time for planting and the time for pulling up, the time for killing and the time for healing, the time for tearing down and the time for building. He sets the time for sorrow and the time for joy, the time for mourning and the time for dancing, the time for making love and the time for not making love, the time for kissing and the time for not kissing. He sets the time for finding and the time for losing, the time for saving and the time for throwing away, the time for tearing and the time for mending, the time for silence and the time to talk. He sets for love and the time for hate, the time for war and the time for peace. (Ecclesiastes 3:8) – Good News Translation

When it was time for you to grow up; you failed to do so because of the seed that grew inside you! When it was time to move forward, you didn't feel the power of your pride anymore. It was time for you to face the real world, but you failed to do so! The world demanded you to decide what you would do in the world and that scared little boy from elementary school realized that he was doomed for! Who were you going to be ditto? Your pride in ditto disappeared because I commanded pride to leave! Tell me my child, my child that grew up to be an author! Who are you going to mimic now? After the spirit called Pride abandoned you, you became afraid because you spent the whole time behaving like a child! You began to despise yourself and that is when I introduced you to the very spirits you write about! I planted the spirit of Addictions in you once you became accustomed to picking up alcohol. My child, my child that has grown up to be an author! You are the biggest fool because even as you write this book, you still are a child! Spirit of Pride was planted in you but then left you! Then the spirit of Addictions was planted in you!

My child, my child that has grown up to be an author! I could care less about your creativity. Name your sins what you want, but you cannot hide from my truth! This is who you are! Call them by their first or last name; call them by a Pokémon or even your other stupid favorite tv shows. You cannot run away from me! I told you I was coming after you! For it is written:

Jesus and his disciples were at supper. The devil had already put into the heart of Judas, the son of Simon Iscariot, the thought of betraying Jesus (John 13:2) - Good News Translation

After Jesus had said this, he was deeply troubled and declared openly, 'I am telling you the truth: one of you is going to betray me.' The disciples looked at one another, completely puzzled about whom he meant. One of the disciples, the one whom Jesus loved, was sitting next to Jesus. Simon Peter motioned to him and said, 'Ask him whom he is talking about.' So, the disciple moved closer to Jesus' side and asked, 'Who is it, Lord?' Jesus answered, 'I will dip some bread in the sauce and give it to him; he is the man.' So, he took a piece of bread, dipped it, and gave it to Judas, the son of Simon Iscariot. As soon as Judas took the bread, Satan entered into him. Jesus said to him, 'Hurry and do what you must!' (John 13:21-27) - Good News Translation

My child, my child that has grown into an author! If Judas, a disciple of the Son of God could not hide from me, what hope do you have? Yes, he ate the bread of Christ, but there was no Spirit of God in his life! What's a body without God's Spirit to empower it? Don't you see he too was once a child? From the very beginning, the seed that lived in him was the spirit called Greed. For it is written:

Six days before the Passover, Jesus went to Bethany, the home of Lazarus, the man he had raised from death. They prepared a dinner for him there, which Martha helped serve; Lazarus was one of those who was sitting at the table with Jesus. Then Mary took a whole pint of very expensive perfume made of pure nard, poured it on Jesus' feet, and wiped them with her hair. The sweet smell of perfume filled the whole house. One

*of Jesus' disciples, Judas Iscariot- the one who was going to betray him-
said, "Why wasn't this perfume sold for three hundred silver coins and
the money given to the poor?" He said this, not because he cared about
the poor, but because he was a thief. He carried the money bag and would
help himself to it.* (John 12:1-6) - Good News Translation

*From the very beginning, he loved money and sought out riches! My child, my
child that has grown up to be an author! Do you see now what I can do with a
single spiritual seed? His greed consumed his pathetic beating heart and grew to
become obsessed with money causing him to even betray the Son of God! For it
is written:*

**But those who want to get rich fall into temptation and are caught in the
trap of many foolish and harmful desires, which pull them down to ruin
and destruction. For the love of money is a source of all kinds of evil.
Some have been so eager to have it that they have wandered away from
the faith and have broken their hearts with many sorrows.** (1 Timothy
6:9-10) - Good News Translation

*Funny how I speak about the love for money; it's begun to consume your pathetic
heart too! One little spiritual seed and look at what you people turn into to! The
power of my spirit called Pride has left you realizing how insecure you really are!
My child, my child that has grown up to become an author! Why don't you let
your readers know about the times in high school when you made fun of those
who suffered from my spirit named Anxiety. Well, in your defense you didn't
know that it was real because that seed inside you blinded you from seeing what's
real. My child, my child that has grown up to be an author! Do you believe in
Anxiety now? I called upon its name when you were vulnerable! Pride blinded
you; Addictions made you hate the reflection you saw in the mirror, but Anxiety
is what really got to you! My child, my child that has grown up to become an
author! Tell us how you sleep? You close your eyes begging for a good night sleep,
but my spirit wakes you up and attacks you! You feel it in your body; you feel
it in your mind; you feel in it in your heart; you feel it in your soul! Author, oh
author write about how it makes you feel! It torments you not only in the night,
but it has gained control of you in the daylight! What's his name again? The
one who sang, 'His palms are sweaty, knees weak, arms are heavy.' I believe his*

name is Slim Shady! What do you think he suffers from? Author, oh author do you think its only about you? Do not worry, you are not the only one who suffers from my spiritual tolls. However, you have really piqued my interest because I warned you to stop writing! Does it give you hope? You think you can beat me? My child, my child who has grown up to become an author! Hide behind whatever title, just know I am coming for you all! For it is written:

And the Lord said, "Simon, Simon! Indeed, Satan has asked for you, that he may sift you as wheat. (Luke 22:31) – New King James Version

I can hear your heart beating author! Are you scared? Listen, I can make a bargain with you. I'll go easy on you if you stop writing this stupid, 'The Secret Is Out,' book. Why don't you just make this little deal with me? You think I do not know about what's pushing you down? You think I don't see you juggling back and forth with my spirits? Anxiety torments you, so your heart begs for a drink because Addiction has you convinced that Anxiety will leave you alone if you listen to it. Author, oh author don't you see they are lying to you? You are such a fool! They say they're fighting one another, but they are actually working together! I've fooled you using just two unclean spirits; I wonder if you could handle more? Oh, that's right! You want to know why I call you my child? Because you're still a child! You are still that insecure child from elementary school that couldn't handle bullies! From such a young age you listened to my spirit's voices and used them to protect you from physical bullies! Now it's those same spirits that are spiritually bullying you! My child, my child that has now grown up to be an author! Remember the first poem of this chapter? It went like this:

'What hurts more? The pain on the outside or the pain inside? Things people can see or things they cannot?'

Yes, that's right! It's the things that you cannot see because those are the things that brutally attack you! I gave you that advice from such a young age. I made you think it would protect you. The irony is it has come right back to attack you like a poisonous snake! Now you got both spiritual and physical attacks on the inside and out! Author, oh author it has been such a pleasure mocking you! 'Poetic Justice,' is what you called it? Yet, you cannot even blame me because *you did it all to yourself! Spirit of Pride, Addictions, Anxiety, please remind the author of a few more of your friends like the spirit of Depression! Do you feel depressed? The cycle that you run in has brought you into heavy financial issues! My child, my child may I also remind you of the pain you've caused your dear ole family. How many times is your own father going to have to bail you out of your financial issues? Have my spirits emotionally drained you? Carelessly taking out loans when your own father specifically said, 'My son, please stop drinking and I'll pay for your tuition!' Oh author, don't you forget? Are you ashamed yet? I remember the dialogue because when he spoke to you, my spirits were advising you this: 'Don't listen to him! You can juggle school and drink! Everyone else does it! He just doesn't understand because he is an old immigrant.' My spirits called you, 'smart and responsible.' However, that was your downfall! The prideful seed I planted from a long time ago called your own father a foolish bully. That prideful seed I planted inside you from long ago hates the answer no! So, you rebelled and got yourself into some ridiculous scenarios! Each one of your university years got worse and worse. Author, oh author I can hear your thoughts yelling, 'Satan shut up!' Author, oh author please tell me who in their right mind rejects free money. Your hard-working father offered to pay the school money! Author, oh author you say you hate me, but I think in reality you really love me! No, you continued year after year racking up your debts! As the debts grew so did my spirits inside you! You created your own adversities! It got to the point when you were too afraid to get a loan that you just let the school interests grow! Does anyone know that? No, of course not because you are too prideful to admit that! Author, oh author in this book you wrote about truth. Why are you not telling the truth about these stories? How embarrassing was it for you when you were too prideful to tell your father the financial debt you got yourself into? You couldn't even do it, so you asked that friend of yours named Andreas! Oh, author don't worry I'll tell your readers that you paid him back! See author, the thing about my spirits are that they get quite expensive! Your hard-working father begged you to quit your impulsive ways by even explaining your family tree. Author, oh author you know it wasn't nice to bring up personal family issues in this book!*

On the other hand, since you don't have any issue airing out your dirty laundry why don't I remind you about family curses! I've encountered everyone's family tree, and one thing about yours is they tend to struggle with my spirits named

Addictions and Pride! Readers did you know that the author is struggling to continue writing. If only the readers could see the tears on this page! You remember all the times' people have warned you! Expect the process of warning involves words like stop and no! Those are words you hate and don't like to hear! Even your younger brothers worry about you! For it is written:

The LORD said to her, 'Two nations are within you; You will give birth to two rival peoples. One will be stronger than the other; The older will serve the younger.' The time came for her to give birth, and she had twin sons. The first one was reddish, and his skin was like a hairy robe, so he was named Esau. The second one was born holding on tightly to the heel of Esau, so he was named Jacob. Isaac was sixty years old when they were born (Genesis 25:23-26) - Good News Translation

Oh author, oh author I can hear your thoughts weeping, 'Please, stop it!' You see readers, the reason why the author is yelling stop is that this is another one of his insecurities. Author, oh author wipe away your tears! Don't you want to prove to me that you're not that elementary little baby? This story has touched you because the older brother is you and the younger one is your brother Imani! Oh, Imani, meaning faith in Swahili; I guess your parents were foreshadowing his name where your name is just ironic! Innocent is the author's name, but I see no innocence! Readers in this story the older brother sells his first-born rights to his younger brother all for a bowl of soup! For it is written:

The boys grew up, and Esau became a skilled hunter, a man who loved the outdoors, but Jacob was a quiet man who stayed home. Isaac preferred Esau because he enjoyed eating the animals Esau killed, but Rebecca preferred Jacob. One day while Jacob was cooking some bean soup, Esau came in from hunting. He was hungry and said to Jacob, 'I'm starving; give me some of that red stuff' Jacob answered, 'I will give it to you if you give me your rights as the first-born son.' Esau said, 'All right! I am about to die; what good will my rights do me?' Esau made the vow and gave his rights to Jacob. (Genesis 25:27) - Good News Translation

Author, oh author does this not sound familiar? What kind of child are you compared to your brother? Wild, impulsive, a drunk, rebellious; stupid and useless! Where your brother has devoted his time at the church! People look up to him while they look down on you! Your insecurity is that you feel like you've let down your first-born rights! It's as though Imani is the older brother! You were offered constant love from your own father, but you rejected it because you loved me more, all so that you can feel free to party! You hate hearing no, so you have become selfish and now some of your own friends have even noticed it! You lie that you're in control, but you weep behind closed doors! That is why you hate being home, you don't know what to call home! You've 'dittoed' your way in life, but now people have seen you for what you really are; a poor child attempting to write a book because it's the only way you can talk to God! You yell, 'Spirit of God this! Spirit of God that!' I know this is your last resort because I've cornered you.

What a journey this has been but once I devour that little faithful seed inside you, your soul will be mine for good! I know you've encountered my spirit named Suicide because it was so close to ending you! Is that why you started writing this book? Author, oh author why don't we make a wager? Let's see what gets done first, this book or your life!"

-The doctrine of Satan

Hardship is something everyone goes through and there is not a single person in the world who has not felt it. From the moment we are born we are subject to hardships. Birth itself is a hardship because the mother must suffer just to give birth to her child.

And he said to the woman, 'I will increase your trouble in pregnancy and your pain in giving birth. In spite of this, you will still have desire for your husband, yet you will be subject to him.' And he said to the man, 'You listened to your wife and ate the fruit which I told you not to eat. Because of what you have done, the ground will be under a curse. You will have to work hard all your life to make it produce enough food for you. It will produce weed and thorns, and you will have to eat wild plants. You will have to work hard and sweat to make soil produce anything until you go back to the soul from which you were formed. You were made from soil, and you will become soil again.' **(Genesis 3:16-19) – Good News Translation**

God was displeased with Adam and Eve for disobeying him, so he pronounced punishments on both men and women. In chapter flesh vs spirit, I mentioned the spiritual meaning behind why it was a sin for Adam and Eve to eat from the forbidden fruit. What I didn't mention was that Adam and Eve's banishment from the garden was not their only punishment. Before their disobedience, there was no suffering. After they left Eden, God introduced what we call adversities and hardships upon our lives. Yes, that's right God allowed difficulties onto the earth. So, then this leads us to ask why? Why would the loving and merciful God allow for his creations to suffer? If it was to punish Adam and Eve, then that's fair but to let it go further to the whole human race? What was his reasoning? The thing about the garden of Eden was it represented a connection with God. Once Adam and Eve disobeyed it tarnished our relationship with God. Removing the two characters from the place where they used to be connected to him was God's way of telling us, "without him we are nothing." Now in my knowledge, I know certain people who will hear that and will become ambitious and challenge that statement because they have completely rejected God. Yet, I cannot critique nor judge them because I have subconsciously lived my life in a way where I challenged that statement as well. Believing that life is better without God because we have set our sights on earthly desires is the biggest lie. My whole life has been an attempt to challenge God and the sad part is I did not even know that I was doing it. In the previous doctrine of Satan poem, it reveals things about myself that I have shamelessly done but it is also an indication of my stupidity because I caused my own adversity and hardships.

Some people ruin themselves by their own stupid actions and then blame the LORD. (Proverbs 19:3) – Good News Translation

I cannot say that I have lived a hard life because my parents have worked hard enough to ensure that I can have the best possible life. Unfortunately, it doesn't matter how privileged one person is, especially when someone acts foolishly; they will get exactly what they deserve. What were my foolish acts? Well, I had accumulated a whole lot of debt because of my impulsive ways. I spent my whole time in university not caring about my studies but rather partying and squandering my opportunities. I have never been good at saving my money but was talented at spending it. There were many other stupid situations that I had gotten myself into and the people who had to pay for it were my parents. In the poem by the doctrine of Satan, it mentioned about a friend bailing me out from incurring tuition interest charges. Yes, it is true, and his name is Andreas Giannou, who covered a 2000$ Carleton University tuition payment because of my irresponsibility. Instead of saving what I had in my savings, I took spontaneous trips with friends which upset my parents which resulted in me getting kicked out. I stayed at my close friend Gesummino Sala's house for a month. During that time, I was blessed with loving hospitality from his mother and sister, but I still could not find any happiness. Deep down I knew I had to try to make amends with my parents. All these stories are examples of how I had created my own misery, but this was all because I was trying to challenge what God had set for my life.

The concept of disobedience not only introduced sin but also hardships onto our lives. When Adam and Eve disobeyed God, they were spiritually saying that they did not need God because they knew better. That may have not of been their intention, but that is what disobedience means which is why it was a sin to go against God's instructions. When they were booted out of the garden, humanity met adversity. If adversity could be defined, what's the first thing that comes up in our minds? Adversity means difficulties or misfortunes that occur in our lives. Now, this is the tricky part because I have talked about the Holy Spirit and how once we receive it, we become God's children. If we follow these steps and instructions that Jesus Christ told us, why are we still subject to adversity? It was mentioned in the chapter flesh vs. spirit. Christ came to free us from our sinful nature so why are we still subject to hardships? If we were to watch the local or national news, it is filled with tragic and painful sufferings. I could list many examples of different hardships, but it would extend the length of this whole book. I could give an idealistic answer to try and help understand why we go through adversity, but the answer itself doesn't make it easier when trying to walk with God. Adversity to us are difficulties and misfortunes, but that is not the real definition and purpose of adversity in the eyes of God. My idealistic answer to why we suffer and go through hardships was that God allowed it so that we are reminded that we need him. From the very beginning, he knew humanity would disobey and challenge him, so he allowed adversity to exist to humble and bring us back to his garden. I would like to say that I fully stand behind it, but that would be a lie. I wrote this chapter not to boast that I have come to understand God's definition of it but to admit that I am trapped by humanities definition of it. What do I mean by that? It was a tough pill to swallow when I looked myself in the mirror and did not recognize myself. I had lived my whole life being someone I was not just so that I could feel secure. I played the role of the Pokémon ditto because I was too prideful to admit that I needed God. That pride grew so strong that it blinded me from the truth, and I lived recklessly and sought out the pleasures of this world. Inevitably bringing on my own self-inflicted adversities but where did it all start? The egotistic mentality that I did not need God. That was my problem. Was I any different from an atheist? Yes, I was different because at least atheists aren't hypocrites. They stand by what they believe in (or don't believe in). An atheist has already made up their minds that God or any spiritual entities don't exist because they have put their faith in their minds. When an atheist hears a claim like, "We need God," they are likely to laugh and will collect whatever empirical evidence they can find to not only resist but defeat that ideology. I wrote that I was worse than an atheist, in terms of my faith, because I claimed to be a follower but behaved like God did not exist.

Remember that there will be difficult times in the last days. People will be selfish, greedy, boastful, and conceited; they will be insulting, disobedient to their parents, ungrateful, and irreligious; they will be unkind, merciless, slanderers, violent and fierce; they will hate the good; they will be treacherous, reckless, and swollen with pride; they will love pleasure rather than God; they will hold to the outward form of our religion, but reject its real power. Keep away from such people. **(2 Timothy 3:1-5) - Good News Translation**

People will behave this way because they have made up their minds that they do not need God and have rejected all things associated with him.

Behind every hardship that occurs on this earth is that statement, but we find it difficult to accept because of what is written in 2 Timothy 3:5: "we want to hold to the outward form of the religion but reject its real power." It seems rather self-centered of me to write about hardships especially when my own misfortunes came due to my own stupid actions. What right do I have to write about defining adversity when everything that has happened in my life could have been avoided? Yes, I have outlined what God sees as adversities but what I think we all struggle with is tackling what humanity defines as adversity. What do I mean by that? Well, I had listed the things that I considered as difficulties and when another person hears them, they will call it a misfortune. No one in the world is pleased when their finances are low; no one in the world is happy when their relationships go south and no one in the world is glad about getting sick. The list could go on, but misfortunes exist everywhere in the world. It doesn't leave anyone out but chases after all our joy and happiness.

When I went to Tanzania, I met one of my uncles who has had his arm sliced off by a bunch of thieves. Due to that tragedy, he cannot land a job because no one wants to hire a man with only one arm. Hearing his story broke my heart, but it hurt even more when he told me how he wishes for a prosthetic arm. Obviously, he cannot afford a prosthetic arm so he cannot go back to work and help support his family. Before all that, he had a job and both arms but one evil act by a random group of people changed his life for the worst and now he suffers for it. Therefore, what am I supposed to say to someone who has experienced such misfortune? Do I reply that his hardship doesn't matter to God? Of course, not! Do I answer him that God wants him to surrender to him first and all will be well? How do you tell someone about God when their life is filled with so much misery? Furthermore, how can I call my misfortune difficult when he's the one that lost an arm? Measuring one hardship with another is the only way for us as humans to appreciate what we have but even then, the difficulties of adversity still weigh on us. This makes it difficult to see what God wants us to see. God's definition of adversity is the process of us realizing that without him we are nothing. Humanities definition of adversity are hardships that are emotionally, physically, mentality or even spirtually draining. This is where I become confused because I cannot wrap my head or heart around how God expects us to be triumphant over our hardships. How does he except us to focus on him? Human misfortunes began the moment Adam and Eve disobeyed God, but did God really intend for us to suffer all our lives? Our disobedience created our suffering but how far are we to be tested until we eventually break? The difference between this chapter and law vs. faith is I understand what adversity is, but I am conflicted with its purpose; wherein law vs. faith I knew the purpose but misunderstood the definitions of the two. How does one ignore the reality of hardships and put their trust in God? I know God cares about what we go through, but it becomes difficult to understand God when our difficulties overwhelm us. The prayer that I need to pray is to understand the purpose of why adversities still exist even when we acknowledge that we want and need God.

"Spirit of God,

I have grown so accustomed to saying everything on my heart. I do it because you're slowly teaching me how to tell the truth. Spirit of God, you've taken me back to my birth country all for the sole reason to separate me from this very environment. You spoke to me in different ways and you have allowed me to see many different things. You are the God that sees all things because nothing can be hidden from you. You have brought me back safely to the land of many opportunities, but I keep messing up! I keep getting myself caught up in avoidable things! You know how much I love you, but I keep letting you down. Why does it feel impossible to serve you? I know I've been a prideful being, I've hurt others; I've been an untrusting being, and I've continued to sin. Yet, you are my witness when I say I'm not lying when I heard your voice on that plane. You said that you would be there for me! Spirit of God, your Scriptures say, 'ask, and we shall receive.' Spirit of God, I have presented my problems to you. I know they began long ago and only exist because of my own sins. The constant negligence to not take responsibility for my actions have worsened my problems. Spirit of God, you know I have nowhere to turn to. For it is written:

A man named Lazarus, who lived in Bethany, became sick. Bethany was the town where Mary and her sister Martha lived. (This Mary was the one who poured the perfume on the Lord's feet and wiped them with her hair; it was her brother Lazarus who was sick,) The sisters sent Jesus a message: 'Lord your dear friend is sick.' When Jesus heard it, he said, 'The final result of this sickness will not be the death of Lazarus; this has happened in order to bring glory to God, and it will be the means by which the Son of God will receive glory.' Jesus loved Martha and her sister and Lazarus. Yet when he received the news that Lazarus was sick, he stayed where he was for two more days. Then he said to the disciples, 'Let us go back to Judea.' 'Teacher,' the disciples answered, 'just a short time ago the people there wanted to stone you; and are you planning to go back?' Jesus said, 'A day has twelve hours, doesn't it? So those who walk in broad daylight do not stumble, for they see the light of this world. But if they walk during the night, they stumble, because they have no light.' Jesus said this and then added, 'Our friend Lazarus has fallen asleep, but I will go and wake him up.' The disciples answered, 'If he is asleep, Lord, he will get well.' Jesus meant that Lazarus had died, but they thought he meant natural sleep. So, Jesus told them plainly, 'Lazarus is dead, but for your sake, I am glad that I was not with him so that you will believe. Let us go to him.' (John 11:1-15) - **Good News Translation**

Spirit of God, you knew that Lazarus was sick way before they sent you the message about his health. Yet, you didn't go to him when he needed you the most. Spirit of God, I was not there but Lazarus must have been crying out your name! He knew you were the Son of God, so he must have said to his sister Martha, 'Sister, sister! Please go call Christ! All the doctors have failed to better me!' Spirit of God, I know you knew the pain he was going through. He believed in you and put his faith in you, but you kept him waiting until it was too late. Spirit of God, he must have given up hope once he knew it was time to go. He must have thought to himself, 'Maybe it was not God's will to save me.' Spirit of God, I am not sick because you have blessed my health. Spirit of God, I know people who are going through hardships. Spirit of God, I know you know about my uncle in Tanzania. When those bandits axed off his arm and stole from him. Although he still lives, he cannot find work because no one wants to hire a man with one arm. Spirit of God, he came to me and asked me for help. I *know you heard his cry for help when he asked me for about $2000USD so he could get a prosthetic arm. I sat there and told him, 'Id do my best to help.' It was your Spirit that spoke to me and said it was your will for me to go to Tanzania! Why did you burden me with that? How can I help others, when I cannot even help myself? Spirit of God, I know you know about my cousin who aspires to be a doctor. He is far more intelligent than I am and that's his dream. Yet, his father lost his job and couldn't pay for his tuition, so he got booted from school. He came to me depressed that one night and begged me to help him get back into school. Spirit of God, you knew these things would happen! It was your voice that told me I had to go there. Now I feel burdened but how can I help? I cannot even help myself! Was that your goal? You know about my hardships, but it just feels like you purposely added more! Every time I've asked you for help in this book you gave me a direct answer. But when I ask about adversities all your Spirit says is, 'Be patient, trust in me, pray, fast, have faith, obey and repeat!' I've prayed about my adversities way before I wrote this book, but that's the one thing you haven't spoken back to me about. Is it because you're still upset with my sins? Do I need to endure much longer? Spirit of God, I do not think I can take much more. You heard the doctrine of Satan's voice speak to me. Out of all chapters, it's mocked me the most in this one! Yet, your Spirit rebukes me and says, 'Be patient, trust in me, pray, fast, have faith, obey and repeat!' Spirit of God, it feels like I'm being disrespectful right now, but you know my heart, so I have to continue to talk. What are you trying to get out of me? What is it that you want to teach me? I listened to your voice and I obeyed and went to church there every day. I felt your Spirit grow inside of me and I trusted, prayed, had faith, obeyed each and every day! I know without that trip I would have never come back to this book and made it what it is. However, I am still going through adversities! I did not work for that whole month, and I know you knew my bills were piling up! Spirit of God, you know that took a hit at my credit score! I cannot even describe that stress! Yet, your Spirit rebuked me and said, 'Be patient, trust in me, pray, fast, have faith, obey and repeat!' Spirit of God are you kidding me! When I landed back home on Canadian soil, I know you heard the doctrine of Satan say to me:*

'One month in Tanzania and look at all your financial issues! This isn't faith but false hope.' 'Be patient,' he says? Please, oh please author, explain to me? Is God going to drop off a bunch of money for you?'

Yes, I know you rebuked his voice, but all you replied to me was, 'Be patient, trust in me, pray, fast, have faith, obey and repeat!' Spirit of God, my heart cannot lie to you, so I might as well tell the truth. Sometimes I feel like I've got a split personality! I know you're real and you've proven it to me numerous times, but my adversity is draining me. I've been patient and trusted you; I've fasted, prayed and obeyed; I've kept the faith again and again, yet my adversities remain. I do not deny your goodness and love for me. Forgive me, if that's what I may have blotted out. I would just like a few answers:

You knew of Lazarus's situation, but you waited four days and that's when his health said, 'too late.' Spirit of God, I know your Word, but at times when I begin to worry about my problems, I lose sight of the truth. Spirit of God, my timeline of 2018 has been strange, but nothing you do is ever straight forward. Your thoughts and ways are just too much for me to understand! For it is written:

"For my thoughts are not your thoughts, nor are your ways my ways," says the LORD. "For as the heavens are higher than the earth, so are my ways higher than your ways, and my thoughts than your thoughts." (Isaiah 55:8-9) – New King James Version

You knew I needed work, but you put me in a position where I had to reject a good job for no job. Spirit of God, when my own dad reads this, he will know that I'm telling the truth. My dad knew about my debts, but he told me I had to go to Tanzania and reject that job. Spirit of God, you know I'm not fond of hearing the answer no. You knew this about me! Yet, who wins a war against the Almighty God? I've been kicked out of my house once and that terrorized me, so you put that thought in my dad's head. None of those events made sense because even he knew the importance of work. Spirit of God, you knew I would have refused to go to Tanzania, so you had to corner me with my greatest fear. You knew I would have disobeyed my earthly father but when he said, 'take the job but move out.' I knew that I couldn't fight against it because financially I couldn't afford it. Spirit of God, you knew I was angry; angry at you because I felt like you had something to do with it! Then you spoke to me on that plane and took away my anger. I guess what I'm saying is: Are you waiting for the time to bring your Spirit glory? When you heard of Lazarus sickness, you said, 'The final result of this sickness will not be the death of Lazarus; this has happened in order to bring glory to God, and it will be the means by which the Son of God will receive glory.' For it is written:

'Take the stone away!' Jesus ordered. Martha, the dead man's sister, answered, 'There will be a bad smell, Lord. He has been buried four days!' Jesus said to her, 'Didn't I tell you that you would see God's glory if you believed?' They took the stone away. Jesus looked up and said, 'I thank you, Father, that you listen to me. I know that you always listen to me, but I say this for the sake of the people here so that they will believe that you sent me.' After he had said this, he called out in a loud voice, 'Lazarus, come out!' He came out, his hands and feet wrapped in grave cloth around his face. 'Untie him,' Jesus told them, 'and let him go.' **(John 11: 38–44) – Good News Translation**

Spirit of God, I may never be able to foresee what you have in store for me. If glory to your name is what you're planning, then I'll continue to be patient, trust, pray, fast, have faith, obey and repeat. If you did not bring me back to Tanzania, who knows where I would be right now. If I took that job, who knows where I would be right now. The way you've been working through me, I struggle to find where you want me to be.

Before I close this prayer, I want to thank you for helping me get this far. Spirit of God, in this chapter I do not just write for the readers but also for myself. You work in mysterious ways, but I still live with adversity. Spirit of God, I've asked many times for an answer, but you never have given me a full explanation. You have yet to answer me like you've responded to me in the chapters: Conquering Egypt and Babylon, flesh vs. spirit, lust vs love, and law vs. faith. I believe that you will remain in me for the rest of my life because I choose to stay in you. But how much longer will I go through these adversities? Please give me more than the answer, 'Be patient, trust in me, pray, fast, have faith, obey and repeat!' I am losing strength and just want to know your purpose in all these hardships. Spirit of God, please answer me.

Amen."

Adversity can either make or break a person. Historically, many have overcome their hardships and are remembered for it. From public figures to just regular people. We find comfort and motivation in their stories because they overcame their problems. I cannot speak or fathom what kind of hardships other people go through but within hardship is a chance to hear God's voice.

That evening they heard the LORD God walking in the garden, and they hid from him among the trees. But the LORD God called out to the man, "Where are you?" He answered, "I heard you in the garden; I was afraid and hid from you because I was naked." **(Genesis 3:8-10) – Good News Translation**

It all traces back to the beginning when Adam hid from God because he had known that he sinned, so he tried to hide from God. That very Scripture exposes our very human DNA because when we do wrong, we become spiritually conflicted. God had already known what Adam did and I'm sure Adam himself knew that God saw everything, but his shame caused him to hide. The reason I spent a good deal of time explaining the book of Genesis in the chapter flesh vs spirit was to make everyone understood what sin did to us. So, how does that chapter have any connection with this one? One thing that I find fascinating about the Word of God is how everything, even the tiny stuff, all tie up together. To the human mind, the Word of God is like a jigsaw puzzle but with the help of the Holy Spirit, the pieces are put together.

Then he said, "Do not draw near this place. Take your sandals off your feet, for the place where you stand is holy ground **(Exodus 3:5) – New King James Version**

Heaven and earth will pass away, but my words will never pass away. **(Matthew 24:35) – Good News Translation**

In the beginning, the Word already existed; the Word was with God, and the Word was God. From the very beginning, the Word was with God. **(John 1:2) – Good News Translation**

Before Moses could approach the burning bush, God had commanded him to take off his sandals because he was standing on holy ground. Why did God make him do this? Are there certain places on earth where we must take off our shoes because God has proclaimed it as holy ground? God instructed Moses to take off his sandals because Moses was in the presence of God, so it served as an act of respect. When we open the Word of God, we must remember they are not mortal words but God's Word that transcends above our thoughts and ways.

For as high as the heavens are higher than the earth, so are my ways higher than your ways and my thoughts than your thoughts. **(Isaiah 55:9) – English Standard Version**

God set the precedence of how holy his words are by telling Moses to take off his sandals. This then leads to the question: Why the sandals? Moses was a Hebrew but was raised by Egyptians. He had walked among sinners and had sinned himself. The sandals in the story represent where we all have journeyed through life and our experiences. The hardships that we go through may define who we might become or who we are but when we enter the presence of God all that is forgotten because of Jesus. If we commit ourselves to study the Word of God, we cannot bring our worldly views to his presence because his Word is holy and true. That is why God told Moses to take off his sandals because they represented the filth(sin) of where he had spent his life walking on. When we read the Word of God, we must like Moses take off our footwear (worldly views and ideologies) because we are entering holy ground (God's divine wisdom). It's not a secret anymore that I have chosen to walk on the path of unrighteousness, so why am I sprawling the pronoun "we" so much? Some people have rejected the unrighteousness path and others choose to live the righteous way, yet they still go through hardships!

A sinner may commit a hundred crimes and still live. Oh yes, I know what they say: "If you obey God, everything will be all right, but it will not go well for the wicked. Their life is like a shadow, and they will die young because they do not obey God." But this is nonsense. Look at what happens in the world: sometimes the righteous get the punishment of the wicked, and the wicked get the reward of the righteous, I say it is useless. **(Ecclesiastes 8:12–14) - Good News Translation**

It makes no difference. The same fate comes to the righteous and the wicked, to the good and the bad, to those who are religious and those who are not, to those who offer sacrifices and those who do not. A good person is no better off than a sinner; one who takes an oath is no better off than one who does not. One fate comes to all alike, and this is as wrong as anything that happens in this world. As long as people live, their minds are full of evil and madness, and suddenly they die. **(Ecclesiastes 9:2-3) - Good News Translation**

I certainly wasn't the first and will not be the last to write about what they think of adversity and hardships. The book of Ecclesiastes was written by king Solomon, the same person who God blessed with tremendous wisdom. Yet, he could not understand it either because it did not make any sense. Culture, technology, politics and times may have changed, but life and all its concept still remain a mystery to us. We are born and then we die, simple as that, which is why Solomon closed his theology of Ecclesiastes by saying the following:

"After all this, there is only one thing to say: Have reverence for God, and obey his commands, because this is all that we are created for. God is going to judge everything we do, whether good or bad, even things done in secret." **(Ecclesiastes 12:13) - Good News Translation**

Everything else that Solomon did, his career, and his wisdom, are all recorded in the History of Solomon. He was king of Jerusalem over all Israel for forty years. He died and was buried in David's city, and his son Rehoboam succeeded him as king. **(1 Kings 11:41-43) - Good News Translation**

In the chapter love vs lust, I had mentioned how king Solomon turned away from God because of his lust for foreign women. They convinced him to worship other gods which angered God and that was the downfall of the famous king. Despite his infinite wisdom, he still turned away from God. The reason why I'm bringing up king Solomon again is to remind us that no amounts of knowledge can protect us from the temptations of sin.

O Timothy! Guard what was committed to your trust, avoiding the profane and idle babblings and contradictions of what is falsely called knowledge- by

professing it some have strayed concerning the faith. Grace be with you. Amen.
(1 Timothy 6:20-21) – New King James Version

God's command to Moses to take off his sandals is a warning to us when we become too dependant on our earthly ideologies. We see, hear and experience many things and soon begin to think that we are wiser than God. We may never say, "I am smarter and wiser than God," but we behave like we are. Whatever path we choose to walk, whether we believe it is righteous or not we are still unworthy in the eyes of God. I could pour what I think is wise unto these pages, but it will not save my soul nor will it save others. I've invested the majority of my life searching for the X that will unveil the wealthy treasure chest and it is within that very search that I have burdened my happiness. I've idolized celebrities and sat behind the computer screen critiquing yet also envying their lives because they seem like they have it all. I've been selfish and prideful which is why I have lost many friends. In this chapter, I've exposed the dark secrets that I've kept to myself not to vent but to explain how little things like pride tarnish one's character. Yet, I still don't feel like its enough to solidify what hardship and misfortune really are because all the things that I suffer from are the results of my own actions. It would've been more appropriate to just pray for those who are suffering from hardships that they did not self inflict onto themselves.

Adversity weighs down on people and tests not only the human heart but the mind, body and spirit. Adversity draws out people's addictions, or in other words what they hold close to their hearts. Adversity draws out the flesh and spirit because it knows they are enemies. Adversity draws out on people's lusts' because if they give in, they may find themselves in greater trouble. Adversity tests the integrity of a person because it fixates on the law. It examines the faith of a person because it strives to appear as an unclimbable mountain. There will be some people that will not see the relevance of adversity with God because they are strongly convinced that everything that happens in life is by coincidence. However, before the earth was made God was "I AM." Now that very statement may confuse people because grammatically it does not make any sense, but there is a reason why God calls himself "I AM." Before the English language or any language for that matter, he was already the Word that had spoken.

In the beginning, the Word already existed; the Word was with God, and the Word was God. **(John 1:1) - Good News Translation**

I am the first and the last, the beginning and the end. **(Revelation 22:13) - Good News Translation**

God cannot and will never be a thing of the past (or in other words something that died) which is why he is "I AM." God never called himself "I Might" because his Word already did since he spoke it from the beginning. He will always be present far past the end of time. To save myself a headache of explaining "I AM" because my brain is incapable of truly understanding it. "I AM" is why we know God is omnipresent. Omnipresent means all present which solidifies his name as the one who is all.

The twenty-four elders fall down before the one who sits on the throne and worships the one who lives forever and ever. They throw their crowns down in front of the throne and say, "Our Lord and God! You are worthy to receive glory, honor, and power. For you created all things, and by your will, they were given existence and life." **(Revelation 4:10-11) - Good News Translation**

Therefore, he has already concluded to us that he transcends time. Time exists because God gave it the power to exist. We use time to help us organize ourselves because if no one respected time, nothing would function properly. On the other hand, even with time, we are still a mess. The only problem with the configuration of time is we have misinterpreted its meaning. In the chapters regarding Egypt and Babylon, I had mentioned how we all worship something because we are spiritual beings. As spiritual beings, we are inevitably subjected to the powers of time because we are all going to eventually die.

No one remembers the wise, and no one remembers the fools. In days to come, we will be forgotten. We must all die- wise and foolish alike. So, life came to mean nothing to me, because everything in it has brought me nothing but trouble. It had all been useless; I had been chasing the wind. **(Ecclesiastes 2:16-17) – Good News Translation**

In the story of Lazarus, Jesus knew that Lazarus was sick and in need of immediate healing because time was not on his side. However, Jesus did not seem to be bothered by time because he knew where time got its power.

When Jesus heard it, he said, "The final result of this sickness will not be the death of Lazarus; this has happened in order to bring glory to God, and it will be the means by which the Son of God will receive glory." **(John 11:4) – Good News Translation**

Jesus didn't rush to the aid of Lazarus. Lazarus's sister must have been under tremendous stress because the sickness was killing her brother. Illnesses and diseases themselves are also subject to time because the longer they remain untreated, the worse we get. None of this is a new phenomenon which is why we have people in the medical sector. They have devoted their lives to helping others when our bodies are under attack from sicknesses or diseases.

Jesus answered them, "People who are well do not need a doctor, but only those who are sick. I have not come to call respectable people to repent, but outcasts." **(Luke 5:31-32) – Good News Translation**

Come to me, all of you who are tired from carrying heavy loads, and I will give you rest. Take my yoke and put it on you, and learn from me, because I am gentle and humble in spirit; and you will find rest. For the yoke I will give you is easy, and the load I will put on you is light. **(Matthew 11:28-30) – Good News Translation**

In the conquering Egypt and Babylon chapter, we went over how those two Scriptures have a spiritual reference to it. In the story of Lazarus, the doctors could not help him. Lazarus was on his deathbed and the reality of death loomed over his life. Jesus acknowledged the role of doctors and never spoke negativity towards the occupation. But in the case of this story, no doctor was able to help Lazarus. Now this dates back 2000 years ago, so the obvious reality is that the doctors were 2000 years behind from the medication and health knowledge we have now. But we are talking about Jesus here! So healing someone wasn't an issue. Yet, he allowed Lazarus to die knowing fully well that he could have healed him. So, what was the point? It all goes back to what I had made clear from the beginning of the book. We have to evaluate the spiritual rather than the physical. At that period of time, the doctors could not heal Lazarus. But even today there exists diseases or specific sickness that are beyond the medical profession's reach and they cannot help every patient from the reality of death. Was God's purpose of the story to discourage the medical profession? Or did I misinterpret the Scripture because I did not remove my shoes which stood on holy ground?

Jesus said to her, "I am the resurrection and the life. Those who believe in me will live, even though they die; and those who live and believe in me will never die. Do you believe this?" "Yes, Lord!" she answered. "I do believe that you are the Messiah, the Son of God, who was to come into the world." **(John 11:25-27) - Good News Translation**

Make any sense? Of course not! In all honesty, it cannot make any sense because time restricts it from making any sense. So, do I just finish the chapter and close with the conclusion that none of this makes any sense? No, personally I have come too far to turn back. There must be an explanation of what Jesus was talking about! The reason as to why we find it difficult to understand what Jesus said is because we have kept our sandals on holy ground. As humans, we rely on time to organize ourselves, but we have also misinterpreted its purpose because we have put our time in other things. How can we understand the elements of the Spirit when our minds are fixated on the things that are destined to diminish? The whole concept of life makes sense because time is its reference. This also makes sense with the concept of death because time tells us that someone is dead. Besides the obvious factors of seeing and touching a person. We see life in others by each passing second, minute, hour, day, month and year. The death of a person is made known to us when they are no longer active with time. Jesus explains explicitly that those who believe will live despite death or will never die. For that to make sense the person must somehow transcend time itself. But our knowledge and common sense tell us that it is impossible.

"I have no demon," Jesus answered. "I honor my Father, but you dishonor me. I am not seeking honor for myself. But there is one who is seeking it and who judges in my favor. I am telling you the truth: whoever obeys my teaching will never die." They said to him, "Now we know for sure that you have a demon! Abraham died, and the prophets died, yet you say that whoever obeys your teaching will never die. Our father Abraham died; you do not claim to be greater than Abraham, do you? And the prophets also died. Who do you think you are?" Jesus answered, "If I were to honor myself, that honor would be worth nothing. The one who honors me is my Father—the very one you say is your God. You have never known him, but I know him. If I were to say that I do not know him, I would be a liar like you. But I do know him, and I obey his word. Your father Abraham rejoiced that he was to see the time of my coming; he saw it and was glad." They said to him, "You are not even fifty years old—and you have seen Abraham?" "I am telling you the truth," Jesus replied. "Before Abraham was born, 'I Am'." Then they picked up stones to throw at him, but Jesus hid himself and left the Temple. **(John 8:48-59) – New King James Version**

In John 8:48-59, we read about how Jesus is telling the Pharisees how those who obey his teaching will never die. But this brought forth a violent situation because the Pharisees questioned how that could be possible if Abraham and the other prophets died. Jesus responded, "Before Abraham was born, 'I AM.'" Which basically means he was before, during and after Abraham's birth, life and death. This absolutely pissed off the Pharisees because time not only doesn't allow it to make sense, but Jesus just proclaimed to them that he was God since 'I AM' is one of God's holy names (Exodus 3:14). So they tried to stone him for this comment. However, because I am such a great narrator and teacher (clearly joking), we know the Pharisees were blinded by the law. They worshipped the law to such a point that it became their god, not knowing that God was right in front of them. Has the way we view, and value time blinded us from seeing God? As I write this, I want to tread very carefully with what I'm saying because I do not want to mistaken wisdom for foolishness. I have written about my upbringing and explained my story, but I cannot claim to have mastered or even come close to understanding adversity. It just seems that adversity co-exists through time because we are fighting against the inevitable fact that we are all going to die. If this is the case, why did God make time so powerful? Yes, Jesus said that if we believe, we can overcome adversity(death) but I'm becoming somewhat weary trying to explain this. My mind has been stretched so far that I too am just chasing the wind.

I, the Philosopher, have been king over Israel in Jerusalem. I determined that I would examine all the things that are done in the world. God has laid a miserable fate upon us. I have seen everything done in this world, and I tell you it is all useless. It is like chasing the wind. You can't straighten out what is crooked; you can't count things that aren't there. I told myself, "I have become a great man, far wiser than anyone who ruled Jerusalem before me. I know what wisdom and knowledge really are. I was determined to learn the difference between knowledge and foolishness, wisdom and madness. But I found out that I might as well be chasing the wind. The wiser you are, the more worries you have; the more you know, the more it hurts. **(Ecclesiastes 1:12-18) - Good News Translation**

"Author, oh author you are now entering holy ground, I order you to take off your shoes!

Readers behold the sacred truth on account of the Holy Spirit of God! For it is written:

A voice cries out, 'Prepare in the wilderness a road for the LORD! Clear the way in the desert for our God! Fill every valley, level every mountain. The hills will become a plain, and the rough country will be made smooth. Then the glory of the LORD will be revealed, and all people will see it. The LORD himself has promised this. A voice cries out, 'Proclaim a message!' 'What message shall I proclaim?' I ask. 'Proclaim that all human beings are like grass; they last no longer than

wildflowers. Grass withers and flowers fade when the LORD sends the wind blowing over them. People are no more enduring than grass. Yes, grass withers and flowers fade, but the Word of our God endures forever.' (Isaiah 40:3-8) - Good News Translation

Author, oh author you have been striving to calm the hearts of the readers with comforting words. However, your words are empty because they fail to proclaim the truth! You are speaking on your behalf and writing on account of your philosophy and thoughts! It is through your own sin to please others where you burden yourself with greater adversity! For it is written:

Does this sound as I am trying to win human approval? No indeed! What I want is God's approval! Am I trying to be popular with people? If I were still trying to do so, I would not be a servant of Christ. (Galatians 1:10) - Good News Translation

Throughout this whole book, my Spirit remained with you and you stayed in me, but one glance at your problems and you abandoned me. I told you to be patient, trust in me, pray, fast, have faith, obey and repeat but you ignored it and called it useless! Author, oh author let's say if I gave you the wisdom to understand time and space, would it save you from the consequences of all your mistakes? Author, oh author have you forgotten who you serve? Author, oh author you are no longer a child that needs to drink milk but a servant who is to eat solids. For it is written:

As a matter of fact, my friends, I could not talk to you as I talk to people who have the Spirit; I had to talk to you as though you belonged to this world, as children in the Christian faith. I had to feed you milk, not solid food because you were not ready for it. And even now you are not ready for it because you still live as people of this world live. When there is jealousy among you and you quarrel with one another, doesn't this prove that you belong to this world, living by its standards? When one of you says, 'I follow Paul,' and another, 'I follow Apollos'- aren't you acting like worldly people? After all, who is Apollos? And who is Paul? We are simply God's servants, by whom you were led to believe. Each one of us does the work which the Lord gave him to do: I planted the seed,

Apollos watered the plant, but it was God who made the plant grow. The one who plants and the one who waters really do not matter. It is God who matters because he makes the plant grow. (1 Corinthians 3:1-7) - **Good News Translation**

Author, oh author may I ask why you wrote this chapter? Yes, that's right your answer is written in your heart! You wrote it because you're still burdened by life! You struggle to find the answers to your problems which is why you consistently failed to understand the responses I have laid right in front of you. Be patient, trust in me, pray, fast, have faith, obey, repeat! However, you have failed to live by the instructions I had given you. Instead, you wanted things to happen under your terms! This chapter burdened you because you would not listen to what I had to say. You expected wisdom to come in the form of long paragraphs like I had given you from other chapters. But my wisdom is gifted to those who love and obey me. For it is written:

But where can wisdom be found? Where can we learn to understand? Wisdom is not to be found among mortals; No one knows its true value. The depths of the oceans and seas say that wisdom is not found there. It cannot be bought with silver or gold. The finest gold and jewels cannot equal its value. It is worth more than gold than a gold vase or finest glass. The value of wisdom is more than coral or crystal or rubies. The finest topaz and the purest gold cannot compare with the value of wisdom. Where, then, is the source of wisdom? Where can we learn to understand? No living creature can see it, not even a bird in flight. Even death and destruction admit they have heard only rumors. God alone knows the way, knows the place where wisdom is found because he sees the ends of the earth, sees everything under the sky. When God gave the wind its power and determined the size of the sea; when God decided where the rain would fall, and the path that the thunderclouds travel; it was then he saw wisdom and tested its worth- He gave it his approval. God said to us humans, 'To be wise, you must have reverence for the Lord. To understand, you must turn from evil.' (Job 28:12-28) - Good News Translation

Author, oh author even king Solomon admitted this, 'To be wise, you must have reverence for the Lord.' You burdened yourself with this chapter because you struggled to find answers and struggled with your hardships. Both author and readers have peace and listen to what the Spirit of God has to say about this chapter.

Write this upon your hearts:

For in your patience you shall be humbled; in your trust you shall never be let down; in your prayers you will always be answered; in your fasting you shall be fed; in your faith you shall reap blessings and thanksgiving; in your obedience you shall see love, and in your repetition you will grow stronger with God! For it is written:

You have been made clean already by the teaching I have given you. Remain united to me, and I will remain united to you. A branch cannot bear fruit by itself; it can do so only if it remains in the vine. In the same way, you cannot bear fruit unless you remain in me. (John 15:3-4) – Good News Translation

Author, oh author you wrote that adversity co-exists through time and time gets its power from me. Surely, I tell you that none have figured out that adversity exists through sin! No one is subject to time when they believe in me because those who believe will not and cannot die. For it is written:

And there are heavenly bodies and earthly bodies; the beauty that belongs to heavenly bodies is different from the beauty that belongs to earthly bodies. The sun has its own beauty, the moon another beauty, and the stars a different beauty; and even among stars, there are different kinds of beauty. This is how it will be when the dead are raised to life. When the body is buried, it is mortal; when raised, it will be immortal. When buried, it is ugly and weak; when raised, it will be beautiful and strong. When buried, it is a physical body; when raised, it will be a spiritual body. There is, of course, a physical body, so there has to be a spiritual body. For the Scriptures says, 'The first man, Adam, was created a living being'; but the last Adam is the life-giving Spirit. It is not the spiritual that comes first, but the physical, and then the spiritual. The first Adam,

made of earth, came from the earth; the second Adam came from heaven. Those who belong to the earth are like the one who was made of earth; those who are of heaven are like the one who came from heaven. Just as we wear the likeness of the man made of earth, so we will wear the likeness of the Man from heaven. What I mean, friends is that what is made of flesh and blood cannot share in God's Kingdom, and what is mortal cannot possess immortality. Listen to this secret truth: we shall not die, but when the last trumpet sounds, we shall all be changed in an instant, as quickly as the blinking of an eye. For when the trumpet sounds the dead will be raised, never to die again, and we shall all be changed. For what is mortal must be changed into what is immortal; what will die must be changed into what cannot die (**1 Corinthians 15:40-53**) – **Good News Translation**

Author and reader let me stretch your thoughts farther apart when I ask you this:

Why did I call the forbidden tree, the tree that gives knowledge of what is good and bad? Author, I can hear your thoughts scrambling for answers but for the sake of truth and sound doctrine, I refrain you from falsely speaking. Yes, I told Adam and Eve to not eat from the fruit. Yes, in the chapter birth of the doctrine you wrote about disobedience, but the answers to your questions about adversities were given from the very beginning! Yes author, Satan tempted Eve, but Satan is only relevant to the story because Eve allowed him to be! Eve listened to the voice, the same voice that you listen to. For it is written:

But the grace that God gives is even stronger. As the Scriptures say, "God resists the proud, but gives grace to the humble." So then, submit yourselves to God. Resist the devil, and he will run away from you. Come near to God, and he will come near to you. Wash your hands, you sinners! Purify your hearts, you hypocrites! Be sorrowful, cry and weep; change your laughter into crying, your joy into gloom! Humble yourselves before the Lord, and he will lift you up. (**James 4:6-10**) – **Good News Translation**

Readers seeing every word on this page: To hear my voice you must take off your shoes because you're now standing on holy ground. Forget your ideologies and evil ways! Repent of your sins and come to me! For it is written:

And yet, I am the God who forgives your sins, and I do this because of who I am. I will not hold your sins against you. (Isaiah 43:25) – Good News Translation

What you consider knowledgeable, forget it and follow the words that come from my lips. Those who do not do this have already rejected me because they are for the world. For it is written:

Unfaithful people! Don't you know that to be the world's friend means to be God's enemy? If you want to be the world's friend, you make yourself God's enemy. (James 4:4) – Good News Translation

The world suffers from the doctrine of Satan because it has allowed itself to listen to Satan's voice. For it is written:

I cannot talk with you much longer, because the ruler of this world is coming. He has no power over me, but the world must know that I love the Father; that is why I do everything as he commands me. Come, let us go from this place. (John 14:30-31) – Good News Translation

Readers listen if you have ears!

All that had heard the story of creation blame Satan for their own sin when it was by man and woman's free will that accepted sin. The tree that gave knowledge of what is good and bad separated all from me because man and woman did not obey nor trust in me. From the very beginning, man and woman behaved on their own and through their sin, they became independent beings. It is this very reason why all suffer because you are all nothing without me. In the chapter love vs lust, the author of these pages asked what love is? I responded to the author saying that, 'I am true love.'

Author, oh author if this is so, why then do you reject true love? I can hear your hearts response, 'Spirit of God, I have not rejected your love.' Readers, it is this very nature that I gave up my Son so that all your sinful nature would die and be buried by the blood of my sacred Lamb! Author, oh author say this to your heart:

Spirit of God, by the power of your Son, forgive my sins because I continue to lie! I rejected your love when I disobeyed your Spirit's voice when it said, 'Be patient, trust in me, pray, fast, have faith, obey and repeat.' Spirit of God, I know you have forgiven me because my prayer is steadfast! I have been no different from Adam nor am I different from Eve. I point fingers and blame others for my sins and when the repercussions came, I shamefully blamed you! Spirit of God, you made us and we disobeyed you; we abandoned you then blamed you; Spirit of God, you chased after us and we ran away from you; Spirit of God, you offered yourself to us and now you wait to see who gives themselves to you! I refuse to be an independent being because I am nothing without you.'

Readers listen if you have ears!

The tree that gave knowledge of what is good and bad gave all the nature to desire sin. It was through your own disobedience that all are subject to the power of time. Surely, I tell you none of you were supposed to be subject to time because only one creature was to be subject to its doom.

Readers open your hearts to the truth! Listen then, if you have ears!

The end of time is to separate those who choose life and those who choose death. For I tell you the lake of fire was not made for humanity. It is a place where my presence has no desire being because all that go there have no desire for me. The one who is and will suffer from the real power of time has desired the lives of my chosen people. For it is written:

When the day came from the heavenly beings to appear before the LORD, Satan was there among them. The LORD asked him, 'What have you been doing?' Satan answered, 'I have been roaming here and there, roaming around the earth.' (Job 1:6-7) - Good News Translation

Readers listen if you have ears!

Eden is a place that transcends time itself! That is why it is hidden from the human eye. It was in Eden that all were supposed to transcend above time because you were told to obey me! However, you disobeyed me because you did not love me as I loved you. Author and readers, do you all want to know why you all hate rejection? Surely, I tell you none of you were made to be rejected! For my love structured your lives so that you all would also love! Since all are made from love, it is that very love that feels sorrow when you are rejected because I could never reject you! This is why when man and woman disobeyed, they dismissed my love but I could never dismiss them. For it is written:

For God loved the world so much that he gave his only Son so that everyone who believes in him may not die but have eternal life. (John 3:16) - Good News Translation

Readers listen if you have ears!

For my love for all of you was so great that I chased after you by giving my own life! Admittedly, there is no greater act of love than by giving one's life for a friend! For I did this because death has no power over me and through my loving action I revealed my power which saves! The Good News has been told! What then are you all going to do with this beautiful testimony? For the story of love has been revealed! Surely, I tell you those who reject me now with that knowledge, I shall dismiss them. For it is written:

If we continue to endure, we shall also rule with him. If we deny him, he also will deny us. (2 Timothy 2:12) - Good News Translation

Readers listen if you have ears!

Long ago you all did not know love, but I showed the world true love. Do not repeat man and woman's mistake from the beginning. Surely, I tell you that my act was final and cannot be repeated! There is no repetition in such an action for its power is too great! Those who reject it have found it in their hearts to reject truth! For it is written:

For we know that Christ has been raised from death and will never die again- death will no longer rule over him. And so, because he died, sin

has no power over him; and now he lives his life in fellowship with God. In the same way, you are to think of yourselves as dead, so far as sin is concerned, but living in fellowship with God through Christ Jesus. (Romans 6:9-11) - Good News Translation

Readers listen if you have ears!

I escorted man and woman out because their hearts had become full of sin. They desired the knowledge of good and evil rather than the one true God that has always loved. Man and woman were separated from my presence due to their disobedience. And because of that, they were in the presence of the one who had desired to destroy them. Author, was it not you that wrote about what I told Ezekiel? About the king of Tyre? For it is written:

The LORD spoke to me, 'Mortal man,' he said, 'tell the ruler of Tyre what I, the Sovereign LORD, am saying to him: Puffed up with pride, you claim to be a god. You say that like a god you sit on a throne, surrounded by the seas. You may pretend to be a god, but no, you are mortal, not divine.' (Ezekiel 28:1-2) - Good News Translation

Man and woman disobeyed me to behave like the king of Tyre! Little did they know they were to be his slaves, slaves to his upcoming punishments through their own sins. Man and woman became beings of wanting things they could not have because the ruler of their world desires the souls he doesn't have! The ruler of that world wants what he cannot have, so he behaves like a tyrant because he wants to rule the things that were never supposed to belong to him. For it is written:

The dead will stare and gape at you. They will ask, 'Is this the man who shook the earth and made kingdoms tremble? Is this the man who destroyed cities and turned the world into a desert? Is this the man who never freed his prisoners or let them go home?' (Isaiah 14:16-17) - Good News Translation

Readers listen if you have ears!

Do not be like this ruler! Puffed up with pride and claiming to be the king over time! For there is only one king. Who rules over all! For it is written:

I will make him my first-born son, the greatest of all kings. I will always keep my promise to him, and my covenant with him will last forever. **(Psalms 89:27-28) - Good News Translation**

Surely, I tell you that no one can escape what is to come at the end of time! Author, oh author you think you know about the power of time! Surely, I tell you it has no power over you or any of your readers if all believe in me. That is why I warn all to not want the things you do not need or want the things that you do not have because he uses them to trap all of you. Even to his own people, he lies and fools them with deceit! Many hear the story of creation and are quick to blame the man and the woman! Yet, all of you live every day being fooled by the villain! For the punishments were written for the serpent, man and woman! For it is written:

Then the LORD God said to the snake, 'You will be punished for this; you alone of all animals must bear this curse; From now on you will crawl on your belly, and you will have to eat the dust as long as you live.' (Genesis 3:14) - Good News Translation

And he said to the women, 'I will increase your trouble in pregnancy and your pain in giving birth. In spite of this, you will still have desire for your husband, yet you will be subject to him.' (Genesis 3:16) - Good News Translation

And he said to the man, 'You listened to your wife and ate the fruit which I told you not to eat. Because of what you have done, the ground will be under a curse. You will have to work hard all your life to make it produce enough food for you. It will produce weeds and thorns, and you will have to eat wild plants. You will have to work hard and sweat to make soil produce anything until you go back to the soil from which you were formed. You were made from soil, and you will become soil again.' (Genesis 3:17-19) - Good News Translation

Readers listen if you have ears!

All were punished! The serpent for his deceit; Adam for his unwillingness to say no to his wife; and Eve for her foolishness! Author, oh author when I spoke to you to be patient, trust in me, pray, fast, have faith, obey and repeat; I spoke so that you would not fall under temptation like Adam and Eve. The thought of disobedience lingered around their minds before the serpent because those who obey me show that they love me. Man and woman disobeyed me because they began to desire themselves. The thought of eating from the tree that gave knowledge of what is good and bad appealed to them because they wanted to be gods themselves. For it is written:

The snake replied, 'That's not true; you will not die. God said that because he knows that when you eat it, you will be like God and know what is good and what is bad.' (Genesis 3:4-5) – Good News Translation

Author, oh author I can hear your heart saying, 'But Spirit of God, the serpent tricked them into thinking that way.'

Readers listen if you have ears!

It was by their own free will that they sinned! The tree that gave knowledge of what is good and bad was not desired because Satan presented it to them but rather was desired because their eyes coveted sin. Those who do not understand will ask, 'Is knowledge sin?' For it is written:

Here are proverbs that will help you recognize wisdom and good advice and understand sayings with deep meaning. They can teach you how to live intelligently and how to be honest, just, and fair. They can make an inexperienced person clever and teach young people how to be resourceful. These proverbs can even add to the knowledge of the wise and give guidance to the educated so that they can understand the hidden meanings of proverbs and the problems that the wise raise. (Proverbs 1:1-6) – Good News Translation

I told you readers, take off your shoes because you are now standing on holy ground!

Listen, those who have ears!

Knowledge is not the same as wisdom. The author of these pages may be knowledgeable of what is good and what is bad, but that does not make him wise to decode truth. He writes what he understands from the knowledge within, but it is when he prays to me when he receives wisdom that is beyond his knowledge. To be a reader does not make you wise but does make you knowledgeable; this is the same for the author! Both are the same and have come from sinful natures, but it is by my Spirit that all will be spiritually wise and fruitful. The knowledge of good may exist within the author and reader but so does the knowledge of evil roam around the minds of both. If this is the case, what then are they to do? Author, oh author tell your readers this:

'Spirit of God, I give you great thanks and praise for everything you have done for me. All the things that you continue to reveal to me I cannot even comprehend the things you do for me. You told me to remove my shoes because I have walked on the path of sin. I've entered many homes that hold different religions and ideologies that have confused me from the truth! I do not write this on behalf of me but by your Spirit, which is why my tongue burns to speak your truth. How can I ever be made new if I have become fond of the lies of this world? How can I ever receive what is holy when I am unclean? Who enters someone's home with their shoes on? Forgive me for entering into your Word with such arrogance and disobedience. I was once puffed up with pride and swallowed all the ideologies and doctrines fed to me. However, you have lifted my flesh and spirit to desire you! I pray that the readers take up their cross and forget the knowledge they have been taught by the world. The tree that gave us knowledge of what is good and bad deluded us from the truth, which is you. I do not want to continue roaming around the earth searching for more knowledge which distances me from you. I've removed my shoes and bowed my head down low to worship you! I have abandoned all the things that I thought was knowledge because it was not truth. I have suffered adversity and hardships through my own sins because I mistaken knowledge for wisdom and wisdom for truth.'

Readers listen if you have ears!

The ruler of this world will disguise himself behind the knowledge of what is good and what is bad. For it is written:

311

Then the devil took Jesus to a very high mountain and showed him all the kingdoms of the world in all their greatness. 'All this I will give you,' the devil said, 'if you kneel down and worship me.' Then Jesus answered, 'Go away Satan! The Scriptures say, 'Worship the Lord your God and serve only him!' Then the devil left Jesus, and angels came and helped him. (Matthew 4:8-11) - Good News Translation

Author and reader pay close attention!

The Son of God rejected the king of Tyre. Do you not see it? The knowledge of what is good and what is bad can be found in your very minds! Will you all acquire the world and lose your soul, or will you reject the world for me to save your soul? For it is written:

For if you want to save your own life, you will lose it; but if you lose your life for my sake, you will find it. Will you gain anything if you win the whole world but lose your life? Of course not! There is nothing you can give to regain your life. (Matthew 16:25-26) – Good News Translation

Author, oh author how have you not written about the story of Job? My servant Job! You desired the answer for this chapter so I will give it to you through his story. For it is written:

'Did you notice my servant Job?' the LORD asked. 'There is no one on earth as faithful and good as he is. He worships me and is careful not to do anything evil.' Satan replied, 'Would Job worship you if he got nothing out of it? You have always protected him and his family and everything he does, and you have given him enough cattle to fill the whole country. But now suppose you take everything he has- he will curse you to your face!' 'All right,' the LORD said to Satan, 'everything he has is in your power, but you must not hurt Job himself.' So, Satan left. One day when Job's children were having a feast at the home of their oldest brother, a messenger came running to Job. 'We were plowing the field with the oxen,' he said, "and the donkeys were in a nearby pasture. Suddenly the Sabeans attacked and stole them all. They killed every one of your servants except for me. I am the only one who escaped to tell you.' Before

he had finished speaking, another servant came and said, 'Lighting struck the sheep and the shepherds and killed them all. I am the only one who escaped to tell you.' Before he finished speaking, another servant came and said, 'Your children were having a feast at the home of your oldest son, when a storm swept in from the desert. It blew the house down and killed them all. I am the only one who escaped to tell you.' Then Job got up tore his clothes in grief. He shaved his head and threw himself face downward on the ground. He said, 'I was born, with nothing, and I will die with nothing. The LORD gave, and now he has taken away. May his name be praised!' In spite of everything that had happened Job did not sin by blaming God. (Job 1:8-22) - **Good News Translation**

When the day came for the heavenly beings to appear before the LORD again, Satan was there among them. The LORD asked him, 'Where have you been?' Satan answered, 'I have been walking here and there, roaming the earth.' 'Did you notice my servant Job? The LORD asked. 'There is no one on earth as faithful and good as he is. He worships me and is careful not to do anything evil. You persuaded me to let you attack him for no reason at all, but Job is still as faithful as ever.' Satan replied, 'A person will give everything in order to stay alive. But now suppose you hurt his body- he will curse you to your face!' So, the LORD said to Satan, 'All right, he is in your power, but you are not to kill him.' Then Satan left the LORD's presence and made sores break out all over Job's body. Job went and sat by the garbage dump and took a piece of broken pottery to scrape his sores. His wife said to him, 'You are still as faithful as ever, aren't you? Why don't you curse God and die?' Job answered, 'You are talking nonsense! When God sends us something good, we welcome it. How can we complain when he sends us trouble?' Even in all this suffering Job said nothing against God. (Job 2:1-10) - **Good News Translation**

Readers do you know the lesson that Job had to learn. The ruler that roams the world desired his soul too! However, for the sake of truth, I allowed Satan to hurt Job and take things away from him.

Readers listen if you have ears!

I needed Job to understand that those things that he had meant nothing! Those who do not understand will read and their hearts will ask, 'What kind of God lets their faithful servant suffer like that?' Readers, your heart beats with such pride because the things you possess are no different from the tree that gave knowledge of what is good and what is bad. Those who refused to remove their shoes are no different from Job's wife! Those who refused to remove their shoes will argue their knowledge of what is good and what is bad. Those who refused to remove their shoes have already bowed down to the one that roams the earth. Those who refuse to remove their shoes will never understand the truth and will always reject it! For it is written:

Everything is pure to those who are themselves pure; but nothing is pure to those who are defiled and unbelieving, for their minds and consciences have been defiled. They claim that they know God, but their actions deny it. They are hateful and disobedient, not fit to do anything good. (Titus 1:15-16) - Good News Translation

The Lord said, 'These people claim to worship me, but their words are meaningless, and their hearts are somewhere else. Their religion is nothing but human rules and traditions, which they have simply memorized. So, I will startle them with one unexpected blow after another. Those who are wise will turn out to be fools, and all their cleverness will be useless.' (Isaiah 29:13-14) - Good News Translation

Readers listen if you have ears!

Surely, I tell you those who remove their shoes will be made new by my Spirit! Those who remove their shoes will do so because they know they are entering holy ground. They will obey my commandments because they love me! They will learn what Job learned about hardships and adversity. They won't ask foolish questions like, 'But Job did not sin against you? He was good to you and worshipped you, yet you allowed Satan to torture him?'

Readers listen if you have ears!

Those who ask such questions are still enslaved with the knowledge of what is good and what is bad.

Author, oh author what good did king Solomon's wisdom do him? In the end, he wrote poems that ended with him saying, 'I'm just chasing the wind.' Author, oh author you spoke to your readers how king Solomon was fruitful and successful because of the wisdom-the wisdom I gave him. Unfortunately, it was the spirit lust that tore Solomon from me.

Author and reader, I warn you even if you acquire all the knowledge that the earth has to offer; it will never get you to know me. For it is written:

When the Judgment Day comes, many will say to me, 'Lord, Lord! In your name, we spoke God's message, by your name we drove out demons and performed miracles!' Then I will say to them, 'I never knew you. Get away from me, you wicked people!' (Matthew 7:22) – Good News Translation

Author and readers pay attention and understand the following message!

Surely, I tell you that rejection that all you so badly hate will not compare to my rejection! I am telling you the truth! For when the trumpet sounds and it will sound louder than when the thunder strikes the ground, you all will remember this message! For none of you were made to be rejected because I had my arms stretched while nails were drilled in me. For my love was shown and given to all of you to receive through your belief! Surely, I tell you, none of you will be concerned about what time it is! For time itself will be preparing itself for its own end! For it is written:

As surely as I am the Living God, says the Lord, everyone will kneel before me, and everyone will confess that I am God. (Romans 14:11) – Good News Translation

For this reason, God raised him to the highest place above and gave him the name that is greater than any other name. And so, in honor of the name Jesus all beings in heaven, on earth, and in the world below will fall on their knees, and all will openly proclaim that Jesus Christ is the Lord, to the glory of God the Father. (Philippians 2:9-11) – Good News Translation

GOD'S TRUTH VS SATAN'S DOCTRINE

Author and readers write this upon your hearts!

For there is no adversity or hardship too big for God to fix! There is no wealth or success too large to deny that Jesus Christ is King! For when the rain falls, he still is King; when the hail strikes, he still is King. For if he can split the Red Sea into two, what problem is there that he cannot fulfill? We once did not have Good News because of sin! We once did not know love like we now do! For the Spirit of God can use anyone and anything to proclaim the truth! To reject him is to deny the truth, how can we be so foolish to do such a thing? By his blood, we are made new and by our faith, we hope to be one with him. For the angels sing,' holy, holy is the God Almighty,' so shall we sing the same! Spirit of God you loved us so shall we return the same love back to you. We may face hardships and adversities but to allow that to come between you and us would be deadly.

There is no greater tragedy than to look at the one who sits at the throne and have him say, 'I do not know you.' For we were made out of love but rejected him, so he chased after us because of his love. He did not care that we rejected him because of his love! He accepted our rejection in hopes for us to see his true love for us. Now we have heard the Good News! As we live in a world that rejects and is filled with hardships and adversities; nothing changes and disrupts our connection with him because we know about the truth! For we will know true hardship and adversity if we decide to proclaim to him, 'we do not need you.'

Readers listen if you have ears!

For it is not by wisdom that people are saved but by their faith in me. For those who believe in me are truly wise because they have given up their sinful nature. They do not need the knowledge of what is good and what is bad to live in truth. For it is written:

Endure what you suffer as being a father's punishment; your suffering shows that God is treating you as his children. Was there ever a child who was not punished by his father? If you are not punished as all his children are, it means you are not real children, but bastards. In the case of our human fathers, they punished us, and we respected them. How much more, then, should we submit to our spiritual Father and live! Our human fathers punished us for a short time, as it seemed right to them;

but God does it for our own good, so that we may share his holiness. When we are punished, it seems to us at the time something to make us sad, not glad. Later, however, those who have been disciplined by such punishment reap the peaceful reward of a righteous life. (Hebrews 12:7-11) - **Good News Translation**

Readers listen if you have ears!

In Job's suffering and hardships, he was rewarded with the truth! That adversity brought Job closer to me because the kingdom of earth is nothing in my eyes nor should it mean anything to you! All the things that I have given life to: From the oceans to the sky, I love all creatures! By taking away the kingdom of earth from Job, his heart shifted to my domain! Readers, why desire a kingdom that is destined to diminish? Job had his livestock destroyed and children were taken from him, and his health was attacked! My servant Job eventually withered to the ground in pain, yet he refused to curse me.

Author, oh author let me ask you. What can I take away from the people of this world until they wither to the ground and curse me? Is it their families? Is it their friends? Is it their money? Is it their homes? Is it their cars? If I took away all these things will they curse me? Author, oh author I told Satan to do everything except one thing. I told him to not touch Job's heart! Surely, I tell you the heart is where a person's true treasure lies. For it is in Job's suffering where you see traces of the knowledge what is good and what is bad. Job may have refused to curse me, but he began to question my ways and started to curse his own self. For it is written:

I am ready to risk my life. I've lost all hope, so what if God kills me? I am going to state my case to him. It may even be that my boldness will save me since no wicked person would dare to face God. Now listen to my words of explanation. I am ready to state my case, because I know I am in the right. Are you coming to accuse me, God? If I do, I am ready to be silent and die. Let me ask for two things; agree to them, and I will not try to hide from you: stop punishing me, and don't crush me with terror. Speak first, O God, and I will answer. Or let me speak, and you answer me. What are my sins? What wrongs have I done? What crimes

am I charged with? Why do you avoid me? Why do you treat me like an enemy? Are you trying to frighten me? I'm nothing but a leaf; you are attacking a piece of dry straw. You bring bitter charges against me, even for what I did when I was young. You bind chains on my feet; you watch every step I take and even examine my footprints. As a result, I crumble like rotten wood, like a moth-eaten coat. (Job 14-28) - **Good News Translation**

Readers listen if you have ears!

It has been revealed that man and woman were removed from Eden because of their sin. Man and woman were once dependant on me, but their disobedience disconnected them from me. Author and readers, you were all disconnected from me and that tree that gave knowledge of what is good and bad made you behave independently so naturally, you all reject me. Author and readers, you saw how Israel struggled! They refused to be patient, trust, pray, fast, have faith, obey and repeat! They complained and complained and asked, 'Spirit of God, who do you think you are?' They asked, 'Spirit of God, what do you want?' They asked, 'When are you going to let us be?' They asked, 'Where is our real king?' They asked, 'Why do we have to obey you?' They asked, 'How are you going to fix this?' Even my servant Moses grew tired of them, and their sins caused him to sin! For it is written:

There was no water where they camped, so the people gathered around Moses and Aaron and complained. 'It would have been better if we had died in front of the LORD's Tent along with the other Israelites. Why have you brought us out this wilderness? Just so that we can die here with our animals. Why did you bring us out of Egypt into this miserable place where nothing will grow? There's no grain, no figs, no grapes, no pomegranates. There is not even any water to drink!' Moses and Aaron moved away from the people and stood at the entrance of the Tent. They bowed down with their faces to the ground, and dazzling light of the LORD's presence appeared to them. The LORD said to Moses, 'Take the stick that is in front of the Covenant Box and then you and Aaron assemble the whole community. There in front of them all, speak to the rock over there and water will gush out of it. In this way, you will bring

water out of the rock for the people, for them and their animals to drink.'
Moses went and got the stick, as the LORD commanded. He and Aaron
assembled the whole community in front of the rock, and Moses said,
'Listen you rebels! Do we have to get water out of this rock for you?'
Then Moses raised the stick and struck the rock twice with it, and a great
stream of water gushed out, and all the people and animals drank. But
the LORD reprimanded Moses and Aaron. He said, 'Because you did
not have enough faith to acknowledge my holy power before the people of
Israel, you will not lead them into the land that I promised to give them.'
This happened at Meribah, where the people of Israel complained against
the LORD, and he showed them that he is holy. **(Numbers 20:2-13) –**
Good News Translation

Despite their complaints, I still showed my love through glory. The roots of all
your nature are displayed in your sins; the origins of all your nature is found
when you go through hardships. Adversity is acknowledged through the roots of
the tree that gave all you the knowledge of what is good and what is bad. That
is why Job's wife said, 'You are still as faithful as ever, aren't you? Why don't
you curse God and die?' The roots of all your nature are like this:

'When God gives, he is good, but when God takes, he is bad!'

Surely, I tell you this knowledge will bring you to death! That is why I told
Adam and Eve to stay away from that tree! You all have mistaken knowledge
as if it were the truth.

Listen, those who have ears!

Those who believe in me are the ones who are truly wise! This is because their
faith is true wisdom; the wisdom that leads to life rather than death. What is
knowledge to the truth? Those who refuse to take off their shoes will remain
independent and always be enslaved by sin. They will say, 'My knowledge is all I
need because God makes no sense!' They will ask, 'Spirit of God, where is your
proof? What evidence do you have that you are the truth?' These same people
are the ones who foolishly ask, 'What is the meaning of life?' They hang with
astrologers who study the stars and philosophers that study their own thoughts.
They have all given themselves titles and decorated themselves with degrees from

their educations. Acquiring more and more knowledge of what is good and what is bad. It is that same thirst that blinds them from the true meaning of life. For it is written:

Jesus answered him, 'I am the way, the truth, and the life; no one goes to the Father except by me.' (John 14:6) - Good News Translation

Author and readers, why do you think king Solomon kept saying, 'I am chasing the wind.' It was I who gave him wisdom, but even with his understanding, he failed to find the meaning of life. Solomon was the son of David! For it is written:

But I will not stop loving David or fail to keep my promise to him. I will not break my covenant with him or take back even one promise I made him. Once and for all I have promised by my holy name: I will never lie to David. He will always have descendants, and I will watch over his kingdom as long as the sun shines. It will be permanent as the moon, that faithful witness in the sky. (Psalms 89:33-37) - Good News Translation

David pleased me not because of his knowledge but by his faith! It was David who spoke, 'Do not banish me from your presence; do not take your Holy spirit away from me.' It was because of David's faith that I began my dynasty with him. For it is written:

The Scripture says that the Messiah will be a descendant of King David and will be born in Bethlehem, the town where David lived. (John 7:42) - Good News Translation

It was by my Spirit that I rebuked the prophet Samuel from picking Eliab as king but chose David because of his heart! For it is written:

When they arrived, Samuel saw Jesse's son Eliab and said to himself, "This man standing here in the LORD's presence is surely the one he has chosen." But the LORD said to him, "Pay no attention to how tall and handsome he is. I have rejected him because I do not judge as people. They look at the outward appearance, but I look at the heart." (1 Samuel 16:7) - Good News Translation

And when he had removed him, he raised up for them David as king, to whom also he gave testimony and said, 'I have found David the son of Jesse, a man after my own heart, who will do all my will.' (Acts 13:22) – **New King James Version**

No matter his sin, David came to me to repent because of his loyal spirit and faith in the everlasting God. Before wisdom was given to Solomon, he was just a man with knowledge of God. What then made Solomon so great? Was it his wealth? Was it his wisdom? Was it because he was king? All these things did not matter to me because before he became those things, it was his faith that made him acknowledge me! It was by his faith that he found wisdom! For it is written:

O LORD God, you have let me succeed my father as king, even though I am very young and don't know how to rule. Here I am among the people you have chosen to be your own, a people who are so many that they cannot be counted. So, give me the wisdom I need to rule your people with justice and to know the difference between good and evil. (1 Kings 3:7-8) – Good News Translation

Author and reader listen then if you have ears!

Before all were born, I knew all of you because I designed you. Despite your sins, I gave my own self to free you! It was my Spirit that warned man and woman to stay away from the tree that gave knowledge of what is good and what is bad. Disobedience started long ago but my love for all of you did not wither! I couldn't let you go. For it is written:

We despised him and rejected him; he endured suffering and pain. No one would even look at him- we ignored him as if he were nothing. But he endured the suffering that should have been ours, the pain that we should have borne. All the while we thought that his suffering was punishment sent by God. But because of our sins, he was wounded beaten because of the evil we did. We are healed by the punishment he suffered, made whole by the blows he received. All of us were like sheep that were lost, each of us going his own way. But the LORD made the punishment fall on him, the punishment all of us deserved. He was treated harshly but endured it humbly; he never said a word. Like a lamb about to be slaughtered, like

321

a sheep about to be sheared, he never said a word. He was arrested and sentenced and led off to die, and no one cared about his fate. He was put to death for the sins of our people. He was placed in a grave with those who are evil, he was buried with the rich, even though he had never committed a crime or told a lie. The LORD says, 'It was my will that he should suffer; his death was a sacrifice to bring forgiveness. And so, he will see his descendants; he will live a long life, and through him, my purpose will succeed. After a life of suffering, he will again have joy; he will know that he did not suffer in vain. My devoted servant, with whom I am pleased, will bear the punishment of many and for his sake, I will forgive them. And so, I will give him a place of honor, a place among the great and powerful. He willingly gave his life and shared the fate of evil men. He took the place of many sinners and prayed that they might be forgiven.' **(Isaiah 53:3-12) - Good News Translation**

Author, oh author do you understand? Author, oh author I have heard your complaints. I have known of all your hardships and pain. You have humbled yourself and accepted that you have sinned. Have you not learned? Author, oh author that I am a forgiving God. What makes you think I have not heard your cries and complaints? What makes you think that I am punishing you? Do not behave like Job when he started to complain about my ways. For it is written:

Empty words, Job! Empty words! No one who is wise would talk the way you do or defend himself with such meaningless words. If you had your way, no one would fear God; no one would pray to him. Your wickedness is evident by what you say, you are trying to hide behind clever words. There is no need for me to condemn you; you are condemned by every word you speak. Do you think you were the first person born? Were you there when God made mountains? Did you overhear the plans God made? Does human wisdom belong to you alone? There is nothing you know that we don't know. We learned our wisdom from gray-haired people-those born before your father. God offers you comfort; why still reject it? We have spoken for him with calm, even words. But you are excited and glare at us in anger. You are angry with God and denounce him **(Job 15:1-13) - Good News Translation**

Author, oh author I forgave your sins and heard your sincere cries. Where did your faith go? Did you not understand law vs. faith? Just as one's faith raises them above the law of death so shall faith raise them above their hardships. I forgave you and responded to you. Author, oh author when I said patience you only waited a day. When I said trust, you put your trust in other things. When I said pray, your heart had no faith. When I said fast, you did not eat the bread that I had given you which is my Word. When I said have faith you lied and said, 'I do.' When I said to obey, you disobeyed. Author, oh author there was no point for me to say repeat because you were living in sin. For it is written:

The LORD said, 'I was ready to answer my people's prayers, but they did not pray. I was ready for them to find me, but they did not even try.' The nation did not pray to me, even though I was ready to answer, 'Here I am, I will help you. I have always been ready to welcome my people, who stubbornly do what is wrong and go their own way.' (Isaiah 65:1-2) - Good News Translation

Your hardship blinded you from the truth because your hardship was caused by sin. Your hardship was infused by the knowledge of what is good and what is bad. Your heart said, 'The Spirit of God is good when he gives but bad when he takes away.' Your knowledge of what was good and what was bad blinded you from the truth! That is why you rejected me when I said, 'be patient, trust in me, pray, fast, have faith, obey and repeat!'

Author, oh author writing this chapter began to be a burden to you because you were too focused on what was good and what was bad rather than the truth. That is why I told you to take off your shoes because you are now standing on holy ground! Surely, I tell you, if Moses behaved like this, he would have never seen the Red Sea split into two. Surely, I tell you, he would have never been remembered as one of the ancient people who won the battle of faith. Author, oh author his adversity was Pharaoh's Egypt and the people of Israel! Author, oh author Moses was my servant, but even his knowledge of what was good and what was bad caused him to sin! I told him to speak to the rock, but instead, he hit the rock! His heart said this, 'These people of Israel are frustrating me so I will show the power of God through my wrath by striking this rock.'

Author, oh author I can hear your heart say, 'Spirit of God this is too much, I understand now.' If this is so, answer this: What do you fear more? Perishing in hell or living in sin? I can hear your heart respond, 'Perishing in hell.' Well, now I tell you this: They are both the same thing! Author, you now know hell was not made for any of you but for those who choose to live without me. If the end is what you fear, then it means you know what the cost of sin is. Your readers will ask, 'How can anyone be perfect? How can anyone ever be worthy of heaven and avoid hell?' Surely, I tell you, none of you were worthy! You have all sinned and because of this, no one is perfect. This is why I gave you all my Son and named him Jesus, so he would save you from yourselves and the enemy of love. Author, oh author you told the readers about my Spirit, so you out of all people must know it is impossible to not sin without my Spirit. It is impossible because of your knowledge of what is good and what is bad. That knowledge has puffed all you up with pride and has made you think you are above me. This is why all suffer! Author, oh author can you not see that without me you will always taste the fruits of that forbidden fruit. For it is written:

Then the LORD God placed the man in the Garden of Eden to cultivate it and guard it. He told him, 'You may eat the fruit of any tree in the garden, except the tree that gives knowledge of what is good and what is bad. You must not eat the fruit of that tree; if you do, you will die the same day.' (Genesis 2:15–17) – Good News Translation

Author, oh author you all have placed crowns on your heads and have named them different names. You all aspire to be something and seek gratification from these things. None of you can be without sin with these crowns on your heads. Those who have placed these crowns on their heads can never understand me, as a matter of fact, they will always reject me. Author, oh author the only way these people will accept me is if I utter the words, 'I will give you the world,' yet I cannot utter those words because that would make me a liar and a God of hate. Why would I offer something that is destined to be destroyed? My own people rejected the Savior and handed him over to the world to be crucified. For it is written:

For the people who live in Jerusalem and their leaders did not know that he is the Savior, nor did they understand the words of the prophets that

are read every Sabbath. Yet they made the prophets' words come true by condemning Jesus. (Acts 13:27) - **Good News Translation**

They rejected my Son because they had 'evil,' 'power,' and 'dominance' as the crowns on their heads. They wanted me to give them the world, but I did not send my Son to give any of you the world. I gave you all my Son so that you may join me in eternity. Author, oh author you once asked why adversity exists. I told you it co-exists through sin, but I will its existence to remind all of you why I saved you! There was not one prophet or follower on this earth who had not seen adversity. Adversity attacks what all you humans consider good and bad to show that all of humanities knowledge is really foolishness. This is because Adam and Eve's disobedience symbolized foolishness when they sinned and hid from me. Author, oh author I have responded to all your questions so now I leave you with this question: Would it then be better to suffer for truth rather than what the world considers good and bad? I can hear your heart's response saying, 'suffer for truth.' Those who are for me will respond the same way because they belong to me. Therefore, author do not be surprised if the world hates you! For it is written:

My dear friends, do not be surprised at the painful test you are suffering, as though something unusual were happening to you. Rather be glad that you are sharing Christ's sufferings, so that you may be full of joy when his glory is revealed. (1 Peter 4:12-13) - **Good News Translation**

The enemy scatters the people who did not want to live for me! If they reject my Spirit and my Words, then they have rejected the truth for what is good and for what is bad; therefore, I will let them be. Who goes into the home of someone else's without an invitation? Author, oh author would you go to a house in which you were not welcome? Of course not! Those who do are called trespassers! This is what the ruler of this world does. For it is written:

The thief comes only in order to steal, kill, and destroy. I have come in order that you might have life- life in all its fullness. (John 10:10) - **Good News Translation**

That is why I let them be because they have shut their doors on me. Those who open their doors for me, I too will open my doors for them. For it is written:

When the Son of Man comes as King and all the angels with him, he will sit on his royal throne, and the people of all nations will be gathered before him. Then he will divide them into two groups, just as a shepherd separates the sheep from the goats. He will put the righteous people at his right and the others at his left. Then the King will say to the people on his right, 'Come, you that are blessed by my Father! Come and possess the kingdom which has been prepared for you ever since the creation of the world. I was hungry, and you fed me, thirsty, and you gave me a drink; I was a stranger, and you received me in your homes, naked, and you clothed me; I was sick, and you took care of me, in prison and you visited me.' The righteous will then answer him, 'When Lord, did we ever see you hungry and feed you, or thirsty and give you a drink? When did we ever see you a stranger and welcome you in our homes, or naked and clothe you? When did we ever see you sick or in prison, and visit you? The King will reply, 'I tell you, whenever you did this for one of the least important of these followers of mine, you did it for me!' Then he will say to those on his left, 'Away from me, you that are under God's curse! Away to the eternal fire which has been prepared for the devil and his angels! I was hungry, but you would not feed me, thirsty but you would not give me a drink; I was a stranger, but you would not welcome me in your homes, naked but you would not clothe me; I was sick and in prison, but you would not take care of me.' Then they will answer him, 'When Lord, did we ever see you hungry or thirsty or a stranger or naked or sick or in prison, and we would not help you?' The King will reply, 'I tell you, whenever you refused to help one of these least important ones, you refused to help me.' These then will be sent off to eternal punishment, but the righteous will go to eternal life. (Matthew 25:31-44) – Good News Translation

Author, oh author do you now understand? For in your prayer you said I gave you more burden, but you were putting your hardships over the hardships of others! Author, surely I tell you what I showed you in Tanzania was not to bring you burden but to open your eyes to me! Those who do not know me will say, 'Oh so the Spirit of God does not care about our problems. We are to suffer all our lives and just give freely without helping ourselves?' Surely, I tell you, those people are destined to be placed on the left side! They are not on the side of truth but are rebellious and selfish beings who are opposed to love! I have already opened your eyes to the truth author! Do not possess such thoughts because they come from the knowledge of what is good and what is bad! Those who are blinded by the knowledge of what is good and what is bad will say to you, 'Oh look at the author who wrote and preached about trusting God! Look at all his problems and hardships, where is his God?' Author, oh author this is what you shall say to them, 'My God lives in me and I have devoted myself to serving the truth! My God that I serve is always with me because I am with him! My God is a provider, so I put my patience, trust, prayer, fasting, faith, obedience and repetition in him!' For it is written:

Abraham answered,' God himself will provide one.' And the two of them walked on together. (Genesis 22:8) - Good News Translation

And Jesus concluded, 'So those who are last will be first, and those who are first will be last.' (Matthew 20:16) - Good News Translation

Author, oh author you have heard the truth; the truth that has been before and the same truth that will continue to be far past the end. I have listened to all your cries, but your mourning came from the knowledge of what is good and what is bad. Author, oh author you once neglected the truth because you did not understand that nothing is impossible for God! For it is written:

Jesus answered, 'What is humanly impossible is possible for God.' (Luke 18:27) - Good News Translation

Author, oh author write this upon your heart:

In my patience, I will find humility; the humility that will give me peace! In my trust, I will never be let down because I serve a God that keeps his Word. In my prayers, I shall always be answered because God answers a sincere heart. In my fasting, I shall be fed because the Word is in me. In my faith, I shall reap blessing because I have believed in what I could not see. In my obedience, I shall see love because those who obey love God. In my repetition of all these things, I shall grow stronger with God! For it is written:

Three times I prayed to the Lord about this and asked him to take it away. But his answer was: 'My grace is all you need, for my power is greatest when you are weak.' I am most happy, then, to be proud of my weaknesses, in order to feel the protection of Christ's power over me. (2 **Corinthians 12:9) – Good News Translation**

You have been made clean already by the teaching I have given you. Remain united to me, and I will remain united to you. A branch cannot bear fruit by itself; it can do so only if it remains in the vine. In the same way, you cannot bear fruit unless you remain in me. (John 15:3-4) - **Good News Translation**

Author, oh author you have two choices: to choose knowledge or to choose truth. I urge you to choose me!

Readers listen if you have ears!

Those who possess my Spirit have already transcended time and space. Readers listen to these wise and true things that I speak. What is considered wise in the world, I will show its flaws and expose its foolishness! The author of these pages said that you all are subject to time, but now I tell you: The people who are subject to time are the ones who belong to the world. My children who believe and worship me cannot be subject to time because they are apart of me. For it is written:

Philip said to him, 'Lord, show us the Father; that is all we need.' Jesus answered, 'For a long time I have been with you all, yet you do not know me, Philip?' Whoever has seen me has seen the Father. Why, then, do you say, 'Show us the Father?' (John 14:8-9) - **Good News Translation**

It is I who gives time its power and before it was, I was already "I AM." When time ends, I will still be "I AM." Those who eat my flesh and drink my blood will be saved! For in my flesh is the bread of life, the very bread that spoke before time itself. In my blood, is the water of life that quenches all your thirsts and satisfies forever and ever. For it is written:

I am the living bread that came down from heaven. If you eat this bread, you will live forever. The bread that I will give you is my flesh, which I give so that the world may live. This started an angry argument among them. 'How can this man give us his flesh to eat?' they asked. Jesus said to them, 'I am telling you the truth; if you do not eat the flesh of the Son of Man and drink his blood, you will not have life in yourselves. Those who eat my flesh and drink my blood have eternal life, and I will raise them to life on the last day. For my flesh is the real food; my blood is the real drink. Those who eat my flesh and drink my blood will live in me, and I live in them. The living Father sent me, and because of him, I live also. In the same way, whoever eats me will live because of me. This, then, is the bread that came down from heaven; it is not like the bread that your ancestors ate, but then later died. Those who eat this bread will live forever.' (John 6:48-58) - **Good News Translation**

Both my Word and my Spirit existed before time was and will exist when time ends! Readers, oh readers surely I tell you that the truth prevails over all knowledge because I am the truth. I told Adam and Eve to not eat from the tree that gives knowledge of what is good and what is bad because they would no longer be able to understand the truth. For it is written:

So, Pilate asked him, 'Are you a king, then?' Jesus answered, 'You say that I am a king. I was born and came into the world for this one purpose, to speak about the truth. Whoever belongs to the truth listens to me.' 'And what is the truth?' Pilate asked. (John 18:37-38) - **Good News Translation**

Readers listen then if you have ears!

The knowledge of good and bad created flesh vs spirit, love vs lust and law vs faith (revealing to all, one of the secret themes for the three conflicts – I Am Nothing Without God). But my sacrifice is truth which made wholeness, mercy, salvation, and grace. What was supposed to be from the beginning has now been made new through flesh and Spirit or better known as the Lamb of God, Jesus Christ!"

-Spirit of God

When things aren't going well in our lives, we tend to panic and stress out. Which is normal because we are human. However, it is that same fair concept that eludes us from the truth. It took me more than 3 months to complete this chapter because I was stressed about employment, finances, relationships and many other things that made me to feel useless. I was just as arrogant and confused as Pontius Pilate when he responded to Jesus, "What is the truth?" I mean when our lives look like they are headed to nothing but shambles, the last thing we're going to care to think about is the truth. Whatever is dragging us down, we tend to panic and try to figure out a quick solution to our problems. Sometimes we get lucky, but other times we become rash and drag ourselves deeper into other problems. Even as I write this out, I can hear my mind questioning myself like, "Well is that good or is that bad?" I have already admitted that all my issues in life have been entirely self-inflicted, so this made writing this chapter even more difficult. I just felt like a hypocrite and wasn't qualified to write about this chapter, but I suddenly remembered one of my favorite truths.

And yet, I am the God who forgives your sins, and I do this because of who I am. I will not hold your sins against you. **(Isaiah 43:25) – Good News Translation**

Come to me all who are weary and burdened, and I will give you rest **(Matthew 11:28) – Good News Translation**

Despite all my mistakes, I remembered those two Scriptures and did the most challenging thing ever. I finally forgave myself because God had already forgiven me. I had to forgive myself in order to understand his voice when he said, "be patient, trust, pray, fast, have faith, obey and repeat." I was allowing my hardships and past mistakes burden my happiness but most importantly hearing the truth. My knowledge of what is good and bad blinded me because I put them above God's Word. This becomes a common issue for us all because we all have gone through things that are different from one another. It is in the Spirit of God poem that the story of Adam and Eve reveals to us how foolish our human nature really is. Does this mean God doesn't care about our problems? Of course not! However, what I had to learn is sort of the same lesson as I had to learn in Egypt and Babylon chapters.

Since we are subject to time and cannot escape its power, we give our idols power by placing value in them through time. I already mentioned in the Egypt and Babylon chapters how to know whether or not we serve an idol. Well now, I am going to speak on how idols let us down. They too are subject to time itself so the worship we give to an idol is useless and insignificant because it will soon be gone as well. Once we put an idol (can legit be anything) before God, we have endangered ourselves in idolizing it. In the case of this chapter, we revere our knowledge above the truth because we allow our hardships to rob us of our happiness. Humanity begins to worry once we sense that we are about to lose something we've built up on a pedestal. Humanity gets upset when the things we call good let us down because our knowledge has classified it as fruitful thinking. What are these things that I keep blabbing about which are classified as good? It could be anything! If we look at the story of Job, God allowed Satan to take almost everything from him. Although Job did not dare curse God, Job's human nature got exposed once he started questioning God's methods (by trying to question God's ways we further distance ourselves from him because it represents unfaithfulness which turns into foolishness). Adversities and hardships create suffering to bring us closer to God when we reject sin and time (because we will live forever through Christ- The Holy Spirit) but it also identities sin and time when we attempt to depart from God. To recall the Egypt and Babylon chapters again, idols use time as a way to get us to worship them. It is this very reason why Jesus describes the relationship with God and humans like the vine and its branches. My explanation about time started to give me a headache because I was missing one key component, time itself has its end. Time has a set date to end because God doesn't tolerate sin and time is given to us as a sign of mercy to those who still live in sin. Which is why Babylon wants our time so that we continue to live in sin and the ruler of Babylon is Satan. Throughout this whole book, I discussed what sin is but never to such a degree where it corresponds with suffering and adversity. It became challenging to write about adversity because I know many people who have devoted themselves to being good people, but they suffer unjustly. It is this same thought process that even burdened king Solomon because he could not understand this. However, I had to remember what God said about humanity.

"There is no one who is righteous, no one who is wise or who worships God. All have turned away from God; they have all gone wrong; no one does what is right, not even one. Their words are full of deadly deceit; wicked lies roll off their tongues, and dangerous threats, like snake's poison, from their lips; their speech is filled with bitter curses. They are quick to hurt and kill; they leave ruin and destruction wherever they go. They have not known peace, nor have they learned reverence for God." **(Romans 3:10-18) – Good News Translation**

Suffering began when we sinned, so we are all subject to the punishment of time because of what we've become. If this is true, what hope do we have?

Here is what I have found out: the best thing we can do is eat and drink and enjoy what we have worked for during the short life that God has given us; this is our fate. **(Ecclesiastes 5:18) – Good News Translation**

Once again, king Solomon weighed his thoughts on the useless and short life that God has given us by saying, "the best thing we can do is eat and drink and enjoy." My Egyptian(addictions) self, used to be content with his thinking but as I mentioned, Mr. Solomon's wisdom only took him so far. Adam and Eve were also blessed by God because they were the first male and female created. Yet, they began to suffer the moment they disobeyed. They set themselves apart from God and attempted to hide from him the moment they acquired the knowledge of what is good and what is bad.

In this chapter, we learn that our knowledge eludes us from the truth. So, what is the truth? The truth is we belong to God! This chapter even goes so far to explain that if we reject God, we are already living in sin because we have rejected the truth. Humanity was always supposed to live with God, but it was our own foolish decision makings that drove us away. I could have never completed this chapter if I kept relying on my knowledge of what is good and what is bad. It is by faith that I have transcended above time itself and got the answer I've always been searching for. Personally, I refuse to ever be trapped by the powers of time because it means death. Does this mean that I am telling everyone to disregard time? Of course not! God gave time its power to show his mercy and love for those who have not known the truth or understood it. It was mentioned in the Spirit of God poem about the act of removing one's shoes. This was said to illustrate humility and obedience to the truth.

In the beginning, I failed to understand why Jesus waited so long to go and heal Lazarus because of my own fear of time. I could not understand it because of my lack of faith. I failed to understand why Jesus had to wait for Lazarus to die just to show God's glory. This could be the same thinking to those who also read the story, but the reason is mind-blowing. Jesus waited for the death of Lazarus so that he could prove his statement, "those who believe in the Son will never die." In Lazarus' resurrection, God's glory was shown because Lazarus' belief in the Son not only overpowered death but showed God's love. It is this very reason why Jesus said, "those who believe can never die," because his love transcends time. How can anyone ever agree with such a notion? It is that very Scripture that trumps all our knowledge of what is good and what is bad.

Timothy, keep safe what has been entrusted to your care. Avoid the profane talk and foolish arguments of what some people wrongly call "knowledge." For some have claimed to possess it, and as a result they have lost the way of faith. God's grace be with you all. **(1 Timothy 6:20-21) – Good News Translation**

What is good knowledge and what is bad knowledge? There is no answer to this question because what is considered good to others may be bad and vice versa. This is a flaw in our knowledge. Humanity once considered slavery good because it was a commodity and the way of business, but times have changed and now we see it as bad knowledge. If the belief is, "there is no God," does the intent of the statement come from the knowledge of what is good? Or the knowledge of what is bad? Well, it really depends who we're asking. It is that very response that makes the knowledge of what is good and what is bad sinful. For we are all under agreement that slavery was once considered good knowledge but is now bad. But the thing is we are not talking about something of the physical. We are talking about an invisible God. If it is thought that God cannot exist because our understandings have failed to prove his existence, aren't we all hypocrites and liars? Historically our knowledge has let us down because of the failure to distinguish between good and bad. How then can we rely on what we think is good or bad? If we struggle to prove the existence of something because we cannot see due to lack of physical evidence. Based off our knowledge, we then would call God an illusion because our knowledge cannot fathom whether something is good or bad if we have never seen it. Or does that just expose what our knowledge really is? An illusion. It has failed us in the physical so how should we trust its judgement of the spiritual- invisible God.

The purpose of science is to disprove illusions because reality is evident. Science's core principles are to provide empirical evidence to explain why reality is not an illusion and to make sure that we are not deluded by the very things we see, feel and touch. However, science itself is flawed because it is embodied by the very knowledge of what is good and what is bad so therefore can it not be argued that science itself is an illusion? "Blasphemy!" is what the whole scientific community would yell. They would rebuttal by saying, "How could science ever be an illusion? It is by science's very discoveries that we have satellites in space; it is by science's discoveries that planes fly. Science has achieved all these things and many more things, so how then could it ever be an illusion? What idiotic person could have the nerve to say such a bold and uneducated statement?" The thing is, I agree with the out-roar and response from the science community because to call science an illusion is foolish. It is something that makes sense and continues to make sense by its achievements in furthering human lives and knowledge. "That is why science rules!" As mentioned by Bill Nye, the science Guy. The most educated person will respond in this matter because of what they know and what science has proven. It has succeeded in disproving illusions because of its tangible methods. The educated person will boast about science but has yet to ever see science. Where do the properties of science come from? In our search to disprove and approve what's real, we have advanced our knowledge. Have we asked ourselves about the origins of science? Of course not, they don't matter to us because they come from us. We believe and rely on science because it does exactly what it was intended to do- provide knowledge. The more knowledgeable we are, the further we excel. Then what's the issue? Well, science cannot be called an illusion because it proves realism through its discoveries. Can this not be the same for God and all his works? Pause.

Science cancels out the idea of God because it has failed to prove perfection. To define God is to define perfection which is why science hates on the idea of God. It hates the idea of God because it is always trying to be perfect. That then leads me to ask: Is science always trying to be perfect? Of course, it is! Humanity is always hungry for more knowledge, whether it is good or bad knowledge. That is why we say, "there is no such thing as a stupid question," because we are always curious about everything. Some may argue that there are stupid questions simply because they will judge what a good or bad question is. Then I ask: Is it a stupid question to ask if God exists? Well, how could it be because that very question is showing how limited our knowledge will always be. Science hates what it cannot prove because science itself is limited to such knowledge. The educated person will respond that science can disprove God's existence through the very things that it has proven. However, an educated person can never ask themselves where science was made. They will call that a silly question because science isn't tangible. But what if we were to refute that there are any silly questions, then who created science? "No, you do not get it," the educated man will respond. "Science is just a concept just like religion." As the educated man will continue to argue. But if all this is true, then isn't everything an illusion? The very thing that proves illusions cannot even prove its own existence. It is only by the acts of science that we know that it exists. Therefore, I say this to the educated man: God exists by the words he has placed in our hearts because through faith

God is no illusion. "That doesn't even make any sense!" responds the educated man. The educated man will continue to say, "faith itself is just a concept which derives from the knowledge of good and bad." So, I rebuttal the educated man with this, "The concept of science and the concept of religion was formed by the knowledge of what is good and what is bad. Then where did our knowledge come from? Before science and religion, there must have been something that formed knowledge itself. That thing is faith because it is by faith that man and woman called the knowledge 'God.'

In the beginning God created the heavens and the earth. **(Genesis 1:1) – New King James Version**

It is by faith that we understand that the universe was created by God's Word, so that what can be seen was made out of what cannot be seen. **(Hebrews 11:3) – Good News Translation**

We once admitted that our knowledge was too limited to know perfection. No matter how far science and religion argue with one another; one thing prevails above both which is faith. Faith, or in other words belief, was given by perfection so that we may come to be one with perfection. Perfection allowed us to be because of love, something that knowledge itself cannot even fathom.

There are four things that are too mysterious for me to understand: an eagle flying in the sky, a snake moving on a rock, a ship finding its way over the sea, and a man and a woman falling in love. **(Proverbs 30:18-19) - Good News Translation**

Perfection loved us so much that it made us in its own image and wanted us to obey it so that we too would live in perfection with it.

Then God said, "And now we will make human beings; they will be like us and resemble us. They will have power over the fish, birds, and all animals, domestic and wild, large and small. So, God created human beings, making them to be like himself. He created them male and female." **(Genesis 1:26-27) - Good News Translation**

Abandoning or rejecting faith is just pure arrogance because we did not get where we are today without it. To have or to gain any sort of knowledge is the act of faith itself. Therefore, can it not be argued that science could have never existed without the existence of God? In sciences attempt to be perfect it lost its way because of the mass amounts of good and bad knowledge it is responsible for. Science is the way it is because God allowed it to be to show us how limited we are and will always be without him. Science creates hardships because it is the act of struggling to know more when we were supposed to never struggle for anything because we were already made in his image(perfect). Science is the way it is because it has abandoned its own maker; science is the way it is because it doesn't care to differentiate good from bad but cares to please knowledge. So, therefore, I ask the educated man this, "When are we all going to stop and think for just one moment and ignore the knowledge of good and bad, to strive for truth?" Are we ready for the truth? I sit here today and cannot even categorize what good or bad knowledge is nor do I care to know. I say that because I am mentally and spiritually unable to define good and bad knowledge because it would mean to be without God. Here is a good and bad statement: Science is amazing and so is religion because it is showing that we are trying to find the truth. That statement is an example of good and bad knowledge because we are so focused on concepts rather than truth. This is the irony: we will always fail because both concepts are limited and are powered by our own knowledge. Therefore, there must be one truth and I have faith, not knowledge, that the only way to find it is to abandon our concepts and go back to the very beginning to the one that is perfect.

For the message about Christ's death on the cross is nonsense to those who are being lost, but for us who are being saved by it is God's power. The Scripture says, "I will destroy the wisdom of the wise and set aside the understanding of scholars." So then, where does that leave the wise? Or the scholars? Or the skillful debaters of this world? God has shown that this world's wisdom is foolishness! For God in his wisdom made it impossible for people to know him by means of their own wisdom. Instead, by means of the so-called "foolish" message we preach, God decided to save those who believe. Jews want miracles for proof, and Greeks look for wisdom. All of us, we proclaim the crucified Christ, a message that is offensive to the Jews and nonsense to the Gentiles; but for those whom God has called, both Jews and Gentiles, this message is Christ, who is the power of God and the wisdom of God. For what seems to be God's foolishness is wiser than human wisdom, and what seems to be God's weakness is stronger than human strength. **(1 Corinthians 2:18-25) – Good News Translation**

To be afraid of time is to be afraid of death. I fretted and stressed about my problems and almost lost my way, which was leading me to give up on this book. Many will ask, how is your life now? I do not see hardships, nor adversities but I see Christ. Does that mean that I do not experience hardships or adversities? No, that is not what I meant because they exist to strengthen my relationship with God. The Spirit of God poem has taught me that hardships and adversities strengthen us to new heights. A height that has no limits, a height that is called 'The Good News' (relationship with Jesus). Hence why I said, "I do not see hardships, nor adversities but I see Christ." It is this which motivated and pushed me to continue writing because there are people who are hungry, poor, sad, alone and are burdened. Due to faith, I have received wisdom that we are and can transcend above time if we do not live in sin but live for Christ's sake. How does one do such a thing? The secret was revealed in the birth of the doctrine chapter when I confessed and repented of my sins and received the Holy Spirit. The journey continued through the chapters and now we are here to receive the secrets about adversities and hardships. The Word is our guide because the Word is God and he has purposely given us the Holy Spirit to teach us about himself, which is in the Word.

In my travels I have been in danger from floods and from robbers, in danger from my own people and from Gentiles; there have been dangers on the high seas and dangers from false friends. There has been work and toil; often I have gone without sleep; I have been hungry and thirsty; I often been without enough food, shelter, or clothing. And not to mention other things, every day I am under the pressure of my concern for all the churches. When someone is weak, then I feel weak too; when someone is led into sin, I am filled with distress. If I must boast about things that shows how weak I am. The God and Father of the Lord

Jesus- blessed be his name forever! - knows that I am not lying. **(2 Corinthians 11:26-31) - Good News Translation**

It was Apostle Paul who wrote about his suffering as a follower of Christ. Apostle Paul did not complain once about his adversities because he had come to know the truth. He mentions "boasting" because it is a typical human trait in which we all do when we all want to receive praise. However, he rebuked his knowledge of what is good and bad for the sake of God's glory. Therefore, the only boasting that he did was to bring thanks and glory to the works of Christ.

Three times I prayed to the Lord about this and asked him to take it away. But his answer was: "My grace is all you need, for my power is greatest when you are weak." I am happy, then, to be proud of my weakness, in order to feel the protection of Christ's power over me. I am content with weakness, insults, hardships, persecutions, and difficulties for Christ's sake. For when I am weak, then I am strong. **(2 Corinthians 12:8-10) - Good News Translation**

No human knowledge can ever comprehend what Apostle Paul meant by this because they will argue against weakness, insults, hardships, persecutions, and difficulties. At the beginning of this chapter, I hesitated to put that Scripture in this book because I could not and did not want to understand it. I mean who enjoys suffering? There is an answer to that question. There are two types of suffering: the suffering of sin and the suffering of the truth. One thing that we all can come to an agreement with is that no one is exempted from hardships and adversity.

In his life on earth Jesus made his prayers and requests with loud cries and tears to God, who could save him from death. Because he was humble and devoted, God heard him. But even though he was God's Son, he learned through his sufferings to be obedient. **(Hebrews 5:7-8) – Good News Translation**

Suffering began because we sinned which separated us from God, then God gave Jesus to the world so that he would suffer for the truth in hopes we would go back to the truth. The Spirit of God's poem mentioned how hell was not made for humanity but for Satan and his demons. But if we choose to live without God, then that is where we will end up. Time, adversity and hardships are all temporary things and since we all live on earth with temporary things, we are subject to their temporary powers. Those who believe in the gospel of Christ are setting themselves above temporary things and only suffer because they have become unionized with Christ who also suffered. Those who believe, suffer for Christ's sake because they have acknowledged his sacrifice which was out of love. One suffers by standing up to unrighteousness because the spiritual ruler is a tyrant who hates righteousness. By unifying ourselves with Jesus, we join the same suffering because we love him back. It is only by flesh that we suffer because Jesus came to earth in the flesh which is why he was called the Son of Man. That is why it will be by the Spirit in which we will be raised because Jesus was raised too. Those who have become one with Christ do not suffer the same way as those who suffer for the sake of knowledge because they are not subject to death. Those who have committed their lives to Christ are committing their lives to everlasting life because Jesus is the Spirit that overcame death. The reward in suffering for Christ is eternal life which will be achieved in the resurrection of our spirits. If we are committed to him, he will be committed to us by sharing his power to us.

Jesus said to her, "I am the resurrection and the life. Those who believe in me will live, even though they die; and those who live and believe in me will never die. Do you believe this?" **(John 11:25-26) – Good News Translation**

This is a true saying: "If we have died with him, we shall live with him. If we continue to endure, we shall also rule with him. If we deny him, he also will deny us. If we are not faithful, he remains faithful, because he cannot be false to himself. **(2 Timothy 2:11-13) – Good News Translation**

CHAPTER 10

SPIRITUAL SUICIDE

God looked at everything he made, and he was pleased. The evening passed, and the morning came - that was the sixth day. **(Genesis 1:31) – Good News Translation**

And so, the whole universe was completed. By the seventh day, God finished what he had been doing and stopped working. He blessed the seventh day and set it apart as a special day because by that day He had completed his creation and stopped working. **(Genesis 2:1-3) - Good News Translation**

On July 19th, 2001 my brother Imani was born and on August 16th, 2007 my youngest brother Isaiah was born. Yes, I am the first born, but Imani was technically the third born which makes Isaiah the fourth born. As I mentioned in the chapter flesh vs. spirit, my parents had a second born and her name was Neema. She unfortunately did not live very long because she died from pneumonia. It was the first time I had encountered death, but I was too young to really understand what it meant. In the chapter flesh vs. spirit, I had mentioned about the nightmare I had about Neema walking around in our family living room in a white gown. Subconsciously I was thinking about her but as indicated in the flesh vs. spirit chapter, we do undergo spiritual warfare in which the devil himself can take the form of loved ones just to mess with us. I've always had an eerie feeling about death ever since the passing of my younger sister. I became paranoid that if the devil can take the form of anyone, then he would always do it. The problem with thinking like this is it gives credit to Satan to where credit is not due. At the beginning of this book, I made him out to be this powerful being but the more I dug into the truth, the more it reveals how powerless he really is. My intake on death has become such a negative thing that I do not keep pictures of people who have died. As I'm writing this, I feel kind of ridiculous sharing this insane behavior but sharing my truth is the whole point of this book. On August of 2018, I visited Tanzania and one of the things that my dad wanted me to do was to go visit the graveyard of my grandmother and aunt who passed away. No one except my family knows this, but I got into an altercation with my dad over the phone because I refused to go to the graveyard. I have spoken about many experiences in this book, but death is a new one that I find extremely uncomfortable to talk about. I think I am this way because of the passing of my little sister. I never dealt with that pain because I was so young, so I bottled it up deep inside until another death occurred. On January 3rd, 2013 a friend of mine who I knew from soccer passed away. His name was Sheldon and I had known him through my soccer teammate who was related to Sheldon. I couldn't believe it! One moment there's life in someone and the next moment they are lifeless. "Things change with just a blink of an eye," was one of the tweets he had posted that night on his Twitter account, which gave everyone goosebumps. On the day that Neema passed away, I remember putting my finger on her palm expecting her to hold onto it, like she always used to. "Why won't she grab my finger, why won't she wake up?" I asked my mother. I continued to press my mom with that question until she started to cry so I stopped asking because I knew something was wrong. I had mentioned that my family was religious, but it was Neema's death that broke religion and drew my mother and father to focus on a relationship with God. The meaning in Swahili for Neema is grace but after her death, it seemed like all hope was lost. However, grace turned into faith on July 19th, 2001 when Imani was born which means faith in Swahili. Unfortunately, my faith was yet to be tested just yet. That was to happen in the year 2018. God knew exactly how to touch my heart as all can see in this book.

What were the implications of Neema's death to me? It would have to be that I became fearful of life and never wanted to understand my purpose because of how short life is. I just became extremely observant of it while hiding in my prideful and lost shell. I was not close to Sheldon, but it was the impact on my teammate and the entire community which made me remember Neema again. It affected the lives of many people but most importantly robbed joy, happiness, and peace from Sheldon's family. It is a devastating feeling to lose someone we love, and any human being can attest to that. A year after Sheldon's death, I was about to experience another loss expect this one was different because it was a close friend of mine who I had known all throughout high school. Cauley and I had taken a few electives together at Carleton University and we had known each other throughout high school. It was just the end of our second year. Right after we finished our last exams, and we had plans for the summer to hangout more. A week after our final exams, I received a call that he had passed away in his sleep and the fear returned once again. Life is very short, but it is also precious and even with the short time Neema, Sheldon, and Cauley spent on this earth they touched the hearts of many.

They said to one another, "Here comes that dreamer. Come on now, let us kill him and throw his body into one of the dry wells. We can say that a wild animal killed him. Then we will see what becomes of his dreams." Reuben heard them and tried to save Joseph. "Let's not kill him," he said. Just throw him into this well in the wilderness, but don't hurt him." He said this, planning to save him from them and send him back to his father. When Joseph came up to his brothers, they ripped off his long robe with full sleeves. Then they took him into the well, which was dry. While they were eating, they suddenly saw a group of Ishmaelites traveling from Gilead to Egypt. Their camels were loaded with spices and resins. Judah said to his brothers, "What will we gain by killing our brother and covering up the murder?" Let's sell him to these Ishmaelites. Then we won't have to hurt him; after all, he is our brother, our own flesh and blood." His brothers agreed, and when some Midianite traders came by, the brothers pulled Joseph out of the well and sold him for twenty pieces of silver to the Ishmaelites, who took him to Egypt. When Reuben came back to the well and found that Joseph was not there, he tore his clothes in sorrow. He returned to his brothers and said, "The boy is not there! What am I going to do?" Then they killed a goat and dipped Joseph's robe in its blood. They took the robe to their father and said, "We found this. Does it belong to your son?" He recognized it and said, "Yes, it is his! Some wild animal has killed him. My son Joseph has been torn to pieces!" Jacob tore his clothes in sorrow and put on sackcloth. He mourned for his son for a long time. All his sons and daughters came to comfort him, but he refused to be comforted and said, "I will go down to the world of the dead still mourning my son." So, he continued to mourn for his son Joseph. **(Genesis 37:19-35) - Good News Translation**

The story of Joseph is similar to Cain and Abel's, but the only difference was his eleven brothers did not go through with the murder of their brother. Jacob, who was Joseph's father, was so devastated and grieved for a long time because he thought his son was killed. The toll of death is unbearable especially if it is our own loved ones that are taken away.

One day two women came and presented themselves before king Solomon. One of them said, "Your Majesty, this woman and I live in the same house, and I gave birth to a baby boy at home while she was there. Two days after my child was born, she also gave birth to a baby boy. Only the two of us were there in the house- no one else was present. Then one night she accidentally rolled over on her baby and smothered it. She got up during the night, took my son from my side while I was asleep, and carried him to her bed; then she put the dead child in my bed. The next morning, when I woke up and was going to nurse my baby, I saw that it was dead. I looked at it more closely and saw that it was not my child." But the other woman said, "No! The living child is mine, and the dead one is yours!" The first woman answered back, "No! The dead child is yours, and the living one is mine!" And so, they argued before the king. Then king Solomon said, "Each of you claims that the living child is hers and that the dead child belongs to the other one." He sent for a sword, and when it was brought, he said, "Cut the living child in two and give each woman half of it." The real mother, her heart full of love for her son, said to the king, "Please, your Majesty, don't kill the child! Give it to her!" But the other woman said, "Don't give it to either of us; go on and cut it in two." Then Solomon said, "Don't kill the child! Give it to the first woman- she is its real mother." **(1 Kings 3:16-28) - Good News Translation**

This Scripture dates to the time when Solomon was king. Since he was filled with so much wisdom, he understood the love of a parent. When death occurs in a family or even outside a family: sorrow, pain, regret, and anger are just a few emotions that people go through. But the strongest feeling that shows is love.

Meanwhile, these three remain: faith, hope, and love; and the greatest of these is love. (1 Corinthians 13:13) - Good News Translation

It is love that drives all these other emotions which is why Paul wrote that love is the greatest of them all. It isn't common for us to mourn for someone who we have never known. It's usually the death of family or someone close to us where we are moved because we love them.

We love because God first loved us. If we say we love God but hate others, we are liars. For we cannot love God, whom we have not seen if we do not love others, whom we have seen. (1 John 4:19) - Good News Translation

Where am I going with all this? How does it relate to suicide and the passing of loved ones? Well, everything that I just mentioned in this chapter has to do with love. I spoke about three individuals. One was family, the second was a soccer friend, and the third was a close friend. Yet, all three of their passing still had an impact on me because of one simple thing- love. In the chapter love vs lust, I prayed for the definition of love and the Spirit of God replied, *"Author, oh author love isn't something tangible that you can pick up. But its power is evident when you feel it, but you're focused on understanding it. Author, oh author love cannot be studied like the way you study books."* It was that response where I discovered that whatever happens to us in this lifetime, the best versions of ourselves are shown when we love one another. I never understood love because I did not take the time to get to know God. In chapter adversity and hardships, I confessed that my biggest issue was pride. Can 'love' exist when things like pride surround our hearts? Well, if I am speaking out of my knowledge of what is good and bad, my answer would be yes. However, that is not where I want to generate my answer from because my knowledge is useless. Love is not real when we have other things mixed with it. As I write this right now, I can be glad at my own character growth because I have come a long way from who I was when I first started writing this book. It was not done by my own power but through my faith and resilience to remain in God.

I named this chapter spiritual suicide to not only talk about the time where I attempted suicide but its spiritual presence. Some may be lucky enough and have never felt like ending their own life, but that doesn't necessarily mean that they've never encountered the spirit. What do I mean by that? Well, I'm not just talking about the physical act of suicide but the spiritual side of it. I began talking about loved ones passing away so that we are all reminded by love. This spirit's root of success relies on love. It strives on making the person lose their sense of love by not only telling the person that love doesn't exist but cannot exist for them. In my experience, I have heard the voice of suicide speak to me which is why I would like to rename its name to the 'spirit that makes people give up'. I name it the spirit that makes people give up because that is it's goal.

My whole life consisted of listening to the voice of sin because it made me feel special. In chapter adversity and hardships, I spoke about living life like the Pokémon ditto which enabled me to copy anyone just so I can fit in. It got to the point where I knew I was like ditto and that personality trait became a voice I listened to. I even went so far that I named the voice something and I found it completely normal because it acted like my shield and sword. I have confessed to a lot of things, but my biggest mistake was relying on that voice because I treated it like it was my god. That voice was in love with sin and became prideful in my sins which prevented me from ever seeing my mistakes. That voice spoke to me like it was my friend and it also wrestled God's voice. It's not like I never knew the bible, but I was so prideful in my sins that I rejected the truth. I was not the best sibling because I only cared about myself and did things that only benefited me. I caused so much grief for my parents that they did not even recognize the child they raised. I hurt a lot of my friends by being selfish and dishonest which put grief on my walk with God. Now I would like to say that is exactly what burdened me in life but that would not be true. I was no stranger to burning bridges with people because the voice of sin would say, "Who needs them!" So, what was the real thing behind my unhappiness? It wasn't my addictions, lust, or understanding flesh and spirit, or law and faith, nor was it my adversities. Although all those things did play a huge role in my depression it wasn't the thing that made me want to give up. I wanted to change my life because of the conviction I got from God's Spirit. This is the awful truth: Although I hurt so many people, that's not what got me wanting to change which is scary because it was like I didn't really care about the consequences of my actions. Was it because of my pride? That is partially the answer, but there was something inside of me that I valued over family, friends or any life situations. This could sound selfish but what broke me was the constant voice from God. Although, I lived such an ungodly life and was picky towards what I wanted to obey, what secretly mattered to me was what God thought of me. That very statement is what God was prepared to expose about myself. It was going to reveal that I was not only being fake to others but myself which made my "faith" a lie. This was because God examined my heart and saw that I didn't care for the people. How can anyone claim to love God, one who we haven't seen, and not love the very people they see everyday? That was who I was.

If we say we love God, but hate others, we are liars. For we cannot love God, whom we have not seen, if we do not love others, whom we have seen. **(1 John 4:20) – Good News Translations**

I bombarded myself with all sorts of false doctrines to justify my sins but when life got tougher it was God's voice that constantly convicted me. It may seem like I'm going off topic from this chapter, but this conviction is what changed me. God's voice is not what made me want to end my life, it was my arrogance and pride that drove me to that road. What do I mean by this?

My child, when the LORD corrects you, pay close attention and take it as a warning. The LORD corrects those he loves, as parents correct a child of whom they are proud. **(Proverbs 3:11-12) - Good News Translation**

347

Have you forgotten the encouraging words which God speaks to you as his children? "My child pay attention when the Lord corrects you, and do not be discouraged when he rebukes you. Because the Lord corrects everyone he loves and punishes everyone he accepts as a child." Endure what you suffer as being a father's punishment; your suffering shows that God is treating you as his child. Was there ever a child who was not punished by his father? If you are not punished, as all his children are, it means you are not real children, but bastards. In the case of our human fathers, they punished us, and we respected them. How much more, then, should we submit to our spiritual Father and live! Our human fathers punished us for a short time, as it seemed right to them; but God does it for our own good, so that we may share his holiness. When we are punished, it seems to us at the time something to make us sad, not glad. Later, however, those who have been disciplined by such punishment reap the peaceful reward of a righteous life. **(Hebrews 12:5-11) – Good News Translation**

Remember in the chapter love vs lust when the Spirit of God said, *"but none of you are really orphans. Instead, you choose to be orphans."* This was my issue, I knew God was speaking to me, and I kept ignoring it because the voice kept convicting me of my actions. For example, it got to the point where I could not even enjoy going out for drinks with my friends because I would hear the voice say, "Why are you out drinking? You were made for much more than this." It got to the point where I would try to bury the voice by drinking more so I could not be conscious of the voice, but that would just ruin my night. I ended up growing accustomed to God's convictions so I would just remain silent and not react to it, but it would never go away. There were nights where the Holy Spirit would tell me to look at someone and I was able to see what they were going through. God's Spirit would say, "Do you see that person? You could help them with what they're going through?" That's just a few examples of what I would hear from God's Spirit and I absolutely hated it! I guess I hated it because I did not want that kind of responsibility, but the thing about God is he knows us better than we know ourselves. Although I hated hearing it, I always felt upset because I started to think about it and for some reason, I realized that I really did want to help.

Okay, let us get back on track. I just admitted that the one thing that I valued over everything was what God thought of me. The only flaw in this thinking was I had deceived myself thinking I was in the clear of God's judgment. Pride can only take someone so far until it turns on the person and that's what happened to me when adversity hit. Once my pride was broken, I had realized that I had lied to myself all these years thinking I was righteous. All the times that I had ignored God's voice suddenly became real when I knew that I was so far from righteous. The moment I had realized what kind of person I had become, it sickened me. I thought to myself, "I am a disgrace, and there is no way God can ever love and forgive me." I had spent so many years ignoring his voice and the moment I thought that he did not love me is when Satan took the chance he had been waiting for. See I do not know what other people value over everything, but I knew what my safe haven was. It doesn't matter who it is or what we've done, once our safe haven is gone that is when we are left most vulnerable. My safe haven was my faith in God and Satan knew that! My pride exposed how phony I really was, and I was unable to bounce back. However, the good news is: Although there was no truth in me, there is truth in God. The very same voice that tried countless of times to correct me or get me to change my ways tried once again.

"My beautiful child, I can hear your heart saying,

'Spirit of God, just leave me alone, I am not worth your forgiveness! I just found out that I've been lying to myself my whole entire life! Why are you so loving? Why are you so forgiving? I kept ignoring your voice, why can't you just let me die! I am not worth this love! It doesn't make any sense; you say you forgive me but what if I do it again? Just leave me alone and let me die!'

My beautiful child, I can see that you're broken! I can see that you feel like all is lost and everyone's abandoned you, but I am here for you. Come back to me! You know I will not hold your sins against you because I love you. My Spirit speaks to you not to condemn but to correct you. I have seen the tears of your heart and I know you're struggling, but I am the God who loves and forgives. For it is written:

The teachers of the Law and Pharisees brought in a woman who had been caught committing adultery, and they made her stand before them all. 'Teacher,' they said to Jesus, 'this woman was caught in the very act of committing adultery. In our Law, Moses commanded that such a woman must be stoned to death. Now, what do you say?' They said this to trap Jesus so that they could accuse him. But he bent over and wrote on the ground with his finger. As they stood there asking him questions, he straightened up and said to her, 'Where are they? Is there no one left to condemn you?' 'No one, sir.' she answered. 'Well, then,' Jesus said, 'I do not condemn you either. Go, but do not sin again.' (John 8:3-11) - **Good News Translation**

Surely, I tell you my child, all sinners are like the woman who was caught committing adultery! For the world points to judge and condemn but I ask, 'Who then is without sin?' For all of you are guilty! However, I came to save you from the powers of sin. My child, my child I can hear your heart saying,

'Stop saying you love me! What did I do to deserve that? I keep failing you and I've lived a life that has denied you. Why are you so forgiving! Stop forgiving me. I don't deserve it! Stop it, Spirit of God, I don't deserve your love, I just don't so please just let me die!'

Oh, my child, do not let sin win! It wants to rule you, you must overcome it. Take my hand and come back to me, my beautiful child!"

-Spirit of God

I couldn't do it and that may not have been the exact thing I heard on March 18th, 2018 but God had intervened with my suicidal thoughts. My safe haven may have been weakened when my pride exposed me for who I really was but what got me to finally admit that I was broken was God's Spirit. The thing about the Holy Spirit is once we've obtained it, it never abandons us. So, what might be going through everyone's head is how did I get to such a low point to my life when I had God's Holy Spirit? As I mentioned from the very beginning of this book, just because a person gets the Holy Spirit doesn't mean life is all sunshine and rainbows. It is the beginning of a new journey with Christ because that person has recognized the truth in Christ. However, it is still on that person to develop that special relationship. This was my issue. I never established any relationship with the Holy Spirit. Despite all that, God's Spirit is so loving that it will speak to us because it longs for a relationship with us.

I kept neglecting its voice because it kept voicing out my mistakes and I didn't like that due to my pride. I had grown up to being someone that hated being told what to do and hearing the word no, so I wrestled with God's voice. As the story was told in the previous chapter, my pride left me once my hardships grew and that was when I realized I needed God. I saw what the Spirit saw and that is when I cracked. I couldn't believe what I saw because my pride blinded me from ever seeing my mistakes. I claimed to value God so much, but once I took a good look at myself, I saw emptiness and I just lost it. I couldn't bring myself to accept 'love' or 'forgiveness' because the moment my pride left, all my 24 years of sins just burdened my heart. "I am not worth your love," was all I could say to God because my safe haven was my faith and I had just found out I spat at my own faith. On top of that was the realization of everything bad I had ever said and done. God's voice did not drag me to suicidal thoughts. God was correcting me in hopes that I would change. However, I had never in my life thought that there was anything wrong with who I was. Well, that is because I had spent my whole life not being myself! When I realized that I had to do something about this toxic personality, I couldn't bring myself to think past that. My thoughts kept replaying all my sins and I began to condemn myself to death. Despite having the Holy Spirit, my brokenness ignored its loving plea and I chose to become a spiritual orphan. It's a shame because the moment I told the Holy Spirit to leave me alone was when I met one of Satan's top-ranking spirits, the spirit that makes people give up.

"Author, oh author why don't you do me a little favor and tell your readers this:

'Transparent as water is the human race but as I mix my poison into their stream, so shall anxiety and depression conquer them! They will doubt themselves once they realize that they are truly naked. They will say, 'Oh, my gosh we're naked!'

That's right you're all naked which is why you're all vulnerable to me! Once they realize they are naked, they will turn translucent. Author this is where it gets deep. Through the guilt of their sins, I will inflict a few scars here and there. This is how they will feel. 'Doctor, I cannot feel my heartbeat? PTSD! Anxiety!' They will all begin to panic! I will continue to tell my spirits to attack. I'll make the human race doubt everything! They will soon look at their physical appearance and think, 'Oh I'm ugly!' While others will struggle from my other vicious spirits. My spirits will say, 'Are you hungry? I wouldn't eat that!' Coming from the north, south, east and west they will be tormented by how they look. I will beat them physically and scar them mentality, and very soon they will be spiritually Opaque! Now it's time to devour them! It's time to attack their spirit! No Spirit of God I see? The suicide is complete!'

I have turned my attention back at you author. You will always be lost because you are in love with my voice! Your name will be remembered next to disgrace because I have kept records of all your sins! Author, it has come the time for your readers to know about your encounter with my top general. Have you forgotten about the spirit of Suicide? How it had you against the ropes? Let us go down memory lane.

It is said that your God does not allow his people to face battles they cannot handle. Well author, it seems like you lost the fight. As the bicycle of life wobbled left and right, you lost control of the handles. Scrapped your knees, which caused cuts and bruises. Do you remember the fight that you and your parents were even having? Don't worry author, it doesn't matter because I knew you were bored with life. You lost all feeling and senses; the pain receptors in your brain were turned off. Author, oh author in this long book of yours, you explained how God once said, 'Let there be light!' and the light showed. However, on that day there was no light in you! So, I asked you, 'Where is your God?' Yet, you just stared at the darkness in your room without a reply. You did not reply, but this is what your stubborn heart said,

'I walk out my house with a mask as my body fully armored holding a shield and sword; I am my own protector. I absorb my own sins and sing my own hymns.'

You could not say Christ because you were too prideful and continued listening to the voice that I had placed in you. So, the Spirit of God let you live on. Stripped, slapped, and spat at. Whipped and wounded were the conditions your Savior went through. Crowds laughed at him and mocked him. Nails drilled inside of him. Suffering and pain until the end. As he mentioned, 'It is finished.' Yet, you still deny him! I guess he did that all for nothing, well for your case! Author, do you recall the chapter adversity? I told the spirit of Pride to impregnate you! Well, it was that day that you would see the child that I had planted inside of you. The mask that your heart spoke of had begun to fade and your armor you thought would always protect you broke into pieces. The sword of pride that you possessed had reached its limits and the shield was a lie, just a knockoff from the truth. You have always known you were living a life full of lies! You just enjoyed sin so much that you indulged in the items I gave you! I will never forget the first time the spirit of Suicide spoke to you! My number one general who took you down and exposed you for who you really were. I was ready to welcome you into my home just like you had welcomed me into yours! The spirit of Suicide spoke,

'Haven't, you had enough? Listen and listen closely. You can make this all end. Forget family and friends. Forget about life, forget your problems, forget everything. It can all be made better if you just forget everything. If peace is what you seek, then go rest in peace. Isn't it the only way to find peace? God will forgive you! He has to forgive you because he said to go to him to find peace!'

Author, I can see you cringing at this memory because you listened to the voice. You were so obedient to the voice. It was the first time you had heard the voice and the spirit of Suicide spoke in such a gentle manner deceiving evil for good. For it is written:

You are doomed! You call evil good and call good evil! You turn darkness into light and light into darkness. You make what is bittersweet, and what is sweet you make bitter. (Isaiah 5:20) – Good News Translation

Yes author, I can hear your thoughts recalling, 'the tone of the voice had a mask!' Don't play stupid because you knew who was behind the mask, but it had trapped you inside your thoughts. The spirit of Suicide had possessed your body and put you in a comatose. The voice was patient with its approach; the voice had roamed the earth and knew your story and weaknesses. I gave power to the voice of Suicide because it had done so well in the past. It had murdered the lives of many; It had broken the faiths of many believers and crushed the heads of the non-believers. For it is written:

Whoever is meant to be captured will surely be captured; whoever is meant to be killed by the sword will surely be killed by the sword. This calls for endurance and faith on the part of God's people. (Revelation 13:10) – Good News Translation

The voice had slowly robbed and killed joy, peace, love, and hope but on that day the voice spoke to destroy. Author, oh author tell your readers because I know you're guilty of listening to that voice. You then began to walk down the stairs with the spirit of suicide latched onto your soul! Author, oh author you should have seen the spirit as it danced and laughed at you! As you got to the kitchen, your heart began to grieve because you had no power over your body. However, you're lucky because something else came into the kitchen! An angel from heaven interrupted the spirit of Suicide's mission, it out-spoke my voice. Do not think that you are victorious because you survived! There is still that scar on your right palm to remind you that it isn't finished. Even though my top general failed the mission, you still picked up the sharp looking object well known as a knife. I remember the fear inside your heart when you stared at the sharp edges. You were still trapped in your mind, so the spirit of Suicide unveiled its mask and said,

'Put your right hand on the kitchen counter and open up your palm. Spread your fingers so far across from one another. Let's play a game! While I take over your body as you wrestle against your thoughts. I know that you're not left-handed so grab the knife with your left hand; it'll make this interesting. The game is a different version of Russian roulette. Now, start outside your thumb. Ready? Set. Go! Now stab the knife in between each one of your fingers! From your thumb to your pinky and back! Steady now, you don't want to miss. Or do you? Now go faster! That's right, I have full control over your body because you're too occupied with your suicidal thoughts. Keep going! Keep going! Faster! Faster! Fas....!'

Author, oh author I initially told the spirit of Suicide to slit your wrists! Yet it failed to get you into doing it. I wonder if its because you were afraid of the knife. Or, was your precious Lord and Savior's voice ringing in your head? You truly lived luckily. Well for now you live. You still have the scar on your right palm, don't you? Remember how exhilarating it was? Feeling your own heart beat out of your palm! No Psalms! Yet, you lived luckily. Well for now you live. It was sort of like Russian roulette expect with no bullets. No guns, oh just imagine how fast that would have been! I almost had you, author! The same way the ropes tighten around the neck of Judas! Watching his life getting taken from him! I did that! But forget him he was bound by sin. How are you feeling nowadays? Feeling better? Not allowing me to come in? I suggest you hold onto Christ forever because if you don't, I will come back for you. You have something I like just like the others! Whenever you're feeling worthless and unloved, remember me, I will take it all in for you. Especially when you're guilty of sin! Yes, you live but watch your back! If I can huff and puff and blow your house down once. I bet I can do it again. Yet, you lived luckily. Well, for now, you live."

-The doctrine of Satan.

When I look back at all that had happened during that time, I begin to wonder what other people's safe havens are? Satan's doctrine had specifically studied who I was because I had accepted things like pride in my life. This makes me think back to chapter battling Egypt and Babylon, where I had talked about addictions and idols. We cannot serve both God and Satan; it just doesn't work. Now it doesn't necessarily mean that a person is a Satanist because Satan is a deceiver so whatever he dangles in front of us may not seem evil, but he knows that we are spiritual beings who put our faith in things. It is part of his knowledge to know this. Faith is the only way we can come to know and be one with God, so what he does is he directs our faith to something else. In my case, I did have faith in God but it was also powerless because I did not live by it. I was no different from the Israelites who had seen God do marvelous things, but they were in love with sin that they couldn't find it within their hearts to submit to God.

They will hold to the outward form of our religion but reject its real power. Keep away from such people. **(2 Timothy 3:5) – Good News Translation**

I was the "such people" because I possessed the knowledge of the religion but rejected its real power. What does it mean to deny its real power? See at the beginning of this book I spoke about the angels that worship God, day and night unconditionally. However, those same angels wish to understand God's unconditional love. Despite that, they still continue their worship because of his awesome power. In my case, I rejected my faith's power because I did not possess a love for God. I used religion as a jacket to disguise my sins when I was indeed naked, shameful and dead. This attempt to use religion became a horrific lie that molded itself with my pride. 2 Timothy 3:5 warns us about such people and to not be such people because we are only fooling ourselves. There are many ways that people can hold to the outward form of the religion: wearing a cross, quoting Scriptures on their social media accounts (guilty), getting some biblical tattoo on themselves (guilty). The list can go on! There are some who can be found in the church, and this is what the Pharisees did which is why Jesus spoke against them!

All in all, it is not on us to search for such people, but the Scriptures specifically warn us to not be those people and to stay away from them. How do we know that if we are those people? Well, I found out that I was that person when my pride got broken down and I kept hearing God's Spirit convict me. I was so disappointed in myself that I allowed the spirit that influences people to give up have authority over my life for a night. I have never in my life been a suicidal person, but that's just what sin can do! It can lead us to situations in which we could have never predicted to be in. I thank God for all that I had been convicted of because it made me wake up and see myself from his view. It did not convict me to say, "You're a sinner, and you're going to hell." Although I feel like I deserved to go to hell, God foresaw our human nature a long time ago and knew it was going to be our downfall.

Although God hates whenever we sin, he knew where the root of our sins was coming from. It all started from the tree that gave knowledge of what is good and bad. As I mentioned numerous times in this book, the wage of sin is death, so God had to do something to save us from both those two dilemmas. By Jesus Christ's death, he paid for the hefty price sin required. By doing so he also left us with the option to possess his Spirit to overcome our sinful nature. That is when the relationship begins, but it is only up to the person to make the first move. This is where the spirit of suicide comes in place because it attempts to prevent a person from ever getting the Spirit. If they do get it, the spirit strives to discourage the person from having a relationship with the Holy Spirit. I do not need to get into the many maneuvers the devil will attempt to break us because it really doesn't matter if we know the truth.

So then, submit yourselves to God. Resist the devil, and he will run away from you. **(James 4:7) – Good News Translation**

Is it that simple though? Yes, it really is but it is easier said than done because the devil will do and say anything to get us from submitting. Even if we submit, we still have to resist and that was my issue. Those who submit will make the decision to receive the Holy Spirit, but the battle doesn't just end there because the person has to resist the devil. Resistance could come in the form of many things. Satan could bring up our pasts to discourage us and make us think God doesn't love us. He could use things like addictions or lust to break our submission to the truth. He could send the spirit of propaganda to cause arguments between our flesh and spirit. The doctrine could even go so far by messing with our knowledge of the law of God which will challenge our faith! I once gave up in life, so the thoughts of ending my life entered my mind. But God loved me so much that those thoughts weren't strong enough to destroy me. The very voice I hated hearing so much was the thing that kept tackling at my pride. In the chapter adversity, the doctrine of Satan poem specifically stated that there will come a time when the spirit of pride would abandon me. The thing that I did not realize was that it was lying because pride does not leave a person by its own free will. It was by God's Holy Spirit inside of me which kept convicting me of my wrongdoings that broke my pride. I feel it in my heart to say that God used my pride against me to help me see my sinful nature.

If you don't punish your children, you don't love them. If you do love them, you will correct them. **(Proverbs 13:24) – Good News Translation**

The most amazing and loving thing that a parent can do is discipline their child. God knew I hated hearing his voice of conviction because it possessed the truth. I hope I am not framing God's convicting voice as the reason for my attempted suicide. I thank God for convicting me because it allowed me to see that I was wrong and was so far from the truth. This is what 2 Timothy meant when it said, "people will reject its real power." I dismissed my faith's real power because I did not want to follow its commandments which is why I hated hearing the word 'no' or that I made a mistake. Anyone who claims to love God will obey his commandments. That is just something that cannot be debated. It is by this very reason why I chose to forget everything I was ever taught or felt to find the truth and write this book. I did that for my faith and my love for God!

If you love me, you will obey my commandments. I will ask the Father, and he will give you another Helper, who will stay with you forever. He is the Spirit, who reveals the truth about God. The world cannot receive him, because it cannot see Him or know Him. But you know Him because He remains with you and is in you. **(John 14:15-17) – Good News Translation**

God's Word irritates people because it contains a truth that is sharper than any double-edged sword.

The Word of God is alive and active, sharper than any double-edged sword. It cuts all the way through, to where should and spirit meet, to where joints and marrow come together. It judges the desires and thoughts of the heart. There is nothing that can be hidden from God; everything in all creation is exposed and lies open before his eyes. And it is to him that we must all give an account of ourselves. **(Hebrews 4:12-13) – Good News Translation**

This sword tormented me because I knew deep down that it was right and I was wrong, so I shoved alcohol, partying, lust, false ideologies and many more things to silence it. I looked back to March 18th, 2018 and I thank God it happened because it was that day that made me admit that I needed God. The saying "Rome wasn't built in a day," is relevant to my story because it took a very long time for me to adjust to God's voice and take the necessary steps to change. The evidence is in this book because what started off as a story to tell became a journey with God's Spirit. The spirit of suicide, or the spirit that makes us give up, is not like the other spirits that used to torment me. It is a spirit that just gets to the point because it only seeks to destroy. Evil spirits all behave differently. The Scripture that mentions: The thief only comes to steal, kill and destroy introduces the process of how spirits operate. To steal, it robs us of our time because we were made to worship God and that requires time; to kill, it kills blessings because we were created blessed and those who love God obey him so he blesses them; and to destroy, is the destruction of our purpose which is to be one with God. For example: When a spirit robs someone of joy, chances are the person will not notice it gone until they start looking for it. When a spirit kills, what that means is it has spiritually murdered a blessing from us. Satan has no power over God, so he targets us through temptations and if we give in, he can kill something that is or was supposed to be for us. Lastly, and hopefully no one reading this will ever face, is destruction. Destruction to the devil means spiritual and physical death. Its main goal is to destroy faith because once a person's faith is gone, they have lost all motivation to be what God intended them to be. It doesn't even matter if the person even knew what God wanted them to be because that spirit has a tight hold on the person's thoughts and emotions.

What gives life is God's Spirit; human power is of no use at all. The words I have spoken to you bring God's life-giving Spirit. **(John 6:63) – Good News Translation**

I have told you this while I am still with you. The Helper, the Holy Spirit, whom the Father will send in my name, will teach you everything and make you remember all that I have told you. Peace is what I leave with you; it is my own peace that I give you. I do not give it as the world does. Do not be worried and upset; do not be afraid. **(John 14:25-27) - Good News Translation**

Some people will go through their whole entire life with demons and evil spirits and never know it. I'm a testimony to that because I lived in sin. If we allow ourselves to continue living in sin it shouldn't surprise us what we will attract.

I have told you this many times before, and now I repeat it with tears: there are many whose lives make them enemies of Christ's death on the cross. They are going to end up in hell, because their god is their bodily desires. They are proud of what they should be ashamed of, and they think only of things that belong to this world. **(Philippians 3:18-19) – Goods News Translation**

This is dangerous because if we remain in our pride and do not have anything within us that convicts us, we will not survive against Satan's doctrine. Even when I received the Holy Spirit, I still unknowingly lived with demons because I was suffering from anxiety, alcoholism, arrogance, pride, lust, and many more things. It really doesn't matter to me what their names were because God's Spirit had a way of getting rid of them.

Do not bow down to any idol or worship it, because I am the LORD your God and I tolerate no rivals. **(Exodus 20:5) - Good News Translation**

If a person possesses the Holy Spirit, it will not abandon them no matter what. It may be harsh in its conviction, but it is only through its conviction where a person will see their sins and make the decision to turn from them. When these spirits were upon my life, the Holy Spirit did not stand for it, so it continued to convict me even more.

The gates of Jericho were kept shut and guarded to keep the Israelites out. No one could enter or leave the city. The LORD said to Joshua, "I am putting into your hands Jericho, with its king and all its brave soldier. You and your soldiers are to march around the city once a day for six days. Seven priests, each carrying a trumpet are to go to the Covenant Box. On the seventh day, you and your soldiers are to march around the city seven times while the priests blow the trumpets. Then they are to sound one long note, as soon as you hear it, all the people are to give a loud shout, and the city walls will collapse. Then the whole army will go into the city. **(Joshua 6:1-5) – Good News Translation**

The reason why I am referring to this Scripture is that the walls of Jericho that were shut and guarded represented my pride. God instructed the Israelites to march around the city for seven days and on the seventh day the priests were to blow through a trumpet. It sounded ridiculous but after the seventh day the walls collapsed, and the Israelites were able to enter the city of Jericho and conquer it. In this case, my pride was like that of the walls of Jericho and inside the walls was a scared little boy who needed God but was too prideful to admit it. I guarded myself with my sins and thought it was a fortress, but the more God's voice convicted me, the weaker the walls got. Yes, I had the Spirit with me, but I trapped myself in my own head. The only way for these walls to go down was through the loud noise of trumpets (God's voice). Although I had accepted God's Spirit, I was still blind because of my pride. The doctrine of Satan wanted to destroy me with the spirit of suicide, but God loved me so much and spared me. If I had not made the decision to go after God's Spirit on January 2018, I don't think I would stand a chance. For in my conviction that I got from God's Spirit, I saw the truth and it reached out to me. It exposed me for who and what I was and said, "Here I am, not to condemn but to forgive you, so that you may see the truth and accept it and have life through me."

Jesus said, "I came to this world to judge so that the blind should see and those who see should become blind." Some Pharisees who were there with him head him say this and asked him, "Surely you don't mean that we are blind, too?" Jesus answered, "If you were blind, then you would not be guilty; but since you claim that you see, this means that you are still guilty." **(John 9:39-41) – Good News Translation**

My blindness came in the form of my pride. Despite all that, I was going to experience the real power of my faith through the Holy Spirit. My blindness was about to turn into sight through God's conviction. The more it convicted me, the more my sight became clearer and my pride broke down. That concludes my story and experience with the deadly spirit of suicide.

"Author and readers,

Write down a list of people that you have said you hate. Then write a list of all the people that have done you wrong. Afterward, write down a list of people you do not get along with. If everyone were to do this, they would title their lists 'My Enemies.' Well today, I tell you those people are the people that you must love. For it is written:

You have heard that it was said, "Love your friends, hate your enemies." But now I tell you: love your enemies and pray for those who persecute you, so that you may become the children of your Father in heaven. For he makes his sunshine on bad and good people alike and gives rain to those who do good and to those who do evil. Why should God reward you if you only love the people who love you? Even the tax collectors do that! And if you speak only to your friends, have you done anything out of the ordinary? Even the pagans do that! You must be perfect- just as your Father in heaven is perfect. (Matthew 5:43-48) - Good News Translation

It is by my Spirit that said, 'the world will hate you because it hated me first'. For it is written:

If the world hates you, just remember that it has hated me first. If you belonged to the world, then the world would love you as its own. But I chose you from this world, and you do not belong to it; that is why the world hates you. (John 15:18-19) - Good News Translation

The reason why the world hated me is because it knew I came to save. Those who belong to the world do not want to be saved because they have become one with the environment of sin. The moment humanity disobeyed me; they were cast out to the world- the world of sin. You all became one with the world because your real enemy stood and accused all of you of your iniquities and filth. For it is written:

In another vision, the LORD showed me the High Priest Joshua standing before the angel of the LORD. And there beside Joshua stood Satan ready to bring an accusation against him. The angel of the LORD said to Satan, "May the LORD, who loves Jerusalem, condemn you. This man is like a stick snatched from the fire." (Zechariah 3:1-2) – Good News Translation

Author and reader, surely I tell you your real enemy attacks you all in your sleep; your real enemy attacks you all in broad daylight. This enemy is one you cannot see but is like a lion that is seeking to devour! For it is written:

Be alert, be on watch! Your enemy, the devil, roams around like a roaring lion, looking for someone to devour. (1 Peter 5:8) – Good News Translation

Author, oh author I must warn you about this enemy because you once allowed him into your home! You've respected his voice and sometimes have mistaken it for mine. Throughout this whole book, you've allowed him to speak which is why you have fallen into temptation and sinned. Your enemy has defiled righteousness, love, and respects nothing! Your enemy has declared war against me, but I have defeated him, so he lashes out at my sheep. Those who are misinformed will be lost and be caught in his traps. Your enemy doesn't hold anything back because he wants to destroy everything in his path. My Spirit said, 'pray for everyone and love everyone' because your enemy has put you all against each other. Those who are for him are already lost, but there are still some who need to be shown the right path. Author, I can hear your heart ask, 'But Spirit of God, how will I know who is willing to be saved? How will I fight what I cannot see?' Surely, I tell you, it is not for you to know but by my Spirit which will guide you to say the right things and voice out the truth. I never said be picky nor did I say choose whomever you want. I said love your enemies and pray for those who persecute you. Author, apply this unto your heart:

Do not change your ways because its Monday; do not change your ways because its Tuesday; do not change your ways because its Wednesday; do not change your ways because its Thursday; do not change your ways because its Friday; do not not change your ways because its Saturday; do not change your ways because its

Sunday. Certainly, do not change what I tell you because you are now apart of me. For it is written:

Jesus Christ is the same yesterday, today, and forever. Do not let all kinds of strange teachings lead you from the right way. It is good to receive inner strength from God's grace, and not by obeying rules about food; those who obey these rules have not been helped by them. (Hebrews 13:8) – Good News Translation

Those who are apart of me have confessed their love for me! They will be one with me and will obey me because they love me. Author, oh author since you have acknowledged your love for me, you will abide by this. The list I told you to write that you enlisted as your 'enemies,' you will treat them as your friends. Even though they will snare at you and call you many names; even if they gossip and reject you. You will cry tears of mercy for them because you know who the real enemy is. For I tell you this because the real enemy is their enemy too! You will pray for them and treat them like they had shared your mother's womb with you because you now know the truth. They will curse at you with their insight of good and bad, but you will go into your prayer closet and say, 'Father forgive them, they do not know what they're doing.' Author, oh author you know very well what the enemy has said to you in the past. You know what he has done to you, but all those things happened to you because you let him! You knew the truth but never obeyed the truth. I have already told you this a long time ago. For it is written:

I am giving you the choice between life and death, between God's blessing and God's curse, and I call heaven and earth to witness the choice you make. Choose life. (Deuteronomy 30:19) – Good News Translation

There are no in-betweens, those who say, 'Spirit of God, we love you,' but still, remain in sin and disobey my Word. I will rebuke them because 'I AM' 'El Roi,' the God who sees! For it is written:

Haggar asked herself, "Have I really seen God and lived to tell about it?" So, she called the LORD, who had spoken to her, "A God Who Sees." (Genesis 16:13) – Good News Translation

Those people are naked and full of sin. They deceive others by using my name, but they forget that I see everything. Author, oh author remember that I AM El Roi. That is why I tell you and your readers this:

Do not lose faith in righteousness and do not be discouraged by wicked acts! Have faith in the Lord that sees everything because all those who remain faithful will be lifted up. For it is written:

Write down clearly on tablets what I reveal to you so that it can be read at a glance. Put in writing, because it is not yet time for it to come true. But the time is coming quickly, and what I show you will come true. It may seem slow in coming but wait for it; it will certainly take place, and it will not be delayed. And this is the message: "Those who are evil will not survive, but those who are righteous will live because they are faithful to God." (Habakkuk 2:2-4) - Good News Translation

Author, I can hear your heart asking, 'Spirit of God if they are on the opposite side of truth, why would I bother with them?' Author, oh author it is by my Spirit that you write the way you do. For not too long ago you were on the other side of truth! You spoke maliciously, got drunk, and lived like the pagans. You ignored my voice for 24 years and lived irreligiously. You ate my proverbs but vomited out their wisdom. For it is written:

There are seven things that the LORD hates and cannot tolerate: A proud look, a lying tongue, hands that kill innocent people, a mind that thinks up wicked plans, feet that hurry off to do evil, a witness who tells one lie after another, and someone who stirs up trouble among friends. (Proverbs 6: 16-19) - Good News Translation

However, some people kept praying for you because it was by my Spirit that they continued to love you. Even though you deliberately rejected my Word and the purpose I set out for you, but my love for you never went away! It is not on you to judge who should be loved and saved because before humanity, I knew all my creations and loved them all the same! For it is written:

Before I formed you in the womb, I knew you, before you were born, I set you apart; I appointed you as a prophet to the nations. (Jeremiah 1:5) – Good News Translation

I said those words to the prophet Jeremiah, but it applies to all my children! Before your mothers and fathers knew each other, I already knew all of you! Before all of you could speak, I made the oceans and the skies! I created the sun, moon, and stars. I did all this to show my glory, for in my glory is love. Author, oh author pay no attention to the sins of others but continue to pray for them because they are under the spell of the real enemy. For it is written:

Whoever continues to sin belongs to the devil, because the devil has sinned from the very beginning. The Son of God appeared for this very reason, to destroy what the devil had done. (1 John 3:8) – Good News Translation

Readers listen!

The author of this chapter titled it suicide all for the sole reason to talk about the wicked spirit that makes people give up. However, it is in this chapter where the author will be reminded that I took what the enemy attempted to do and turned it against him!

Author, oh author I can hear your heart asking, 'Spirit of God how did you turn it against him?' Author, oh author have you forgotten everything about that night? You think I did not see what the enemy was attempting to do to you? For it was I who sent my own angels that night to protect you. The angel called you by your name and its voice spoke, 'hope, joy, love, and peace.' It was my angel that gave you strength because it reminded you about eternal life! Author, oh author I heard your heart that night. It was crying and felt defeated. It was listening to the very mask you made which the spirit of suicide hid in! However, I spoke to your heart, and it heard this,

'All the things you thought you lost will be found times ten with me. My child it is time to turn your life around because you attempted to gain the world and almost lost your soul. Turn away from your sins and listen to the sound of my voice!'

Author, oh author it was that day that made you want to write this book! You did not recognize my angel's voice because you were still on the other side, far from truth but I was there that night. It was my will for you to soon know my voice and now you do! I can hear your heart asking, 'Spirit of God, I do not fear men or women alike, but I do not want to sound insensitive to them but why did you save me? Many other people suffer from the spirit of suicide, and some are lucky to fight it, but others aren't. If you know that we are suffering from such vile spirits why didn't you save them? The world has called it mental health issues, but I am not a fool to the spiritual. If your love is equal to everyone why was I spared? Those who are not spared what then comes about for them? Will you show mercy? What are their fates?'

Author, oh author let me ask you this, 'Why is it that you suffered from the spirit of suicide? How was it that you allowed it into your life? If you are wise enough to know that mental health issues are really the enemies secret, how did it enter you undetected?' Surely, I tell you, the answer is in the previous chapter! Didn't I tell you? Didn't I teach you about hardships and adversities? Those who suffer from such vile spirits only suffer because they continue to live their lives in sin. Those who commit suicide are suffering from the costs of sin. For it is written:

For sin pays its wage- death, but God's free gift is eternal life in union with Christ Jesus our Lord. (Romans 6:23) - Good News Translation

Can you surely tell me that those who suffer for my sake would ever attempt to take their own life? It would make their walk with faith rather useless. As a matter of fact, their claim in the faith would be exposed as a lie! Why would they sacrifice themselves when Christ himself did that for them? For it is written:

But he endured the suffering that should have been ours, the pain that we should have borne. All the while we thought that his suffering was punishment sent by God. But because of our sins, he was wounded, beaten because of the evil we did. We are healed by the punishment he suffered, made whole by the blows he received. All of us were like sheep that were lost, each of us going his own way. But the LORD made the punishment fall on him, the punishment all of us deserved. (Isaiah 53:4–6) - Good News Translation

The LORD says, "It was my will that he should suffer; his death was a sacrifice to bring forgiveness. And so, he will see his descendants; he will live a long life, and through him, my purpose will succeed. **(Isaiah 53:10) - Good News Translation**

Our High Priest is not one who cannot feel sympathy for our weaknesses. On the contrary, we have a High Priest who was tempted in every way that we are but did not sin. **(Hebrews 4:15) - Good News Translation**

Author, oh author I can hear your heart asking, "But Spirit of God, there are some who have been victimized by other people's sins and because of this, they do not feel loved and the spirit of suicide attacks them. What then of their fate?" Author, oh author with such knowledge it is the very reason why I told Simon Peter, 'Upon this rock, I shall build my church and the not even the gates of Hades shall prevail against it!" For it is written:

And I also say to you that you are Peter, and on this rock, I will build my church, and the gates of Hades shall not prevail against it. And I will give you the keys of the kingdom of heaven, and whatever you bind on earth will be bound in heaven, and whatever you loose on earth will be loosed in heaven." (Matthew 18:19) – New King James Version

Surely, I tell you all this because of your faith in the living God! For the keys of the kingdom of heaven are in the hands of those who submit to my Spirit and believe in me. Author, oh author your heart pleas for those who are unknowing of my Word. Surely, I tell you this is the reason why I have told you, none of you are each others' enemies!

Author, oh author accept this truth and announce it to all!

'The Lord God has seen what the spirit of suicide has done, and it is why I told all believers to go and not only preach the gospel but to declare freedom to those spiritually bound by the gates of hell. Those who believe in me have the authority over any vile spirits! For it is written:

Go your way; behold, I send you out as lambs among wolves. (Luke 10:3) – New King James Version

For those who speak of my name in faith the heavens shall obey and will break all chains on earth. Now go and act on this Good News for it will be by your faith that the lost and innocent shall know this truth and be free from such spirits! For the gates of Hades will tremble at the sight of you!'

Author, oh author do not be afraid! Surely, I tell you that fear which you feel was not given by me but by sin! For it is written:

For God has not given us a spirit of fear, but of power and of love and of a sound mind. (2 Timothy 1:7) – New King James Version

It is that spirit that I have written in you that thinks of those who have fallen victim to the spirit of suicide which makes you ask me such questions. Author, oh author your spirit yearns for these people because it was written within you to help such people! Go out and share this information so that none fall under victim to this spirit! There are some who will reject you but if they do, continue to pray for them because you know how your enemy operates! For it is written:

'He who hears you hears me, he who rejects you rejects me, and he who rejects me rejects him who sent me." (Luke 10:16) – New King James Version

Author, oh author I have given you the power to not only rebuke the enemy from your life but also the lives of others! Be at peace, for my peace will be with you! For it is written:

Then the seventy returned with joy, saying, "Lord, even the demons are subject to us in your name." And he said to them, "I saw Satan fall like lighting from heaven. Behold, I give you the authority to trample on serpents and scorpions, and over all the power of the enemy, and nothing shall by any means hurt you. Nevertheless, do not rejoice in this, that the spirits are subject to you, but rather rejoice because your names are written in heaven." (Luke 10:17-20) – New King James Version

Readers write this upon your hearts and memorize it in faith because the power will be released from your tongues!

'For by the power and glory of Jesus Christ, all spiritual warfare that exists in either my life or my family - I decree and declare the abolishment of all spirits that work for Satan's doctrine! For it is not by my power but by the power of the Holy Spirit of God that has heard my prayer! For the words that come out of my mouth have made the heavens rumble and the earth shake. For all the demons with names that exist in my life, I shall call them out one by one and they all shall flee! May they hear my voice and be reminded that I am the child of the living God, the God who made heaven and earth. For it is written:

Now I saw heaven opened, and behold, a white horse. And he who sat on him was called Faithful and True, and in righteousness he judges and makes war. His eyes were like a flame of fire, and on his head were many crowns. He had a name written that no one knew except himself. He was clothed with a robe dripped in blood and his name is called The Word of God. And the armies in heaven, clothed in fine linen, white and clean, followed him on white horses. Now out of his mouth goes a sharp sword, that with it he should strike the nations. And he himself will rule them with a rod of iron. He himself treads the winepress of the fierceness and wrath of Almighty God. And he has on his robe and on his thigh a name written: 'KING OF KINGS AND LORD OF LORDS.' (Revelations 19:11-16) – New King James Version**

For those who have been burdened and tormented by the king of tyrants shall sing that Scripture to his kingdom and remind him of the KING OF KINGS AND LORD OF LORDS! They will shout, 'That is our God!' And by faith all the chains that had 'torture and torment' engraved in steel will be broken and they shall cheer, 'Glory be to the Lord Jesus Christ for he has liberated me from torture and torment!' AMEN!'

Author, oh author for I Am El Roi, the God who sees! For mercy and love exists within me. The spirit of suicide works tirelessly for Satan and those who listen to its voice have ears, so it is up to them to either accept or reject its lies! Those who possess my Spirit will obey my commandments to go and preach my Word which speaks mercy and love! Those who listen to my Word have ears, so it is up to them to either accept or reject the truth! For I will ask such people, 'I had sent my lambs out to speak to you, but you rejected them? You closed off your hearts to those who offered you love, and you returned hate to them. But you found comfort in the words of the enemy?' For it is written:

Jesus answered them, "I told you, and you do not believe. The works that I do in my Father's name, they bear witness of me. But you do not believe, because you are not of my sheep, as I said to you. My sheep hear my voice, and I know them, and they follow me. And I give them eternal life, and they shall never perish; neither shall anyone snatch them out of my hand. (John 10:25-28) – New King James Version

For those who find comfort in the words of the enemy have given the enemy their freewill and by faith they will listen because they are not my sheep. That is the fate of those who have fallen under victim of the sins of others and then obey the spirit of suicide. But the blood of those who are slain by the spirit of suicide are on the hands of the people who claim to love me but did not go out and preach my Word! For greater is my mercy to those who weren't shown love by my lambs but woe to those who knew of my love but ignored the unloved. For it is written:

But he who did not know, yet committed things deserving of stripes shall be beaten with few. For everyone to whom much is given, from him much will be required; and to whom much has committed, of him they will ask the more. (Luke 12: 48) – New King James Version

So, their faith in me will be exposed as a lie and they will have to answer to this because my sheep follow my ways! For faith is seen through works and it is by faith that a person is put right with me! So, author, if your heart weeps for such people, go out and by faith your actions will save such people because my Spirit lives in you. It is in your actions where your hands shall not have bloodshed but even if they reject you, mourn in prayer so that they might receive the strength to overcome that destructive spirit!

Author, oh author I warn you all about the enemy because he has become one with sin. Sin only leads to one road and it is to the world of the dead. I am telling all you the truth, sin draws people to death! The spirit of suicide attempts to mimic my Spirit! My Spirit tells them I love them, where the spirit of suicide tells them love does not exist for them! My Spirit wants to be one with all so that you may have eternal life, where the spirit of suicide wants people to surrender to it so it may claim a death certificate. It does so with deceit and lies while lurking in the darkness. It latches onto people seeking to get them to surrender to the wages of sin-death. My Spirit longs to be one with all so that all may be immune to death and sin because Christ defeated both in his sacrifice. For it is written:

Since the children, as he calls them, are people of flesh and blood, Jesus himself became like them and shared their human nature. He did this so that through his death he might destroy the devil, who has the power over death, and in this way set free those who were slaves all their lives because of their fear of death. (Hebrews 2:14-15) – Good News Translation

For in my Son's sacrifice, he showed the world his love for all, but it is in a person's sacrifice for my Spirit where they show their love for me! Author, oh author don't you see why I told you to turn away from your sins? For it is written:

For anything that is clearly revealed becomes light. That is why it is said, "Wake up sleeper and rise from death, and Christ will shine on you." (Ephesians 5:14) – Good News Translation

Author, oh author you asked why you were spared and why others weren't? Surely, I tell you it is by grace that your heart even heard my voice that night, even though you didn't know it was mine. That is why I must remind you all that you are not enemies of one another. Your enemy is always looking to devour! Author, oh author tell your readers this:

'What the spirit of suicide attempted has shown you what it's like to be without me! What the enemy has attempted has shown you what its like to live in sin. The author of this book was once stubborn and thought he could live without me. My love allowed him to live that way but look at what almost happened that fatal night!'

Author and readers pay attention,

Let me reveal to all of you what is hidden in the dark. Your enemy attempts to steal, kill and destroy the happiness of people. Your enemy has disguised himself behind sin because once you commit to it, he stands to accuse you through guilt! The spirit of suicide is just as relentless as its other friends, but the prince of darkness loves his association with it because it attacks at all frontiers. That destructive spirit manipulates the thoughts of my beautiful creations by telling them to surrender to death! It doesn't want any of you to repent and if you do, it puts a time clock on your sins. Those who reason with the voice of sin will say to themselves, 'What I just did, there is no coming back so what's the point?' That destructive spirit has become so boastful in its work that it has even entered the threshold of churches! Why do you think some feel discouraged? It is that destructive spirit that intimidates my beautiful creations from entering churches. For it is written:

Then he said, "Daniel, don't be afraid. God has heard your prayers ever since the first day you decided to humble yourself in order to gain understanding. I have come in answer to your prayer. The angel prince of the kingdom of Persia opposed me for twenty-one days. Then Michael, one of the chief angels, came to help me because I had been left there alone in Persia. (Daniel 10:12-13) - Good News Translation

Author and readers beware of this destructive spirit because its primary goal is more than just taking one's own life from themselves. This destructive spirit attempts to oppose people's prayers by making them give up on forgiveness and faith. For my servant, Daniel had prayed to me and because I loved Daniel, I had sent my angels to him so that he would receive my reply. However, the enemy sent this destructive spirit to attempt to oppose one of my angels! Surely, I tell you all, do not lose faith or give up hope. For it is written:

What are the angels, then? They are spirits who serve God and are sent by him to help those who are to receive salvation. (Hebrews 1:14) – Good News Translation

That destructive spirit even fights my angels to discourage the faith of my people! What if my servant Daniel began to lose faith? What if my servant Daniel thought to himself, 'I have prayed, but the Lord has not answered me?' Surely, I tell you if Daniel gave up, he would have turned away from me and would have never received my message from the angel. It is this very reason why I tell you all to turn away from your sins and become one with me. For it is written:

Those who are children of God do not continue to sin, for God's very nature is in them; and because God is their Father, they cannot continue to sin. (1 John 3:9) - Good News Translation

That destructive spirit operates to not only oppose you all but even my own angels! It does this because it knows my angels are the messengers for my beautiful creations. For it is written:

At sunset, he came to a holy place and camped there. He lay down to sleep, resting his head on a stone. He dreamed that he saw a stairway reaching from earth to heaven, with angels going up and coming down on it. (Genesis 28:11-12) - Good News Translation

Author and reader imagine if my servant Daniel gave up and quit praying? It was his patience, trust, prayer, fasting, faith, obedience and repetition which kept him immune from that vile spirit. 21 days had passed, but he did not give up and he received the answer to his prayer. This destructive spirit will use the knowledge of your earthly clocks to make all of you impatient, but I have already spoken about this matter. For it is written:

For we do not wrestle against flesh and blood, but against the principalities, against the powers, against the rulers of the darkness of this age, against spiritual hosts of wickedness in the heavenly places. (Ephesians 6:12) – New King James Version

Those who do not know me and reject my truth will be doomed by these destructive spiritual forces! Those who refuse to turn away from their sins can never hear my voice even when my angels are present. Author, oh author you once asked why you were spared. I told you that it was by grace, but also by the prayers of those who prayed for you! That is why I ask you to pray for all because none of you are enemies of one another. Surely I tell you, your prayers will not go unheard, just as my servant Daniel's prayers were not. Your enemy will attempt to oppose my angels, but it is by my power that the enemy's plans will always fail! Yet, it is also by my Spirit in which you will remain in me so that you will reject sin and hear my voice. For it is written:

Therefore submit to God. Resist the devil and he will flee from you. Draw near to God and he will draw near to you. Cleanse your hands, you sinners; and purify your hearts, you double-minded. Lament and mourn and weep! Let your laughter be turned to mourning and your joy to gloom. Humble yourselves in the sight of the Lord, and he will lift you up. (James 4:7-10) – **New King James Version**

Author and readers remain in me even when it seems like things have gone bleak. I have already told you the truth about hardships and adversities. Now I ask you to be prayer warriors! For David did not defeat Goliath by playing shield and sword! Nor did he defeat Goliath by his size, but by his faith in the Lord. For it is written:

David answered, "You are coming against me with sword, spear, and javelin but I come against you in the name of the LORD Almighty, the God of the Israelite armies, which you have defied." (1 Samuel 17:45) – Good News Translation

For it is by my Spirit that defeats the spirit that attempts to make all give up on the truth! For it is written:

But you belong to God, my children, and have defeated the false prophets because the Spirit who is in you is more powerful than the spirit in those who belong to the world. (1 John 4:4) - Good News Translation

Attention author! It is my voice and my Word in which people will be victorious against the enemy. Author, can't you see the truth? The truth behind this chapter? You went through all this because you listened to the enemy's voice. Therefore, I place this warning onto you because I AM El Roi. If you turn away from me, I have seen what the enemy has plotted, and it will be 100 times worse than what you went through! He has set out traps for you and will use whoever and whatever to tempt you to turn away from me, but you must remain faithful! For it is written:

Be sure that the book of the Law is always read in your worship. Study it day and night, and make sure that you obey everything written in it. Then you will be prosperous and successful. Remember that I have

commanded you to be determined and confident! Do not be afraid or discouraged, for I, the LORD your God, am with you wherever you go. (Joshua 1:8-9) - Good News Translation

Your enemy has no power over me and since you are with me, he has no power over you! Attention author! Pray for your friends, family and those who you do not get along with. Pray for those who have hurt you and have said horrible things about you. Be patient with them, love and forgive them. Do not live like them or your words will mean nothing! For it is written:

Imitate me, then, just I imitate Christ. (1 Corinthians 11:1) - Good News Translation

Attention Author! Take this cup that is filled with mercy and salvation and drink it! Attention Author! Take this cup that is filled with the blood of Christ and let it fill you with wholeness! Attention Author! Be filled with the Spirit of God, now and forever! For it is written:

Do not get drunk with wine, which will only ruin you; instead, be filled with the Spirit. Speak to one another with the words of psalms, hymns, and sacred songs; sing hymns and psalms to the Lord with praise in your hearts. In the name of our Lord Jesus Christ, always give thanks for everything to God the Father. (Ephesians 5:18-20) - Good News Translation

Attention author! Be filled with the Spirit so that your words will always be clean and true. If you infuse yourself with anything else, your words will mean nothing! You will do all this not to bring yourself glory but to glorify my name! It is by my Spirit that you will do this because when my name is exalted, people will see my love. You will not do all this for your sake but for the sake of those who have yet to know my voice. You will not do all this because you fear your enemy but for the sake of those who do not know who the real enemy is. You will not do all this because you want to be praised but to bring praise to me.

Attention author! Do not be afraid of those who will challenge you! Surely, I tell you, in your obedience they will see your change. For it is not by your power that you will do all these things but by my power because you heard my voice and

accepted the truth. Who can judge the Lord God? What sin do I have? What lies have I ever told? If you live for me, who then can judge you? They will only say, 'That author speaks to the holy living God, we cannot trap him because he lives for the truth.' Author, I can hear your heart saying, 'Spirit of God when will I be ready? I have already disgraced my name because I am regarded as a sinner. Everyone knows this through my past, and they have all counted my sins. I do not think I have the strength to do this. Yes, your words are true, but I've lived a life filled with lies. Who will listen to what I have to say?' They will say, 'Look it's the boy who cried wolf.' 'I feel so stupid because you named me author, but I've spent many months of my life hiding behind this book. It is only by your Spirit that I can hear what you say, but who will believe me that you are with me?'

Attention author!

Have you not learned anything from this journey? For it is written:

Anyone who is joined to Christ is a new being; the old is gone, the new has come. All this is done by God, who through changed us from enemies into his friends and gave us the task of making others his friends also. Our message is that God was making all human beings his friends through Christ. God did not keep an account of their sins, and he has given us the message which tells how he makes them friends. Here we are, then, speaking for Christ, as though God himself were making his appeal through us. We plead on Christ's behalf: let God change you from enemies into his friends! Christ was without sin, but for our sake God made him share our sin in order that in union with him we might share the righteousness of God. (2 Corinthians 5:16–21) – Good News Translation

Do not be afraid of this new challenge; do not be scared of this task because I will be with you. It is not up to you to worry about what people will think of you. They are not your enemies! It is through your change in me that you pray for them, so they will know the real enemy and come to see the truth, just as you have seen the truth.

Attention author! You do not live for yourself anymore so your actions will be selfless.

Attention author! You do not live in pride anymore so your actions will be that of humility.

Attention author! It is not people who take away sin, but it is the power of my Son which has made you clean. Have you forgotten about Saul who is now known as apostle Paul? For it is written:

They kept stoning Stephen as he called out to the Lord, "Lord Jesus, receive my spirit!" He knelt down and cried out in a loud voice, "Lord! Do not remember this sin against them!" He said this and died. (Acts 7:59-60) - Good News Translation

And Saul approved of his murder. That very day the church in Jerusalem began to suffer cruel persecution. All the believers, except the apostles, were scattered throughout the provinces of Judea and Samaria. Some devout men buried Stephen, mourning for him with loud cries. But Saul tried to destroy the church; going from house to house, he dragged out the believers, both men, and women, and threw them into jail. (Acts 8:1-3) - Good News Translation

As Saul was coming near the city of Damascus, suddenly a light from the sky flashed around him. He fell to the ground and heard a voice saying to him, "Saul, Saul! Why do you persecute me?" "Who are you, Lord?" he asked. "I am Jesus, whom you persecute," the voice said. "But get up and go into the city, where you will be told what you must do." (Acts 9:3-6) - Good News Translation

Despite his sins, I chose him and shown a light on him. When I spoke to him, he bowed to the Most High and cried in my arms. Saul was known as the man who persecuted the church, but I forgave him. For it is written:

I give thanks to Christ Jesus our Lord, who has given me strength for my work. I thank him for considering me worthy and appointing me to serve him, even though in the past I spoke evil of him. But God was merciful

to me because I did not yet have faith and so did not know what I was doing. And our Lord poured out his abundant grace on me and gave me the faith and love which is ours in union with Christ Jesus. This is a true saying, to be completely accepted and believed: Christ Jesus came into the world to save sinners. I am the worst of them, but God was merciful to me in order that Christ Jesus might show his full patience in dealing with me, the worst of sinners, as an example for all those who would later believe in him and receive eternal life. To the eternal King, immortal and invisible, the only God– to him be honor and glory forever and ever! Amen. (1 Timothy 1:12-17) – Good News Translation

The Jewish people hated him based on his past and his sins, but he remained in me and I remained in him. Author, oh author your real fear is what people will say about your change. They will say, 'no man changes that drastically.' Yet you forget that it was not by your power that changed you but by mine. Has it not sunk in yet? No man nor woman can spiritually change by their own power, but it is by their sacrifice and reverence in me that they are changed in Spirit. Those who suffer in sin and see its true nature will soon become disgusted with it. They will hate their own clothes and rip them off but then they will be afraid to be in the light because of their nakedness. Author, oh author these people will search through the earth's resources but will never find peace. This is the message I have for those people. For it is written:

I alone know the plans I have for you, plans to bring you prosperity and not disaster, plans to bring about the future you hope for. Then you will call to me. You will come and pray to me, and I will answer you. You will seek me, and you will find me because you will seek me with all your heart. Yes, I say, you will find me, and I will restore you to your land. I will gather you from every country and from every place to which I have scattered you, and I will bring you back to the land from which I had sent you away into exile. I, the LORD, have spoken. **(Jeremiah 29:11-14) – Good News Translation**

Those who suffer in sin will soon become adamant about hearing the truth. Author, oh author do not be afraid because sin has lied to your eyes. It tells those who are not with it that its people are joyous and at peace. It even flirts with the

eyes of those who are on the side of truth by telling them they are missing out. Do not listen to the voice of sin because it lies through its teeth! Stay on course with the truth and pray for those who are being deceived by the voice of sin! Your enemy has closed off their hearts, shut off their hearing and blinded their sight.

Attention author! Pray for those people and do not despise them. You have opened up your heart to me and asked to be filled with my Spirit. You opened your mouth and I fed you bread and nursed you water, that gave you strength.

Attention author! To fully change you had to rebuke the enemy's voice and turn away from sin. Would it be a lie to say that you do not know how to conquer both Egypt and Babylon? Would it be a lie to say that you do not know how to overcome your flesh with my Spirit? Would it be a lie to say that you do not know how to overcome lust with my love? Would it be a lie to say you understand the law because of your faith? Would it be a lie to say that you understand and possess faith, so you obey my laws? Would it be a lie to say that you know how to prevail above the hardships that come from sin? If all this is true, who then can oppose you? If all this is the food you eat and the water that you drink, who then can judge you? If I have said that you are forgiven, who then can condemn you? Is it not true that whatever I bless, no one can curse? Who can curse what I have blessed? Let that go to debate! All that has happened was done because you once drank from the cup of sin. It had lied to you because it told you that you belong to it. Surely I tell you, you have already defeated sin because of your faith in me! It once wrestled you to the ground and commanded you to surrender; however, it is by mercy and love that you were saved. Your enemy has now seen that you've abandoned him, so he is trying to scare you by ridiculing you in your thoughts. Do you not think this happened Saul who is now known as Paul? For it is written:

He went straight to the synagogues and began to preach that Jesus was the Son of God. All who heard him were amazed and asked, "Isn't he the one who in Jerusalem was killing those who worship that man Jesus? And didn't he come here for the very purpose of arresting those people and taking them back to the chief priests?" But Saul's preaching became even more powerful, and his proofs that Jesus was the Messiah were so convincing that the Jews who lived in Damascus could not answer him.

After many days had gone by, the Jews met together and made plans to kill Saul, but he was told of their plan. Day and night, they watched the city gates in order to kill him. But one-night Saul's followers took him and let him down through an opening in the wall, lowering him in a basket. (Acts 9:20-25) – **Good News Translation**

Attention author! You named this chapter suicide so that people will know about the wicked spirit that leads people into death. Now I will flip the script on you and remind you about my Spirit that gives all strength. Tell this to your readers:

'My Spirit has been poured out to defeat all spiritual principalities. It triumphed over all the enemy's powers and it is the light that shines on the world. My Spirit is inviting through the words that I speak. My Spirit cannot be seen, but its presence is known to those who receive it. My Spirit cannot be taken away because I do not abandon those who love me. My Spirit sings hymns of joy to the broken and is like a guide in the night to those who are lost. My Spirit cleans the wounds that have been exposed and infected. My Spirit gives insight and teaches people about the truth so they may accept my love. My Spirit is a stamp of victory and renewal to those who think they have expired. My Spirit tolerates no rivals because I am the God that has no competitors. My Spirit is your protector and defender which slays the head of your enemy, the Leviathan. For it is written:

With your mighty strength you divided the sea and smashed the heads of the sea monsters; you crushed the heads of the monster Leviathan and fed his body to desert animals. (Psalms 74:13-14) – **Good News Translation**

My Spirit allows those who receive it to see the traps that the enemy plans to lay out before they are laid out. My Spirit connects people to me because I love them, and they love me. My Spirit forgives and keeps no record of wrongdoing because the person who has received it will no longer desire sin. My Spirit feeds the hungry and heals the sick. My Spirit casts out evil spirits and makes them quiver in fear. My Spirit clothes the naked in holy garments, so they become a light to the world. My Spirit lifts people from the powers of death so they may live in eternal life. My Spirit weeps for the lost because it knows I want my beautiful creations back. My Spirit rebukes false claims and reveals the truth! My Spirit is called Helper because it knows the people on earth cannot live alone without it. It is my Spirit that is kind in heart and forgives the sins of others.

Those who take a cup filled with my Spirit will never thirst again because they will have tasted truth! Those who take the cup filled with my Spirit will no longer crave the rotten things their bodies crave. Those who take the cup filled with my Spirit will no longer be victimized by wicked spirits because my Spirit has defeated the evil forces in the heavenly world.'

Attention author! Do not be afraid! You have always asked, and you have received from me. It is not by you that you have written with such authority, that authority comes from me. That is why my Son prayed for his sheep and gave his life for all of you so that you may receive me and get to know me. He prayed for the found and the lost alike, the confused and the proud; the blind and the sick; the sinners and those who continue to keep the faith.

He did all this because he knows that your enemy desires all of you. I gave what humanity calls mortal lives so that you may see my power through your faiths' and experience eternal life. My Son lowered himself beneath all of you just so that all of you would be lifted up! It was through the prophets which I spoke that all this would happen. My truth that was merely just words to all of you became a reality so that all of you would know the God that you serve. To all believers and non-believers, the truth is available and up for grabs, what shall all of you do? Accept it!

Author and readers write this upon your hearts! For it is written:

I will sprinkle clean water on you and make you clean from all your idols and everything else that has defiled you. I will give you a new heart and a new mind. I will take away your stubborn heart of stone and give you an obedient heart. I will put my spirit in you and will see to it that you follow my laws and keep all the commands I have given you. Then you will live in the land I gave your ancestors. You will be my people, and I will be your God. I will save you from everything that defiles you. I will command the grain to be plentiful so that you will not have any more famines. I will increase the yield of your fruit trees and your fields so that

there will be no more famines to disgrace you among the nations. You will remember your evil conduct and the wrongs that you committed, and you will be disgusted with yourselves because of your sins and your iniquities. **(Ezekiel 36:25-31) - Good News Translation**

Author, I can hear your heart asking, 'Spirit of God, what if I fail and let you down? What if I make a mistake and crumble? How is it that you trust me with this responsibility? Can I just remain to be an author?' Author, oh author you speak like this because the destruction spirit is still trying to remain in you! Your enemy is trying to snatch you away and bring you to the fire! Your enemy is trying to present sin as joyful, but no longer will you hear his voice in your thoughts! I have spoken this upon your life! Throughout this whole book, you have asked and have received. Now I tell you for the sake of all, I have rebuked the spirit that always speaks negatively about you! It will no longer surround you nor will it ever torment you because I have removed it. It is by my Spirit that I tell you, you will no longer desire any sort of alcohol for your addiction is now broken!

Author, oh author there will come a time when you will no longer voice out my words through the ink of a pen but by the way you walk and speak out loud for me. You will open your mouth to large crowds of people and profess that 'I AM, Elohim, Yahweh, Abba, El Elyon, El Roi, El Shaddai, Yahweh Yireh, Yahweh Nissi, Jehovah Rapha, Yahweh Shalom.' For it is written:

And God said to Moses, "I AM WHO I AM." And he said, "Thus you shall say to the children of Israel, 'I AM has sent me to you.'" (Exodus 3:14) – New King James Version

And because you are sons, God has sent forth the Spirit of his Son into your hearts, crying out, "Abba, Father!" (Galatians 4:6) – New King James Version

I thank the LORD for his justice; I sing praises to the LORD, the Highest. (Psalms 7:17) - Good News Translation

Hagar asked herself, "Have I really seen God and lived to tell about it?" So, she called the LORD, who had spoken to her, "A God Who Sees." (Genesis 16:13) - Good News Translation

Whoever goes to the LORD for safety, whoever remains under the protection of the Almighty, can say to him, "You are my defender and protector. You are the God; in you, I trust" (Psalms 91:1) - Good News Translation

Abraham named that place "The LORD Provides." And even today people say, "On the LORD'S mountain he provides." (Genesis 22:14) - Good News Translation

Moses built an altar and named it "The LORD is my Banner." (Exodus 17:15) - Good News Translation

He said, "If you will obey me completely by doing what I consider right and by keeping my commands. I will not punish you with any of the diseases that I brought on the Egyptians. I am the LORD, the one who heals you." (Exodus 15:26) - Good News Translation

But the LORD told him, "Peace. Don't be afraid. You will not die. Gideon built an altar to the LORD there and named it "The LORD is Peace." (Judges 6:23) - Good News Translation

Attention author! Surrender all your doubts, mistakes, worries and sins because they are no longer yours, for I have taken them away. It is by my Spirit that you are not to suffer from sin because you will not tolerate sin or its voice. It is by my Spirit that those who receive me will no longer be victimized by any vile spirits. Those foul spirits that have tormented and tortured people will be sent back to where they came from. For it is written:

Since you have accepted Christ Jesus as Lord, live in union with him. Keep your roots deep in him, build your lives on him, and become stronger in your faith, as you were taught. And be filled with thanksgiving. See to it, that no one enslaves you by means of the worthless deceit of human wisdom, which comes from the teachings handed down by human beings

and from the ruling spirits of the universe, and not from Christ. For the full content of divine nature lives in Christ, in his humanity and you have been given full life in union with him. He is supreme over every spiritual ruler and authority. (Colossians 2:6-10) – Good News Translation

Author, it is by my Spirit that you will no longer listen nor hear the voice that spreads lies about the truth. I, the Spirit of God, have spoken."

-Spirit of God

CHAPTER 11

SUBMISSION TO THE TRUTH PART I

"Spirit of God,

I give you great thanks and praise for all that you've done for me. However, you know the inside of my heart and the dark secrets that my thoughts come up with. What you have spoken to me for this chapter has put me in great discomfort. For it is written:

An angel from heaven appeared to him and strengthened him. In great anguish he prayed even more fervently; his sweat was like drops of blood falling to the ground. (Luke 22:43–44) – Good News Translation

Spirit of God, you know I fear to write about this chapter because I feel that it is highly unpopular and my thoughts are telling me, 'you will cause controversy.' I feel so ashamed that I even have such thoughts, but it's the very reason why you spoke into me to write about this chapter. I am still learning in faith, but this prayer is simply for strength. There is nothing that is hidden from you so why bother keeping it from you. As you placed this great message in me, I pray that you will help me write about my greatest fear. In my submission to you is obedience; in my submission to you is love; in my submission to you is the power of the Word. In my submission to you there is the Spirit that doesn't allow me to thirst. Help me write in such a way, where my fear does not jeopardize the message. Spirit of God, I tried to ignore your message, but you kept speaking to me in my dreams. Spirit of God, I tried to ignore writing about this chapter, but you kept speaking to me during the day. Spirit of God, I tried to ignore writing about this chapter, but you even used my own brother to speak to me about it. I get it now; I have heard your voice. Please just help me like you helped the ancient people who have won the race of faith. Spirit of God, you have spoken upon my life and my life will always remain in your hands. I have heard your voice, and it has been such a great honor. Sometimes I do wonder what your thoughts are like. How I wonder what would happen to my face if I ever got to see you in person. For it is written:

When Moses went down from Mount Sinai carrying the Ten Commandments, his face was shining because he had been speaking with the LORD; but he did not know it. Aaron and all the people looked at Moses and saw that his face was shining, and they were afraid to go near him. But Moses called them, and Aaron and all the leaders of the community went to him, and Moses spoke with them. After that, all the people of Israel gathered around him, and Moses gave them all the laws that the LORD had given him on Mount Sinai. When Moses had finished speaking with them, he covered his face with a veil. Whenever Moses went into the Tent of the LORD's presence to speak to the LORD, he would take the veil off. When he came out, he would tell the people of Israel everything that he had been commanded to say, and they would see that his face was shining. Then he would put the veil back on until the next time he went to speak with the LORD. (Exodus 34:29-35) - Good News Translation

I thank you for being a part of me, but this isn't just one-time favor but a forever thing. For it is written:

Do not banish me from your presence; do not take your holy spirit away from me. (Psalms 51:10-11) - Good News Translation

Spirit of God, help subdue my thoughts and emotions! I do not trust them because they've spent years being victimized by the enemy's doctrine! You have placed this mission unto my heart to write a message about submitting to the truth. Take my hand and help me write the message you instilled in my heart. Spirit of God, throughout this whole book you spiritually nurtured out my sinful nature and because of this you have shown me the path that leads to the sacred door that not many will not find. For it is written:

Go in through the narrow gate because the gate to Hell is wide and the road that leads to it is easy, and there are many who travel it. But the gate to life is narrow, and the way that leads to it is hard, and there are few people who find it. **(Matthew 7:13-14) – Good News Translation**

It is for this very reason why you placed this message onto my heart so that many will know what it will take to walk through the narrow gate. As fearful as I am to write about this chapter, I know there is no other way to find you without it! For it is written:

Then Jesus said to his disciples, "If any of you want to come with me, you must forget yourself, carry your cross and follow me." (Matthew 16:24) – Good News Translation

If you are ashamed of me and my teaching, then the Son of Man will be ashamed of you when he comes in his glory and in the glory of the Father and of the holy angels. (Luke 9:26) – Good News Translation

I'm ready to take up my cross and follow you. Therefore, I surrender my will in exchange for yours. Spirit of God, not many will be able to understand such words but show mercy to them because it is difficult to give up all that we know. However, you know their hearts and stories. That is why I have faith that you have your plans to get them to hear your voice just as I have heard yours. For it is written:

I alone know the plans I have for you, plans to bring you prosperity and not disaster, plans to bring about the future you hope for. Then you will call to me. You will come and pray to me, and I will answer you. (Jeremiah 29:11-12) – Good News Translation

I tremble in fear because my will has been all that I have relied on, but it is by this chapter where all will know the power of the truth. For it is written:

When I came to you, my friends, to preach God's secret truth, I did not use big words and great learning. While I was with you, I made up my mind to forget everything except Jesus Christ and especially his death on the cross. So, when I came to you, I was weak and trembled all over with

fear, and my teaching and message were not delivered with skillful words of human wisdom, but with convincing proof of the power of God's Spirit. Your faith, then, does not rest on human wisdom but on God's power. **(1 Corinthians 2:1-5) - Good News Translation**

Spirit of God, I can hear your voice in my heart quoting a specific Scripture while saying, 'Do not fear nor worry about the thoughts that are attempting to make you stop. Continue in prayer and trust in the Word, and I will be with you.' For it is written:

The Word of God is alive and active, sharper than any double-edged sword. It cuts all the way through, to where soul and spirit meet, to where joints and marrow come together. It judges the desires and thoughts of the heart. There is nothing that can be hidden from God; everything in all creation is exposed and lies open before his eyes. And it is to him that we must all give an account of ourselves. (Hebrews 4:12-13) - Good News Translation

Spirit of God guide me in my sentences and help me by instilling within me the same wisdom you gifted king Solomon. But I do not ask for that gift to boast that God made me wise, for we have all come to realize that wisdom does not save. But it is through the submission of the truth that we are welcomed into your kingdom.

I seal this prayer with the name that is above all names, Jesus Christ, for it is written:

For this reason, God raised him to the highest place above and gave him the name that is greater than any other name. And so, in honor of the name of Jesus all beings in heaven, on earth, and in the world below will fall on their knees and all will openly proclaim that Jesus Christ is Lord, to the glory of God the Father. (Philippians 2:9-11) - Good News Translation

Amen."

First and foremost, I have to get something off my chest. Pause. That statement is rather redundant since I have gotten 10 chapters off my chest. But I feel it in my spirit to remind everyone that I am not perfect. But my journey has brought me this far because of the Holy Spirit. I feel my spirit pushing me to say that because I named this chapter submission to truth. Although this is not part of the message that the Holy Spirit urged me to write, my spirit wants to write this so all can recognize who I was. By now, everyone should know my life story. But how does a story like mine become this book? Throughout this book there have been poems by the doctrine of Satan and also by the Spirit of God. But if I were to put my feet in the readers shoes how is it that one person can write from both God and Satan? If I were a non-believer and picked up this book, wouldn't I not think such thoughts? Or even better, if I was a believer and picked up this book, wouldn't I think the author of this book is a false prophet or even the antichrist himself? This is why I have to remind everyone that I am no different than them because I have flaws and from the very beginning, I was a sinner. As the book continued, I continued to reveal more of my sinful nature but what was stopping me from manipulating the truth? Besides the fact that I would gain nothing from doing so...

For if he who comes preaches another Jesus whom we have not preached, or if you receive a different spirit which you have not received, or a different gospel which you have not accepted- you may well put up with it. **(2 Corinthians 11:4) – New King James Version**

Beloved, do not believe every spirit, but test the spirits, whether they are of God, because many false prophets have gone out into the world. By this you know the Spirit of God: Every spirit that confesses that Jesus Christ has come in the flesh is of God, and every spirit that does not confess that Jesus Christ has come in the flesh is not of God. And this is the spirit of the antichrist, which you have heard was coming, and is now already in the world. **(1 John 4:1-3) – New King James Version**

I bring this up because of how serious the truth is and all readers including myself must hold onto that till the very end. If we do not submit to Jesus, we will submit to the antichrist. I am a sinner and I made sure that everyone knows it because maybe just maybe it can touch the hearts of those who suffered what I suffered. It is through Jesus Christ, that has brought me to name this chapter submission to the truth because his Spirit has told me to submit to him. The two Scriptures which I quoted was for all to know how to tell the difference between the Spirit of God and the spirit of the antichrist. Just as God made himself into flesh to reveal the truth, the devil is going to do the same to distort the truth. Unfortunately, it is not God's will for me to go in great detail about the antichrist for this book. So how was it that I was able to write poems in the form of Satan's doctrine? It's actually very easy and that is not me bragging, but it is a confession that brings me great discomfort. In the chapter adversity and hardships, I spoke about how adversity and hardships began because of sin. It was through my sinful nature where I was able to write in such a way where it came from the standpoint of the devil.

He who sins is of the devil, for the devil has sinned from the beginning. For this purpose, the Son of God was manifested, that he might destroy the works of the devil. **(1 John 3:8) – New King James Version**

1 John 3:8 states that those who sin are of the devil because the devil has sinned from the beginning. I am being blunt, but the boldness of the statement is true. Hence why I named the book God's truth vs Satan's doctrine because I lived in sin which gifted me the access to write about the doctrine. But because of Jesus it was not even a fight that I had to engage in, but a decision that I had to make which brings forth this chapter.

So then, because you are lukewarm, and neither cold nor hot, I will vomit you out of my mouth. **(Revelations 3:16) – New King James Version**

I began writing this book on March of 2018 and thought I had finished in August 2018. When I finished that draft and gave it to a family friend to edit. He seemed pleased with the work, but he told me something was missing. The first draft was called the doctrine of Satan, not God's truth vs Satan's doctrine. But what I failed to understand was that draft was a book just about sin. Revelations 3:16 mentions how God will vomit us out of his mouth and that is exactly what he did. When I was in Tanzania, it was God's Spirit that rejected the book. During my time in Tanzania, God worked with me each day and the more I spent time in his Word, I became more accustomed to his voice. It was then when the Holy Spirit revealed a spirit that was not of God's. What do I mean by that? I was obsessed with selling this book by attracting the audience with the name Satan. Little did I know that the real truth was I had developed a deep relationship with the enemy without knowing it. In a way I was like the antichrist. The strategy that kept me bonded to him was my love for the things of the world, or in other words sin. I wasn't willing to change anything about my book because I wanted to sell it, just to say I wrote a book and accomplished something. But this is what 1 John 4:1-3 meant. The spirit of the antichrist now exists in the world. It possesses all knowledge of the doctrine because it embodies Satan. As I look back now on my journey and how God rejected my first draft, I am relieved because the spiritual presence of the devil was trying to use what God had willed in my life for his own motives. "Okay, now you're just being dramatic," that's exactly what I would think if I picked up this book and read what I just said. But the reason why I am sharing this is because Jesus resides in me through the Holy Spirit. I developed a relationship with him which then prohibited me from interacting with those sinful thoughts. It is for this very reason why I will never again write a doctrine of Satan poem because it is the Holy Spirit's will for me to write about how one submits to the truth. Not to write about the spirit of the antichrist, who is already in the world. I began this chapter with a prayer and closed it in faith that the Holy Spirit will guide me to write for not just the readers but myself. My spirit is just as much in jeopardy of the doctrine of Satan as anyone else in the world which is why I need to make sure that all who read this make a choice. I struggle every day with Satan's tactics so do not think that I am exempted from it, if anything I feel more pressure on my life because of my knowledge of the truth.

After my prayer, I asked how one is to believe whether or not I am speaking on behalf of God or behalf of the devil himself. I provided the Scripture which comes from the Word which weaponizes all readers to know how to answer that question.

You are of God, little children, and have overcome them, because he who is in you is greater than he who is in the world. They are of the world. Therefore, they speak as of the world and the world hears them. We are of God. He who knows God hears us; he who is not of God does not hear us. By this we know the spirit of truth and the spirit of error. **(1 John 4:4–6) – New King James Version**

All those who read this, know this: I am a sinner and my nature is what the dictionary calls evil. I have lied, stolen, cheated, hurt and cursed people. I have been selfish and hateful towards people on purpose. I was addicted to pornography and obsessed with sexual immorality. I loved drinking more than I loved my family and friends. I, alike Saul who is better known now as apostle Paul, have denied Christ and persecuted the people of God by letting down those who have prayed for me (Only I know what I mean by that and I have chosen not to elaborate it in this book). I also have not willingly given my tithes and offerings to God. All that I have listed are the sins that I have been guilty of and I do not have record of how many times I have committed them. It was this evil nature that gave me the ability to write the doctrine of Satan poems and understand them. But because of Jesus Christ, I destroyed that first draft called, "The doctrine of Satan," and named what all are reading now, "The Secret is Out: God's truth vs Satan's doctrine." Although the spirit of the antichrist exists in the world today, 1 John 4:4-6 states that God's Spirit (Holy Spirit) is greater than he (antichrist) who is of the world. The one who knows all about his doctrine lives in the world and knows how to win the world over by getting them to submit to sin. That is why it is written in 1 John 3:8, "the Son of God was manifested, that he might destroy the works of the devil." The reason Apostle John wrote "might" is because we all have free will to choose Jesus Christ. Apostle John was foreshadowing the future because he was given visions of the end of times. Jesus Christ came to save us from sin so that we "might" have eternal life "if" we choose him. The "if" goes hand in hand with the "might" because that measures faith and relationship, and those who "do" choose him "will" receive eternal life. Whereas the devil will set forth his manifestation through the antichrist, who will get those who did not choose Jesus to submit to sin. Even though sin doesn't have power over us, it is only true if we go to the one that gives us power over it, which is Jesus Christ. Anyone who doesn't submit to Jesus has put themselves at spiritual risk of giving their free will to the antichrist, who will get them to submit to sin. When the time comes, he will take form of someone and win over the world; those who do not have God's Spirit will listen to him.

Do not let anyone deceive you in any way. For the Day will not come until the final Rebellion takes place and the Wicked One appears, who is destined to hell. He will oppose every so-called god or object of worship and will put himself above them all. He will even go in and sit down in God's Temple and claim to be God. Don't you remember? I told you all this while I was with you. Yet there is something that keeps this from happening now, and you know what it is. At the proper time, then, the Wicked One will appear. The Mysterious Wickedness is already at work, but what is going to happen will not happen until the one who holds it back is taken out of the way. Then the Wicked One will be revealed, but when the Lord Jesus comes, he will kill him with the breath from his mouth and destroy him with his dazzling presence. The Wicked One will come with the power of Satan and perform all kinds of false miracles and wonders and use every kind of wicked deceit on those who will perish. They will perish because they did not welcome and love the truth so as to be saved. And so, God sends the power of error to work in them so that they believe what is false. The result is that all who have not believed the truth, but have taken pleasure in sin, will be condemned. **(2 Thessalonians 2:3-12) – Good News Translation**

Then I stood on the sand of the sea. And a beast rising up out of the sea, having seven heads and ten horns, and on his heads a blasphemous name. Now the beast which I saw was like a leopard, his feet were like the feet of a bear, and his mouth like the mouth of a lion. The dragon gave him his power, his throne, and great authority. And I saw one of his heads as if it had been mortally wounded, and his deadly wound was healed. And all the world marveled and followed the beast. So they worshipped the dragon who gave authority to the beast; and they worshipped the beast, saying, "Who is like the beast? Who is able to make war against him?" And he was given a mouth speaking great things and blasphemies, and he was given authority to continue for forty-two months. Then he opened his mouth in blasphemy against God, to blaspheme his name, his tabernacle, and those who dwell in heaven. It was granted to him to make war with the saints and to overcome them. And authority was given him over every tribe, tongue, and nation. All who dwell on the earth will worship him, whose name have not been written in the Book of Life of the Lamb slain from the foundation of the world. **(Revelations 13:1-8) – New King James Version**

He causes all, both small and great, rich and poor, free and slave, to receive a mark on their right hand or on their foreheads, and that no one may buy or sell except one who has the mark or the name of the beast, or the number of his name. Here is wisdom. Let him who has understanding calculate the number of the beast, for it is the number of a man: His number is 666. **(Revelations 13:16-18) – New King James Version**

Now that I have provided the evidence from the Word itself about the antichrist's characteristics, I will address my own questions. It was by mercy from God that the first draft was never published because if it did get published, I most likely would be a disciple of the devil. I would have never gone through this journey and the chapters that are would never illustrate the victory of God's truth. That is not me saying God has not won but I myself would have never received his victory. But the beautiful testimony is in this chapter because the rumours of when or where the antichrist is, should not scare anyone who possess God's Spirit. Jesus, who died for our sins gave us power over that spirit through his Spirit. Although I included the doctrine of Satan in this book, it was done not by my initial plan or logic. It was done through grace and salvation! Despite my sinful nature, he never abandoned me and what the devil initially had planned was used to expose what sin really is. It didn't take talent to write the doctrine of Satan poem's because they represented my sin. But just as the Spirit of God said in the previous chapter, *"Author, it is by my Spirit that you will no longer listen nor hear the voice that spreads lies about the truth. I, the Spirit of God have spoken."* It is the reason why I will not and cannot write from a sinful standpoint. I do not write to please anyone which is why I know this chapter is controversial but those who hate it, only hate it because they are of the world. Do not take that as judgement because I prayed for every person who reads this because there exists a spirit that is preparing for a submission to Satan's doctrine and it is moving quickly. If there still exists a belief that I am of the antichrist or writing about a false gospel remember this: Yes, Satan knows the Scriptures, but it is against his nature to speak the truth. Although I possess a sinful nature, it is by the Holy Spirit that allows me to live as a child of God who hates sin. For what demon, or evil spirit lives for Christ? I spoke of the world but exposed the one who attempts to control it. Not once did I speak in favour of the world but in favour of God. I announced that Jesus Christ came in flesh and died for our sins, for Paul wrote those who deny this are not of God. My spirit and all its vulnerabilities have been laid out so that my life can be used as an example. So, do what the Spirit of God instructed Apostle John and, "test every spirit, whether they are of God, because many false prophets have gone into the world." I have given all the tools to know how one can tell the difference. Furthermore, take also what the Spirit of God instructed Apostle Paul and, "if someone speaks of another Jesus, which the Word has not spoken of or different spirit or gospel, do away with it." I give all this out of love, not the love the world knows or claims to know, but the love that comes from God which is perfect. The true love spoken in the chapter love vs lust. I have not written about another Jesus nor have I lied about his gospel. What's even more amazing is because of God's love, he never abandoned me even in my sinful nature which is available in the previous chapters. It exposes the character traits of sin which can be viewed as a warning to the antichrist's tactics but no longer will it be seen in this chapter, the last or any future books I write.

That being said, it is time for me to address what God has placed in my heart. This chapter is called submission to the truth because it will challenge many others to decide who they want to live for. It is time to finally discuss the unpopular message which I know will also be labeled as the controversial message.

From Corruption in Heaven, Birth of the doctrine, Battling Egypt and Babylon, Conquering Egypt and Babylon, Flesh vs Spirit, Love vs Lust, Law vs Faith, Adversity and Hardships to Spiritual Suicide. Everyone has read my journey that has led me to here. All chapters were important and significant in my spiritual growth and relationship with God. Hopefully it will play a part in the lives of others, but all that God has helped me through were just a glimpse of his glory. To solidify a relationship with God, one must really ask themselves whether they are going to submit to him or not. Yes, I used the word submit and I am aware how using such a word sounds derogatory because its as if I am asking or telling everyone to surrender their free will.

Therefore submit to God. Resist the devil and he will flee from you. Draw near to God and he will draw near to you. Cleanse your hands, you sinners; and purify your hearts, you doubleminded. Lament and mourn and weep! Let your laughter be turned to mourning and your joy to gloom. Humble yourselves in the sight of the Lord, and he will lift you up. **(James 4:7-10) – New King James Version**

I have never been in the business to preach a message of fear because it was not fear that lead me to God but rather an urge to know about his love. However, I cannot sugar code anything in this controversial chapter. Apostle James did not do it and it was God's Spirit that led him to write that bold statement. If the previous chapters brought comfort, joy, relief, happiness, hope or wisdom then blessed be to God for helping me do so. But all those things are temporary! Every single one of them. What the Spirit of God led Apostle James to write was love which is eternal because it comes from God. I truly thought as I was finishing up the previous chapters that I would come out as the author who wrote how to live a Godly life and I would live a life full of sunshine and rainbows. Not just for myself but for others but the reality is that is not the purpose of the gospel. The purpose of the gospel was to destroy what the devil had done and for his beautiful creations to acknowledge his sacrifice and go back to God. As beautiful as the earth is, we all know it will not be here much longer. It has existed for billions of years and sustained us for thousands of years, but years is

GOD'S TRUTH VS SATAN'S DOCTRINE

just a translation of time. Time is not on anyone's side, nor is it on the earth's side but the purpose of this chapter is not to drift too much into the end of days (Book of Revelations). The world was made for us as an act of love from God, but then sin entered the world and none of us had the power to overcome it. Therefore, God sent himself down and gave us a name which had the power to overcome it due to his sacrifice which was translated into another act of love. Except that act of love was the greatest act of love because it overcame the whole world's sins.

'Heaven is my throne, and the earth is my footstool. What house will you build for me? Says the LORD, or what is the place of my rest? Has my hand not made all these things?' **(Acts 7:49-50)- New King James Version**

So where am I going with all this? What is it that's going to make everyone go, "Oh my God, what did he just say?!" In the chapter adversity and hardships, the Spirit of God poem mentioned: *"Author, oh author the only way these people will accept me is if I utter the words, 'I will give you the world,' yet I cannot utter those words because that would make me a liar and a God of hate. Why would I offer something that is destined to be destroyed?"* The meaning behind those words relate back to the chapter battling Egypt and Babylon because the world was not saved but defeated. It is the people of the world that God loves but the one who resides in the world is the one who is meant to be destroyed (The devil). Going back to what Apostle James wrote. I will break down what he meant and why he meant it. To submit to God is to love God with all our heart, soul and mind.

"Teacher, which is the greatest commandment in the law?" Jesus said to him, "You shall love the LORD your God with all your heart, with all your soul, and with all your mind.' This is the first and great commandment. **(Matthew 22:36-28) – New King James Version**

We now know from the Word that obedience is the way we show God we love him. Now in the chapter conquering Egypt and Babylon, I broke down spiritual warfare against things like depression, anxiety and addictions. But I didn't just discuss spiritual matter but also the mind, body, and heart. Therefore, if we know that showing love to God is by obeying him then let us do so. Secondly, the first and greatest commandment is to love him with all our heart, soul and mind then we solve the greatest truth of submitting to God. But there's a problem. How does one get their heart, body, soul and mind to love/obey God? This is where the Holy Spirit comes in and the act of being born again solidifies all elements that make us who we are. The Spirit of God allows for us to be one with Christ, where the baptism of the water (being born again) is a declaration of being a new being in the eyes of God. Boom! I think I just got everyone thinking, "what did he just say?" Let me simplify what I just said. It is within a pregnant woman's womb where her child stays, but how does the woman know she is going into labour? It is when her water breaks. She is made aware that it is time for her child to be born. When the child comes out of their mother's womb, they are covered in blood but also a colourless fluid which resembles water. I have already made it known to everyone that we are all born sinners the moment we come out of our mother's womb. But the representation of the water breaking from a woman significances birth, or prelabour rupture of membranes (Yes, I googled that one). In the chapter love vs lust, one of the Spirit of God poems addressed the definition of love and how birth represent firsts. This applies to all of us because that water breaking represents the first birth of that person.

Jesus answered, "Most assuredly, I say to you, unless one is born of water and the Spirit, he cannot enter the kingdom of God. That which is born of the flesh is flesh, and that which is born of the Spirit is spirit. **(John 3:5-6) – New King James Version**

We recognize the day of our birth as our birthdays because it was the day our flesh was recognized to the world. This is the same for heaven and why it is called being born again! Our birthdays are the recognition of our flesh being born, whereas the baptism of water is the recognition of our spirit being united with the Spirit (Jesus). Hence the reason why it is called being born again. Which is why Jesus himself got baptized because even though he is the begotten Son of God, he came in human flesh. This process could not be cheated, and this should give us an indication of his truthful heart because he did not even need to do that but did so for us.

Then Jesus came from Galilee to John at the Jordan to be baptized by him. And John tried to prevent him saying, "I need to be baptized by you and are you coming to me?" But Jesus answered and said to him, "Permit it to be so now, for thus it is fitting for us to fulfill all righteousness." Then he allowed him. When he had been baptized, Jesus came up immediately from the water; and behold, the heavens were opened to him, and saw the Spirit of God descending like a dove and alighting upon him. And suddenly a voice from heaven, saying, "This is my beloved Son, in whom I am well pleased." **(Matthew 3:13-17) – New King James Version**

Remember how I basically used the simple example of a pregnant woman going into labour? How when a child comes out of her mother's womb, the child is covered in blood and colourless fluids that resemble water? If birth represents firsts, then it is rather foolish for us to debate what death represents because when we die that's it. Or is it? This is the beautiful testimony of what Jesus represents:

But when they came to Jesus and saw that he was already dead, they did not break his legs. But one of the soldiers pierced his side with a spear, and immediately blood and water came out. And he who has seen has testified, and his testimony is true; and he know that he is telling the truth, so that you may believe. For these things were done that the Scripture should be fulfilled, "Not one of his bones shall be broken." And again, another Scripture says, "They shall look on him whom they pierced." **(John 19:33-37) – New King James Version**

What does all this mean? The Son of God living in Spirit of human flesh was dead but when he was pierced in his side, water and blood came out which we know represents birth. Similar to what happens when a woman is giving birth and the child comes out covered in blood and water-like substance. In order words, the statement of 'death represents last' is not valid in Christ. John 19:33-37 foreshadowed two things! The first: Although his flesh was dead at that specific moment, the water and blood represented his Spirit being poured out to the world. The second: It signified new life (born again but in Spirit) because although the flesh dies, the spirit will live and will only live if the person believes in Jesus Christ. A person who believes receives the blood (forgiveness of sins) and water (Holy Spirit) that came out of Jesus Christ' side which lifts them into eternity (heaven). Completing the victory of salvation because the blood separates us from sin (reversing what Adam and Eve did) and the Spirit connects us with God which gives us authorization to live with the Father and the Son in heaven. This is why baptism is a must because it shows that we believe in his promise.

What shall we say then? Shall we continue in sin that grace may abound? Certainly not! How shall we who died to sin live any longer in it? Or do you not know that as many of us as were baptized into Christ Jesus were baptized into his death? Therefore we were buried with him through baptism into death, that just as Christ was raised from the dead by the glory of the Father, even so we also should walk in newness of life. For if we have been united together in the likeness of his death, certainly we also shall be in the likeness of his resurrection, knowing this, that our old man was crucified with him, that the body of sin might be done away with, that we should no longer be slaves of sin. For he who has died has been freed from sin. Now if we died with Christ, we believe that we shall also live with him, knowing that Christ, having been raised from the dead, dies no more. Death no longer has dominion over him. For the death that he died, he died to sin once for all; but the life that he lives, he lives to God. Likewise, you also, reckon yourselves to be dead indeed to sin, but alive to God in Christ Jesus our Lord. **(Romans 6:1-11) – New King James Version**

If the Spirit of God, who raised Jesus from death, lives in you, then he who raised Christ from death will also give life to your mortal bodies by the presence of his Spirit in you. So then, my friends, we have an obligation, but it is not to live as our human nature wants us to. For if you live according to your human nature, you are going to die; but if by the Spirit you put to death your sinful actions, you will live. **(Romans 8:11-13) – New King James Version**

Everyone must die once, and after that be judged by God. In the same manner Christ also was offered in sacrifice once to take away the sins of many. He will appear a second time, not to deal with sin, but to save those who are waiting for him. **(Hebrews 9:27-28) – New King James Version**

The act of baptism (being born again) is something that I did not really understand. I made that known in the earlier chapters and I dug so deep in the Word for my own assurance. But the thing that pleases God, and I am not talking about my own life but all lives, is he knew we would have a hard time understanding all this.

But without faith it is impossible to please him, for he who comes to God must believe that he is, and that he is a rewarder of those who diligently seek him. **(Hebrews 11:6) – New King James Version**

The process of submission requires faith and faith is shown through action. Those who demonstrate action are diligently seeking him. In other words, what the author of Hebrews is stating is that faith cannot be forced onto someone. This was not something that was forced down on me. Remember that all are reading about my journey with God! I lived with much pressure living in a home that worshipped and honored God while I deliberately rejected it because of my love for sin. All that I've revealed to everyone reading this is true and in summary I truly did not see any value or worth in myself. Without God I am nothing, and I do not mean that I am not worth anything or am not valuable. I say that because he knew I felt that way and because of this he reminded me of my value and what I was worth through him. He taught me the love that I knew I could not find here in the world. Readers, do not read this like my parents forced this down on me or some preacher came to my house and said, "You're going to hell!" Do not be deceived! Before all of creation (angels, humans, heaven and earth) he existed and was true and perfect love. Because of how I lived and what I had done in the past, I cannot write in the standpoint of pressuring or forcing people to believe in God. No one forced the gospel on me. It was me, myself and I who made the decision to do so myself and the last thing I want people to believe is that God hates us. That perception is not of human perception but demonic perception which is why I did everything I can to expose Satan's doctrine.

Now the Spirit expressly says that in latter times some will depart from the faith, giving heed to deceiving spirits and doctrines of demons, speaking lies in hypocrisy, having their own conscience seared with a hot iron, forbidding to marry, and commanding to abstain from foods which God created to be received with thanksgiving by those who believe and know the truth. For every creature of God is good, and nothing is to be refused if it is received with thanksgiving; for it is sanctified by the Word of God and prayer. **(1 Timothy 4:1-5) – New King James Version**

Hate originated from the devil, so he enforces his propaganda that God is the one who hates but God does not hate us. God hates sin because it was never apart of him, nor was it supposed to be apart of us.

But you, beloved, building yourselves up on your most holy faith praying in the Holy Spirit, keep yourselves in the love of God, looking for mercy of our Lord Jesus Christ unto eternal life. And on some have compassion, making a distinction; but others save with fear, pulling them out of the fire, hating even the garment defiled by the flesh. **(Jude 1:20-23) – New King James Version**

From the very beginning the devil has always been a liar. In all his lies there is a common denominator: steal, kill and destroy. Apostle James began his bold writings with the sentence of submitting to God which I just explained. He then proceeded to say, "resist the devil and he will flee from you." How do we resist the devil? Why do we even need to if we have submitted to God? This is what I had to learn and why this chapter is extremely important. I've talked and talked about different topics in this book but never gave instruction on how to remain firm in the faith. Hence why the Holy Spirit has placed this message in my heart to include in the book. Apostle James wrote in an interesting tone when writing James 4:7-10. It was a tone of humility, a humility towards God because the Spirit knows the hearts of the proud and the proud will not accept the gospel due to their knowledge of what is good and bad. "Lament and mourn and weep! Let laughter be turned to mourning and joy to gloom." These words do not sound like words of encouragement at all so why write them? Because James knew of what the people of the future would face. What the devil prepared has grown and the spirit of the antichrist is swallowing the hearts of non-believers with one key spirit- pride. Someone who is prideful in their nature will never be able to see God. It was because of pride which allowed Satan to become the being he is today because he wanted to be called, "The Most High."

Where do wars and fights come from among you? Do they not come from your desires for pleasure that war in your members? You lust and do not have. You murder and covet and cannot obtain. You fight and war. Yet you do not have because you do not ask. You ask and do not receive, because you ask amiss, that you may spend it on your pleasures. Adulterers and adulteresses! Do you not know that friendship with the world is enmity with God? Whoever therefore wants to be a friend of the world makes himself an enemy of God. Or do you think that the Scripture says in vain, "The Spirit who dwells in us yearns jealously?" But he gives more grace. Therefore, he says, "God resists the proud, but gives grace to the humble." **(James 4:1-6) – New King James Version**

We are spiritual beings who crave spiritual attention but if we are not spiritually educated, we will seek out that attention in the world. Beware everyone! Yes, I said beware. I said beware because of the evil tyrant who roams the world seeking to devour us. He too is a spiritual being who has set forth his spiritual dominion on the earth. I said this was going to be a controversial chapter because it embodies things that no one wants to hear or can understand through the physical lenses. I know this because I hated this part of the truth because we soon begin to realize that we need to make a decision. We are either hot or cold, not lukewarm! If you say, you believe in God this is the gospel! Yes, readers I repeat, if you believe in God this is the gospel! So read it, weep to it, mourn to it, turn your laughter into sadness and your joy into gloominess because we cannot serve two masters. We will either submit to God and resist the devil or submit to the devil and resist God.

I am the LORD, that is my name; and my glory I will not give to another, nor my praise to carved images. **(Isaiah 42:8) – New King James Version**

No one can serve two masters; for either he will hate the one and love the other, or else he will be loyal to the one and despise the other. You cannot serve God and mammon. **(Matthew 6:24) – New King James Version**

Do not love the world or things in the world. If anyone loves the world, the love of the Father is not in him. For all that is in the world- the lust of the flesh, the lust of the eyes, and the pride of life- is not of the Father but is of the world. And the world is passing away, and the lust of it; but he who does the will of God abides forever. **(1 John 2:15-17) – New King James Version**

I do not apologize for my boldness, if anything I write this in sadness because my old self (the doctrine of Satan loving self) attempts to fight against the will of God. But James wrote to mourn, cry and be of gloom because when we decide to submit to God, we are preparing a funeral of our sinful selves. Except this funeral is not of the physical but of the spiritual so if we decide to submit, it requires us to humble ourselves to God. I will be blatantly honest here. I hated when I read Scriptures that started off with, "Purify yourselves you sinners!" I hated it because I was like, "that sounds so judging and hateful," but I promise everyone reading this, it is not judgement, it is an act of mercy which stems from love. It is salvation and grace which stems from love. Judgement is not done by God while we still have breath, judgement is done when we die physically!

"And being in torments in Hades, he lifts up his eyes and saw Abraham afar off, and Lazarus in his bosom. Then he cried and said, 'Father Abraham, have mercy on me, and send Lazarus that he may dip the tip of his finger in water and cool my tongue; for I am tormented in this flame.' But Abraham said, 'Son, remember that in your lifetime you received your good things, and likewise Lazarus evil things; but now he is comforted, and you are tormented. And besides all this, between us and you there is a great gulf fixed, so that those who want to pass from here to you cannot, nor can those from there pass to us.' Then he said, 'I beg you therefore father, that you would send him to my father's house, for I have five brothers, that he may testify to them, lest they also come to this place of torment.' Abraham said to him, 'They have Moses and the prophets; let them hear them.' And he said, 'No father Abraham; but if one goes to them

from the dead, they will repent.' But he said to him, 'If they do not hear Moses and the prophets, neither will they be persuaded though one rise from the dead.'" **(Luke 16:23-31)- New King James Version**

I am not trying to scare anyone by bringing up that story. I have to tell all the truth so what else am I to do? Am I supposed to hide this from everyone? There are those who know far more than I do but I am blessed to have this wonderful relationship with the Spirit who gives me insight on such things. I speak on the lives of those who do not know. What are they going to do with such information? Does it piss them off? Will they reject it? What I write has been given to me by the Spirit, but I am not exempted by it. In my heavenly imagination, God will know how to judge me accordingly because I will not have any excuse. When it is time for me to take my last breath, will I so joyfully utter the most beautiful set of last words? (This is what I would say when my hour of death comes)

For I am already being poured out as a drink offering, and the time of my departure is at hand. I have fought the good fight, I have finished the race, I have kept the faith. Finally, there is laid up for me the crown of righteousness, which the Lord, the righteous Judge, will give to me on that Day, and not to me only but also to all who have loved his appearing. **(2 Timothy 4:6-8) – New King James Version**

A prideful heart cannot accept the gospel of Jesus, but I had a prideful heart as well. Therefore, if one has a prideful heart or isn't sure if they do, then pray diligently to God to remove it. Trust me, he will know how to do so because he knows all his beautiful creations. I urge everyone to humble themselves and repent to God because the cost of living in sin is not a transaction we can afford. Remember the Spirit of God poem said in the chapter adversity, *"What do you fear more? Perishing in Hell or living in sin? I can hear your heart respond, 'Perishing in Hell.' Well, now I tell you this: They are both the same thing! Author, you now know Hell was not made for any of you but for those who choose to live without me. If the end is what you fear, then it means you know what the cost of sin is."*

As promised, I will now talk about how to resist the devil. I spoke about a spiritual funeral not to long ago but did not really go into depth about it. Physical funerals are when we go and mourn for our loved ones. We are accepting that they are no longer with us and we hope that they are in heaven but unfortunately that is not up to us. Yes, I just said that but also remember I will not lie about the Word of God. I do not possess the spirit of the antichrist so I will not feed anyone what they want to hear.

Little children, it is the last hour; and as you have heard that the antichrist is coming, even now many antichrists have come, by which we know that is the last hour. They went out from us, but they were not of us; for if they had been of us, they would have continued with us; but they went out that they might be made manifest, that none of them were of us. But you have anointing from the Holy One, and you know all things. I have not written to you because you do not know the truth, but because you know it, and that no lie is of the truth. **(1 John 2:18-21) – New King James Version**

Who is a liar but he who denies that Jesus is the Christ? He is antichrist who denies the Father and the Son. Whoever denies the Son does not have the Father either; he who acknowledges the Son has the Father also. **(1 John 2:22-23) – New King James Version**

"So, Mr. Author are you saying that my 'so and so' who passed away last year did not go to heaven?" No, that is not what I am saying at all! I could not have such knowledge of such things because I am not God. Of course, we must mourn for our loved ones because they are our loved ones! What I am trying to do is compare spiritual death to physical death. When someone passes away, all their loved ones gather and honor that person's life. Even after that person's death they are remembered for the time they spent with us.

You must put to death, then, the earthly desires at work in you, such as sexual immorality, indecency, lust, evil passions, and greed (for greed is a form of idolatry). Because of such things God's anger will come upon those who do not obey him. **(Colossians 3:5-7) – Good News Translation**

407

And those who are Christ's have crucified the flesh with its passions and desires. **(Galatians 5:24) – New King James Version**

What did Apostle Paul mean by all this? I have to explain this because some might not understand, or others might misinterpret it. Remember the whole, "repent of your sins, weep, mourn and turn gloom," statement made by Apostle James? This is what it means to put to death our earthly desires which include sexual immorality, indecency, lust, evil passions and greed. Why is it that one would weep, mourn and turn gloom for such things? Here's the thing, when we read such things, we know they are bad but the part that we all struggle with is the repent part. I mentioned before, I did not like the phrase, "repent you sinners!" I did not like it because of pride. The spirit of pride will hold back the hearts of many from mourning for their spiritual freedom in Christ because they will call it weakness, or stupid. James wrote what he wrote because death is in the same discussion as a funeral, but we are not crying for the bad things we have done but for salvation and grace which is available to us through Christ. A prideful heart will be rejected by God which is why it is written in James 4:6, "God resists the proud, but gives grace to the humble." I am not referring to anyone else's death, I am referring to our own self. Because when we die, it is a "me" thing not a "we" thing.

For we must all appear before the judgement seat of Christ, that each one may receive the things done in the body, according to what he has done, whether good or bad. **(2 Corinthians 5:10) – New King James Version**

So Christ was offered once to bear the sins of many. To those who eagerly wait for him he will appear a second time, apart from sin, for salvation. **(Hebrews 9:28) – New King James Version**

Our family members or best friends will not be there neither will our spiritual leaders. No one will be able to defend us. For they themselves are to be judged as well, judged by the living God who offered himself to save us from sin so that we will receive salvation.

Just as we mourn for our loved ones when they pass away, we must (I really want to capitalize and bold that) mourn for our lives for the sake of

Christ. The only difference is we must not remember or commemorate our old selves for if we do such things we are essentially saying, "I miss the devil." I'll just use the story of Lot's wife as an example. God destroyed Sodom and Gomorrah for its evil sins but spared Lot and his family. But he warned them not to turn around and look back at the city. Unfortunately for Lot's wife, she did not listen and looked back because a piece of her loved the sinful city. That story is a metaphorical example of how a prideful heart behaves. It will receive God's grace and love. That person will experience God's glory and submit themselves to Christ. But Egypt or Babylon, for example, will tempt them and their hearts will remember the temporary pleasures of those nations and with pride they will look back and be doomed. For when Lot's wife turned around, she turned into a pillar of salt.

But his wife looked back behind him, and she became a pillar of salt. **(Genesis 19:26) – New King James Version**

I have to take a short break from all this for just a few sentences and say one thing. The Holy Spirit put this message in my heart, and I was afraid to write it because I have the submit part all patented down but it is the resist part that really intimidates me. It burdens me because the Spirit has placed it in my heart to write about, but I do not want to be a hypocrite. This is my selfish proclamation to all reading this: I write in this manner for the sake of myself because I cannot turn back and start to miss my old self. Yes, I just said that, but I really need all the readers to think about their lives with this one Scripture (because I am thinking about mine).

When he had called the people to himself, with his disciples also, he said to them, "Whoever desires to come after me, let him deny himself, and take up his cross, and follow me. For whoever desires to save his life will lose it, but whoever loses his life for my sake and the gospel's will save it. For what will it profit a man if he gains the whole world, and loses his own soul? Or what will a man give in exchange for his soul? For whoever is ashamed of me and my words in this adulterous and sinful generation, of him the Son of Man also will be ashamed when he comes in the glory of his Father with the holy angels. **(Mark 8:34-38) – New King James Version**

Here is my generous and sorrowful proclamation for everyone. I received this message from the Holy Spirit of God and write it on my heart but I, as the author, must walk and talk this message for the rest of my life. I must do this to give hope and encouragement for all so that those who see me, see a person who was sinful like themselves but was able to put to death my natural desires for the sake of Christ. I place that onus and responsibility on myself (for myself). Although no one asked me to do that for their lives, I do it for the one named Jesus Christ. For it was he who did what he did for all of us, which is why the Holy Spirit told me to write this message because it is bigger than me. Imagine the humiliation and embarrassment now if I turn my heart away from Christ? That will be my pain to bear and no one will be able to save me from such a punishment. But blessed be to God Jesus Christ who knew his people would fear their old selves, so he gave us the Holiest of Spirits-his own. He gave us his Spirit to properly bury our old selves so we may live in union with him. Does this mean I am incapable of making mistakes? No, not at all because my journey supersedes this whole book and there are things still unknown to me which God will put my heart to the test. I do not know what those things or experiences are going to be but if God is for me, what then can be against me? For all the experiences which I have written are of the old, so the Spirit of God is preparing me for the new.

But of him you are in Christ Jesus, who became for us wisdom from God- and righteousness and sanctification and redemption- that, as it is written, "He who glories, let him glory in the LORD." **(1 Corinthians 1:30-31) – New King James Version**

Do you not know that you are the temple of God and that the Spirit of God dwells in you? If anyone defiles the temple of God, God will destroy him. For the temple of God is holy, which temple you are. **(1 Corinthians 3:16-17) – New King James Version**

Therefore, if anyone is in Christ, he is a new creation; old things have passed away; behold, all things have become new. Now all things are of God, who has reconciled us to himself through Jesus Christ, and has given us the ministry of reconciliation, that is, that God was in Christ reconciling the world to himself, not imputing their trespasses to them, and has committed to us the Word of reconciliation. (2 Corinthians 5:17-19) – New King James Version

Alright break over! Let's get back to submission of the truth. I addressed what needs to be done in regard to putting to death our natural desires. But there is one more thing I want to address, and it pertains to the funeral of natural selves. Because I have spent so much time in my sinful self, I know how a sinful heart and mind feels and thinks. This is how a sinful mind and heart will respond, "That sounds so stupid, what do you mean by putting to death our natural selves?" They will reject it and call it nonsense so let's think about physical funerals. We have become so selfish about our lives because they are "our lives" but let me remind everyone that our lives are not actually our lives. What do I mean by that?

For you were bought at a price; therefore, glorify God in your body and in your spirit, which are God's. (1 Corinthians 6:20) – New King James Version

Before Christ, our lives were still not our lives! Our lives belonged to sin and the reason why no one knew that is because they loved sin, so they freely lived in it. Before Adam and Eve ate from the tree that gave knowledge of what was good and bad, their lives belonged to God because God gave them life.

There has never been a minute in time where our lives belonged to us. Yes, we touch our flesh and choose to eat and drink what we want. We make our own decisions and choose who we want to associate with, but the reality is our lives are not our own. This is the reality of the spiritual realm; we have always belonged to God. However, this is who God is- he did not create us to boss us but to love us all in the hopes that we would love him back. This is what sin is- it is separation from God, and

411

it demands the payment of death. This is who Satan is- he hates God, so he goes after what God loves by using sin because it destroys us since we are who God loves. After Eden, we were a commodity of the devil because of sin. We did not belong to God even though we were created by him because God does not associate with sin. Israel became God's people through covenant but broke that covenant to run back to the thing that God was trying to save them from. But his love never faded so he came to earth, the land of sinners and lived amongst us in flesh. In order to sacrifice himself because only his blood was pure enough to purify all sins and it sealed the unbreakable covenant which is called the Good News. Sin demanded death, so he gave it what it wanted but sin did not have any power over him because he was sinless. After three days his Spirit raised him to the heavens. He then poured out his Spirit so that we would receive it as the mark of righteousness that provides power over death to raise us from the dead and be worthy of heaven.

At that time, I will answer the prayers of my people Israel. I will make rain fall on the earth, and the earth will produce grain and grapes and olives. I will establish my people in the land and make them prosper. I will show love to those who were called "Unloved," and to those who were called "Not-My-People." I will say, "You are my people," and they will answer, "You are our God." **(Hosea 2:21-23) – Good News Translation**

So therefore, if we are to say he is not our God, so be it. If we are to say, it is my life and I can do with it what I want, so be it. But let me remind everyone, if such proclamations are made then let me tell that person what then is true. That person's life will never be theirs because it will belong to something else. It could be their employer, but in reality, God is not that person's master, it is money. Therefore, money has robbed them of their hearts and because of this they have idolized greed and the worship of idols is the worship of the devil (Please refer back to the Egypt and Babylon chapters). If God is not our God, then Jesus is not our Savior which means our master is sin. Sin is ruled by the one who first sinned and his name is Satan. Hence the Word has done nothing for us, and this book is of no meaning. If we think that putting to death our natural desires and evil ways is nonsense, then why do we say that a person is in a better place when they die?

Who is wise and understanding among you? Let him show by good conduct that his works are dine in the meekness of wisdom. But if you have bitter envy and self-seeking in your hearts, do not boast and lie against the truth. This wisdom does not descend from above, but is earthly, sensual, demonic. For where envy, and self-seeking exist, confusion and every evil thing are there. **(James 3:13–16) – New King James Version**

We hope for such things when someone passes but all it really does is reveal our arrogance and pride towards the truth. We will say things like, "He/She is in a better place." But what is that better place? To even have such a discussion we trigger the conversation of God. We possess hope for a better place at the moment of death but do not possess it in the time of life. That wasn't a question nor a formulation of a thought but rather a firm and bold statement of those who are still of the world. What kind of hypocrisy is that? Please do not possess such a mindset. What then are we to do when someone dies? Do we not hope that they are to go to heaven? Of course, we pray and hope for that because of our faith in God but that is what I am getting across. Faith! It is by faith that we hope for such things when someone dies. Some will say, "Oh author, that was extremely harsh what you just said because it seems like you are attacking those who have passed." No, I am not. I needed to instil that mindset so that we all can understand what it takes to resist the devil. Let us pray and hope for our loved ones to be in heaven but let us not fool ourselves that our lives belong to ourselves. Some will say, "Oh author, God gave us freewill to do what we please and as long as we are good people, we are good." If that is the mindset then I have failed everyone reading this book because that is not the gospel of Jesus. God gave us that freewill out of love, it was not given for us to squander it in sin because it is sin that destroys us. No one can outsmart sin nor can they find a loophole by it; it is what it is and does what it does - steal, kill and destroy. I cannot offer this book any more depth on it because all chapters support each other, and God has been with me to write what needed to be written. Therefore, I will now close part 1 of submission to the truth.

CHAPTER 12

SUBMISSION TO THE TRUTH PART II

In continuation of part 1, this chapter will complete the message of submission of the truth. We already went over how one submits to God and we also spoke about resisting the devil. In this chapter, I will provide 4 steps on how to ensure submitting to God and resisting the devil becomes a habit that is conformed into our very character. The controversial chapter ends in part II which is this chapter.

Now these four steps were actually given to me by my younger brother Imani. He gave them to me as the steps to help me never backslide and they are also the same steps he lives by. Well, now those steps have been incorporated into this message. The four steps are prayer, bible reading, spiritual dieting and church attendance.

It is kind of self-explanatory why we need to pray but for the sake of the truth, I will explain it. In the earlier chapters, I was so far from who I am now, but not once did I converse with God. As the chapters continued, I made sure everyone would see how I prayed to God.

How I wish my people would listen to me; how I wish they would obey me! **(Psalms 81:13) – Good News Translation**

I want your constant love, not your animal sacrifices. I would rather my people know me than burn offerings to me. **(Hoses 6:6) – Good News Translation**

I once thought I was never good at praying because it seemed awkward or sometimes, I found myself thinking, "I can't say that to God." The thing about prayer is it is a form of communication and I had to learn that God already knows what we want or need. If this is the case what was the point of holding back?

And Abraham came near and said, "Would you also destroy the righteous with the wicked? Suppose there were fifty righteous within the city; would you also destroy the place and not spare it for the fifty righteous that were in it? Far be it from you to do such a thing as this, to slay the righteous with the wicked, so that the righteous should be as the wicked; far be it from you! Shall not the judge of all the earth do right?" So the LORD said, "If I find in Sodom fifty righteous within the city, then I will spare all the place for their sakes." Then Abraham answered and said, "Indeed now, I who am but dust and ashes have taken it upon myself to speak to the Lord: Suppose there were five less than fifty righteous; would you destroy all of the city for lack of five?" So he said, "If I find there forty-five, I will not destroy it." And he spoke to him yet again and said, "Suppose there should be forty found there?" So he said, "I will not do it for the sake of forty." Then he said, "Let not the Lord be angry, and I will speak: Suppose thirty should be found there?" So he said, "I will not do it if I find thirty there." And he said, "Indeed now I have taken it upon myself to speak to the Lord: Suppose you find twenty should be found there?" So he said, "I will not destroy it for the sake of twenty." Then he said, "Let not the Lord be angry, and I will speak but once more: Suppose ten should be found there?" And he said, "I will not destroy it for the sake of ten." So the LORD went his way as soon as he finished speaking with Abraham; and Abraham returned to his place. **(Genesis 18:23-33)- New King James Version**

I picked this dialogue on purpose because when I read it, I found Abraham to be annoying. It got to the point where I thought God was going to smite him, or something, for continuously asking him about his will. But that is the perception the devil wants us to have of God because he kept listening to Abraham and answered him. Abraham addressed God 6 different times about the same topic and God did not once snap at him. He asked God if he was going to spare 50, to 45, to 40, to 30, to 20, and finally 10 people. I honestly felt like cringing after the 3rd time Abraham asked God about the 40 people. I thought God was going to snap and be like, "Stop asking me questions!" Yet, he never did that and kept responding and stayed by Abraham's side. I found this dialogue as a beautiful example to use on how we should pray to God. Obviously not the same context but the comfort level and respect Abraham showed God really opened up my mind on how I can talk to God.

The LORD would speak with Moses face-to-face, just as someone speaks with a friend. Then Moses would return to the camp. But the young man who was his helper, Joshua son of Nun, stayed in the Tent. **(Exodus 33:11) – Good News Translation**

In Exodus 33:11, it says that God spoke to Moses face-to-face like someone who speaks with a friend. I found that also comforting and beautiful. Which got me to think if Abraham could not annoy God with all those questions and Moses spoke to God like a friend, what was stopping me from doing the same? This communication thing with God is our way to develop a relationship with God and its the one thing he longs from us. If we think to ourselves, "I do not know how to pray to God," we are lying to ourselves. If we can communicate with our friends, families, coworkers, strangers and sometimes some of us even talk to ourselves (guilty of this a lot). If this is the case, then we should have no problem speaking to God. I used to bottle things up inside and never confided in anyone about my burdens. It's not that I didn't have good people around to trust, but I was too prideful to admit that I had something burdening me. As my pride broke off and the Spirit of God revealed to me the truth about myself, I couldn't bear to look at myself. In the chapter adversity, I spoke about how I got bullied because of my skin color. I felt uncomfortable being in my body, mind, and spirit. Being racially abused is bad enough, but there is nothing more excruciating than having our spirits broken.

I will take you to be my people, and I will be your God, and you shall know that I am the LORD your God, who has brought you out from under the burdens of the Egyptians. I will bring you into the land that I swore to give to Abraham,

to Isaac, and to Jacob. I will give it to you for a possession. I am the LORD.'"
Moses spoke thus to the people of Israel, but they did not listen to Moses,
because of their broken spirit and harsh slavery. **(Exodus 6:7-9) – English**
Standard Version

When we find out about our faults, especially if we're too prideful
to see them, it is the perfect time to talk to God. This does not just
categorize people who are broken but anyone! God gave us the power
of speech to speak so we need to use that ability to talk to him. We see
that I eventually started to speak to God about everything in this book
because I saw what bottling things up inside was doing to me.

So Hannah arose after they had finished eating and drinking in Shiloh. Now
Eli the priest was sitting on the seat by the doorpost of the tabernacle of the
LORD. And she was in bitterness of soul and prayed to the LORD and wept in
anguish. Then she made a vow and said, "O LORD of hosts, if You will indeed
look on the affliction of Your maidservant and remember me, and not forget Your
maidservant, but will give Your maidservant a male child, then I will give him
to the LORD all the days of his life, and no razor shall come upon his head."
And it happened, as she continued praying before the LORD, that Eli watched
her mouth. Now Hannah spoke in her heart; only her lips moved, but her voice
was not heard. Therefore Eli thought she was drunk. So Eli said to her, "How
long will you be drunk? Put your wine away from you!" But Hannah answered
and said, "No, my lord, I am a woman of sorrowful spirit. I have drunk neither
wine nor intoxicating drink but have poured out my soul before the LORD. Do
not consider your maidservant a wicked woman, for out of the abundance of my
complaint and grief I have spoken until now." Then Eli answered and said,
"Go in peace, and the God of Israel grant your petition which you have asked
of Him." **(1 Samuel 1:9-17) – New King James Version**

Hannah wanted a child so badly, but she never got pregnant, so she
prayed to God desperately. The priest Eli saw her moving her lips, but
she wasn't making a sound, so he accused her of being drunk. What
I take from this story is it doesn't matter how we pray to God. God
still heard her prayer because it came from the heart. She eventually
got pregnant and gave birth to her son Samuel, who ended up being a

prophet. She kept her promise to God, but it all began with her prayer to God. It's not like God did not know that Hannah wanted a child, but it all goes back to that communication thing. By communicating we build a relationship with God. In the chapter adversity, I showed how distressed I was with all the hardships that I was going through and did not hold back my feelings or thoughts. I may have sounded annoying to any human but based off what I learned from Abraham, speaking to God doesn't annoy him. The only way we can annoy God is by deliberately disobeying him or sinning when we know something is a sin. Does it sound silly to mutter to God in public? To other people yes, but God doesn't care how we do it, as long as we do it. It could be anywhere, but if we have faith, he will answer us. It could be intimidating if a person doesn't know anything about God, but that person should not be discouraged.

Second step is bible reading and this is important because it is the Word of God. Bible reading is like food for our souls just as regular food satisfies our bodies and gives us strength. The Word of God satisfies our souls and keeps us strong spiritually.

But Jesus answered, "The Scripture says, 'Human beings cannot live on bread alone, but need every Word that God speaks.'" **(Matthew 4:4) - Good News Translation**

I come from a family that has raised me up to know the Word of God, so I was not a stranger to the bible. Nonetheless, my knowledge of the Word really excelled when I made a choice to know the truth. My mother taught me a lot about the Scriptures when I was younger. She made me memorize Psalms 23, 51, and 136 by heart which is why I can quote them with ease. She taught me what to read every morning before I did anything which were the Proverbs. The proverbs show the incredible wisdom which God had blessed king Solomon with.

Now when the queen of Sheba heard of the fame of Solomon concerning the name of the Lord, she came to test him with hard questions. She came to Jerusalem with a very great retinue, with camels that bore spices, very much gold, and precious

stones; and when she came to Solomon, she spoke with him about all that was in her heart. So Solomon answered all her questions; there was nothing so difficult for the king that he could not explain it to her. And when the queen of Sheba had seen all the wisdom of Solomon, the house that he had built, the food on his table, the seating of his servants, the service of his waiters and their apparel, his cupbearers, and his entryway by which he went up to the house of the Lord, there was no more spirit in her. Then she said to the king: "It was a true report which I heard in my own land about your words and your wisdom. However, I did not believe the words until I came and saw with my own eyes; and indeed, the half was not told me. Your wisdom and prosperity exceed the fame of which I heard. Happy are your men and happy are these your servants, who stand continually before you and hear your wisdom! Blessed be the Lord your God, who delighted in you, setting you on the throne of Israel! Because the Lord has loved Israel forever, therefore He made you king, to do justice and righteousness."
(1 Kings 10:1-9) – New King James Version

I believe my mother told me to read the proverbs every day because she wanted to instill in me the wisdom of king Solomon so that one day, I would be wise and successful as him. If it helps anyone, the technique that she taught me was to read the chapter which corresponded with the date (This is for the book of proverbs). If it were the 5th, I would read proverbs chapter 5. She did this because there are 31 chapters in the book of proverbs which is usually how many days there are in a month, excluding February (good ole leap year). Bible reading is not only required for people who don't know anything about God but for those who think they are experts. I had some knowledge, but it was really my thirst for the truth and my connection with the Holy Spirit that helped me know his Word. By understanding the Word, we will know more about God. This is the perfect time to talk about the Holy Spirit and its importance because it can reveal the many deep secrets within the bible.

When, however, the Spirit comes, who reveals the truth about God, he will lead you into all the truth. He will not speak on his own authority, but he will speak of what he hears and will tell you things to come. **(John 16:13) – Good News Translation**

The bible is not an ordinary book. There are many questions about the beginning and even more about the end. There are tons of conflicts which were caused by Satan but are pertained on us. The resolution seems difficult to understand because it relates to things we cannot see. This is what I say about the bible which made my search for the truth within it smoother.

God said, "Do not come any closer. Take off your sandals, because you are standing on holy ground." **(Exodus 3:5) - Good News Translation**

I had mentioned this in the chapter adversity, regarding taking off our footwear. The footwear represents the filth of places we've walked in our lives which mean our thoughts, experiences, ideologies, laws, philosophies, etc. We hold all these things so dearly in our hearts and minds. It is impossible for anyone to know who God is if we come with the attitude that we know more than him. As a matter of fact, everything in the bible will sound gibberish to that person because they have not respected God's holiness.

And the LORD said to him, "What is that in your hand?" He said, "A rod." And he said, "Cast it on the ground." So he cast it on the ground, and it became a serpent; and Moses fled from it. Then the LORD said to Moses, "Reach out your hand and take it by the tail" (and he reached out his hand and caught it, and it became a rod in his hand), "that they may believe that the LORD God of their fathers, the God of Abraham, the God of Isaac, and the God of Jacob, has appeared to you." Furthermore, the LORD said to him, "Now put your hand in your bosom." And he put his hand in his bosom, and when he took it out, behold, his hand was leprous, like snow. And he said, "Put your hand in your bosom again." So he put his hand in his bosom again, and drew it out of his bosom, and behold, it was restored like his other flesh. "Then it will be, if they do not believe you, nor heed the message of the first sign, that they may believe the message of the latter sign. And it shall be, if they do not believe even these two signs, or listen to your voice, that you shall take water from the river and pour it on the dry land. The water which you take from the river will become blood on the dry land." **(Exodus 4:2-9) – New King James Version**

Moses obeyed God and took off his sandals and the moment he did, all that he knew was blown away. Miracles and wonders happened before Moses because of his trust in God. God worked many miracles through Moses, wonders that baffled the Israelites and it also put Egypt in ruins. Now does this mean we will be able to turn sticks into snakes or cause the Nile to turn to blood? As amazing as that would be, those miracles were bestowed unto Moses to get the people of Israel to believe that God was with him.

In his disciples' presence, Jesus performed many other miracles which are not written down in this book. But these have been written in order that you may believe that Jesus is the Messiah, the Son of God and that through faith in him you may have life. (John 20:30) – Good News Translation

Now, there are many other things that Jesus did. If they were all written down one by one, I suppose that the whole world could not hold the books that would be written. (John 21:25) – Good News Translation

The purpose of all these miracles written in the Scriptures are to help us believe in God. Moses got to experience firsthand of God's power and showed the stubborn Israelites that God was with him. I am using the reference of Moses being on holy ground because before he was blessed with the power of miracles, he had to show reverence to God. All that he learned growing up in Egypt had to be forgotten in order to know God.

And Moses and Aaron went in unto Pharaoh, and they did so as the LORD had commanded: and Aaron cast down his rod before Pharaoh, and before his servants, and it became a serpent. Then Pharaoh also called the wise men and the sorcerers: now the magicians of Egypt, they also did in like manner with their enchantments. For they cast down every man his rod, and they became serpents: but Aaron's rod swallowed up their rods. And he hardened Pharaoh's heart, that he hearkened not unto them as the LORD had said. (Exodus 7:10-13) – King James Version

God commanded Moses to take off his sandals so that nothing could interfere with Moses' process to get to know him. The same goes with the Word because they may appear to just be words, but as I have mentioned in previous chapters, the Word is God.

For the word of God is living and powerful, and sharper than any two-edged sword, piercing even to the division of soul and spirit, and of joints and marrow, and is a discerner of the thoughts and intents of the heart. **(Hebrews 4:12) – New King James Version**

Jesus performed miracles so that we too would believe, and it is recorded through the gospels of Matthew, Mark, Luke, and John. All who were close with Jesus gave their own versions of what he did and how he behaved. "The bible was written by people, not God himself," many will say. Yes, this is true, but every single writer within the bible did not write for their own benefit or will but by God's. The people of the Old Testament (prophets) wrote what they saw and heard through the signs and wonders of the Mighty God of Israel. Whereas in the New Testament, the writings involve the life of Christ and the influence of the Holy Spirit. All Scripture that was written was because God had been working through them to voice out his message.

For I testify to everyone who hears the words of the prophecy of this book: If anyone adds to these things, God will add to him the plagues that are written in this book; and if anyone takes away from the words of the book of this prophecy, God shall take away his part from the Book of Life, from the holy city, and from the things which are written in this book. **(Revelations 22:18-19) – New King James Version**

Faith is something that can be misconstrued because of our human nature to doubt everything. That is Satan's number one goal within his doctrine to make us question our faith in God. Which is why he will attempt to manipulate the meaning behind the words just to lead us astray from what God's Word means. He has also been bold enough to create his own religions by taking things out of the original Word of God so that we would be led astray. It's the reason why I asked God to help me understand the Word because I did not want my interpretations of the Word to come from my own knowledge, that is when his Spirit led me to Exodus 4:2-9. If anyone wants to understand who God is, we have to be willing to surrender our so-called knowledge and focus on God (take off your shoes, for the Word is Holy ground).

Everyone else is concerned only on their own affairs, not with the cause of Jesus Christ. **(Philippians 2:21) - Good News Translation**

So let no one judge you in food or in drink, or regarding a festival or a new moon or sabbaths, which are a shadow of things to come, but the substance is of Christ. Let no one cheat you of your reward, taking delight in false humility and worship of angels, intruding into those things which he has not seen, vainly puffed up by his fleshly mind, and not holding fast to the Head, from whom all the body, nourished and knit together by joints and ligaments, grows with the increase that is from God. **(Colossians 2:16-19) – New King James Version**

What I thought I knew about God to what I have been taught by the Holy Spirit has left me speechless. Am I finished? Do I now know everything? If I think such things, I have just told myself the biggest lie because I still possess limited knowledge of God. To know all of God is to be God, remember that everyone! That is the beautiful thing about a relationship with him, God is infinite and our journey with him will never end.

Moses once looked at his walking stick as just an ordinary stick. But the moment he took off his sandals and showed reverence to God's holiness. That same stick had to power to change into a snake, turn the Nile waters into blood, and split the Red Sea into two! He changed Moses in ways the people of Israel could not imagine, and the Israelites could not even look Moses in the face whenever he finished speaking to God.

I once saw the bible as something that would judge my way of life with its list of dos' and do not's, but that is not what it is. Yes, it can come across like that, but once we know the source that influenced the writers to write the way they did, we see the real power of God. There were times where I thought a specific Scripture meant something but the moment I prayed to the Spirit, it revealed what was unknown to my knowledge. For example, in the chapter law vs. Faith, I was stumped with Romans 13 regarding state authorities because I, like anyone, read the text with my own understanding. I struggled with Romans 13 because it felt like that Scripture was contradicting God's commandments. That is when I prayed to the Spirit (Jesus) for guidance. The Spirit knows the secrets of God and although the bible was written by humans, it was God's will to work through those certain writers. Those writers themselves took a leap of faith to get to know God and he answered them. God got them to record what they saw, and they heard and wrote so the future generations may also believe as they did. Seeing doesn't necessarily mean someone will believe nor is reading, but these people did it anyway because of their own faith in God. The moment they took off their footwear and showed faith, God worked through them with miracles and revelations beyond their imaginations. Anyone who does know me on a personal level could have never of guessed that I knew this much, but the thing is I never knew this much. This book says, "written by Innocent Nangoma," but all that I have written was because I took a leap of faith. God took what I misunderstood and opened my eyes to a love that never ends.

Then he opened their minds to understand the Scriptures. **(Luke 24:25) – Good News Translation**

The third step is spiritual dieting and this one is a tricky one. No, I am not talking about our food intake or physical exercises, although they are important. Spiritual dieting pertains to what we see, hear and even say. I am not going to tell anyone what to listen to or watch. However, I will admit that one of my favorite artists is J. Cole and its not just his lyrical talents but the messages behind his lyrics that make him my favourite hip-hop artist. But I haven't really kept in touch with any of his new music as religiously as I used to.

If you give these instructions to the believers, you will be a good servant of Christ Jesus, as you feed yourself spiritually on the words of faith and of the true teaching which you have followed. But keep away from those godless legends, which are not worth telling. Physical exercise has some value, but spiritual exercise is valuable in every way, because it promises life both for the present and for the future. **(1 Timothy 4: 6-8) – Good News Translation**

I did not quote that specific Scripture to judge any musical artist or celebrities but to bring attention to who we praise and idolize. I will always respect someone like J. Cole and his craft, but I refuse to idolize anyone anymore. I already admitted I have no interest in hearing what good or bad knowledge is because it deviates from the truth and if I have strayed from the truth, I will no longer submit to the truth. Does this mean people should stop listening to all genres except gospel music? No, of course not!

"We are allowed to do anything," so they say. That is true, but not everything is good. "We are allowed to do anything"- but not everything is helpful. **(1 Corinthians 10:23) - Good News Translation**

Spiritual diet is no different from our physical diet and the way we can think about it is simple. We all know we are all made differently. Some people exercise differently, and other people eat differently. All this is right by our physical capabilities and appearances. We coordinate our diets based on our physique and our physical capabilities. This is the same for the spiritual because what spiritually convicts me, may not spiritually convict someone else. However, anyone reading this must tread carefully and not take that sentence as literal as it sounds.

Eat whatever is sold in the meat market without raising any question on the ground of conscience. For "the earth is the Lord's, and the fullness thereof." If one of the unbelievers invites you to dinner and you are disposed to go, eat whatever is set before you without raising any question on the ground of conscience. But if someone says to you, "This has been offered in sacrifice," then do not eat it, for the sake of the one who informed you, and for the sake of conscience— I do not mean your conscience, but his. For why should my liberty be determined by someone else's conscience? If I partake with thankfulness, why am I denounced because of that for which I give thanks? So, whether you eat or drink, or whatever you do, do all to the glory of God. Give no offense to Jews or to Greeks or to the church of God, just as I try to please everyone in everything I do, not seeking my own advantage, but that of many, that they may be saved. **(1 Corinthians 10:25-33) – English Standard Version**

Apostle Paul wrote this to help us understand spiritual dieting because of its ties with submitting to the truth. Many debates may arise regarding how one should behave, but there can come no good from such discussions because it would result in the judgment of others.

So flee youthful passions and pursue righteousness, faith, love, and peace, along with those who call on the Lord from a pure heart. Have nothing to do with foolish, ignorant controversies; you know that they breed quarrels. And the Lord's servant must not be quarrelsome but kind to everyone, able to teach, patiently enduring evil, correcting his opponents with gentleness. God may perhaps grant them repentance leading to a knowledge of the truth, and they may come to their senses and escape from the snare of the devil, after being captured by him to do his will. **(2 Timothy 2:22-26) – English Standard Version**

How then can we all come together and know what God requires of us? I wrote to tread carefully about spiritual conviction only because the doctrine of Satan will try and manipulate that statement. Yes, we are all free to do whatever we want but when it comes to spiritual dieting, it becomes complex because we are all different. This difference may cause confusion because we like to compare ourselves with one another which could lead us to false doctrines. This is where the submission comes in and the first steps to knowing the difference between God's truth versus Satan's doctrine. Being baptized by the water and by the Holy Spirit and the name Jesus Christ. It is only then when one will know and understand what God requires of them. What do I mean by that? Well in the Egypt and Babylon chapters, I mentioned how I relied on alcohol to help cope with my depression and guilt. Therefore for me, I must refrain from drinking because when I do the Holy Spirit convicts me because it knows that I once put alcohol first rather than trusting God.

Drinking too much makes you loud and foolish. It's stupid to get drunk. **(Proverbs 20:1) – Good News Translation**

If I want to be the person God wants me to be, I have to find the self-control within the Spirit to say no to alcohol. That being said, I am not condoning drinking but nor am I prohibiting it because it is available to us since God made it. We are accountable to ourselves and if there is something that we are doing that we know will lead us to sin, why bother tempt ourselves and continue doing it? I can count how many times I've smoked weed. Approximately 10-15 times in my whole life and they were only in situations where I was with a certain group of friends. However, I do not really like smoking and it isn't something that I desire so for me it isn't something that spiritually convicts me because I just don't like it and know better. I have no attachment to it at all so I never do it and why should I? Because it feels good to get high? Fortunately for me, I do know my limitations and I always knew I had an addictive personality which is why I have never done any other drugs. Will I gain anything from getting high? For me, I do not need it nor do I like the feeling which is why it is easy for me to say no to it. But for others it controls their lives. I can confidently say that I reject marijuana in my life, but that does not come in the form of judgement because I know how it feels to be controlled by something. That something for me is alcohol which is why I have to stay away from it. Apostle Paul wrote in this matter not to set strict earthly rules, but he abided by God's commandments which were given to him by the Spirit. It is this very reason why he writes, "I try to please everyone in all that I do, not thinking of my own good, but the good of all, so that they might be saved." This statement did not mean he lived to please people for the sake of their sinful pleasures but the sake of their salvation with the power of the truth. Are we not right with God if we smoke or drink? No, that is not how it works, and I made that clear in the law vs faith and Egypt and Babylon chapters. But I also made it clear that if we are spiritually tamed by such things it is a form of idolatry. So, the question we must ask ourselves is: What is alcohol and drugs offering us that God cannot offer? It is in that very answer where we will know the source of why we crave what we crave.

Alcohol is for people who are dying, for those who are in misery. Let them drink and forget their poverty and unhappiness. **(Proverbs 31:6-7) – Good News Translation**

God knows everyone's hearts and stories because he designed us and can see everything we do. My spiritual dieting will always be different from another because once someone receives God's Holy Spirit, the Spirit will examine the person's strengths and weaknesses. Through its examination, it will know the persons calling based on how God designed them because the Spirit pleads on our behalf to God. Paul urges us not to judge but simply encourage, pray and forgive others.

Therefore let us not pass judgment on one another any longer, but rather decide never to put a stumbling block or hindrance in the way of a brother. I know and am persuaded in the Lord Jesus that nothing is unclean in itself, but it is unclean for anyone who thinks it unclean. For if your brother is grieved by what you eat, you are no longer walking in love. By what you eat, do not destroy the one for whom Christ died. So do not let what you regard as good be spoken of as evil. For the kingdom of God is not a matter of eating and drinking but of righteousness and peace and joy in the Holy Spirit. Whoever thus serves Christ is acceptable to God and approved by men. So then let us pursue what makes for peace and for mutual upbuilding. Do not, for the sake of food, destroy the work of God. Everything is indeed clean, but it is wrong for anyone to make another stumble by what he eats. It is good not to eat meat or drink wine or do anything that causes your brother to stumble. The faith that you have, keep between yourself and God. Blessed is the one who has no reason to pass judgment on himself for what he approves. But whoever has doubts is condemned if he eats, because the eating is not from faith. For whatever does not proceed from faith is sin. **(Romans 14:13-23) – English Standard Version**

If someone who has not received the Holy Spirit, they are in danger of misinterpreting this message because their behavior will be based on their knowledge of what is good and bad. To adequately fulfill a healthy spiritual diet, God's Spirit must be present so one can tell the difference between God's truth and Satan's doctrine. Anyone who reads this cannot claim that I said its okay to get drunk or high because that is not what I said nor is that even wisdom. A true submission to the God's truth and resistance to the devil will do away from all these things because they are the activities of the world. So, if the Spirit of God is not in anyone who reads this- understand that last statement. The reliance of alcohol and drugs is the search of spiritual comfort in earthly matters (remember who roams the earth, seeking to devour).

Be sober, be vigilant; because your adversary the devil walks about like a roaring lion, seeking whom he may devour. **(1 Peter 5:8) – New King James Version**

This leads to my second part of spiritual dieting because some television series and films are no longer ashamed or even care about their direct and explicit reference to demonic things.

The light of the body is the eye: if therefore thine eye be single; thy whole body shall be full of light. But if thine eye be evil; thy whole body shall be full of darkness. If therefore the light that is in thee be darkness, how great is that darkness! **(Matthew 6:22-23) - King James Version**

What does that even mean? Jesus warns us about how our eyes are like the lamp for the body, which in other words means our eyes are the gateway to either spiritual light or spiritual darkness. If what we put in front of us is darkness and we know its darkness, then our bodies will absorb it. On the other hand, if we know its light, then our bodies will shine. Jesus doesn't just stop there because he knows how Satan can deceive us into thinking that something is good when it is in fact, bad for us. Just as physical dieting is essential for our bodies, so is spiritual dieting important for our souls.

Last but not least, is church attendance. Why is this important? I admitted in the earlier chapters how I used to hate going to church because it bored me. However, the church is important because it keeps us in union with the people of Christ. Those who believe and love God should know that Jesus wanted us in church and act as disciples for one another.

"Again, I say unto you, that if two of you shall agree on earth as concerning anything that they ask, it will be done for them by my Father in heaven. For where two or three are gathered together in my name, I am there in the midst of them." **(Matthew 18:19-20) -New King James Version**

So then, faith comes from hearing the message, and the message comes through preaching Christ. **(Romans 10:17) – Good News Translation**

And let us consider one another in order to stir up love and good works, not forsaking the assembling of ourselves together, as is the manner of some, but exhorting one another, and so much the more as you see the Day approaching. **(Hebrews 10:24-25) – New King James Version**

Jesus himself did not travel alone but picked out 12 disciples and preached all over.

When Jesus came into the region of Caesarea Philippi, He asked His disciples, saying, "Who do men say that I, the Son of Man, am?" So they said, "Some say John the Baptist, some Elijah, and others Jeremiah or one of the prophets." He said to them, "But who do you say that I am?" Simon Peter answered and said, "You are the Christ, the Son of the living God." Jesus answered and said to him, "Blessed are you, Simon Bar-Jonah, for flesh and blood has not revealed this to you, but my Father who is in heaven. And I also say to you that you are Peter, and on this rock, I will build my church, and the gates of Hades shall not prevail against it. **(Matthew 16:13-18) – New King James Version**

What the church represents is togetherness and it doesn't matter who we are, we all need that. Yes, it is true that prayer is an indication that we are communicating with God, but God does not want us to be alone here on earth. Before Jesus began his gospel, he went out and searched for 12 disciples and was never alone. The foundation of the church started for one sole reason so that we would be together in the body of Christ. Even though God sent down the Holy Spirit, he wanted the Apostles to go out and make more disciples, which in hindsight means they were to be the church.

Go then, to all peoples everywhere and make them my disciples: baptize them in the name of the Father, the Son, and the Holy Spirit, and teach them to obey everything I have commanded you. And I will be with you always, to the end of the age. **(Matthew 28:19-20) – New King James Version**

That is why in the chapter flesh vs spirit, the Spirit of God poem stated: *"Human beings are all different but are all alive for one purpose. You will gather together and form churches. Some will make buildings, and some will use their own houses. Some will use schools, and others will use their own workspaces. But they are all the church because they are both flesh and spirit so human beings unite together because I am your one true purpose."* It has become some sort of false knowledge that the church is just a building or institution when it in fact takes a person, who believes in the gospel of Jesus Christ, to be the church. It is by this very reason why Jesus instructed his disciples to go make more because it is all our purpose to be one with God. It did not just end with the disciples but grew because they went out and preached the gospel of Jesus Christ. Does this mean anyone without the Spirit cannot be the church? Of course not! If that were the case, then no one would be in church because everyone in it had to make a choice to submit to God and receive his Spirit. The one who professes by faith that Jesus Christ is the Lord and Savior has recognized the truth from their hearts. This is why Jesus said to Peter, "Blessed are you, Simon Bar-Jonah, for flesh and blood has not revealed this to you, but my Father who is in heaven. And I also say to you, that you are Peter, and on this rock, I will build my church, and the gates of Hades shall not prevail against it." This did not mean that Peter is the church, but he became a living organism of the church. He received this powerful proclamation from Jesus Christ because he proclaimed that Jesus is the begotten Son of the living God.

But the righteousness of faith speaks in this way, "Do not say in your heart, 'Who will ascend into heaven?'" (that is, to bring Christ down from above) or, "'Who will descend into the abyss?'" (that is, to bring Christ up from the dead). But does it say? "The word is near you, in your mouth and in your heart"(that is, the word of faith which we preach): that if you confess with your mouth that the Lord Jesus and believe in your heart that God has raised him from the dead, you will be saved. For with the heart one believes unto righteousness, and with the mouth confession is made unto salvation. For the Scripture says, "Whoever believes on him will not be put to shame." For there is no distinction between Jew and Greek, for the same Lord over all is rich to all who call upon him. For "whoever calls on the name of the LORD shall be saved." **(Romans 10:6-13) – New King James Version**

Yes, it is true that we can become the church as individuals by our faith in Jesus Christ. That however doesn't mean that we are to be alone which is why we recognize the institution of the church. For the church is the gathering of people who believe together that Christ lives in them. Those who become the church through the renewal of the Holy Spirit, go to church. But those same people who do this must remember that there was once a time where they were not for the church or living like the church.

You will seek me, and you will find me because you will seek me with all your heart. **(Jeremiah 29:13) - Good News Translation**

By remembering such things, they must remember what it was like and be disciples to those outside of themselves and the physical structure of the church. This does not mean that the people in church should treat the people out of church differently but should be living according to how Christ lived.

Imitate me, just as I also imitate Christ. **(1 Corinthians 11:1) – New King James Version**

Do not be fooled, "Bad companions ruin good character." Come back to your right senses and stop your sinful ways. I declare to your shame that some of you do not know God. **(1 Corinthians 15:33-34) - Good News Translation**

Paul, an apostle of Jesus Christ, by the commandment of God our Saviour, and Lord Jesus Christ, which is our hope. To Timothy, a true son in the faith: Grace, mercy, and peace from God our Father and Jesus Christ our Lord. As I urged you when I went into Macedonia—remain in Ephesus that you may charge some that they teach no other doctrine, nor give heed to fables and endless genealogies, which cause disputes rather than godly edification which is in faith. Now the purpose of the commandment is love from a pure heart, from a good conscience, and from sincere faith, from which some, having strayed, have turned aside to idle talk, desiring to be teachers of the law, understanding neither what they say nor the things which they affirm. But we know that the law is good if one uses it lawfully, knowing this: that the law is not made for a righteous person, but for the lawless and insubordinate, for the ungodly and for sinners, for the unholy and profane, for murderers of fathers and murderers of mothers, for manslayers, for fornicators, for sodomites, for kidnappers, for liars, for perjurers, and if there is any other thing that is contrary to sound doctrine, according to the glorious gospel of the blessed God which was committed to my trust. **(1 Timothy 1:1-11) – New King James Version**

Let all who are under a yoke as bondservants regard their own masters as worthy of all honor, so that the name of God and the teaching may not be reviled. Those who have believing masters must not be disrespectful on the ground that they are brothers; rather they must serve all the better since those who benefit by their good service are believers and beloved. Teach and urge these things. If anyone teaches a different doctrine and does not agree with the sound words of our Lord Jesus Christ and the teaching that accords with godliness, he is puffed up with conceit and understands nothing. He has an unhealthy craving for controversy and for quarrels about words, which produce envy, dissension, slander, evil suspicions, and constant friction among people who are depraved in mind and deprived of the truth, imagining that godliness is a means of gain. **(1 Timothy 6:1-5) – English Standard Version**

1 Timothy 6:1-5 is an important part of church attendance, and I say this because I have found in my own personal experiences that some churches are being led by people who have hidden motives. This is one of the most important things that has to be noted when devoting time towards a church. There is nothing that irritates me more than going to a church that has a leader whose hidden motives are to manipulate people by using God's Word to become rich. That being said, I am not writing this for people to start investigating the church leaders because they are still anointed by God to be leaders so respect must be shown.

Now Korah the son of Izhar, son of Kohath, son of Levi, and Dathan and Abiram the sons of Eliab, and on the son of Peleth, sons of Reuben, took men. And they rose up before Moses, with a number of the people of Israel, 250 chiefs of the congregation, chosen from the assembly, well-known men. They assembled

themselves together against Moses and against Aaron and said to them, "You have gone too far! For all in the congregation are holy, every one of them, and the LORD is among them. Why then do you exalt yourselves above the assembly of the LORD?" When Moses heard it, he fell on his face, and he said to Korah and all his company, "In the morning the LORD will show who is his, and who is holy, and will bring him near to him. The one whom he chooses he will bring near to him. Do this: take censers, Korah and all his company; put fire in them and put incense on them before the LORD tomorrow, and the man whom the LORD chooses shall be the holy one. You have gone too far, sons of Levi!"
(Numbers 16:1-7) – English Standard Version

This passage dates back to the time of Moses and the Israelites. Some people did not like the leadership of Moses and accused him of doing things from his own will and not God's. I will get to my point regarding false teachings within the church, but I also must emphasize the importance of respecting the leader of a church because it is a serious matter. This altercation between Moses and the people is not something that should be taken lightly. I am not saying this to scare anyone but just to set the proper mindset towards leadership within the church. God had appointed Moses to lead the people of Israel and since this was so, to defy Moses was like challenging God. Does this mean that God loves a leader of the church more than he loves those who aren't in high positions? No, God loves all us all the same, but those who devote their lives to the church are brought to a higher standard because of their responsibilities for God's people. They are sacrificing their time for the sake of the people in the church so that they can lead them spiritually.

And Moses said, "Hereby you shall know that the LORD has sent me to do all these works, and that it has not been of my own accord. If these men die as all men die, or if they are visited by the fate of all mankind, then the LORD has not sent me. But if the LORD creates something new, and the ground opens its mouth and swallows them up with all that belongs to them, and they go down alive into Sheol, then you shall know that these men have despised the LORD." And as soon as he had finished speaking all these words, the ground under them split apart. And the earth opened its mouth and swallowed them up, with their households and all the people who belonged to Korah and all their goods. So they and all that belonged to them went down alive into Sheol and the earth closed over them, and they perished from the midst of the assembly. **(Numbers 16:28-33) – English Standard Version**

What did we just read? Well, everything done in the Old Testament was done to set precedence for us. This precedence is like a warning for us to respect our leaders. This doesn't mean that the earth will open up and swallow us if we have an issue with a leader of a church. What I'm trying to explain, without freaking anyone out, is respect must be shown even if we think negatively about a pastor of a church.

And Moses sent to call Dathan and Abiram the sons of Eliab, and they said, "We will not come up. Is it a small thing that you have brought us up out of a land flowing with milk and honey, to kill us in the wilderness, that you must also make yourself a prince over us? Moreover, you have not brought us into a land flowing with milk and honey, nor given us inheritance of fields and vineyards. Will you put out the eyes of these men? We will not come up." And Moses was very angry and said to the LORD, *"Do not respect their offering. I have not taken one donkey from them, and I have not harmed one of them."* **(Numbers 16:12-15) – English Standard Version**

Moses became angry with the people who opposed him because all he was doing was listening to God's will. This clearly upset him because they were accusing him of doing things on the accord of his own will. Everything he had done in his leadership was done because God had instructed him to do so. All these events that occurred between Moses and the people opposing him are relevant to church attendance. Some people have gotten into the habit of verbally bashing a church because they did not like the teaching that a pastor gave. This is a common thing today because if something does not align with their lifestyle, they will reject the teaching of that church. But if a teaching comes from the Word, then the leader of that church did not commit a sin, but it is the person who heard it that was offended by their own sins. Such things have and are already happening which foreshadows the end of time. For it paves the path for the coming of the one who will be the antichrist because he will preach in favour of sin.

For the time will come when they will not endure sound doctrine, but according to their own desires, because they have itching ears, they will heap up for themselves teachers; and they will turn their ears away from the truth, and be turned aside to fables. **(2 Timothy 4:3-4) – New King James Version**

My narrative on church attendance is still to denounce and warn people of false teachings but also to emphasize the importance of respect towards the leader. There seems to be a frequent pattern for lack of church attendance because people lack the respect for church leaders. The reasoning behind the lack of respect is no different from Korah, Dathan, and Abiram who started the rebellion against Moses. Throughout this book, I had heard God convict me of things that I did not like to hear because I enjoyed doing those things. But I had to make a choice to live for sin or live for truth.

And I pleaded with the LORD at that time, saying, 'O Lord GOD, you have only begun to show your servant your greatness and your mighty hand. For what god is there in heaven or on earth who can do such works and mighty acts as yours? Please let me go over and see the good land beyond the Jordan, that good hill country and Lebanon.' But the LORD was angry with me because of you and would not listen to me. And the LORD said to me, 'Enough from you; do not speak to me of this matter again. Go up to the top of Pisgah and lift up your eyes westward and northward and southward and eastward, and look at it with your eyes, for you shall not go over this Jordan. **(Deuteronomy 3:23-27) – English Standard Version**

In chapter adversity, I had mentioned how Moses disobeyed God when God told him to speak to the rock so water would gush from it. Instead, Moses hit the rock with his stick because the Israelites were irritating him. It honestly doesn't seem like such a big thing. I mean he hit the rock rather than speaking to it. Either way, the water still gushed from the rock. What was the big deal then? The people of Israel were complaining to Moses how they had no water and how God should have just left them in Egypt. This angered Moses and made him react by disobeying God. This 'small' matter ended up costing Moses entrance to the promised land that God had spoken to all of Israel. What does this story have to do with church attendance? Well Moses is regarded as a prophet like no other. He was the leader of Israel but since he disobeyed God, he was not allowed to enter the promised land (all it took was one mistake). God has his way of executing his justice towards those who are leaders far differently than those who are not because of their position and responsibility. This is what I needed to state before continuing my narrative on the dangers of false teachings within the church. Whoever takes on the responsibility of being a spiritual leader within the church must know that they will be judged at a higher degree because of their knowledge of the truth. Moses' mistake may seem so small to us when we read it but because of his position, God held him accountable to a greater degree than most. Moses longed to enter the promised land with the Israelites but due to his disobedience, he lost that opportunity and Joshua took over as the leader of Israel.

I direct the attention and narrative back to the dangers of false teachings and poor leadership because they do happen and exist to this very day. In Tanzania, my aunt who has devoted her life to God had something despicable happen to her. One Sunday evening we visited a different church that her friend invited us to. During the service, one of the ministers who was the church's accountant spent a good 15 minutes pressuring people to give money to the church. He used certain Scriptures to intimidate the congregation into providing more even after they had already given their tithes. He used phrases like," if you want God to heal you or hear your prayers you must give now! God will hold this against you if you do not give!" Like I said before, I am no stranger to the Word of God, and it was at that moment where I felt the Spirit inside me warn me about his antics. I watched how people were searching through their wallets and purses just to give more to the basket that was being passed around. Even my little brother Isaiah was like, "they only care about people's money." The funny thing is my aunt got upset with me for accusing a minister of manipulating people. She called me rude and disrespectful, but later that night she had a strange dream about someone from that church. In the dream, she saw a person stealing her offering. Later that week, the church issued an announcement that the accountant in charge of the church's finances was taking from the building funds.

But this I say: he who sows sparingly will also reap sparingly, and he who sows bountifully will also reap bountifully. So let each one give as he purposes in his heart, not grudgingly or of necessity; for God loves a cheerful giver. And God is able to make all grace abound toward you, that you, always having all sufficiency in all things, may have an abundance for every good work. As it is written: "He has dispersed abroad; he has given to the poor; his righteousness endures forever." Now may he who supplies seed to the sower, and bread for food, supply and multiply the seed you have sown and increase the fruits of your righteousness, while you are enriched in everything for all liberality, which causes thanksgiving through us to God. For the administration of this service not only supplies the needs of the saints, but also is abounding through many thanksgivings to God, while, through the proof of this ministry, they glorify God for the obedience of your confession to the gospel of Christ, and for your liberal sharing with them and all men, and by their prayer for you, who long for you because of the exceeding grace of God in you. "Thanks be to God for His indescribable gift!" **(2 Corinthians 9:6-15) – New King James Version**

There is nothing more despicable than having a member of the church who is trying to take advantage of people's faiths. It is one of many reasons why people have a hard time going to God because they cannot even trust the very institution of the faith! I have elaborated on prayer, bible reading, and spiritual dieting because they are the steppingstones of finding the right church. If someone who does not pray often, read the Word of God and has no idea what a healthy spiritual diet is-chances are they are going to be victims of such antics. Which is sad to say because such individuals are hungry to know the truth but become turned off to pursuing it when things like this occur. Those who are victims of such things are at risk of being manipulated but what's even worse is if they lose their faith in God because of the sin of another person. God has his way of punishing these individuals or churches, if such things take place.

There is nothing that can be hidden from God; everything in all creation is exposed and lies open before his eyes. And it is to him that we must all give an account of ourselves. **(Hebrews 4: 13) – Good News Translation**

Like the accountant was caught stealing from building funds. He was in charge of hyping up the congregation to give, but he was applying pressure for more money. He did that so when the actual amount needed for a specific modification in the church was met, he would pocket the rest. The pastor of the church relieved him of his duties and he obviously did not return to the church. Most of the time it might not even be the church itself but a particular individual who is behind the scenes that try to make a quick buck.

I brought up 2 Corinthians 9:6-15 because Paul is explaining the reward of giving. Tithes and offering are a way to show God that we appreciate everything in our lives. Paul explicitly says, "he who sows sparingly will also reap sparingly, and he who sows bountifully will also reap bountifully." I sincerely like Paul's explanation regarding giving because he doesn't intimidate anyone into giving. However, he does state that when we do give to whichever church we are devoted to, it doesn't go unnoticed in the eyes of God.

Then Jacob made a vow, saying, "If God will be with me, and keep me in this way that I am going, and give me bread to eat and clothing to put on, so that I come back to my father's house in peace, then the LORD shall be my God. And this stone which I have set as a pillar shall be God's house, and of all that you give me I will surely give a tenth to you." **(Genesis 28:20-22) – New King James Version**

Tithes and offerings are not things that ministers or leaders of the churches have made up because it is a concept from the Word (Old Testament). The meaning tithe means tenth, which is why it is common practice to give 10% of our earnings to God. I used Genesis 28:20-22 as an example because Jacob gave a tenth of what he had to God just to show his thanks for everything God had done for him. Now I am not here to debate anything with anyone regarding tithes and offerings because it is something that I need to begin doing as well. I tend to justify not giving because of bills or things that I claim to need but its because I have never possessed a giving spirit.

"For I am the LORD, I do not change; therefore you are not consumed, O sons of Jacob. Yet from the days of your fathers you have gone away from my ordinances and have not kept them. Return to me, and I will return to you," Says the LORD of hosts. "But you said, 'In what way shall we return?'" **(Malachi 3:6-7)- New King James Version**

This is a powerful message delivered by the prophet Malachi, who is speaking to the people of Israel. It is in this time where God is reminding the Israelites of how Jacob always gave to God because he realized that all that he had was given to him by God.

"Will a man rob God? Yet you have robbed me! But you say, 'In what way have we robbed you? In tithes and offerings. You are cursed with a curse, for you have robbed me, even this whole nation. Bring all the tithes into the storehouse, that there may be food in my house, and try me now in this," Says the LORD of hosts, "If I will not open for you the windows of heaven and pour out for you such blessing that there will be room enough to receive it." And I will rebuke the devourer for your sakes, so that he will not destroy the fruit of your ground, nor shall the vine fail to bear fruit for you in the field." Says the LORD of hosts; "And all nations will call you blessed, for you will be a delightful land," says the LORD of hosts. **(Malachi 3:8-12) – New King James Version**

What God says in this Scripture absolutely blew my mind and caused all the hairs on my body to stand. Why? Well I will explain the meaning behind God's rant here. I have always kept it in my nature to never put God to the test when I pray because I remember when Satan approached Jesus and asked him to turn the rocks into loaves of bread.

But Jesus answered, "The Scripture says, 'Do not put the Lord your God to the test.'" **(Luke 4:12) – Good News Translation**

But in Malachi 3:8-12 God states, "And try me this." In other words, what that means is, "put my words to the test" or "put me to the test."

Like he legit is saying to us, "I dare you to give me your tithes and offerings and watch how I will bless you. I will bless you with so much, you won't have enough room to store what I give you." Now because I know my sinful nature too well, the way it will interpret this Scripture is: "If I test God's tithing claim, I can go to the casino and win a million dollars." If we think such thoughts, we need to do like Apostle James and pray to God with humility to change the heart that is still in love with money. When God says bless abundantly, he speaks of things that are in our lives that can sustain success, peace, love and happiness. It can be a blessing on one's health, family, relationships, occupation, goals or aspirations. There is no greater blessing than the blessing that changes our character for the better of not just society but for ourselves mentality, physically, emotionally and spiritually. If we compare Paul's, "the more we give, the more we will be blessed," to what God said through Malachi, imagine the blessings! Now this is something new for me that I myself am working hard on because I have a poor giving spirit. Which is not an excuse because Malachi 3:8-12 begins by saying, "Will a man rob God? Yet you have robbed me!" What does this mean? Well as I mentioned in Part I of submission to the truth, our lives are not our own. Therefore, our properties, jobs, cars, money or anything for that matter does not belong to us. Some will say, "Okay author, relax there because pretty sure it does belong to us."

Then the Pharisees went and plotted how they might entangle him in his talk. And they sent to him their disciple with the Herodians, saying, "Teacher, we know that you are true, and teach the way of God in truth; nor do you care about anyone, for you do not regard the person of me. Tell us, therefore, what do you think? Is it lawful to pay taxes to Caesar, or not? But Jesus perceived their wickedness, and said, "Why do you test me, you hypocrites? Show me the tax money." So they brought him a denarius. And he said to them, "Whose image and inscription is this?" They said to him, "Caesar's." And he said to them, "Render therefore to Caesar the things that are Caesar's, and to God the things that are God's." When they heard these words, they marveled, and left him and went their way. **(Matthew 22:15-22) – New King James Version**

What I find funny about this story is if we technically think about it, everything belongs to God. The Pharisees tried to trap Jesus because they thought he would speak poorly about the Roman empire, but he silenced them with his wisdom. I have never had the giving heart because of how selfish I used to be, and I would justify my selfishness with worthless excuses. "I have so many bills, or I got to go shopping for clothes," were just some of the excuses I would give. When God spoke to me on that plane and spoke of my cockiness, I did not know that one day I would be referring it to tithes and offerings. Yet here we are right now and that was said by the Spirit because it examined everything in me. Seeing those who did not have the means to live like I do broke my heart and it was then when my appreciation of God began. Whatever excuse we make to not give to God, we must remember what God has done for our lives. Many will say, "I worked hard to get where I am today, God did not do it." That statement is an ignorant one because all the things that we possess would have not existed without God. If we possess it, it is because God has blessed us with creation which is why it exists. Since God has willed for its existence, it can be obtained by anyone who works hard for it. I'll give a two simple examples. On the first page of my passport it states: "This passport is the property of the Government of Canada." Although it is my passport, it belongs to the Government of Canada because I am a Canadian citizen. Or another example is a credit card. If we look at the back of our credit cards it will state: "This card is the property and issued by the Bank of ★★★★★ and must be returned upon request." My passport may have my name on it, but it is still the property of the Canadian Government. But if we were to ask: What did they use to make the passport? If we look at the manufacturing process, it all goes back to God. Even the tools used to make the passports are God's. Our credit cards may have our names on it but upon request the banks can take it from us because it is the property of the bank. But if we look at the manufacturing process of the initial credit card, it all goes back to God. Even the things used to make the credit cards are God's. Caesar may have had his face and inscription on the denarius but what was used to make that denarius? Now after explaining all this, we would think that is what God meant when he said, "Will a man rob God?" But that is just my way of getting everyone to realize that nothing really belongs to us. The reality is God doesn't need our money. He specifically says, "Heaven is my throne, and the earth is my footstool!" This is what blows my mind because he doesn't need our money but the purpose of Malachi 3:8-12 are in the following two reasons. He asks us to give for our own good because a generous heart cannot ever be controlled by money. Secondly, Malachi 3:8-12 mentions a curse because those who do not give tithes have robbed God. But the cause of the curse is not what we except. Because we know that God does not need our money, why then did he speak of a curse? See the thing is, he never said that, "he would curse us," but said that, "we are cursed with a curse," which essentially means we are cursing ourselves. Apostle Paul distinctly states, "God loves a cheerful giver," and those who give are blessed. Therefore, those who do not give are robbing God of an opportunity to bless them which is why God says, "You are cursed with a curse, for you have robbed me." I'll go even deeper with the explanation: The sentence, "cursed with a curse," means that our hearts are cursed with the slavery of greed and since our hearts are cursed, are actions are too because we do not allow God to bless us. Furthermore, when we give to God, we show gratitude for the things in our lives because we acknowledge that he has blessed us with those things.

Now Jesus sat opposite the treasury and saw how the people put money into the treasury. And many who were rich put in much. Then one poor widow came and threw in two mites, which make a quadrans. So He called His disciples to Himself and said to them, "Assuredly, I say to you that this poor widow has put in more than all those who have given to the treasury; for they all put in out of their abundance, but she out of her poverty put in all that she had, her whole livelihood." **(Mark 12:41-44) – New King James Version**

Poor or rich? It doesn't matter where someone is in the spectrum of wealth. What God sees is an earnest giver who knows that God is the one who provides. Nothing gets in the way of a giver who has faith in God and that is exhibited by the poor lady in Mark 12:41-44. My aunt in Tanzania is not rich, but it doesn't stop her from giving to God. She always had faith that God would provide. I observed her closely each day and saw how she would give, and it amazed me. I became jealous of her faith and not the type of jealousy that directed hate towards her, but I began to hate my own selfish heart. How could I be jealous of her, when I do not suffer the way she does? The reason why I hated my own heart is that I have been fortunate all my life but never gave to God. This is what God wanted me to see when I was in Tanzania. I believe he knew there would come a day when I would have to speak about this and relate it to church attendance (here we are).

I can continue to ramble on about selecting the proper church, but that would then give people the impression that there is a perfect church. The thing is there cannot be a perfect church without the Spirit of God dwelling in that church. This unpopular message is not just for readers but for every church that claims to deliver the gospel of Jesus Christ. There are small churches, large churches, megachurches; some will sing different songs and others will have longer services than others. See all that does not matter to God! The perfect church is the church that puts God first over everything, obeys his commandments and is not fooled or compromised by any false doctrines. The perfect church does not discriminate on color, race, gender, or sexual orientation because we are all sinners that are seeking the truth to become righteous people in the eyes of God. Long ago, Jews did not consider Gentiles as God's people because they did not follow the Jewish laws. That Jewish law was then abolished by Jesus Christ, as I have mentioned in the law vs. faith chapter because it does not put us right with God. What puts us right with God is our faith in Jesus Christ.

Peter began to speak: "I now realize that it is true that God treats everyone on the same basis." **(Acts 10:34) – Good News Translation**

I was in the city of Joppa praying; and in a trance I saw a vision, an object descending like a great sheet, let down from heaven by four corners; and it came to me. When I observed it intently and considered, I saw four-footed animals of the earth, wild beasts, creeping things, and birds of the air. And I heard a voice saying to me, 'Rise, Peter; kill and eat.' But I said, 'Not so, Lord! For nothing common or unclean has at any time entered my mouth.' But the voice answered

me again from heaven, 'What God has cleansed you must not call common.'
Now this was done three times, and all were drawn up again into heaven. At
that very moment, three men stood before the house where I was, having been
sent to me from Caesarea. Then the Spirit told me to go with them, doubting
nothing. Moreover, these six brethren accompanied me, and we entered the man's
house. And he told us how he had seen an angel standing in his house, who said
to him, 'Send men to Joppa, and call for Simon whose surname is Peter, who
will tell you words by which you and all your household will be saved.' And as
I began to speak, the Holy Spirit fell upon them, as upon us at the beginning.
Then I remembered the Word of the Lord, how he said, 'John indeed baptized
with water, but you shall be baptized with the Holy Spirit.' If therefore God gave
them the same gift as he gave us when we believed on the Lord Jesus Christ,
who was I that I could withstand God?" **(Acts 11: 5-17) – New King**
James Version

Now the apostles and elders came together to consider this matter. And when
there had been much dispute, Peter rose up and said to them: "Men and brethren,
you know that a good while ago God chose among us, that by my mouth the
Gentiles should hear the Word of the gospel and believe. So God, who knows
the heart, acknowledged them by giving them the Holy Spirit, just as he did
to us, and made no distinction between us and them, purifying their hearts by
faith. Now therefore, why do you test God by putting a yoke on the neck of the
disciples which neither our fathers nor we were able to bear? But we believe that
through the grace of the Lord Jesus Christ we shall be saved in the same manner
as they." **(Acts 15:6-11) - New King James Version**

Yet not even Titus who was with me, being a Greek, was compelled to be
circumcised. And this occurred because of false brethren secretly brought in (who
came in by stealth to spy out our liberty which we have in Christ Jesus, that
they might bring us into bondage), to whom we did not yield submission even
for an hour, that the truth of the gospel might continue with you. But from those
who seemed to be something—whatever they were, it makes no difference to me;
God shows personal favoritism to no man—for those who seemed to be something
added nothing to me. **(Galatians 2:3-6) – New King James Version**

Now when Peter had come to Antioch, I withstood him to his face, because he was to be blamed; for before certain men came from James, he would eat with the Gentiles; but when they came, he withdrew and separated himself, fearing those who were of the circumcision. And the rest of the Jews also played the hypocrite with him, so that even Barnabas was carried away with their hypocrisy. But when I saw that they were not straightforward about the truth of the gospel, I said to Peter before them all, "If you, being a Jew, live in the manner of Gentiles and not as the Jews, why do you compel Gentiles to live as Jews? **(Galatians 2:11-14) – New King James Version**

Therefore remember that you, once Gentiles in the flesh—who are called Uncircumcision by what is called the Circumcision made in the flesh by hands—that at that time you were without Christ, being aliens from the commonwealth of Israel and strangers from the covenants of promise, having no hope and without God in the world. But now in Christ Jesus you who once were far off have been brought near by the blood of Christ. For he himself is our peace, who has made both one, and has broken down the middle wall of separation, having abolished in his flesh the enmity, that is, the law of commandments contained in ordinances, so as to create in himself one new man from the two, thus making peace, and that he might reconcile them both to God in one body through the cross, thereby putting to death the enmity. And he came and preached peace to you who were afar off and to those who were near. For through him we both have access by one Spirit to the Father. Now, therefore, you are no longer strangers and foreigners, but fellow citizens with the saints and members of the household of God, having been built on the foundation of the apostles and prophets, Jesus Christ himself being the chief cornerstone, in whom the whole building, being fitted together, grows into a holy temple in the Lord, in whom you also are being built together for a dwelling place of God in the Spirit. **(Ephesians 2:11-22) – New King James Version**

We are to come together as loving people seeking God. Paul had to oppose Peter because this is the most important thing that ties in with praying, bible reading, spiritual dieting, and church attendance. The sins that we have done do not stain us from God's love. Apostle Peter had to learn this so he could treat the Gentiles with love. I cannot stress this enough because this book is what it is because I admitted my sins and asked God to forgive me. When I did that God blessed me with the Holy Spirit, which has not only helped me write in this way, but it acts as the foreseer of my actions. It is my best friend. I was gifted with the Holy Spirit because I admitted my sins which shows I do not want to repeat them. Therefore, if I not a Jew, who asked God for forgiveness and received not only that but his Spirit. What kind of lies in the world are we listening to that is stopping everyone from doing the same? We have become so fixated on categorizing sins into different categories. We forget that sin is all the same in God's eyes. The phrase 'to be saved,' is the act of believing in the gospel of Jesus Christ which involves repentance and being born again. By doing so, we transcend over the cause of our sins and the sins themselves. If someone rejects this, they have declared themselves an enemy of God because they believe that they are without sin and do not need saving. The Holy Spirit itself is telling me, "there are no poems or long paragraphs that can be written to convince or change such people because they have already rejected Christ's love." Thus, I write for those who are curious or do not know all these things! Maybe there are some people who are as hungry as I am to know the truth.

A church that deviates from what I just spoke about is a church that displeases God. There should not be any division or conflicts between churches because they are supposed to be on the same side. A church that has only a particular race should strive to invite every race. A church should not have it within its mission statement to unite one specific group of people. Conflict within the body of Christ just means that a particular church has fallen under the traps of the devil himself. I could write on and on about what a church should be and shouldn't, but I am trespassing closer to judgment rather than guidance. It is God himself who will judge the churches that mislead people from the truth or disrupt the faiths of believers and ruin the curiosity of non-believers. My prayers go out to those who have been victimized by the sins of others within a church. Nonetheless, we must not allow ourselves to lose faith in God for when such things occur. I could give more warnings regarding churches because the sad truth is a church becomes a church by the coming of human beings who believe in God. But because we are human, we make mistakes and hurt others. Jesus knew this even about his own disciples, which is why I state this: A church that denies the Word, Jesus Christ and the need of the Holy Spirit is a church that should be avoided. We do not need to gossip or speak rudely about it because we must have faith that God will either correct that church or place judgment on that church.

False prophets appeared in the past among the people, and in the same way false teachers will appear among you. They will bring in destructive, untrue doctrines, and will deny the master who redeemed them, and so they will bring upon themselves sudden destruction. Even so, many will follow their immoral ways; and because of what they do, others will speak evil of the way of truth. In their greed these false teachers will make a profit out of telling you made-up stories. For a long time now, their judge has been ready, and their Destroyer has been wide awake! **(2 Peter 2:1-3) – New King James Version**

Any leader in the church should be led by the Holy Spirit, and it will be evident by how they live their own lives.

This is a faithful saying: If a man desires the position of a bishop, he desires a good work. A bishop then must be blameless, the husband of one wife, temperate, sober-minded, of good behavior, hospitable, able to teach, not given to wine, not violent, not greedy for money, but gentle, not quarrelsome, not covetous, one who rules his own house well, having his children in submission with all reverence. (for if a man does not know how to rule his own house, how will he take care of the church of God?); not a novice, lest being puffed up with pride he fall into the same condemnation as the devil. Moreover, he must have a good testimony among those who are outside, lest he fall into reproach and the snare of the devil. **(1 Timothy 3:1-7) – New King James Version**

When they finished praying, the place where they were meeting was shaken. They were all filled with the Holy Spirit and began to proclaim God's message with boldness. **(Acts 4:31) - Good News Translation**

I would hate to hear that someone followed all three steps to have their faiths crushed because of the wrongdoing of a church or a certain individual within a church. In addition to that sentence, the four steps are not in order and do not have to go in any particular order. As long as they are followed it will stabilize submission to God and the resistance of the devil. Which is why I have given everyone the tools to be confident in Jesus Christ so that no one's faith will become a victim of Satan's doctrine. We as humans may be flawed by our desires to give into sin, but that desire is destroyed by the gift that God gives to us. No one should believe the lie that the Holy Spirit is bogus because without it, we are not saved, and all churches are doomed.

When his disciples heard it, they were greatly astonished, saying, "Who then can be saved?" But Jesus looked at them and said to them, "With men this is impossible, but with God all things are possible." **(Matthew 19:25-26) – New King James Version**

Then Mary said to the angel, "How can this be, since I do not know a man?" And the angel answered and said to her, "The Holy Spirit will come upon you, and the power of the Highest will overshadow you; therefore, also, that Holy One who is to be born will be called the Son of God. **(Luke 1:34-35) – New King James Version**

There was one day I was walking out of work to cross the street to catch a bus to go back home when the Holy Spirit asked me, "Which would you rather: Having the book sell only 5 copies and all 5 of them become saved or sell 100 million copies but not have a single soul saved?" I pondered on that question the whole bus ride home because it was conflicting with my will and God's will. Little did I know that the very question was a test of submitting to the truth. It would be an absolute lie to say that I do not wish success for this book. When the Spirit asked me that question, I realized that this chapter was unpopular and controversial for myself as well.

Then all the tax collectors and the sinners drew near to Him to hear him. And the Pharisees and scribes complained, saying, "This man receives sinners and eats with them." So he spoke this parable to them, saying: "What man of you, having a hundred sheep, if he loses one of them, does not leave the ninety-nine in the wilderness, and go after the one which is lost until he finds it? And when he has found it, he lays it on his shoulders, rejoicing. And when he comes home, he calls together his friends and neighbors, saying to them, 'Rejoice with me, for I have found my sheep which was lost!' I say to you that likewise there will be more joy in heaven over one sinner who repents than over ninety-nine just persons who need no repentance. **(Luke 15:1-7) - New King James Version**

God put this chapter into my heart on purpose because despite all that has been written before this, none of it means anything if we are not willing to put God first. We will always be trapped in the cycle of sin. It will continue until time has had enough of us and finally takes what it is destined to take. When that great day comes for all of us to give an account of ourselves, will God deny us because we had heard the truth and spoke about it, but failed to submit to it?

"Not everyone who says to me, 'Lord, Lord,' shall enter the kingdom of heaven, but he who does the will of my Father in heaven. Many will say to me in that day, 'Lord, Lord, have we not prophesied in your name, cast out demons in your name, and done many wonders in your name?' And then I will declare to them, 'I never knew you; depart from me, you who practice lawlessness!' **(Matthew 7:21-23) – New King James Version**

The Spirit of God asked me that question because it wanted me to understand that just because I call out, "Spirit of God," and he answers me back, it does not guarantee anything for my entrance in his kingdom. This is the difficult pill that everyone must swallow because Jesus submitted to his suffering for our sake just to save us. Which means if we want to get to know him and follow him, we must submit to him.

He went a little farther on, threw himself face downward on the ground, and prayed, "My Father, if possible, take this cup of suffering from me! Yet not what I want, but what you want." **(Matthew 26:39) - Good News Translation**

Jesus knew the suffering that he was about to go through, so he prayed about it but even in his prayer we can see how he denies his body's will and puts the Father's first. It became a flesh vs spirit battle for Jesus. His flesh was about to experience unimaginable pain that he did not deserve but did it all for us. That is why this chapter is the most important and why I myself had to learn that my will does not matter when it comes in terms with God's will. Just because someone is blessed to hear God's voice does not mean that they have given themselves to God entirely. In the chapter love vs lust, I spoke about love and what it means and where it comes from. The knowledge and understanding of love mean nothing if we do not know its source, which is God. God so loved the world that he gave his only begotten Son. What's stopping us from giving ourselves to him to show our love back? I was completely adamant getting a tattoo on my left shoulder down about Jesus but when it came time to live for him, that was a different story. This 'love' that the world so famously adores quoting has become misguided and empty which is why we all stumble from finding the truth or even understanding it. I have been blessed enough to talk to God at will. But if I squander that gift by living for my will rather than his, I will be one of those 'wicked people' that Jesus tells to get away from him. It is that very reason why the Spirit of God asked me that question because if my heart is only prepared to obtain royalties rather than save souls, I have missed the point of the truth. As a matter of fact, I should just listen to the lies coming from the doctrine of Satan and burn this book. If God did not place this burden on my heart to write about submitting to the truth, it would have not taken a long time for me to eventually lose my way into the dark abyss of hell. I have talked about all the horrible things I have done in my life but one thing that I now can rejoice over is how the Spirit has corrected me. The four steps are tools to help submit to the truth and resist the devil. Christ did all these things when he was on earth. Before Jesus did anything, he prayed to show us its importance. All four steps go hand and hand with one another and are pivotal in our submission to the truth. None of those four steps are greater than one another because they unify each other to our submission to the truth. If someone does not pray how can they ever have a relationship with God? If someone does not read the Word of God how can they know God and rebuke Satan's false doctrines? If someone does not have a healthy spiritual diet, they shouldn't be surprised when they are tempted into doing the very things they despise. If someone does not go to church how can they grow in the body of Christ? If they are not surrounding themselves with fellow believers who are they surrounding themselves with?

Demas fell in love with this present world and has deserted me, going off to Thessalonica. Crescens went to Galatia and Titus to Dalmatia. **(2 Timothy 4:10) – Good News Translation**

Apostle Paul wrote about his friend Demas, who was once a believer and full of faith but abandoned it for the sins of the world. All in all, the sequence of such things occurs when we are not fully submitted to the truth. Even after this book, I still have an accountability to myself to keep going and fight the good fight of faith. It's not up to my parents, or my brothers or even my pastor. My responsibility is to focus on God and carry my own cross. The question we need to all ask ourselves is this: Are we ready to surrender our own wills for the will of Gods? The reason why God accepted Abraham was that his faith did not wither when God asked him to sacrifice his only son. God did not allow Abraham to go through with it, but Abraham was fully submitted to the truth of God that the circumstances did not hinder his faith.

By faith Abraham, when he was tested, offered up Isaac, and he who had received the promises offered up his only begotten son, of whom it was said, "In Isaac your seed shall be called," concluding that God was able to raise him up, even from the dead, from which he also received him in a figurative sense. **(Hebrews 11:17-19) – New King James Version**

Everyone has a gift in them that God has written within which will show God's glory and love to others. It is a gift that God gave us which cannot be taken away from us. Especially not by Satan himself. However, this doesn't mean Satan hasn't figured out a way to prevent us from ever amounting to it. Since Satan cannot take what God has given us, he does two things. The first thing Satan does is he makes sure we never find that gift that God has for our lives through his lies. Secondly, if the gift is evident to the person, he can still use his doctrine to fool the person into submitting to his will by perverting what the gift was supposed to be. In other words, Satan will take what God had destined for us and make it work for his will. For example, if God had given someone the gift to sing, he will attempt to make them never amount to that or get that person to sing about sinful things.

For as we have many members in one body, but all the members do not have the same function, so we, being many, are one body in Christ, and individually members of one another. Having then gifts differing according to the grace that is given to us, let us use them: if prophecy, let us prophesy in proportion to our faith; or ministry, let us use it in our ministering; he who teaches, in teaching; he who exhorts, in exhortation; he who gives, with liberality; he who leads, with diligence; he who shows mercy, with cheerfulness. **(Romans 12:4-8) – New King James Version**

My gifts through the Spirit will not be the same as another but we are not to fret about our gifts except be glad and give thanks to God. They have been written within our spirit and cannot be taken away by anyone or anything which should indicate how valuable we are to him.

There are diversities of gifts, but the same Spirit. There are differences of ministries, but the same Lord. And there are diversities of activities, but it is the same God who works all in all. But the manifestation of the Spirit is given to each one for the profit of all: for to one is given the Word of wisdom through the Spirit, to another the Word of knowledge through the same Spirit, to another faith by the same Spirit, to another gifts of healings by the same Spirit, to another the working of miracles, to another prophecy, to another discerning of spirits, to another different kinds of tongues, to another the interpretation of tongues. But one and the same Spirit works all these things, distributing to each one individually as he wills. **(1 Corinthians 12:4-11) – New King James Version**

Nonetheless, our gifts should not lead us astray because even if we become aware of our gifts, the important thing we must acknowledge is our submission to God which is our one true purpose. We must not allow our gifts to deviate from our one true purpose. Abraham was already told about his promise and what God had written for his life.

When Abram was ninety-nine years old, the LORD appeared to Abram and said to him, "I am Almighty God; walk before me and be blameless. And I will make my covenant between me and you and will multiply you exceedingly." Then Abram fell on his face, and God talked with him, saying: "As for me, behold, my covenant is with you, and you shall be a father of many nations. No longer shall your name be called Abram, but your name shall be Abraham; for I have made you a father of many nations. I will make you exceedingly fruitful; and I will make nations of you, and kings shall come from you. **(Genesis 17:1-6) – New King James Version**

The thing that I'm trying to get across is when the Holy Spirit asked me that question about selling 5 versus 100 million copies. I became upset with myself because I knew God wanted me to answer 5, but my will fantasized about the 100 million copies. I mean who doesn't want to sell that many copies of their own book? However, the question wasn't to burden my gifts, but it was to test whether or not I understood my purpose which is to follow the will of God. If God wants to reach 5 people, who am I to question God's plans? If I truly loved God, I would not allow myself to get upset about such a matter because my purpose was utilized through my submission to the truth. Selling 100 million copies and not touching one soul, what good would that be in the eyes of God? If I answered 100 million, it would just show that I never really cared for the truth. Abraham's faith was not focused on the descendants or even his promised son Isaac but trusting and pleasing God. That is the definition of submitting to the truth! Putting aside our will for the glory of God.

Now it happened as they journey on the road, that someone said to him, "Lord, I will follow you wherever you go." And Jesus said to him, "Foxes have holes and birds of the air have nests, but the Son of Man has nowhere to lay his head." Then he said to another, "Follow me." But he said, "Lord, let me first go bury my father." Jesus said to him, "Let the dead bury their own dead, but you go and preach the kingdom of God." And another also asked, "Lord, I will follow you, but let me first go and bid them farewell who are at my house." But Jesus said to him, "Non one, having put his hand to the plow, and looking back, is fit for the kingdom of God." **(Luke 9:57-62) –New King James Version**

In that Scripture, we find that Jesus speaks to three kinds of people. They all seem like they want to follow Jesus, but Jesus sees inside their hearts that something is preventing them from fully committing to him. The first man states that he is ready to follow Jesus wherever he goes, but Jesus' poetic response indicates that the person is not ready for the spiritual and physical commitments required to follow him. He responds to the man, "foxes have holes, and birds have nests, but the Son of Man has no place to lie down and rest." The contrast between foxes and birds to himself represent powerful imagery of the potential toll one must be prepared to face when following God. I can relate to this because there are some days when I wake up emotional and upset for no absolute reason. It is days like these when we have to get up and pray before doing anything. But sometimes, we will use the excuse and say, "I'm too tired to pray," or we will say, "I don't have enough time to pray." I am a prime example of that because before I go to bed I will use the, "I'm too tired to pray," excuse but I am more than willing to lie in my bed and watch Netflix before going to sleep. I'm just giving simple examples, but if I were to expand further in my explanation of what Christ meant, it would include things like hardships and adversities. It is when we find out that someone in our family has passed away. Will we still find the strength to pray and worship God? It is when someone finds out they've been diagnosed with cancer. Will they still find the strength to pray and worship God? It is when someone has suffered a miscarriage. Will they still find the strength to pray and worship God? These sound like extreme situations, but they are realistic and have happened to many people. I personally cannot imagine how I would feel but the question in the matter is if they do occur will we turn away from God? Will we, like the foxes go into our holes or like the birds go into our nests?

The second man that Christ had said, "Follow me," gave the response that he had to bury his father. When I heard Jesus' answer, I was a bit puzzled. "Let the dead bury their own dead. You go and proclaim the Kingdom of God." Remember Jesus hardly ever meant anything in the physical but rather the spiritual. This refers back to who we surround ourselves with. If they are spiritually not sound with God, they may be the reason why we cannot give ourselves wholly to God. In other words, the spiritually dead are the ones who have no intention of ever turning to God which is why Jesus says, "let the dead bury their own dead." When I first read the Scripture, I could not believe Jesus' response because it sounded so cold, but he did not mean that we are not to bury our loved ones. Instead, he meant the spiritual responsibilities of proclaiming the Kingdom of God which speaks about spiritual life and revival. There's a difference between preaching to the spiritually lost and mourning for the spiritually dead. We are to love and speak about the truth of God to everyone even if they reject it. But if we surround ourselves with the spiritually dead because we missed when we were once dead, then we are destined to face the same spiritual death as them.

For if, after they have escaped the pollutions of the world through the knowledge of the Lord and Savior Jesus Christ, they are again entangled in them and overcome, the latter end is worse for them than the beginning. For it would have been better for them not to have known the way of righteousness, than having known it, to turn from the holy commandment delivered to them. But it has happened to them according to the true proverb: "A dog returns to his own vomit," and, "a sow, having washed, to her wallowing in the mire." **(2 Peter 2:20-22) – New King James Version**

Last but not least is the third man who told Jesus, "I will follow you but first let me say good-bye to my family." This one is straight forward because Jesus responds, "anyone who starts to plow and then keeps looking back is of no use for the Kingdom of God." It may seem similar to the second man, but the difference is the third man was unsure if he wanted to really follow Christ. Where the second man was sure, but his heart was in the wrong place. To help better understand, I'll translate Jesus's responses for both the second and third man. For the second man, he essentially said, "do not worry about the spiritually dead but preach about the truth of God and they will hear it. But if they do not listen, then you have done your part." For the third man, he meant, "You are not fit for the Kingdom of God because you are unsure of the truth and refuse to put me first."

Now behold, one came and said to him, "Good Teacher, what good thing shall I do that I may have eternal life?" So he said to him, "Why do you call me good? No one is good but One, that is, God. But if you want to enter into life, keep the commandments." He said to him, "Which ones?" Jesus said, "You shall not murder,' 'You shall not commit adultery,' 'You shall not steal,' 'You shall not bear false witness,' 'Honor your father and your mother,' and, 'You shall love your neighbour as yourself.'" The young man said to him, "All these things I have kept from my youth. What do I still lack?" Jesus said to him, "If you want to be perfect, go, sell what you have and give to the poor, and you will have treasure in heaven; and come, follow me." But when the young man heard that saying, he went away sorrowful, for he had great possessions. Then Jesus said to his disciples, "Assuredly, I say to you that it is hard for a rich man to enter the kingdom of heaven. And again, I say to you, it is easier for a camel to go through the eye of a needle than for a rich man to enter the kingdom of God." **(Matthew 19:16–24) – New King James Version**

The last and final unpopular and controversial message is this one because Jesus explicitly explains how difficult it would be for a rich person to enter the Kingdom of God. Now, this might seem easy to write about because I am not rich, nor do I come from a wealthy family but who doesn't want to be rich? This then leads to the question: Is it a sin to be rich? Of course not!

For we brought nothing into this world, and it is certain we can carry nothing out. And having food and clothing, with these we shall be content. But those who desire to be rich fall into temptation and a snare, and into many foolish and harmful lusts which drown men in destruction and perdition. For the love of money is a root of all kinds of evil, for which some have strayed from the faith in their greediness and pierced themselves through with many sorrows. **(1 Timothy 6:7–10) – New King James Version**

Keep your lives free from the love of money and be satisfied with what you have. For God has said, "I will never leave you; I will never abandon you." **(Hebrews 13:5) - Good News Translation**

The reason why Jesus told the rich man to give up all that he had was not a command for all the rich. But Jesus simply knew that his heart was in his money and because of this he could never really love God. 1 Timothy 6:7-10 speaks of the dangers of pursuing the rich life because that pursuit traps the heart to love money. Apostle Paul reminds us that we are brought into this world with nothing and we will leave this world with nothing. Therefore, to chase after money is rather pointless. The love of money is the root to all kinds of evil. Does this mean if someone is rich, they cannot love God? Absolutely not! Because there are hard working people who got rich but still put God first. The whole purpose of this chapter is to not denounce anyone or tell anyone how they should live their lives because God will eventually judge everyone accordingly. If we related back to chapter adversity and hardships, we could catch that I exhibited a love for money because I thought that by having it, it would solve all my problems. I had to learn through the Spirit of God, that my hardships and adversities were not going to be solved by money but trusting in God. See the thing is, if God blessed me with a pile of money, I would have said thanks and forgotten about him. It was through my adversity and hardships that helped press my spirit into praying to a level I had never reached. God was more concerned with my heart. God can provide to us at any time but if our hearts are in love with money, we wont truly love him. I have found it true that before God blesses people, he develops the person's character so that when the blessing arrives, they will not forget who blessed them. In the case of the rich man, his heart had treasured his wealth and possessions. He did not see any room to fit Jesus, so he walked away upset.

I made great works. I built houses and planted vineyards for myself. I made myself gardens and parks and planted in them all kinds of fruit trees. I made myself pools from which to water the forest of growing trees. I bought male and female slaves and had slaves who were born in my house. I had also great possessions of herds and flocks, more than any who had been before me in Jerusalem. I also gathered for myself silver and gold and the treasure of kings and provinces. I got singers, both men and women, and many concubines, the delight of the sons of man. So I became great and surpassed all who were before me in Jerusalem. Also my wisdom remained with me. And whatever my eyes desired I did not keep from them. I kept my heart from no pleasure, for my heart found pleasure in all my toil, and this was my reward for all my toil. Then I considered all that my hands had done and the toil I had expended in doing it, and behold, all was vanity and a striving after wind, and there was nothing to be gained under the sun. **(Ecclesiastes 2:4-11) – English Standard Version**

Since I am not rich, I cannot relate to the life of the rich, but I know someone in the Scriptures which can relate to the rich experience. The richest man known to Scripture is hands down king Solomon, and it is said that he received about $40 billion in gold each year as a tribute from other nations. Israel at the time ruled almost every nation, so they paid king Solomon in taxes. That is just what he received in taxes (or tributes whatever they called it back then), so we can only imagine what his actual net worth was. In Ecclesiastes 2:4-11, king Solomon is ranting about how useless his hard work and riches are and proceeded on saying, "it was like chasing the wind- of no use at all." The reason as to why I'm bringing up king Solomon's words is to remind those who are not rich that money can be just as deceitful as sin.

Command those who are rich in this present age not to be haughty, nor to trust in uncertain riches but in the living God, who gives us richly all things to enjoy. Let them do good, that they be rich in good works, ready to give, willing to share, storing up for themselves a good foundation for the time to come, that they may lay hold on eternal life. **(1 Timothy 6:17-19) – New King James Version**

Those who have it, enjoy it! But do not let it rule the heart. The rich man, who could have been "perfect" as Jesus described, let money get in the way of having a relationship with Jesus Christ.

Then Peter said in reply, "See, we have left everything and followed you. What then will we have?" Jesus said to them, "Truly, I say to you, in the new world, when the Son of Man will sit on his glorious throne, you who have followed me will also sit on twelve thrones, judging the twelve tribes of Israel. And everyone who has left houses or brothers or sisters or father or mother or children or lands, for my name's sake, will receive a hundredfold and will inherit eternal life. But many who are first will be last, and the last first. **(Matthew 19:27-30) – English Standard Version**

Rich or poor? It doesn't matter, we are all responsible for how we direct our lives. It becomes difficult for anyone to submit to the truth when they have valued other things before God. The rich value their possessions, so what do others who are not wealthy value? It all goes back to what we store up in our hearts because there are some rich individuals who have no care for their riches and there are some who have enough but want more. There is no silver lining when it comes to the hearts of people. I say this because I do not trust my own heart at all which is why I have become cautious of myself. Only God knows what is real and false within my heart and I am alerted by the Holy Spirit when the false emotions begin to disrupt my walk with God.

Jesus answered, "Love the Lord your God with all your heart, with all your soul, and with all your mind." **(Matthew 22:27) - Good News Translation**

Everyone's story is different, and not all are born on August 5th, 1994. Some readers will be younger, and some will be older, but all the conditions of God's truth apply to them. As my journey continues, I pray to the living God who made heaven and earth, that any of the readers will either begin or continue their journey with the truth. I gave the readers this chapter because it will be a formidable strategy for submitting to the truth. We are victorious in Jesus Christ! That is why at the start of this chapter I prayed for guidance because God wanted me to emphasize to not only the readers but myself that all those chapters and stories will mean nothing if we do not submit to the truth. This is the chapter that matters because the truth speaks to all of us and asks for its creations to go back to him.

When his disciples heard it, they were exceedingly amazed, saying, "Who then can be saved?" But Jesus beheld them, and said unto them, "with men this is impossible; but with God all things are possible." **(Matthew 19:25-26) - King James Version**

Jesus knew it would be impossible for us to be saved which is why he stated that with God everything is possible. Was it not evident, even with the Holy Spirit within me, that I still let God down at times?

For the righteous falls seven times and rises again, but the wicked stumble in times of calamity. **(Proverbs 24:16) – English Standard Version**

This will happen to many, but we have to remember to get up! It will inevitably happen if the person has yet to submit to God. Anyone who does will witness the power of the Holy Spirit. I gave the four steps as a guide, but those four steps are of no use if we do not have the Holy Spirit because it is our connection to our shepherd (Jesus Christ). It is only by God that we are put right, so how can I ever advise how anyone should live their lives? I have made a choice to abide by God's Word and since his words are true, who then can judge me? I do not live life to analyze or study how people conduct their lives because I do not hold such jurisdiction to do so. That power belongs to God, but I do have a burden placed in my heart to worry and pray for how people live their lives. We must be cautious of how we live our lives and who we surround ourselves with. The things that entertains us may seem harmless and may even be fun but remember that there are spiritual forces out there. Do not become so passive and comfortable with the world's doctrines and what it preaches. I am not declaring that everything the world does is sinful, but the biggest lie the devil will tell us is that he is not up to anything. He is always plotting something against us. This journey began with me wanting to find the truth at any cost. I became such a master at lying that I couldn't find it within myself to live for the truth. I mean, how could I? Therefore, I became subject to the powers of the biggest liar himself! Do I write this for the benefit of myself? Actually yes, I do because as I write this message, I place a covenant within myself to be faithful to the very truth I have obtained from God. However, I also write this message for the benefit of others because I did not just wake up one day and make all this up. The evidence of that is in the part I of submission to the truth because I spoke about humility and the repentance of sins. I had to humble myself and accept my faults all in hopes for God to forgive and renew me. I do not need to go out and search for people's approval of my change because that was done by God. What I have written down was given to me by God in Spirit. The same way God had passed down the Ten Commandments to Moses on the tablets. The tablets in this case is a renewed heart that kick started my relationship with God. Moses had to walk up to Mount Sinai to receive the revelation from God. The Scriptures did not say God came down from the mountain to see Moses.

In the third month after the children of Israel had gone out of the land of Egypt, on the same day, they came to the Wilderness of Sinai. For they had departed from Rephidim, had come to the Wilderness of Sinai, and camped in the wilderness. So Israel camped there before the mountain. And Moses went up to God, and the LORD called to him from the mountain, saying, "Thus you shall say to the house of Jacob, and tell the children of Israel: You have seen what I did to the Egyptians, and how I bore you on eagles' wings and brought you to myself. (**Exodus 19:1-3**) – **New King James Version**

It is within that very story which indicates to everyone that it is on us to walk to God. No one can force us, and no one should because it would not be genuine. Moses went alone while the Israelites remained on the ground and lived their sinful ways. They started to worship a golden calf because they began to give in to their sinful nature! They had lived in Egypt for over 400 years and saw the way the Egyptians lived. Therefore, they adopted that lifestyle. That's why I speak in such a manner because I have recognized Satan's doctrine in my very environment! I made the decision to go to the one that is 'truth' so that I may not bow down to the golden calves of this day in age. I did that! The only difference though is the things that I have written are not commandments but a story of a journey to God's own heart. It was my journey on Mount Sinai that convicted me of my sins. It was my journey on Mount Sinai that allowed me to write the Spirit of God poems because I stopped at nothing to know him. I will not judge anyone because everyone has the free will to go to the truth on their own to receive forgiveness. I will not judge anyone's life because there is a day for that and the judge who will proclaim judgment is fair and just. His fairness and justice are seen through the act of love in the sacrifice of Jesus Christ. My purpose to write in this manner is for everyone to go to God and allow him to renew them. My journey to get to this submission to the truth has been a long one (a very long one) because I had to live by trial and error. I tried different ways to avoid submitting to the truth and it only ended in error. So, in reality, if that happened to me, what conclusion will the rest find? Yes, we are all different, and yes certain things might convict my spirit versus someone else's. However, if there is one truth, then my suggestion is to be as cautious as I have become in the way I live my life. For example, if God's Spirit doesn't convict a person when they commit murder then that person should really panic. I will not even get into the matter of a person who does not have God's Spirit and their own conscience does not convict them. Receiving God's Spirit is a blessing and a gift from God but like every gift, they must be taken care of. Just because a person has the Holy Spirit doesn't necessarily mean they are right with God. I have already stated how one gets right with God in this book. What needs to be understood is when the truth is spoken it will touch and may even irritate because it contains God's power. When someone listens and realizes the truth, they should seek out for the Holy Spirit, but that is not the final step. It only takes submission to the truth for us to harness its true power because through it we get to know God.

And so, I tell all of you: what you prohibit on earth will be prohibited in heaven, and what you permit on earth will be permitted in heaven. **(Matthew 18:18) – Good News Translation**

And whatever you ask in my name, that I will do, that the Father may be glorified in the Son. If you ask anything in my name, I will do it. **(John 14:13-14) – New King James Version**

He who believes and is baptized will be saved; but he who does not believe will be condemned. And these signs will follow those who believe: In my name they will cast out demons; they will speak with new tongues; they will take up serpents; and if they drink anything deadly, it will by no means hurt them; they will lay hands on the sick, and they will recover." **(Mark 16:16-18) – New King James Version**

These powers that Jesus speaks about are associated with the Holy Spirit. They are powers that I have yet to ever perform because it is the beginning of my journey with the Spirit. Does this mean we should pick up snakes or drink poison because we have the Spirit? Of course not! The power of the Spirit is harnessed through our faith with God, which knows no limit. By saying this, it means that we have full authority to use the power of Christ's name for the sake of his glory. This power should not be mistaken as some sort of superpower that is illustrated in the comics of the Marvel or DC books (nerdy side kicking in again). This glorious power that Christ speaks about goes hand in hand with the relationship we develop with God.

Now when the apostles who were at Jerusalem heard that Samaria had received the Word of God, they sent Peter and John to them, who, when they had come down, prayed for them that they might receive the Holy Spirit. For as yet he had fallen upon none of them. They had only been baptized in the name of the Lord Jesus. Then they laid hands on them, and they received the Holy Spirit. And when Simon saw that through the laying on of the apostles' hands the Holy Spirit was given, he offered them money, saying, "Give me this power also, that anyone on whom I lay hands may receive the Holy Spirit." But Peter said to him, "Your money perish with you, because you thought that the gift of God could be purchased with money! You have neither part nor portion in this matter, for your heart is not right in the sight of God. Repent therefore of this your wickedness and pray God if perhaps the thought of your heart may be forgiven you. For I see that you are poisoned by bitterness and bound by iniquity." Then Simon answered and said, "Pray to the Lord for me, that none of the things which you have spoken may come upon me." **(Acts 8:14-24) – New King James Version**

Jesus had to teach his disciples that just because they had the authority to perform miracles in God's name, it didn't mean they could start smiting people they didn't like. It had to go hand in hand with God's Spirit. The Scriptures clearly state that we have the authority to permit or prohibit anything on earth and the heavens will respond, but this must be explained thoroughly. As I mentioned in the chapter flesh vs. spirit, the Spirit produces many gifts. The Spirit acts as our helper and friend in exchange for having Christ's physical being beside us. This was done so that all can be united with him. Jesus Christ had to teach his disciples many things and for them to be educated, they had to spend time with him. This is the same with the Spirit, the more we communicate with it, the closer we get with Christ. It will teach us how to behave but most importantly further our relationship with God.

When the days drew near for him to be taken up, he set his face to go to Jerusalem. And he sent messengers ahead of him, who went and entered a village of the Samaritans, to make preparations for him. But the people did not receive him, because his face was set toward Jerusalem. And when his disciples James and John saw it, they said, "Lord, do you want us to tell fire to come down from heaven and consume them?" But he turned and rebuked them. **(Luke 9:51–55) English Standard Version**

Jesus rebuked James and John to show them that the power of the Spirit does not and will not respond to evil motives. It operates with the heart that submits to the truth and all that the Spirit produces. That is why it was the same John, who rebuked Simon in the book of Acts because he had learned from Jesus about mercy and love. These incredible things that Jesus said can only be done through the person who has devoted themselves to know God.

What you say can preserve life or destroy it; so, you must accept the consequences of your words. **(Proverbs 18:21) – Good News Translation**

But no man can tame the tongue. It is an unruly evil, full of deadly poison. With it we bless our God and Father, and with it we curse men, who have been made in the similitude of God. Out of the same mouth proceed blessing and cursing. My brethren, these things ought not to be so. **(James 3:8–10) – New King James Version**

Reading God's Word is the first step to getting to know him but having the Spirit will take it to new heights. This was my problem before receiving the Spirit. I could not comprehend who he was without the Holy Spirit. Our feelings and thoughts will never comprehend God's power or who he is. If his ways and thoughts are higher than ours. How then can our thoughts and ways understand his? That is why the Spirit is a must because it paves the way for us to live righteously with the power of his words.

I conclude and close my case about how one lives because the truth has spoken to me through the Spirit on how I should live based on my submission to the truth. If someone does not have the truth within them, they will possess some piece of Satan's doctrine. One will ask, how could that be? It is because Satan is the father of all lies and there does not exist any truth in him. How then can we not put it past him to go to great lengths to manipulate philosophies, science, religion, laws, politics, entertainment and many more things? His doctrine may not always appear to be demonic, but he is cynical enough to even go straight to the very truth itself and pervert how we receive God's words. Pontus Pilate once asked, "What is the truth?" I picture this in my spiritual imagination: Satan got a flashing lightbulb above his head and decided to prepare his doctrine so that it would make us oblivious to the truth (It's just my imagination). At the end of the day, I urge all to be mindful of how they live. I have told you what I did to find the truth and even though at times I did not like what I heard, it was through God's Spirit that showed me why I have to be strict with my conduct. Sin is fun and entertaining, but it leads to death (physical is inevitable but spiritual is a forever). The truth hurts and may convict, but the road that it leads to is eternal life.

Have I won the race of faith? Am I now a role model to society? See that's the thing, this is a journey not story. This book doesn't end with a, "And he lived happily ever after!" My happily ever after comes in the promise which Christ speaks of. That promise is entering the Kingdom of heaven and helping anyone else do the same. But for the time being, it is important to understand the five themes of this book: Holy Spirit, Journey Not Story, I Am Nothing Without God, Purpose and Victory! For within this book exists all five of these themes that keep us intact for the glory of God's truth. Therefore, all that read this have received these themes in faith because each specific chapter is represented by one of those five themes and those with wisdom will be able to figure it out. But the submission to the truth chapter represents the theme victory which is why I began with a prayer so that we all might receive what is no longer a secret- victory in God's truth! So, pray for me just as I have prayed for you, under the reason that we all remain in God's truth.

Nonetheless, I do worry about others because I had to experience the powers of Satan's doctrine to break me down. Does that mean it takes the devil himself to break people down to turn to God? Absolutely not! The devil doesn't have any intention of anyone ever turning to God. His motive is plain and simple which is to steal, kill and destroy. It is only by mercy that God can coordinate the deliverance of people from Satan's mercilessness. Those who go down the same path as I have walked, I solemnly warn them to just turn around and chase after God immediately. I knew the truth but deliberately rejected it because I wanted to sin! I lived carelessly and impulsively which allowed the spiritual voices from the enemy to torment me the way it did. Our human nature cannot be trusted without God's Spirit because it craves to submit to its environment. Some may argue that their nature is good, so they do not need God to guard their nature. Those people who support this position have already deceived themselves. Our nature does not stay constant because it is nurtured by our environment. If the environment that we live within is sinful, what then will our nature follow? It is by this reason why I urge people to seek the Spirit, so it feeds more of God's nature within us. We cannot change our environments on our own, but if we can change ourselves through the very power of the truth! Together we can potentially change our environments. We should not be fooled by our knowledge of what is good and bad but strive for the truth to be righteous in the eyes of the perfect God. That is the purpose and finalization of submitting to the truth!

"Author, oh author in the beginning, you could not see what I had planned for you. You were once like the blind leading the blind. Your heart was stubborn and hard as a rock. You loved the world so much you were willing to give yourself to it. You ignored my voice because you had yet to know that it was my voice! Thus, I had to work with you slowly so you would see my glory. I worked with you slowly but steadily so you would be ready for the race of faith! For it is written:

So I run straight toward the goal in order to win the prize, which God's call through Christ Jesus to the life above. (Philippians 3:14) – Good News Translation

Your spirit was like the gunk in the eyes of a person who first wakes up from a deep sleep. For it is written:

467

For anything that is clearly revealed becomes light. That is why it is said, "Wake up sleeper and rise from death, and Christ will shine on you." (Ephesians 5:14) - Good News Translation

As your eyes opened up, your heart opened up to my voice. As your ears began to listen so did your mind being to slowly obey. Author, oh author I saw your sinful nature and I tried to reveal it to you! That one Wednesday bible study at your church. My Spirit said, 'Author, oh author look over there at the creature that attempts to hide behind your front door! Its deceived you making you think that it is leaving the temple that I have set forth in you.' But you did not understand that vision. That creature was the ancient serpent, known as the devil, he ran and hid because my presence filled your whole being. Yet, after the service, you did not take it seriously and instead of praying to me you just went to bed. Author, oh author can't you see whenever you did not pray because you thought everything was fine, the enemy crept back into your temple! The accuser of people, the one who starts corruption returned because you kept leaving the door open! You did not abide by Joshua's words! For it is written:

And if it seems evil to you to serve the LORD, choose for yourselves this day whom you will serve, whether the gods which your fathers served that were on the other side of the River, or the gods of the Amorites, in whose land you dwell. But as for me and my house, we will serve the LORD." (Joshua 24:15) – New King James Version

Author, oh author you have preached the message! You were once in love with the world and its sins. It is by this reason why in the chapters Corruption in heaven and birth of the doctrine, you did not hear my voice. It is by this reason why Egypt and Babylon appeased you because you were in love with your emotions. It is by this reason why conflict continued between your flesh and spirit. Your flesh knelt down to the ground and licked the dirt and filth from it because it desired where it came from. For it is written:

Then the LORD God took some soil from the ground and formed man out of it; he breathed life-giving breath into his nostrils, and the man began to live. (Genesis 2:7) - Good News Translation

Your soul was disturbed by your flesh's actions because it was no fool to where it came from! Therefore, they began to hate each other because the flesh had contaminated the soul's appearance, so the soul began to lust after vile things. It is by this reason you mistaken love for lust because your great love known as the world does not know love. Author, oh author the world has listened to the enemy's doctrine which is why the world behaves immorally. It promotes lust sexually and violently! It tells the youth that it is love, so they soon begin to perform immoral sexual acts which you had no shame participating in. The enemy whispered to the world that knowledge comes from experimenting so one, two and three to infinity; the whole world then began to complain. They cry about diseases; they quarrel about abortions! Author, oh author do you not think I have not seen such things long ago? They have disguised this sin in the form of a pill but author, oh author I am no fool! I have seen these wicked acts and have called it an abomination! For it is written:

When the LORD your God cuts off before you the nations whom you go in to dispossess, and you dispossess them and dwell in their land, take care that you be not ensnared to follow them, after they have been destroyed before you, and that you do not inquire about their gods, saying, 'How did these nations serve their gods?—that I also may do the same.' You shall not worship the LORD your God in that way, for every abominable thing that the LORD hates they have done for their gods, for they even burn their sons and their daughters in the fire to their gods. (Deuteronomy 12:29-31) – English Standard Version

Do not hand over any of your children to be used in the worship of the god Molech, because that would bring disgrace on the name of God, the LORD. (Leviticus 18:21) - Good News Translation

Author, oh author you know the enemy roams country to country hurting and breaking the hearts of many. He has perverted the senses of people, so they behave violently! They say immoral things to one another and promote it as well. It is this very reason why laws change. They change the laws to accommodate all their sins! My statutes and commandments have been pushed at the back of their minds or have been called unlawful! They then struggle to find order because the world is controlled by a lying tyrant. They wonder why they can't find peace and wonder why they are lost. They search all over the earth for what's right, but they realize it has no worth. Author, oh author those are my beautiful creations! Oh, my beautiful creations they've allowed themselves to be enslaved and reject my love that offers freedom and victory! There are some who are losing their faith and have forgotten their maker! They ask, 'What is faith? Can we touch it? Can we download it as an application?' They have become senseless people because the idols they worship have consumed them. They worship beings, other human beings! They are rude, violent and corrupt! They have lost their will to love because they do not trust anyone! They can't listen to reason, so they soon begin to give up! Author, oh author their sins soon catch up to them and when all hell breaks loose, they yell, 'Oh my God!' They are quick to throw the blame at me, so I ask them what have I done? They cannot reply because they do not know my voice! If only they knew my voice! For it is written:

And yet the LORD is waiting to be merciful to you. He is ready to take pity on you because he always does what is right. Happy are those who put their trust in the LORD. (Isaiah 3:18) – Good News Translation

It is by this reason why the chapter suicide was written because you felt all this pain! From the very beginning since the first chapter. Author, oh author I saw the enemy's plan, but it is I who knew when to act at the right time. For it is written:

But when the right time finally came, God sent his own Son. He came as the son of a human mother and lived under Jewish Law. (Galatians 4:4) – Good News Translation

I knew the enemy's plan before he had thought it out. Author give thanks to those who prayed for you! The people from church prayed; your parents prayed; your brothers prayed; your relatives prayed! I heard all their cries and just when the enemy thought he had won. I acted at the right moment and saved you from his attack. For it is written:

So, I am going to take her into the desert again; there I will win her back with words of love. (Hosea 1:14) – Good News Translation

His plan for you was death, but that was not my plan for you. Author, oh author have you not learned anything yet? I frustrate the plans of your enemies, and the devil himself fumed and roared in anger. For it is written:

I declared and saved and proclaimed, when there was no strange god among you; and you are my witnesses, "declares the LORD, "and I am God. Also, henceforth I am he; there is none who can deliver from my hand; I work, and who can turn it back?" Thus, says the LORD, your Redeemer, the Holy One of Israel: "For your sake I send to Babylon and bring them all down as fugitives, even the Chaldeans, in the ships in which they rejoice. I am the LORD, your Holy One, the Creator of Israel, your King." Thus, says the LORD, who makes a way in the sea, a path in the mighty waters. (Isaiah 43:12-16) – English Standard Version

The Lord brings the counsel of the nations to nothing; he frustrates the plans of the peoples. The counsel of the LORD stands forever, the plans of his heart to all generations. (Psalms 33:10-11) – English Standard Version

Author, oh author I had to strike down your legs and reteach you how to walk; I took your broken heart and mended it back together. For it is written:

He heals the broken-hearted and bandages their wounds. (Psalms 147:3) - Good News Translation

I took your evil thoughts and drowned them with a strong current flood. Some will remember your sins and call out your past by saying, 'How can this be? He said this and did that!' Author, oh author I have seen all your sins and forgiven them all! For it is written:

'Do not remember the former things, nor consider the things of old. Behold, I will do a new thing, now it shall spring forth; shall you not know it? I will even make a road in the wilderness and rivers in the desert. (Isaiah 43:18-19) – New King James Version

GOD'S TRUTH VS SATAN'S DOCTRINE

You prepare a banquet for me, where all my enemies can see me; you welcome me as an honored guest and fill my cup to the brim. (Psalms 23:5) - Good News Translation

Author, oh author you confessed your sins and worshipped my holy name, so I breathed into you my Holy Spirit; the Spirit that pleas to me on your behalf! It may have taken some time for you to understand the power of the Spirit, but I needed you to trust in me. You kept falling down and whenever you fell you cried out to me and admitted, 'Spirit of God, I'm still a child that has failed to grow up!' Author, oh author you think I did not know this? For it is written:

For though by this time you ought to be teachers, you need someone to teach you again the first principles of the oracles of God; and you have come to need milk and not solid food. For everyone who partakes only of milk is unskilled in the Word of righteousness, for he is a babe. But solid food belongs to those who are of full age, that is, those who by reason of use have their senses exercised to discern both good and evil. (Hebrews 5:12-14) – New King James Version

You beat yourself up because the Spirit convicted you but as I spoke to you in the chapter suicide, you will no longer be friends with the entity that almost destroyed you. Author, oh author I brought you back to your own country where your mother gave birth to you; I had to reset you. I isolated you from all distractions and raised you up properly. I taught you my commandments all over again, and you began to recognize my voice. I nursed you back spiritually and was pleased when you took your first steps. I remember when you tripped and fell. That fall hurt you and you cried out, 'Abba Father!' So I brought you back up into my arms. I had to remind you to always get up whenever you fall. When you were hungry, I did not give you solid foods but gave you the spiritual milk required.

Each passing day I taught you the many proverbs that were blessed unto king Solomon. Watching you grow each and every day I did not let you out of my sight. Author, oh author even when you failed me, I did not turn my back on you because I love you! You couldn't believe it; you didn't understand it even when I explained it you because no one in the world has seen such a love; a love that overwhelms all. This is why I taught you to turn away from your sins because sin harasses people with guilt and shame, so they reject my love and forgiveness. I showed you the spiritually broken that your human eyes could not see. The evil that the world exhibits can be seen through human eyes, but my Spirit that lives within you has taught you to show them the same love I showed you! Author, oh author take pity on them just as I showed pity on you! I spoke into your heart different poems so that they can reach the hearts of the broken. I watched you grow spiritually and was pleased. Author, oh author don't you remember all this? Despite your sins, I did not stop working through you. I needed to mold you into the being that I had willed for; I needed to prepare you to become something for your readers. Author, oh author that is the beautiful testimony! I am the God that does not look down upon the stories of a person; instead, I look up at the person and take what they consider worthless and make it a glorious revelation. Author, oh author I did not care to examine your story, I came to remind you that you are loved and worth it! No sin is too great for me to not forgive; no story is too messy for me not to clean; no pain is too big for me not to heal! I am telling you the truth, I am the God that welcomes the lost and broken; the God that welcomes the outcasts and sick; the God that welcomes sinners who seek to be forgiven; the God that is pleased with the righteous! For it is written:

"Blessed are the poor in spirit: for theirs is the kingdom of heaven. Blessed are they that mourn for they shall be comforted. Blessed are the meek: for they shall inherit the earth. Blessed are they which do hunger and thirst after righteousness: for they shall be filled. Blessed are the merciful: for they shall obtain mercy. Blessed are the pure in heart: for they shall see God. Blessed are the peacemakers: for they shall be called the children of God. Blessed are they which are persecuted for righteousness' sake: for theirs is the kingdom of heaven." (Matthew 5:3-10) - King James Version

Author, oh author prepare yourself for the upcoming journey and new challenges I have set for you! You are no longer a child that requires spiritual milk because you have written about the one thing, I longed from you! For in your submission to the truth you will find love; in your submission you will obey; in your submission to the truth, you will reap blessings; in your submission is the Word that will be with you forever and ever!"

- Spirit of God

CHAPTER 13

CONCLUSION

"Spirit of God,

I have found out what made me sin; I've found out what made me depressed and what caused me to run away from you. My depression started long ago but I just never knew it. I realized I was not happy with my life, so I started writing this book. Many things have come and gone; many things are still here but are destined to diminish. However, one thing that still stands next to me is you. Consistently loving and forgiving me while also reminding me that your Word will always exist. I had a ton of guilt, worries, and regret yet when you spoke to me and took me into your arms. You showed me the mountain that I feared to climb. You made that mountain shrink to the size of an insect. I do not need to go into any more detail of what you can do. I've used as much Scripture as the Spirit has guided me too. For it is written:

So we are even more confident of the message proclaimed by the prophets. You will do well to pay attention to it because it is like a lamp shining in a dark place until the Day dawns and the light of the morning star shines in your hearts. Above all else, however, remember that none of us can explain by ourselves a prophecy in the Scriptures. For no prophetic message ever came just from the human will, but people were under control of the Holy Spirit as they spoke the message that came from God. (2 Peter 1:20-21) - Good News Translation

Therefore, I give great thanks to your Holy Spirit for giving me an unexplainable insight of the Scriptures. Even the Scriptures I thought I had understood, you made me see new things. I do not know how far this journey will go; however, I know this book has spoken to the readers. I've talked about my sins; I've let it all known. I prayed and spoke to you and you answered them all. At the start of this book, I did not know what you wanted from me. What I mean is that I did not understand what my purpose in life was to be. Chapter after chapter you were probably looking at me, patiently waiting for when I would see the glory that was right in front of me. You kept calling me 'Author, oh author' and now I know why. On August 5th, 1994 you wrote it inside of me. You sat at your holy throne designing me and when you were finished you looked at your courtyard filled with all your heavenly beings and was pleased." For it is written:

You created every part of me; you put me together in my mother's womb. I praise you because you are to be feared; all you do is strange and wonderful. I know it with all my heart. When my bones were being formed, carefully put together in my mother's womb, when I was growing there– you saw me before I was born. The days allotted to me had all been recorded in your book, before any of them ever began. (Psalms 139:13– 16) – Good News Translation

The Spirit of God said,

"Here is another one of my beautiful creations that I've made and now he must go into the world and search for me. This child will be born in Dar-es-Salem, Tanzania! I will do as I did to all and write something upon his heart and not even Satan can take it away. This child born on August 5th, 1994 will write about me and I will use him and transform him into one of my many miracles. But before all this is done, he will disgrace his own name and hurt his loved ones. He will have people turn their back on him and he will feel betrayed. His flesh will crave and long for almost anything and everything because it will be seeking validation, but he will never find it. He will fail and curse the day that he was born. However, I have written something inside of him, that not even Satan can take away! He will begin to hear my voice in churches; he will hear my voice when he's alone. He will hear my voice in all sorts of transportations: in cars, buses, planes, and trains. He will hear my voice in every location: every village, town, city, and nation. Wherever he goes he will hear my voice because I wrote it upon his heart. He will think it is torment and not recognize that it comes from *me so he will reject it. Therefore, Satan will attempt to destroy him by sending him wicked and evil spiritual voices. It will torment this child for real and ruin everything he touches. His parents won't know how to save him, and his siblings will cry on behalf of his torment; nor will his friends be able to understand him. However, he will not be destroyed because he will soon acknowledge what I put inside of him. He will wander into the wilderness like my people Israel did. For it is written:*

So the LORD's anger was aroused against Israel, and he made them wander in the wilderness forty years, until all the generation that had done evil in the sight of the LORD was gone. And look! You have risen in your fathers' place, a brood of sinful men, to increase still more the fierce anger of the LORD against Israel. For if you turn away from following him, he will once again leave them in the wilderness, and you will destroy all these people." (Numbers 32:13-15) – New King James Version

He will wander in the wilderness until he puts to death his sin! Once he does this, he will mistake the wilderness as home but that is not what I have planned for him so he will never feel settled. He will then go insane like king Nebuchadnezzar because he will look into a mirror and not recognize who he is because he still listens to the voice of sin. For it is written:

You will be driven away from human society and will live with wild animals. For seven years you will eat grass like an ox and sleep in the open air, where the dew will fall on you. Then you will admit that the Supreme God controls all human kingdoms and that he can give them to anyone he chooses. (Daniel 4:24-25) - Good News Translation

He will hear many languages but not understand them because he refused to listen to what I placed inside of him. However, there is a time I've placed when my voice will out-speak all the noise in his head! He will hear my voice and begin to weep because he once denied the truth. He will shout out, 'Abba Father,' and I will reply, 'my beautiful son.' He will ask for forgiveness and I will forgive him. He will learn my language and inherit my tongue. He will realize nothing could ever satisfy him because he belongs to me. He will fall sometimes but he will hear my voice saying, 'Get up!' For it is written:

*The LORD guides us in the way we should go and protects those who
please him. If they fall, they will not stay down, because the LORD will
help them up.* (Psalms 37:23-24) - Good News Translation

*He will realize he must remain true to what I wrote inside of him. Many will
recognize his change but will continue to reject him because of his past because
he used to sin. However, this must happen so that what I wrote inside of him
will come true. For his name will no longer be the name the world once saw him
as. His new name is the thing I wrote within him and it will be like a fire that
cannot be put out. Many will not understand his new name because it comes from
me. The name that I have given him is Author because that is his purpose! Just
like the law was named 'Law' to reveal to all that they have sinned so have I
named him Author so that he may know my will and his purpose. I did not give
him this name for him to boast nor for him to be praised but for him to reveal to
all that I have written something in everyone. The name that I have given him
will bring my name glory! For it is written:*

**And at the end of the days I, Nebuchadnezzar lifted up my eyes to heaven,
and my understanding returned unto me, and I blessed the Most High
and I praised and honored him who lives forever: For his dominion is an
everlasting dominion, and His kingdom is from generation to generation.
All the inhabitants of the earth are reputed as nothing, And among the
inhabitants of the earth. No one can restrain his hand or say to him,
"What have you done?" At the same time my reason retuned to me, and
for the glory of my kingdom, my honor and splendor returned to me. My
counselors and nobles resorted to me, I was restored to my kingdom, and
excellent majesty was added to me. Now I, Nebuchadnezzar, praise and
extol and honor the King of heaven, all of whose works are truth, and
his justice. And those who walk in pride he is able to put down.** (Daniel
4:34-37) – New King James Version

*This is what I have written in him and as long as he remains true to what I
wrote in him the fire that burns within him will never go out. He will live for
me and belong to me! He will pray for the sick and help those in need. His
readers will read every page and be touched by the words that I have helped him
write. Some will attempt to praise him, but he must rebuke them and say, 'I*

am nothing without God.' Others will challenge him, but he will never play shield and sword because I am his protector. He will help those who hated him, and he will love those who curse him. He will do all these things because he has familiarized himself to my voice. He will remember the chapters and all the stories he has lived through. He will understand the cries of the broken and those who battle Egypt and Babylon, flesh vs spirit, love vs lust, law vs faith, adversity and spiritual suicide! He will do this with the power of my Word! What he used to think was challenging, he will see as nothing because I will always be with him. For it is written:

He gives me new strength. He guides me in the right paths, as he has promised. Even if I go through the deepest darkness, I will not be afraid, LORD, for you are with me. Your shepherd's rod and staff protect me. (Psalms 23:3-4) – Good News Translation

He will not wither because he will remember to be patient, trust, pray, fast, have faith, obey and repeat! He will do all these things because he will have decided to stay true to what I have written inside him. The name author will spread and those who meet him or read this will begin to hear my voice. They too will realize their purpose; the purpose to come back to me. For I want my beautiful creations back! Therefore, I say this: Author, oh author stay true to me and the words that I have written within."

"Thank you, Holy Spirit, for everything! You have given me sound and true doctrine."

-Author & Innocent Nangoma

Printed in the United States
By Bookmasters

Printed in the United States
By Bookmasters